Early Verse by
Rudyard Kipling

1. Kipling in his later years in India. 1887–8?

Early Verse by Rudyard Kipling

1879–1889

Unpublished, Uncollected, and Rarely Collected Poems

EDITED BY
ANDREW RUTHERFORD

CLARENDON PRESS · OXFORD
1986

Oxford University Press, Walton Street, Oxford OX2 6DP
Oxford New York Toronto
Delhi Bombay Calcutta Madras Karachi
Kuala Lumpur Singapore Hong Kong Tokyo
Nairobi Dar es Salaam Cape Town
Melbourne Auckland

and associated companies in
Beirut Berlin Ibadan Nicosia

Oxford is a trade mark of Oxford University Press

Published in the United States
by Oxford University Press, New York

British Library Cataloguing in Publication Data
Kipling, Rudyard
[Poems. Selections] Early verse by Rudyard Kipling
1879–1889: unpublished, uncollected, and rarely
collected poems.
I. Title   II. Rutherford, Andrew, 1929–
821'.8   PR4851
ISBN 0–19–812323-X

Library of Congress Cataloging in Publication Data
Kipling, Rudyard, 1865–1936.
Early verse by Rudyard Kipling, 1879–1889.
Includes indexes.
I. Rutherford, Andrew.   II. Title.
PR4852.R87 1986   821'.8   85–21478
ISBN 0–19–812323-X

Set by Promenade Graphics Ltd., Cheltenham.
Printed in Great Britain by
The Alden Press, Oxford.

TO MY WIFE

ACKNOWLEDGEMENTS

I WISH to express my gratitude to the University of Aberdeen and the Carnegie Trust for the Universities of Scotland for their financial support for my work on this project.

For permission to use manuscript material I should like to thank the following: the National Trust, as copyright holders in the Literary Estate of Rudyard Kipling; Earl Baldwin of Bewdley; the Bohemian Club, San Francisco; the British Library, including the India Office Library and Records; the Bancroft Library, University of California at Berkeley; the Rare Book and Special Collections Division, Library of Congress; the Department of Rare Books, Cornell University Library; the Kipling Collection, Dalhousie University Library; the Houghton Library, Harvard University; the Huntington Library, San Marino, California; the Lilly Library, Indiana University; Margaret E. Macdonald; the Macmillan Press Ltd; the Henry W. and Albert A. Berg Collection, the New York Public Library, Astor, Lenox, and Tilden Foundations; the Pierpont Morgan Library; Princeton University Library; Charles Scribner's Sons; the University of Sussex Library; and the Rudyard Kipling Collection, George Arents Research Library, Syracuse University, Syracuse, NY. I am also indebted to the National Trust for permission to use published works by Kipling which are still subject to copyright, and to the Hutchinson Publishing Group Ltd for permission to reprint one item.

Many colleagues, friends, and correspondents have provided me with information. In particular, I should like to thank Flora Alexander, E. M. Batley, Ian Baxter, Christopher Baugh, Ellison Bishop, Jacqueline S. Bratton, Margaret Brunyate, John Burt, Herbert Cahoon, Michael Candler, Bridget P. Carr, Neil Cossons, J. A. Edwards, Sara S. Hodson, Elizabeth Inglis, Ian Jack, George Jackson, Jonathan B. Katz, A. V. Kelly, Lady Lorna Howard, Lisa A. F. Lewis, Stephen Ferguson, David J. Matthews, William Matheson, Randolph Quirk, Richard B. Rutherford, John Shearman, Christopher Shackle, Nora F. Stovel, Lola Szladits, Karen Smith, Isobel Tait, R. C. Taylor, E. Talbot Rice, Peter Van Wingen, Andrew Walls, Dorothy Walker, George J. Watson, Peter Williams, and William Witte. The staff of the India Office Library and the Manuscripts Section of the University of Sussex Library have been particularly helpful.

I owe a special debt of gratitude to Thomas Pinney, whose work on Kipling's letters will make smooth the path of future scholars, and who has been generous in sharing his discoveries with me. I am also indebted to Barbara Rosenbaum, who has allowed me to see her work in progress towards the compilation of the Kipling section of the *Index of English Literary Manuscripts*. I owe much to Michael Smethurst, the Librarian of the University of Aberdeen, for his efforts on my behalf; and I am grateful to Kim Scott Walwyn of Oxford University Press for her advice and encouragement. My deepest indebtedness is to my wife, without whose unfailing support and active help I could not have brought this work to completion.

CONTENTS

APPENDICES

LIST OF ILLUSTRATIONS

ABBREVIATIONS

Baldwin Papers	The Baldwin Papers relating to the Kipling Family 1875–1945, University of Sussex Library, Manuscripts Section.
Berg Collection	The Henry W. and Albert A. Berg Collection, the New York Public Library, Astor, Lenox, and Tilden Foundations.
BL	British Library.
CMG	*Civil and Military Gazette*
Definitive Edition	*Rudyard Kipling's Verse. Definitive Edition*, London, 1940 (frequently reprinted).
Hobson-Jobson	Henry Yule and A. C. Burnell, *Hobson-Jobson. A Glossary of Colloquial Anglo-Indian Words and Phrases, and of Kindred Terms, Etymological, Historical, Geographical and Discursive*, new edn., ed. William Crooke, London, 1903.
Huntington Library	The Huntington Library, San Marino, California.
KP	The Kipling Papers, University of Sussex Library, Manuscripts Section.
Notebooks 1, 2 and 3	Notebooks of poems, KP 24/3, KP 24/2, and KP 24/1 (see below, pp. 23–7).
Readers' Guide	*The Readers' Guide to Rudyard Kipling's Work*, ed. R. E. Harbord, Canterbury and Bournemouth, 1961–72.
Scrapbooks 1, 2, 3, and 4	Scrapbooks of cuttings of Kipling's newspaper publications, KP 28/1, KP 28/2, KP 28/3, and KP 28/4 (see below, p. 31).
Something of Myself	Rudyard Kipling, *Something of Myself For My Friends Known and Unknown*, London, 1937.
Stewart and Yeats	James McG. Stewart, *Rudyard Kipling. A Bibliographical Catalogue*, ed. A. W. Yeats, Toronto, 1959.
Sundry Phansies	Notebook of poems so entitled in the Berg Collection (see above).
USCC	*United Services College Chronicle.*

INTRODUCTION

I GENERAL

This volume contains over three hundred poems or fragments of poems by Rudyard Kipling, none of which is included in the self-styled Definitive Edition of his verse. Written in the years 1879 to 1882, when he was a schoolboy at the United Services College, Westward Ho!, and 1882 to 1889, when he was a young journalist in India, they provide remarkable insights into his early development and preoccupations as a poet.

Many of these verses were never published by Kipling, but sent in MS copies to friends and relations who formed an inner circle of confidants, some of whom also received more ambitious collections of poems in MS in notebook form. Some other verses which he published in the school magazine (the *United Services College Chronicle*) and a great many which appeared in Anglo-Indian newspapers—especially the *Civil and Military Gazette*, the *Pioneer*, the *Pioneer Mail*, and the *Week's News*—were never collected in volume form. Others again *were* collected, but only in a few special de luxe editions—the *Early Verse* volumes of the Outward Bound Edition and the Edition de Luxe in 1900, and their equivalents in the posthumous Sussex and Burwash Editions which added a few extra items from this period. Of the two hundred and eighty-nine titles in the present collection (some of which include a number of separate items) seventy-seven appeared in the Sussex and Burwash Editions, ninety-seven were published but not collected by Kipling, while the remainder derive from MS or type-script sources. Taken together the poems in these three categories constitute a major extension of the canon of Kipling's verse as hitherto presented to the general reading public.

The volume begins with a thirteen-year-old schoolboy's attempt to place a poem in an American magazine for children. It ends with the author's emergence at the age of twenty-three as a major figure on the London and indeed the international literary scene. (The publication of 'The Ballad of East and West' in December 1889 may be seen as marking the end of his apprenticeship to poetry.) The contents show *inter alia* Kipling's frequent imitation of authors he admired, his gift for parody, his eager experimentation with form and technique, his poetic exploration of imagined characters and situations, and his early commitment to a more personal, passionate, and confessional poetry than he was to practise in later years, though this coexisted with the humorous and extrovert persona which he normally presented to his fellow schoolboys. The poems of his Indian period (October 1882 to March 1889) chart his varying responses to experience there. There are expressions of nostalgia and homesickness. There are celebrations of Anglo-Indian life and comic-satiric commentaries on it. There is an engagement with issues of the day: many of his verses are inspired or provoked by news items currently appearing in the press, and Indian political aspirations, the treatment of women in Hindu society, corruption among senior officials, and the follies of government at municipal, provincial, and imperial levels all provoke him to derisive or indignant comment. In lighter vein he shows a gift for *vers de société*: his humour plays on members of the supreme government at Simla, whom he knew personally through his parents' friendship with Lord Dufferin, viceroy from 1884 to 1888, while at their best his more personal verses to close friends or members of the family combine wit and charm. It is a body of verse uneven in quality, but of considerable interest, social and historical as well as biographical and literary.

2 SCHOOL YEARS

Poetry was important to Kipling from an early age. In the five years when he and his sister Trix[1] were separated from their parents by sad Anglo-Indian necessity, books were a refuge from the miseries he had to endure at Southsea in what he called 'the House of Desolation'. Near the end of his life he could still recall poems that had delighted him in these childhood years: 'On another plane was an old magazine with Wordsworth's "I climbed the dark brow of the mighty Helvellyn". I knew nothing of its meaning but the words moved and pleased. So did other extracts from the poems of "A. Tennyson".'[2] Kipling also recalls, though not by name, two books of poems that had impressed him very deeply. (These have been identified as *Poems Written for a Child*, 1868, by Manella Bute Sedley and her sister Elizabeth Anne Hart, and *Child Nature*, 1869, by Mrs Hart alone.)[3]

---

[1] Alice Macdonald Kipling; later Mrs Fleming; nicknamed 'Trix' because her father had called her 'a tricksy baby'. Born 11 June 1868; Rudyard born 30 Dec. 1865.

[2] *Something of Myself*, p. 7. The line quoted is from Scott's 'Hellvellyn', not from Wordsworth.

[3] Roger Lancelyn Green, *Kipling and the Children*, London, 1965, pp. 40–2.

There comes to my mind here a memory of two books of verse about child-life which I have tried in vain to identify. One—blue and fat—described 'nine white wolves' coming 'over the wold' and stirred me to the deeps; and also certain savages who 'thought the name of England was something that could not burn.'

The other book—brown and fat—was full of lovely tales in strange metres. A girl was turned into a water-rat 'as a matter of course'; an Urchin cured an old man of gout by means of a cool cabbage-leaf, and somehow 'forty wicked Goblins' were mixed up in the plot; and a 'Darling' got out on the house-leads with a broom and tried to sweep stars off the skies. It must have been an unusual book for that age, but I have never been able to recover it, any more than I have a song that a nursemaid sang at low-tide in the face of the sunset on Littlehampton Sands when I was less than six. But the impression of wonder, excitement and terror and the red bars of failing light is as clear as ever.[4]

Further extensions of his literary and emotional experience came during his Christmas visits to the Burne-Jones household at The Grange, North End Lane, Fulham, where he was welcomed by his beloved Aunt Georgiana. Revelling in the love and affection of which he was starved for the remainder of the year, Kipling enjoyed the company of his cousins and the other children, and also of friendly grown-ups like 'Uncle Ned' (Edward Burne-Jones) and William Morris, 'our Deputy Uncle Topsy': 'There was an incessant come and go of young people and grown-ups all willing to play with us—except an elderly person called "Browning", who took no proper interest in the skirmishes which happened to be raging on his entry.'[5] Fuller appreciation of the Pre-Raphaelite milieu was to come later, but already Kipling responded to some of the drawings and paintings on which Burne-Jones was engaged, and he sensed the importance accorded to art and literature by the whole circle.

Some of his earliest surviving poems were to be written in 1879–80 for a family magazine, the *Scribbler*, produced by the Burne-Jones and Morris children; but even before then he had made some juvenile attempts at composition. Edith Plowden, who had been befriended by the Kipling parents in Lahore, recalled how early in 1877 'the mail brought letters from Rudyard and Trix containing their first literary attempts'. In his would-be novel Rudyard described his heroine lying on a sofa, 'the snowy whiteness of her face hands and feet proclaim-[ing] her aristocratic birth'; but he also sent a love poem of which Miss

---

[4] *Something of Myself*, pp. 8–9.
[5] Ibid., p. 12. Cf. Georgiana Burne-Jones, *Memorials of Edward Burne-Jones*, London, 1904, vol. ii, pp. 45–6.

Plowden could recall one fragment: ' "Up to its feathered head the barb / Has pierced into my heart." There was a refrain to each verse "Margaret Margaret I love but thee!" '[6] Two other pieces of juvenilia, 'The Legend of the Cedar Swamp' and 'The Carolina', survive from these very early years as literary curiosities, and are printed in Appendix A of this edition.

The deterioration of Rudyard's eyesight and what seems to have been a kind of nervous breakdown led to his mother's return from India and his removal from the House of Desolation in March or April 1877. For the next nine months he was under her care, and as well as giving him emotional support in that period of recuperation, she warmly encouraged his literary enthusiasms. Lively, intelligent, witty, and well read, Alice Kipling was one of a family of poetry-lovers who also wrote poems of their own; and she shared with her husband, John Lockwood Kipling, a deep interest in poetry past and present. Edith Plowden describes how, in the cultured atmosphere of their home in Lahore, they used to read *Aurora Leigh* aloud and discuss it, how they also read poems by Rossetti and Swinburne (both of whom they had met through the Burne-Joneses), and how Browning had a special place in their poetic pantheon: indeed their shared enthusiasm for his work had been a key discovery when they first met at a picnic at Rudyard Lake in Staffordshire.[7] Undoubtedly, Alice would have helped to guide her son's reading at this period, as well as confirming his love of books:

By the end of that long holiday [*he wrote*] I understood that my Mother had written verses, that my Father 'wrote things' also; that books and pictures were among the most important affairs in the world; that I could read as much as I chose and ask the meaning of things from any one I met. I had found out, too, that one could take pen and paper and set down what one thought, and that nobody accused one of 'showing off' by so doing. I read a good deal; *Sidonia the Sorceress*; Emerson's poems; and Bret Harte's stories; and I learned all sorts of verses for the pleasure of repeating them to myself in bed.[8]

This sustaining influence was not removed when Kipling left for school at the United Services College, Westward Ho!, in January 1878, since Alice Kipling remained in England till the autumn of 1880. She was joined in 1878 by her husband, on an eight-month furlough in the course of which he had to organize the Indian Section of

---

[6] Edith Plowden, *Fond Memory* (MS reminiscences), Baldwin Papers, 1/19.

[7] Baldwin Papers, 1/12, 1/14.

[8] *Something of Myself*, p. 20. *Sidonia the Sorceress*, by Johann Wilhelm Meinhold (1797-1851), was a favourite Pre-Raphaelite text.

Arts and Manufactures at the Paris Exhibition of that year; and Rudyard, who accompanied him to Paris, came to see that visit as the start of his long-lasting love for France and French culture.[9] Before she herself left for India, Alice found a congenial home for the children with three elderly ladies whom Kipling later called 'the Ladies of Warwick Gardens'—Miss Georgiana Craik, a minor novelist, her sister Miss Mary Craik, and their friend Miss Winnard. Kipling later described them as 'three dear ladies who lived off the far end of Kensington High Street . . . in a house filled with books, peace, kindliness, patience and what today would be called "culture" '.

One of the ladies wrote novels on her knee, by the fireside, sitting just outside the edge of conversation, beneath two clay pipes tied with black ribbon, which once Carlyle had smoked. All the people one was taken to see either wrote or painted pictures or, as in the case of a Mr and Miss de Morgan, ornamented tiles . . . Somewhere in the background were people called Jean Ingelow and Christina Rossetti, but I was never lucky enough to see those good spirits. And there was choice in the walls of bookshelves of anything one liked . . . [10]

With such a background it is hardly surprising that at school, once the first period of bullying and victimization had passed, the role Kipling assumed was that of poet, aesthete, and literary intellectual.

In later years he was often tempted to assume the mask of a Philistine, asserting the inferiority of art or literature to action. Writing on Westward Ho! itself, for example, he was to reflect that 'surely it must be better to turn out men who do real work than men who write about what they think about what other people have done or ought to do.'[11] Yet in his years there he was, according to one of his closest associates, 'wholly devoted to *belles lettres* and poetry'.[12] Beresford's book *Schooldays with Kipling* is envious and acidulous in tone and given to exaggeration of a partly facetious nature, but we cannot ignore his description of Kipling as 'the Epicurean Giglamps, the art and literature crank, the anti-sport, anti-athletic highbrow'[13] Lord Birkenhead quotes another contemporary to the same effect: 'It always amused us that he should have become so fervidly the prophet of Action and the laureate of the Deed; for as a boy—and I never knew him after—he was a bookworm,

---

[9] *Something of Myself*, pp. 24–5. Cf. *Souvenirs of France*, New York, 1933, pp. 1–20.
[10] Ibid., pp. 21–2.
[11] *Land and Sea Tales for Scouts and Guides*, London, 1923, p. 258 (from 'An English School', first published in 1893).
[12] G. C. Beresford, *Schooldays with Kipling*, London, 1936, p. 113.
[13] Ibid., p. 298. 'Giglamps' or 'Gigger' was the nickname given to Kipling because of his spectacles.

entirely absorbed in the life of books, unathletic, unsociable, and sad to say—decidedly fat.'[14] In March 1888, moreover, his friend Edmonia Hill recorded her meeting in Allahabad with two young subalterns who were at Westward Ho! at the same time as Kipling, and their telling her that 'he was so brilliant and cynical that he was most cordially hated by his fellow students'.[15] This is not to discount Kipling's animal high spirits, his delight in schoolboy escapades, his zest for life, and his camaraderie with Dunsterville ('Stalky') and Beresford ('M'Turk'). Indeed the relationship between them, celebrated long afterwards in *Stalky and Co.*, is the subject of one of Kipling's earliest surviving poems (see p. 45 below). Yet Dunsterville himself recalls that the first effect of his friendship with the other two was 'to improve [his] taste in literature. The period of Ned Kelly and Jack Harkaway was succeeded by Ruskin, Carlyle, and Walt Whitman.'[16] And Beresford has much to say about Kipling's enthusiasm for books, his omnivorous reading, his 'wild desire to embrace English literature as a whole, and French as far as possible'.[17]

It is not possible to chart the sequence of his reading, but we know that in poetry it included Tennyson, Browning, Swinburne, Matthew Arnold, Sir Edwin Arnold, Elizabeth Barrett Browning, D. G. Rossetti, Christina Rossetti, Fitzgerald, Wordsworth, Keats, Shelley, Longfellow, Emerson, Whittier, Poe, Whitman, Bret Harte, Joaquin Miller, C. G. Leland, and James Thomson, whose 'City of Dreadful Night' shook Kipling, he tells us, to his unformed core.[18] A printed questionnaire which he filled in when he was still at school[19] records his view that poetry 'is never to be treated lightly under any circumstances'. It lists his favourite poets as Whittier, Emerson, Browning, Tennyson, and Poe, mentions writing as one of his favourite pursuits, and quotes Emerson's 'Letters' as the finest passage of poetry he can remember by heart. In 'An English School' he recalls how one of the masters gave him the run of his library, where he found 'all the English poets from Chaucer to Matthew Arnold'.[20] 'Swinburne's poems I must have come across first at the Aunt's', he reflects in *Something of Myself*: 'Tennyson and *Aurora Leigh* came in the way of nature to me in the

[14] H. M. Swanwick, quoted in Lord Birkenhead, *Rudyard Kipling*, New York, 1978, p. 56.
[15] Edmonia Hill, 'The Young Kipling', *Atlantic Monthly*, vol. clvii (1936), p. 408.
[16] L. C. Dunsterville, *Stalky's Reminiscences*, London, 1928, p. 43.
[17] *Schooldays with Kipling*, p. 244.
[18] *Something of Myself*, p. 33.
[19] Department of Rare Books, Cornell University Library.
[20] *Land and Sea Tales*, p. 268.

holidays, and C—— in form once literally threw *Men and Women* at my head. Here I found "The Bishop orders his Tomb", "Love among the Ruins" and "Fra Lippo Lippi", a not too remote—I dare to think—ancestor of mine.'[21] One might suppose that his parents would already have introduced him to Browning; but his works now became one of Kipling's main enthusiasms. Edith Plowden records that 'both Rudyard and Trix when children had a real passion for Browning. They read his poems voraciously, [and] could recite them by the page.'[22] As well as old favourites there were new discoveries, and something of Kipling's delight at the revelation of unexplored riches in English poetry is conveyed in a passage in *Stalky and Co.*, describing Beetle's reactions when, as editor of the school magazine, he was made free of the Head's study:

There were scores and scores of ancient dramatists; there were Hakluyt, his voyages; French translations of Muscovite authors called Pushkin and Lermontoff; little tales of a heady and bewildering nature, interspersed with unusual songs—Peacock was that writer's name: there was Borrow's *Lavengro*; an odd theme, purporting to be a translation of something called a 'Rubáiyát', which the Head said was a poem not yet come to its own; there were hundreds of volumes of verse—Crashaw; Dryden; Alexander Smith; L.E.L.; Lydia Sigourney; Fletcher and a purple island; Donne; Marlowe's *Faust*; and —this made M'Turk (to whom Beetle conveyed it) sheer drunk for three days—Ossian; *The Earthly Paradise*; *Atalanta in Calydon*; and Rossetti—to name only a few. Then the Head, drifting in under pretence of playing censor to the paper, would read here a verse and here another of these poets, opening up avenues. And, slow-breathing, with half-shut eyes above his cigar, would he speak of great men living, and journals, long dead, founded in their riotous youth; of years when all the planets were little new-lit stars trying to find their places in the uncaring void, and he, the Head, knew them as young men know one another.[23]

The Head in real life was Cormell Price, a friend of Burne-Jones and the Macdonald family[24] since his schooldays in Birmingham. He had been a member of the Pre-Raphaelite set since his Oxford days, when he and Swinburne had helped Morris, Burne-Jones and Rossetti

[21] *Something of Myself*, p. 34. 'C——' was W. C. Crofts, the master who provided one of the models for Mr King in *Stalky and Co.*

[22] Baldwin Papers, 1/14. (Cf. 1/20, pp. 2, 16–17.)

[23] *Stalky and Co.*, London, 1899, pp. 217–8.

[24] Alice Kipling and Georgiana Burne-Jones were two of the Macdonald sisters. The third, Agnes, married Edward John Poynter, later President of the Royal Acdemy; the fourth, Louisa, married Alfred Baldwin, a wealthy iron-master; and the fifth, Edith, who remained unmarried, was to be one of Kipling's closest confidants throughout his adolescence. (See A. W. Baldwin, *The Macdonald Sisters*, London, 1960, *passim*.)

with the frescos for the Oxford Union, and he had contributed to the
Oxford and Cambridge Magazine which Morris and Burne-Jones pro-
duced in 1856.[25] Another account of his influence is to be found in
'An English School', where Kipling tells of private Russian classes in
which 'the Head would sometimes tell him about . . . his own early
days at college when Morris and Swinburne and Rossetti and other
people who afterwards became great, were all young, and the Head
was young with them, and they wrote wonderful things in the college
magazines.'[26] Clearly strong encouragement was being given to
Kipling in his own literary aspirations, and this was reinforced in 1881
when the Head made him responsible for the school magazine, the
United Services College Chronicle.

   In considering his work at this stage in his life it is useful to dis-
tinguish between poems written for circulation among his school-
fellows, or poems which he was willing to circulate in this way even if
they had been written for other purposes, and poems of a more private
nature, to be shared only with confidants like his parents, Miss Plow-
den, the ladies of Warwick Gardens, his aunt Edith Macdonald, Mrs
Tavenor Perry (see below, p. 12), and Florence Garrard, the girl
whom he met and fell in love with in the course of 1880.

   For the school he wrote varieties of public poetry of an unambitious
nature. He discovered 'that personal and well-pointed limericks on my
companions worked well', and his lampooning took a more extended
form in an adaptation of Dante in the metre of *Hiawatha*: 'I bought a
fat, American cloth-bound notebook, and set to work on an *Inferno*,
into which I put, under appropriate torture, all my friends and most of
the masters . . . Then, "as rare things will", my book vanished, and I
lost interest in the *Hiawatha* metre.'[27] His lampoons on school person-
alities are recalled in *Stalky and Co.*, but none seem to have survived,
with the doubtful exception of a limerick ('There once was a master
called Osborne') cited by Beresford as possibly being 'by some other
songster'.[28] As time went on Kipling enjoyed a measure of esteem or
notoriety as the school bard. By tradition, he tells us, the yearly theatri-
cals 'ended with the School-Saga, the "*Vive la Compagnie!*" in which
the Senior boy of the School chanted the story of the School for the
past twelve months. It was very long and very difficult to make up,

   [25] Roger Lancelyn Green, *Kipling and the Children*, pp. 51–3.
   [26] *The Youth's Companion*, 19 Oct. 1893, pp. 506–7, cited by Roger Lancelyn Green,
Kipling and the Children, p. 68. Cf. *Land and Sea Tales*, p. 269.
   [27] *Something of Myself*, pp. 33–4.
   [28] *Schooldays with Kipling*, p. 179.

though all the poets of all the forms had been at work on it for weeks.' But Beresford's account makes it clear that at the end of the winter term of 1881 Kipling's own contribution supplanted all others (though 'Alas!' he concludes, 'Every line of this peerless but not deathless ode has perished.')[29] Beresford also professes to recall a composition by Kipling on 'The Siege of Plevna' (an episode in the Russo-Turkish war of 1877–8), done as an exercise in the English class:

Of this specimen of Gigger's poesy, which incidentally was in blank verse, there has survived only one notable line. The bard describes how he, strolling round Plevna with his reporter's notebook open in his hand, observed among many other horrors the corpse of a Turkish boy on the ramparts. A vulture had pounced upon it, and, at the poet's approach, the bird of prey fluttered off, bearing aloft, high into the blue empyrean, 'Yards upon yards of the poor boy's entrails'.

And the tone of the school is well conveyed by the class-master's marginal comment, 'Are you sure it was not a string of sausages you saw?'[30]

It is not surprising that the dominant mode of the poems Kipling offered to school readers was facetious and parodic. There are a few exceptions. 'A Legend of Devonshire' is sombre in tone. 'Ave Imperatrix', written on the occasion of an attempt to assassinate Queen Victoria in March 1882, strikes a patriotic, imperial note uncharacteristic of him at this stage, and wholly unexpected by his associates.[31] The same note is sustained in his prize poem 'The Battle of Assaye'; but these two items are exceptional among his early verses, which otherwise eschew imperial or military themes. More typically, he writes in a light-hearted vein, indulging in schoolboy humour, adapting the form and style of poets like Milton, Keats, Tennyson, Browning, and Swinburne to vignettes of school experience, and showing occasional ingenuity in, for example, his translation of an ode by Horace into Devonshire dialect.[32]

The school magazine provided a ready outlet for such verses, but they form only a minute proportion of his output in these years. He wrote prolifically and with great enthusiasm: 'After my second year at school, the tide of writing set in', he recalled long afterwards: 'There were few atrocities of form or metre that I did not perpetrate, and I enjoyed them all.'[33] Many poems were written in the school holidays,

[29] *Land and Sea Tales*, p. 266; *Schooldays with Kipling*, p. 220.
[30] *Schooldays with Kipling*, pp. 278–9.
[31] Ibid., pp. 289–93. This poem (included in the Definitive Edition) was probably influenced by Wilde's 'Ave Imperatrix'.
[32] See below, p. 160.   [33] *Something of Myself*, p. 33.

many others during term, but all were kept jealously guarded from even his closest friends at Westward Ho! Beresford mentions 'poems that Gigger showed to nobody and objected to anybody's looking at'.[34]

Inspection of the verses inscribed in his Russia-leather, gilt-edged, cream-laid MS. books would not have been at all welcomed; and, in fact, these sanctuaries were never violated, never opened by careless or unworthy hands. The leather-bound books were guarded by a taboo; one of the few sacred words honoured by schoolboys covered them with its protection: 'Private'. It would not be sportsmanlike to intrude on private documents, and that settled it; the verses had the same sanctity as home letters.[35]

These private verses were more serious in tone and more poetically ambitious than those published in the *United Services College Chronicle*. They draw on a wider range of literary models, and they show Kipling the adolescent inhabiting a very different emotional world from that of *Stalky and Co*. His poem 'Two Lives',[36] for example, is both a literary exercise (as suggested by his later comment 'Not bad—a direct Shakespeare crib which I thought vastly fine when I wrote it') and an attempt to convey his sense of living in divided and distinguished worlds—the everyday world of school routine and the world of emotional intensities connected largely with his hopeless passion for Flo Garrard, the prototype of Maisie in *The Light that Failed*. Many of the poems seem to derive from and articulate his own experiences, often of unhappy love. Others are based on observation, like the young prostitute's soliloquy in 'Overheard', or the Cockney housemaid's plea in 'Credat Judaeus'. Some have, no doubt, elements of fantasy and wish-fulfilment. Some are attempts to project himself imaginatively into experiences—of bereavement, for example, in 'The Story of Paul Vaugel' and 'The Trouble of Curtiss'—which he has not known at first hand, but which move his sympathies. In some he uses the dramatic monologue to explore themes like the opposition of paganism and Christianity in 'How the Goddess Awakened', or psychological states like the fear of death in 'This Side the Styx'. Some dabble, not very successfully, in satire. Some exploit the sonnet's capacity to serve as a vehicle for introspective self-analysis. All reveal imaginative, emotional, and literary preoccupations concealed from members of his peer group and shared only with an inner circle of friends and relations.

His parents were among the first recipients of his verses throughout this period. Writing of 1879 Edith Plowden recalled that

[34] *Schooldays with Kipling*, p. 212.
[35] Ibid., p. 284.
[36] See below, p. 137.

Rudyard started writing poetry and in one letter to his father said, 'I am writing a poem it begins like this

> A cry in the silent night
> A white face turned to the wall,
> A pang—and then in the minds of men
> Forgotten! and that is all.'[37]

John Lockwood Kipling wrote to Miss Plowden herself on 5 October 1880 that 'it would be affectation to ignore his very decided talents and powers. He sends me (or rather Mrs Kipling sends) a copy of verses— "The Lesson" which might be to the address of Miss Flora Garrard or possibly to you. In any case they are prettily turned . . . '[38] On returning to India that autumn Alice Kipling, homesick and depressed, was afraid that she might lose touch with her son's development:

> If it isn't too much trouble, dear [*she wrote to Miss Plowden on 26 November 1880*], I wish when Ruddy sends you any verses you would let me have a copy. He promised I should have all he did—but he is not sending them—and as time & distance do their fatal work I am sure that his mother will know less of him than any other woman of his acquaintance.[39]

Her fears, however, proved to be unfounded: his parents continued to receive his compositions, and indeed they arranged for a volume of his verses, *Schoolboy Lyrics*, to be published in Lahore in a limited edition in December 1881, for private circulation. This was done without his knowledge or approval; and if his sister Trix is to be believed—in her old age she was not an entirely reliable witness—he was much put out to find that his private verses had been made public even to this extent:

> Mrs Kipling [*she recalled*] wanted her boy's clever verses preserved in a permanent form—feeling—as she said after—that if he never wrote any more it would still be interesting to keep.
> Mr Kipling—always a little doubtful—thought it unnecessary—of course the boy was clever but it would be a pity if he got swelled head.
> Ruddy knew nothing of the matter and only saw one of the little books when he came out to Lahore. Then—Mother told me long after—he was very angry, told her that she had taken and made use of something he needed and valued, and sulked for two days.[40]

In the meantime, however, he continued to write, and to send his verses to his parents in Lahore. 'As to Ruddy,' Alice wrote to Edith

---

[37] Baldwin Papers, 1/14. Cf. p. 53 below.
[38] KP 1/10.
[39] Ibid.
[40] KP 32/32 (no date).

Plowden on 28 April 1882, 'he fairly takes my breath away—literally pelting me with poems week after week. It is hard to think he finds any time for school work in the midst of his other interests.'[41] And a notebook has been preserved in which his parents transcribed poems he had sent them.

He also sent poems to Florence Garrard, to whom many of them were indeed addressed; to Edith Macdonald, who was his closest confidante in matters of both literature and love; to Edith Plowden, who remembered that 'he wrote constantly sending me all his fresh poems written on notepaper';[42] and to Mrs Tavenor Perry, a kind of mother substitute whom he addressed as 'Mater' in his letters from school. In February 1882, moreover, he began preparing two notebook anthologies of poems fair-copied in his own hand, which he seems to have presented to Edith Macdonald and Florence Garrard before sailing for India. Both have been preserved. A third notebook of his poems as he had first composed them was given to Edith Plowden before his departure, but this was returned to him in 1915 at his request and deliberately destroyed. Another notebook—probably a continuation of that given to Miss Plowden—has survived, with poems dating from early 1882 to early 1884, covering the transition from England to India, and including marginal comments made by Kipling in 1883–4 on some of his own earlier compositions.[43]

For a comment made at the time, with painful honesty, we may turn to 'An Ending', dated 11 April 1882 and addressed presumably to Florence Garrard:

> Now that I have accomplished a little,
>   Very little truly, but still a little—
> Made, painfully some, joyfully others, bitterly many,—
> Made, as a boy makes them,—imperfect meaning to be perfect.
> Failures many, but telling of what was intended,
> They are yours and yours only—
> By the power and the dominance that you have over me,
>   Yours and yours only.[44]

There is a kind of naked sensitivity revealed here which is suppressed or hidden in the years that were to follow.

---

[41] KP 1/10.

[42] Baldwin Papers, 1/20.

[43] For further details of these and other sources, see below, pp. 23ff.

[44] See below, pp. 141–2.

3 INDIA AND AFTER

Kipling sailed for India on SS *Brindisi* on 20 September 1882, some three months before his seventeenth birthday. Arriving at Bombay on 18 October, he went on to join his parents at Lahore, the capital of the Punjab, where he took up his post as sub-editor of the *Civil and Military Gazette*. So began the period of his life which he was to describe in his autobiography as 'Seven Years Hard'. The editorial staff consisted of only two Europeans; the newspaper appeared six days a week throughout the year, except for one day's break at Christmas and Easter, so that the work was unremitting; and his editor, Stephen Wheeler, was a hard taskmaster. 'My Chief took me in hand, and for three years or so I loathed him', Kipling wrote in *Something of Myself*. 'He had to break me in, and I knew nothing.'[45] The process may have been necessary, but it was not a pleasant one: 'Ruddy is . . . getting on well—' his father wrote in 1883, 'having mastered the details of his work in a very short time. His chief Mr Wheeler is very tetchy and irritable and by dint of his exercises in patience and forbearance—the boy is in training for Heaven as well as for Editorship.'[46]

E. Kay Robinson, who succeeded Wheeler as editor in 1886, tells us that besides occasional reporting outside the office, Kipling's daily work on the *Civil and Military Gazette* was, briefly:

(1) to prepare for the press all the telegrams of the day; (2) to provide all the extracts and paragraphs [*i.e. from Anglo-Indian, Indian, English, and other newspapers*]; (3) to make headed articles out of official reports, etc.; (4) to write such editorial notes as he might have time for; (5) to look generally after all sports, out-station and local intelligence; (6) to read all proofs except the editorial matter.[47]

He had also to vet the presentation and content of external contributions to the paper. He reviewed new books and theatrical performances. He reported on race-meetings and official functions like the opening of new bridges or hospitals. He provided regular features on 'The Week in Lahore'; and when taking his one month's holiday a year, he sometimes acted as special correspondent from Simla. He was sent from time to time on special assignments—to cover, for example, the Rawalpindi Durbar of 1885, when the Viceroy received the Amir of Afghanistan on a state visit, or the installation of a new Maharajah of

---

[45] *Something of Myself*, pp. 40–1.
[46] KP 1/10.
[47] 'Mr Kipling as Journalist', *The Academy*, vol. i (1896). Cited in *Kipling : Interviews and Recollections*, ed. Harold Orel, London, 1983, vol. i, p. 87.

Kashmir in 1886. He was assiduous in the production of 'scraps' or editorial notes on current issues and miscellaneous topics, and his Diary for 1885 shows his continual concern about keeping up the level of his contributions—the more so since he was paid ten rupees a column for these in addition to his basic stipend. If Wheeler was ill or on leave, Kipling had sometimes to take sole responsibility for the production of the paper.

It was a regimen which at first seemed incompatible with any writing of his own. 'One of the first things a sub editor has to learn is to altogether give up original writing', he told the Padre at Westward Ho! in a letter of 17 November 1882.[48] Gradually, however, he began to write again in such spare time as he could find, and in 1882–3 there is a trickle of poems which afterwards became a flood. All his verses, as he later said, were 'digressions from office work'.[49] Indeed his entire output of poetry and fiction in these Indian years has to be seen against the background of his journalistic commitments which continued unabated; and he deeply resented any suggestion that he sacrificed professional to personal concerns. An allegation by George Allen, one of the proprietors of the *Civil and Military Gazette*, that he was averse to routine work, produced an explosion in a letter of 30 April 1886, addressed to Kay Robinson:

Now I'll speak distinctly as the drunkard said. The whole settlement and routine of the old rag from the end of the leader to the beginning of the advertisements is in my hands and mine only; my respected chief contributing a blue pencil mark now and then and a healthy snarl just to soothe me. The telegrams also and such scraps as I or my father may write are my share likewise; and these things call me to office half one golden hour before, and let me out, always three-quarters, sometimes a whole hour behind my chief. My sabbath is enlivened by the official visits of the printer and my evenings after dinner are made merry by his demands. So much for the routine to which I am averse . . . on my word I fancy Allen must think I write my 'skits' in office hours. This is not so. You may bet your journalistic boots that if my worthy chief found any portion of the work which he did not conceive to be his share falling on his shoulders I should hear about it pretty sharply. The rhymed rubbish and the stuff like 'Section 420 I.P.C.' is written out of office for my own personal amusement . . . and then—O my friend—is damned as waste of time and only put in with a running lecture on the sinfulness of writing such stuff.[50]

---

[48] Kipling Collection, Dalhousie University Library.

[49] 'My First Book', *The Complete Works of Rudyard Kipling*, Sussex Edn., vol. xxx (1938), p. 3.

[50] KP 17/25. 'Section 420 I.P.C.' [Indian Penal Code] was the original title of the story 'In the House of Suddhoo', later collected in *Plain Tales from the Hills*.

Nevertheless, 'put in' it was; and at the very lowest estimate his verses served as 'fillers': Kipling recalled how Mian Rukn Din, the Muslim foreman on the News side, would say 'Your potery very good, sir; just coming proper length to-day. You giving more soon? One-third column just proper. Always can take on third page.'[51] But when Kay Robinson took over as editor, with instructions from the chief proprietor to 'put some sparkle into the paper',[52] he was shrewd enough to give Kipling his head, so that the *Civil and Military Gazette* became a major outlet for his poetry and fiction. He had also been welcomed as an occasional contributor by the *Gazette's* sister paper, the *Pioneer*, with its weekly supplement the *Pioneer Mail*, which was published at Allahabad in the North-West Provinces but which had a circulation throughout India. The *Pioneer* had published two of his poems (later collected in *Departmental Ditties*) in December 1884, and had subsequently indicated 'willingness to take anything [he] might choose to send'[53]—an offer of which he was quick to take advantage. Towards the end of 1887 he was transferred from Lahore to Allahabad, to work full-time for the *Pioneer*, and from then onwards, apart from a month in the early summer of 1888 when he returned to Lahore to act as editor, he published regularly in the *Pioneer* and only occasionally in the *Civil and Military Gazette*. In January 1888, moreover, the *Pioneer* launched a new weekly publication, the *Week's News*, after an advertising campaign in which Kipling's work was featured as a special attraction; and not surprisingly it carried many of his new productions. These were the main journals for which he wrote in India, but over the years he placed a few poems elsewhere—in the *Englishman*, an influential daily published in Calcutta, in the weekly *Indian Planter's Gazette and Sporting News*, and in the more dignified pages of the quarterly *Calcutta Review*. And he had the satisfaction of finding that his verses, whatever paper they first appeared in, were likely to be reprinted with due acknowledgements by others up and down the country. (The extent of these reprintings has never been charted by bibliographers: the versions produced have, of course, no textual authority, but they help to document the immediate appeal his verses had for his Anglo-Indian public.)

He also ventured into book form, first of all with *Echoes. By Two Writers*, published in the autumn of 1884. Of his poems written in

[51] 'My First Book', Sussex Edn., vol. xxx, p. 4. Cf. *Something of Myself*, p. 41.
[52] E. Kay Robinson, 'Kipling in India', *McClure's Magazine*, vol. vii (1896), p. 101.
[53] Letter to Edith Macdonald, dated 30 July 1885 (Library of Congress).

India in 1882–3 some had been sent privately to friends; a few had been published—one in the *United Services College Chronicle*, two or three others in the *Civil and Military Gazette* and other papers; but the rest had been confided only to the pages of his notebook. 1884 saw a notable increase in his self-confidence. There are again contributions to the school magazine and verses to friends, including a neatly turned Valentine 'To A.E.W'; but there are also more items in the *Civil and Military Gazette*, which include his first treatment of a barrack-room theme in 'The Story of Tommy', a telling attack on the departing Viceroy in 'Lord Ripon's Reverie', and ditties like 'The May Voyage' and 'The Descent of the Punkah' on common features of Anglo-Indian life. His main endeavours were, however, directed to the preparation of *Echoes*. Alice Kipling had returned to England in August 1883 to bring her daughter out to India, and 'the family square' was re-established in Lahore by January 1884. Rudyard and Trix, both of whom delighted in literary games, embarked now on this volume of parodies and imitations (which was extended to include some original pieces); and it is an interesting sidelight on the shared literary culture of Anglo-India that it was not thought necessary in the original publication to identify the authors imitated.

Ten of Kipling's thirty-one or thirty-two contributions date from his schoolboy years, and four from his Indian work of 1882–3: the rest are new. Some are sheer literary fun, like the parodies of Browning in 'The Flight of the Bucket' and Tennyson in 'The Cursing of Stephen'; but others, though light-hearted in tone, are serious enough in their intent. Kipling had argued, only half ironically, in 'Music for the Middle-Aged' that conventional drawing-room ballads needed to be reworked to accord with and express the facts of Anglo-Indian experience:[54] he is now adopting the same policy towards the work of well-established poets, and the parodic humour can amuse readers without subverting the documentary and psychological veracity of poems like 'A Vision of India', 'The City of the Heart', 'Laocoön', 'Nursery Rhymes for Little Anglo-Indians', 'The Maid of the Meerschaum', and 'Estunt the Griff'. The volume illustrates with remarkable clarity his transition from private to public poetry—from the earlier self represented here by poems like 'Failure' and 'A Locked Way' or a more recent work like 'London Town', to the bard of Anglo-India, writing for Anglo-Indian audiences in Anglo-Indian poetic modes about Anglo-Indian experience. It was a transition that involved both

[54] See below, pp. 220–2

gains and losses—one that determined the nature of his whole future development as a poet.[55]

Echoes was received enthusiastically by both press and public: 'By the way,' Kipling wrote to Edith Macdonald on 21 November 1884, 'that book has been most favourably noticed all round India and the whole edition is sold out.'[56] *Quartette*, published in December 1885 as the Christmas Annual of the *Civil and Military Gazette*, was equally successful. Written by 'Four Anglo-Indian Writers'—Kipling himself, Trix, and their parents—it contained three of his stories and five of his poems (one of which dated from his school-days and three from his early years in India). In spite of the very favourable reviews *Quartette* received, John Lockwood Kipling saw dangers in his son's rapid rise to popularity: 'The temptations to vulgar smartness, to over emphasis and other vices are tremendous', he told Margaret Burne-Jones in a letter of 31 January 1886: 'One test of success here is frequent quotation by other papers. And the boy is much quoted—also it is not always his best work that goes the round.'[57] The danger was not only aesthetic, though at worst Kipling's chosen mode of light verse lapses to the facile and the humdrum: there was also, more fundamentally, the danger of too close a rapport, too complete an identification, with his public. Not withstanding his occasional revulsion from Anglo-India (see below, p. 250), there was a thin division between distilling shared experience and values in his verse and acting as a mouthpiece for the lowest common denominator of Anglo-Indian prejudice.

This is not a serious problem in his best work of the period—in *Departmental Ditties*, for example, which was published in the summer of 1886 and set the seal on his reputation as *the* poet of Anglo-India, winning him unstinted praises from the Viceroy downwards. (His father wrote from Simla that 'Lord Dufferin, who frequently comes in to our sketching room, professed to be greatly struck by the uncommon combination of satire with grace and delicacy also with what he calls the boy's "infallible ear" for rhythm & cadence.'[58] The problem can become acute, however, in some of his overtly political poetry: his hostility to emergent Indian nationalism, for example, can issue in ugly racial stereotypes as it does in his early verses 'On a Recent Petition'. Yet his conservatism is more principled than such poems might suggest. He was among the critics of the newly founded Congress who

---

[55] Cf. Louis L. Cornell, *Kipling in India*, London and New York, 1966, pp. 87–9.
[56] Library of Congress.
[57] KP 1/1.
[58] KP 1/10.

argued that it was unrepresentative of Indian opinion—that it took little account of the Muslim population, or the rulers of Princely States, or indeed the mass of the Hindus who were indifferent to the claims urged on their behalf by an educated minority. On a deeper level, there was already an irreconcilable conflict in the Raj between liberal–democratic and benevolently authoritarian theories of government. Philip Woodruff refers to the contrast, by the end of the century, 'between on the one hand the ideal of a liberal empire, an India held in trust, and on the other the reality of despotic power wielded by Platonic Guardians in the interest of order and tranquillity.'[59] In the sphere of government Kipling was a Platonist, believing that good government was demonstrably better than self-government for India, and that good government was best provided by a dedicated élite of Britons. Hence his contempt for aspirant Babus and 'enlightened' viceroys on the one hand, and his merciless condemnation on the other of officials who fell short of the ideal and brought British rule into discredit. (See his poems on the Madras and Hyderabad scandals, pp. 331–2, 338–41, 345–6, and 415–21 below.)

In terms of contemporary controversy, he agreed with those who held that social and moral reforms in India should have higher priority than political change. He was horrified, as he told Margaret Burne-Jones in September 1885, by the numbers who died 'from purely preventible causes' like starvation and disease;[60] and he whole-heartedly endorsed the pragmatism of British officials who laboured to improve conditions in a practical way. ('As far as "Imperialism" went,' he told André Chevrillon years later, 'my only conception of it was that which I saw around me—men devoted to burdensome tasks under difficult conditions without much assistance or any immediate hope of reward, working for impersonal ends.')[61] Conversely, he despised Indians on elected municipal committees who neglected practical improvements it was in their power to make: their failure to improve sanitation, for example, was for him an illustration of their incapacity for government. He was also sharply critical on moral grounds of the treatment of women in Hindu society, especially over infant marriage and the wretched lot of Hindu widows. It was a cultural, not a racial problem, and one susceptible of a solution through reform; but he saw the failure of political activists to tackle this social evil in their own community as evidence of both hypocrisy and inhumanity. The status of women

[59] *The Men Who Ruled India*, London, 1954, vol. ii (*The Guardians*), p. 17.
[60] KP 11/6.   [61] KP 25/3.

became for him one of the indices of genuine as opposed to sham civilization and progress.

Such views were controversial but by no means indefensible in the context of the 1880s. What matters now is the level of poetic skill with which they are articulated. We do not need to be monarchists to enjoy 'Absalom and Achitophel', or Catholic reactionaries to enjoy Waugh's fiction; nor do we need to be old-style imperialists to enjoy the zest, the exuberance, the irreverent and at times outrageous wit of poems like 'Trial by Judge' and 'The Indian Delegates'.

The same qualities (and the same comic opera techniques based on Gilbert and Sullivan) are used to discredit the pretentiousness and folly of the Government of India in poems like 'Parturiunt Montes' and 'O Baal, Hear Us!' These derive an added piquancy from Kipling's knowing personally many of those involved in the activities or policies he ridicules. He first visited Simla for a month's leave in the summer of 1883, but he returned in 1885 for three-and-a-half months' sojourn there as special correspondent for the *Civil and Military Gazette*. In one of his father's letters we get a glimpse of him, one cheek disfigured by a 'Lahore sore', practising waltzing in preparation for this assignment—his proprietors having told him that as he was going to represent the paper, he *must* waltz well.[62] Simla was the most fashionable of hill-stations; it was also the location for the Government of India and the Government of the Punjab throughout the hot season; and its concentration of power and pleasure won it the nickname of Olympus throughout Anglo-India. Kipling soon found that he had the entrée to the highest circles, initially because Lord Dufferin was quick to appreciate the intelligence and wit of his parents—'Dulness and Mrs Kipling cannot exist in the same room', he once declared[63]—and the family came to figure frequently on invitation lists to viceregal entertainments.

Of course—we went everywhere [*Trix wrote to Stanley Baldwin in 1945, with pardonable exaggeration*]—Lord Dufferin put us on the Govt. House 'Free List'—which meant invitations to *all* the balls & dances—& At Homes—& many dinners–instead of one—every season at Simla—And Lord Roberts[64] did the same & so did our own Punjab L.G. [Lieutenant-Governor]—Lord Dufferin's saying that 'Dullness and Mrs Kipling were never in the same room together'—brought us many a pleasant invitation.[65]

[62] KP 1/10: letter to Edith Plowden, 16 Mar. 1885.
[63] A. W. Baldwin, *The Macdonald Sisters*, p. 126.
[64] The Commander-in-Chief, India. See p. 282 below.
[65] KP 1/20.

Increasingly fêted for his own literary achievements, Kipling
returned to Simla each year for his annual leave, and in spite of his
youth he soon came to know all the leading members of government.
On 30 January 1886, for example, the *Civil and Military Gazette* pub-
lished his 'Rupaiyat of Omar Kal'vin', a skit on the budget proposals
just presented by Sir Auckland Colvin, the Financial Member of
Council; and this immediately procured him 'the great satisfaction of a
delightful note' from Sir Auckland, 'complimenting me like anything
and saying "that it was a joy to find that the days of wit and delicate
humour are not yet dead in the land".' 'I wonder', Kipling reflected,
'how long I should have had to wait at home before the Chancellor of
the Exchequer congratulated me on an attack on his financial
policy . . .'[66] Not all great men, however, reacted with such equani-
mity to his attacks. Sir William Wilson Hunter,[67] pilloried in the *Pio-
neer* of 1 June 1888 in a poem 'To the Address of W.W.H.', replied
crushingly: 'I have . . . received your little pasquinade in the *Pioneer*
sent to my address. It is, I think, to be regretted that you devote to
clever trifles of this sort talents which are capable of much better
things. They practically fix your standard at that of the gymkhana and
the mess-room . . .'[68]

The challenge is not an unfair one. Kipling's verses in these years
were less endeavours of art than diversions for himself and for his
readers. 'They arrived merrily,' he reflected afterwards, 'being born
out of the life about me, and they were very bad indeed; but the joy of
doing them was pay a thousand times their worth.'[69] Some had also a
polemic function, reinforcing his journalistic attacks on evil, foolish-
ness, or error: 'If prose doesn't go home,' he wrote in a summary of his
own practice, 'hack out some verses with a lilting refrain that will take
and catch the public ear and you have helped to scotch a snake.'[70]
Many were occasional pieces, inspired by news items and written
quickly so as to constitute a kind of running commentary on events of
the day. Many derived from his own observation, sympathetic or sar-
donic, of varieties of Anglo-Indian life—at Simla, in the Plains, or in
subcategories like the pigsticking and racing fraternities, or the world
of private soldiers represented by Mulvaney and the anonymous

[66] Letter to W. C. Crofts, 18 Feb. 1886 (Kipling Collection, Dalhousie University
Library).
[67] See below, p. 308.
[68] F. H. Skrine, *The Life of Sir William Wilson Hunter*, London, 1901, pp. 374–5.
[69] 'My First Book', Sussex Edn., vol. xxx, p. 4.
[70] KP 11/6: letter to Margaret Burne-Jones, 26 Sept. 1885.

spokesman of 'A Levée in the Plains'. Others again were more per-
sonal in nature—private and informal verses addressed to friends or
members of his family, often in the form of verse-letters or inscriptions
in copies of his published works. This body of poetry taken as a whole
is more light-hearted than Sir Alfred Lyall's *Verses Written in India*,[71]
to which Kipling pays tribute; and far more accomplished than the
undeservedly popular *Lays of Ind* by 'Aliph Cheem'[72] ('Comical, Satiri-
cal and Descriptive Poems illustrative of English Life in India'), which
appeared for the first time in 1871 and ran through seven editions by
1883. Yet Kipling's own work is itself uneven in quality: some of it
seems rather casual or slapdash. Occasionally he took up poems writ-
ten years before and revised them for publication; but most were pro-
duced rapidly, for immediate consumption, with great zest but little
labour. He himself encourages us to see them in the context of Anglo-
Indian newspaper verse, which by its very nature was ephemeral,
though his verses 'had the good fortune to last a little longer than some
others':

I was in very good company [*in the pages of the* Civil and Military Gazette], for
there is always an undercurrent of song, a little bitter for the most part, run-
ning through the Indian papers . . . Sometimes a man in Bangalore would be
moved to song, and a man on the Bombay side would answer him, and a man
in Bengal would answer back, till at last we would all be crowing together, like
cocks before daybreak, when it is too dark to see your fellow . . . The news-
paper files showed that, forty years ago, the men sang of just the same subjects
as we did—of heat, loneliness, love, lack of promotion, poverty, sport, and
war.[73]

He associates himself very closely with his fellow-practitioners who
wrote under pen-names like 'Pekin', 'Latakia', 'Cigarette', 'O', 'T.W.',
and 'Foresight'; and sometimes, it must be admitted, his own works
are not readily distinguishable from those of the best of his contempor-
aries. That is why, given their addiction to anonymity, there will always
be some *dubia* beyond the strict limits of the canon. What distinguishes
his *œuvre* as a whole is its copiousness, freshness, vigour, ingenuity,
irreverence, and irrepressible vitality. Yet it remains true, as Sir Wil-
liam Wilson Hunter said, that 'his talents are capable of much better
things'.

   Prose fiction in fact engages his creative talents more deeply and

---

[71] First published in book form in 1889; but individual items were widely known from
earlier publication in newspapers.
[72] Captain W. Yeldham of the 18th Hussars.
[73] 'My First Book', Sussex Edn., vol. xxx, pp. 4–5.

more continuously than poetry in his later years in India. A few short stories had appeared much earlier—'The Gate of the Hundred Sorrows' in September 1884 and 'The Dream of Duncan Parrenness' in December of the same year. He had taken great pains with 'The Strange Ride of Morrowbie Jukes', published in *Quartette* along with 'The Phantom Rickshaw' and 'The Unlimited "Draw" of Tick Boileau'; but at this time his projected novel, *Mother Maturin*, was still a distraction. 'In the House of Suddhoo' appeared in April 1886; but it was not till the autumn of that year that he really discovered his *métier* as a writer of short stories. The series of *Plain Tales from the Hills* began in November in the *Civil and Military Gazette*, and many of the stories appeared there prior to their publication in book form in January 1888. By then he had embarked on the more ambitious journalism of *Letters of Marque*, *The City of Dreadful Night*, and other features collected in *From Sea to Sea*; but more important was his intensified commitment to prose fiction. The stories which were collected in 1888–9 in *Soldiers Three*, *The Story of the Gadsbys*, *In Black and White*, *Under the Deodars*, *The Phantom Rickshaw*, and *Wee Willie Winkie* were all written in these Indian years, as were others which remained uncollected and others again which were to figure in *The Smith Administration* and *Life's Handicap*. It was a remarkable period of creativity, in which his verses can be seen as digressions not merely from office work but from his main artistic endeavours.[74] Yet our knowledge of Kipling and of Anglo-India would be poorer without them.

[74] 'I am not a poet and never shall be', he wrote to Caroline Taylor on 9 Dec. 1889, '—but only a writer who varies fiction with verse.' (KP 16/5.)

TEXTUAL INTRODUCTION

1 MANUSCRIPT SOURCES

A large number of Kipling's early poems survive in manuscript—mostly in holograph versions, but some in transcriptions by other hands—while some have been preserved in typescript copies. Many are to be found among the Kipling Papers in the University of Sussex Library; many are located in other libraries in Britain, Canada, and the United States; while some of those which have figured in sales catalogues remain, presumably, in private hands.

In addition to individual items which were enclosed with letters, inscribed on the flyleaves of presentation volumes, or scribbled in the margin of school-books or on menus, programme cards, spare diary or scrapbook pages and odd sheets of paper, there are several important notebook collections of his early verses. In *Schooldays with Kipling* Beresford refers frequently to Gigger's practice of copying his poems into 'Russia-leather, gilt-edged, cream-laid MS. books'.[1] Four such notebooks—if we discount the hyperbole of his description—do in fact survive, three in the Kipling Papers at Sussex and one in the Berg Collection in the New York Public Library. A fifth, which may well have been the earliest of them all, was destroyed by Kipling after Miss Plowden had returned it to him in October 1915.[2]

Before he went back to India in Nov 1882 [*she recalled in her old age*], he gave me a thick school copy-book filled with his poems, written straight off. His father, as an opening illustration, drew in sepia a procession of poets led by Love (a little cupid) followed by Homer with his hand on Love's head, then came Dante, Chaucer, Shakespeare, Rossetti, Browning, Russell Lowel [*sic*], closed by a spectacled little Rudyard following with adoring spectacled eyes, pen in hand and copybook under [his arm].[3]

Kipling gives his own account of the volume and its fate in *Something of Myself*:

[The poems in *Schoolboy Lyrics*] had been first written in a stiff, marble-backed MS. book, the front page of which the Father had inset with a scandalous sepia-sketch of Tennyson and Browning in procession, and a spectacled

---

[1] *Schooldays with Kipling*, p. 284. Cf. pp. 150, 198, 254.
[2] See Kipling's letters of 15 Jan., 14 Oct., and 20 Oct. 1915 (Baldwin Papers, 2/30).
[3] Typescript for a talk to the Kipling Society in June 1938 (Baldwin Papers, 1/20). Kipling left for India in Sept., not Nov. 1882.

schoolboy bringing up the rear. I gave it, when I left school, to a woman who returned it to me many years later—for which she will take an even higher place in Heaven than her natural goodness ensures—and I burnt it, lest it should fall into the hands of 'lesser breeds without the (Copyright) law'.[4]

Nevertheless, he preserved the front cover with his father's sketch, which is reproduced opposite. He also preserved, perhaps inadvertently, three other notebooks.

Notebook 1

One of these (KP 24/3), which I refer to as Notebook 1, appears to be a continuation of the volume given to Miss Plowden. The first page, which is numbered '51', begins near the end of 'The Story of Paul Vaugel', which was written in the Christmas holidays of 1881–2. The second item, 'Les Amours Faciles', is dated 2 February 1882; and the last item in the notebook, two draft stanzas of 'On Fort Duty' on a page with the misleading title 'Revenge—a ballad of the Fleet',[5] is dated February 1884. The contents are nearly all dated, and these dated items are in strictly chronological order, with only four exceptions: one poem of a later date ('A Creed') written in, presumably, on a page that had been left blank; one poem of earlier date ('A Reminiscence'), clearly identified as such by Kipling; one poem ('Woking Necropolis') dated 7 June by what is almost certainly a slip of the pen for 7 July; and one poem dated 2 February ('Les Amours Faciles') immediately preceding 'How it Seemed to Us', dated 30 January. Undated items could theoretically have been written in on blank pages at a later date, but in view of the chronological arrangement of the collection as a whole, it seems reasonable to suppose that they were written in the sequence in which they are recorded here. This seems indeed to be a working notebook in which Kipling inscribed each poem as it was composed, though as corrections are slight it is probable that the poems were transcribed from rough drafts, as Beresford indicates was Kipling's normal practice. Quite apart from its providing holograph versions of fifty-nine poems or fragments of poems, some of which are available in no other version, this collection is of special interest for the evidence it provides on dates and order of composition, for the fact that it covers the transition from England to India, and for its containing marginal comments by Kipling in 1883–4 on some of his own earlier compositions. (These comments are recorded in this edition in the headnotes to the poems concerned.)

---

[4] *Something of Myself*, pp. 206–7.   [5] See below, p. 279.

2. The schoolboy Kipling joining a procession of the great poets: sketch by his father, c.1880 (**KP** 3/4).

Notebook 2

A second notebook (KP 24/2), which I refer to as Notebook 2, contains copies of twenty-eight poems transcribed by his father and mother, presumably from holograph copies he had sent to them in India. All but five of these poems are dated, though not with complete reliability, and these five can be dated from other sources. The earliest items are 'The Page's Song' and 'Failure', both here dated 'Winter term 1881', but dated 25 December 1881 in Notebook 3 (see below); and 'Bring me a message of hope, O Sea', dated Xmas Day 1881. The latest item is 'Prescience' ('For a season there must be pain'), later published as 'The Widower' in the *Civil and Military Gazette* for 8 August 1887, used as the source for a chapter-heading in one version of *The Light that Failed*, and collected in 1912 in *Songs from Books*. Here it is dated July 1882, but in Notebook 1, where it figures as 'Patience', it is dated 15 June. The poems in this notebook, therefore, are all products of the period December 1881 to June 1882, and are therefore subsequent to the poems sent to his parents and published by them in *Schoolboy Lyrics* (see below). They are not arranged in chronological order. They do not have the authority of holograph versions, since although they derive from fair copies it is impossible to tell whether variants, especially in accidentals, are attributable to the author's revisions or to regularizing and minor errors in transcription by his parents. In one case, however, this notebook provides the only surviving version of a poem—the verse-letter from Kipling to his sister with the heading 'Given from the Cuckoo's Nest to the Beloved Infant—Greeting' (see below, pp. 113–15).

Notebook 3

Another notebook (KP 24/1), which I refer to as Notebook 3, is in effect an anthology in MS form, holograph throughout. It has a title-page with the title 'POEMS', and a drawing of a devilkin with the rubric 'Portrait of the Author'. This is followed by a verse dedication ('The Dedication of this Book—which is written to a Woman') dated 3 February 1882. Then comes a series of thirty-nine poems written in fair copies on the right-hand pages of the notebook, which are numbered from 1 to 74. These are followed by a two-page, full-spread 'Index to the Poems Written in this Book', with a decorative heading on the left-hand page. All the poems in this series are dated, but they are not in chronological order. Apart from one item 'Haste', dated 25

June 1880, the earliest poem is 'Reckoning', dated 8 August 1881; and the latest is 'The Attainment', dated 28 May 1882. A second series of fourteen poems is written in fair copies on left-hand pages which are numbered in a separate sequence 1 to 38, with pages 20 to 24 being left blank and unnumbered; and there is a separate 'Index to the Poems Written in the Second Part of this Book'. None of the poems in this second series is dated, but all except one ('Rejection') can be dated from other sources. They are not in chronological order. Apart from three earlier items—'Crossing the Rubicon' (1879–80); 'The Reading of the Will' (published as 'Reading the Will' in *Schoolboy Lyrics*, 1881); and 'The Story of Paul Vaugel', incomplete (Christmas holidays, 1881–2)—they are all poems written in the period June to August 1882, the latest being 'The Sign of the Flower', dated 16 August 1882. The notebook ends with the poem 'To You' ('A memory of our sojourn by the Sea'), with a gloss in a different hand identifying the 'you' with Edith Macdonald, to whom the volume was presumably presented before Kipling left for India in September. This last poem is undated, but in Notebook 1 where it figures as 'A Reminiscence', it is dated 'Orig. Aug. 1881'.

Sundry Phansies

The fourth surviving notebook, *Sundry Phansies*, in the Berg Collection of the New York Public Library, is another holograph anthology. It was presented to Florence Garrard, presumably before he sailed for India since it does not include the few early poems written in India that are clearly addressed to her. The title-page is very elaborate, with a design of devilkins and a decorative scroll bearing the legend '1882 FEBRU-ARY SUNDRY PHANSIES WRIT BY ONE KIPLING'. The next page has a note which reads 'I must apologise for the writing and spelling throughout the book—They are both nearly as bad as the poetry'. Then comes a series of thirty-two poems, written in fair copies on the right-hand pages which are numbered 1 to 86 (page 54 being devoted to an elaborate title-page for 'The Story of Paul Vaugel'). It ends with an 'Index to the Phansies writ in this Book'. None of the poems is dated, but twenty-four can be dated from other sources. The verse dedication which opens the volume is the same as the opening poem in Notebook 3, which was dated 3 February 1882. Apart from two earlier items, 'Crossing the Rubicon' (1879–80) and 'The Flight' (i.e. 'Haste', 25 June 1880), the other poems which can be confidently dated are all

products of 1881 and very early 1882. Of the remainder, I would attri-
bute 'Chivalry' to 1880 (see below, p. 54), and 'L'Envoi' ('Rhymes, or
of grief or of sorrow') is described in a later copy as 'written in "81" '.[6]
Sundry Phansies, therefore, while apparently begun at the same time as
Notebook 3, is more retrospective in character. There remain, how-
ever, some undated poems—'Quaeritur' ('Is Life to be measured by
grains?'), 'Conspiracy', 'Song' ('I bound his soul'), 'A Visitation',
'Brighton Beach', and 'Resolve', which may well have been written in
1882; and it must be a matter of conjecture how long a period Kipling
devoted to the completion of this volume. His breach with Flo Garrard
in May 1882 (see below, p. 143) is not conclusive, since communica-
tion was re-established between them, and it was not till 1884 that he
had his final rejection.[7] For what it is worth, however, my impression is
that the collection belongs to the earlier part of the year 1882.

There are many overlaps between the contents of the various note-
books, which are listed in Appendix B; but each has unique items not
preserved in any other version.

2 PRINTED SOURCES

I have not drawn on pirated or unauthorized printings, of which there
were many in Kipling's lifetime, but only on 'legitimate' publications
containing poems that are unquestionably his though they do not
figure in the Definitive Edition of his verse or in collections of his
prose. Such poems are to be found in the following editions, news-
papers or periodicals:

The United Services College Chronicle

Seven issues of the school magazine, which was revived under
Kipling's editorship, appeared between 30 June 1881 and 24 July
1882. They contained fourteen poems by Kipling, one of them ('Told
in the Dormitory') in three instalments; and of the fourteen only one
('Ave Imperatrix') was included in the Definitive Edition. After leaving
school he had a further eight poems published in the magazine
between December 1882 and March 1889; and of these only two,

---

[6] Inscription in copy of *Departmental Ditties* sent to Florence Garrard (Berg Collec-
tion).
[7] See his letter to Margaret Burne-Jones dated May–June 1886 (KP 11/6).

reprinted there from *Departmental Ditties*, were included in the Definitive Edition. As editor Kipling was responsible both for the preparation of copy and for proof-correcting; but after leaving school he had to depend on his successors to see his verses through the press.

Schoolboy Lyrics

Kipling's parents had this volume of his verses published in Lahore in a limited edition for private circulation, in December 1881. This was done without his knowledge or consent (see above, p. 11). The volume was printed by the *Civil and Military Gazette* Press, and his parents presumably corrected the proofs, having previously prepared the copy by transcribing holograph verses he had sent to them. It contained twenty-three poems, none of which is included in the Definitive Edition, though twenty-two were collected in the Outward Bound, De Luxe, Sussex, and Burwash Editions.

The World

One poem of Kipling's ('Two Lives'), written and accepted for publication while he was still at school, appeared in this journal on 8 November 1882, by which date he was in Lahore. (See below, p. 137.) It was collected only in the Sussex and Burwash Editions.

Echoes, By Two Writers

This volume of parodies, imitations, and original works by Kipling and his sister Trix was published in Lahore in the autumn of 1884, though advance copies were in his hands by early August. It was printed by the *Civil and Military Gazette* Press, and Kipling himself oversaw its production. It contained thirty-nine poems, thirty-two (or possibly thirty-one) of which were by Kipling. None was included in the Definitive Edition; but thirty-two were collected in the Outward Bound, De Luxe, Sussex, and Burwash Editions. The attribution of only seven poems to Trix is based on indications by Kipling in a number of presentation copies dated 1884, and confirmed by his including the other thirty-two in the Outward Bound and De Luxe Editions. Trix, however, complained subsequently that when it came to sorting out the verses in *Echoes*, he claimed several of hers; and in a copy presented to Mrs Hill in 1888 eleven poems (including the usual seven) are crossed out as if they were being repudiated.[8] Since, however, one of the four items in dispute ('The Ballad of the King's Daughter') appears in Notebook 3 and *Sundry Phansies*, and another ('Tobacco') in the margin of one of his schoolbooks, Trix's claim to this group can be discounted. 'Jane Smith', however, is still a disputed case. Louis Cornell argues that 'Trix's authorship of this poem is attested by a note in her handwriting in the copy of *Echoes* sent to the Misses Craik.'[9] It is certainly attributed to her in the copies presented to Edith Macdonald and Mrs Alfred Baldwin.[10] The case is unclear, and it is even possible that they co-operated on this poem.

Quartette

This Christmas Annual 'By Four Anglo-Indian Writers' was the work of Kipling, his sister, his father, and his mother. It appeared in December 1885, having been printed by the *Civil and Military Gazette* Press. Kipling himself oversaw its production, and in a long letter to Margaret Burne-Jones he describes the tribulations this involved:

Ram Dass, excellent Hindu that he is brings me pages on pages each viler than the first:—'Sar I cannot understand' says he, and I have to go through it all again. If Quartette comes out without a howling misprint in every other line it will be by the blessing of Providence alone. I never met such awful people in my life. . . . Imagine 513 mistakes in one galley of five pages! The family seem to be rather amused than afflicted by 'those absurd misprints' but it's anything but fun for me.[11]

The volume contained three stories by Kipling and five poems. None of the latter were included in the Definitive Edition, nor were they collected elsewhere.

The Calcutta Review

This quarterly review published four poems by Kipling between October 1885 and July 1886. Of these only one, 'The Explanation' ['The Legend of Love'] was included in the Definitive Edition, but a second, 'The Vision of Hamid Ali', was collected in the Sussex and Burwash Editions. The other two were 'The Seven Nights of Creation' and 'King Solomon's Horses'.

[8] Stewart and Yeats, pp. 13–14.
[9] *Kipling in India*, p. 71.
[10] Baldwin Papers, 2/39, 2/40.
[11] KP 11/6.

Departmental Ditties

The entire contents of the First Edition of 1886 are included in the Definitive Edition. The Second Edition, also published in 1886, contained the poem 'Lucifer', which was not included in subsequent editions of the volume or in the Definitive Edition, but which was collected in the Outward Bound, De Luxe, Sussex, and Burwash Editions. The Third Edition of 1888 contained the poem 'Diana of Ephesus', first published in the *Englishman* on 18 March 1887. It was not included in subsequent editions of any kind until it was collected in the Sussex and Burwash Editions.

Anglo-Indian Newspapers

See above, pp. 13–22, and below, pp. 37–8. The greatest problem here has always been that of identifying as Kipling's poems which he published anonymously or under pseudonyms. There is, of course, no difficulty about items published over his own name or his initials, items retrospectively acknowledged by their inclusion in collected volumes of his verse, or items published over pseudonyms or initials (such as 'Esau Mull' and E. M.) which are clearly identifiable as his; but there are many others the attribution of which has been more or less speculative. The most authoritative discussions of this problem are to be found in L. H. Chandler's *Summary of the Work of Rudyard Kipling, Including Items Ascribed to Him*, New York, 1930, pp. 330–52, Stewart and Yeats, especially pp. 534–41, and Louis Cornell's *Kipling in India*, especially pp. 167–84 and 192–203; and to these I am deeply indebted. I have, however, been able to draw on important new evidence. Firstly, there are among the Kipling Papers at the University of Sussex Kipling's scrapbooks of press cuttings of his own work (KP 28/1, KP 28/2, KP 28/3, and KP 28/4, which I refer to as Scrapbooks 1, 2, 3, and 4 respectively). These do not contain all his publications, but they include nothing that is not his own; and they have enabled me to establish beyond doubt his authorship of many items hitherto uncertain. They have also made possible, directly or indirectly, the identification as Kipling's of poems never previously attributed to him. Secondly, I have been able to draw on a wide range of Kipling's unpublished letters at Sussex and elsewhere, references in which often serve to authenticate poems otherwise in doubt, as do references in his unpublished diary for 1885. Thirdly, I have made use of Kipling's own marginalia in L. H. Chandler's *Summary* and in a typed First-Line

Index to Kipling's verse also compiled by Chandler. Kipling's own copies of these were preserved at his daughter's former home at Wimpole Hall; and his repudiations of particular items—'Not mine. R. K.' is a typical formula—are of great importance. They are not wholly reliable, since his memory sometimes played him false and on a few occasions we find him repudiating works which are demonstrably his; yet his disclaimers constitute in general a prima-facie case against attributing such items to him, unless there is independent evidence to confirm the attribution. That he does *not* repudiate an item does not prove that he acknowledges it as his: we do not know how systematically he scanned the lists of attributions. But his denials of authorship cannot readily be brushed aside.

When the evidence has all been sifted, there remain some items in the Anglo-Indian Press which might be Kipling's, but for which I can find no firm evidence of authorship: these I have relegated to the category of *dubia*, and excluded from this volume.

Outward Bound Edition

New York, Charles Scribner's Sons, 1897–1937, vol. xvii, *Early Verse*, 1900.

As his correspondence with Scribner's shows, Kipling took a keen interest in the planning and preparation of this edition, the first eleven volumes of which appeared in 1897. At one stage he had intended to exclude *Departmental Ditties*: 'I want to suppress 'em because they are unusual bad, and will not be included in any English edition that I may make,' he wrote to Scribner's on 4 April 1897. 'This is my great chance for eliminating some doggerel that I am much discontented with'.[12] In accordance with this decision, the first volume of verse to appear in the edition, *Verses 1889–1896* (vol. xi, 1897), consisted only of *Barrack-Room Ballads and Other Verses* and *The Seven Seas*, together with 'My New-Cut Ashlar' from *Life's Handicap*. By 14 July 1899, however, he had formed 'the intention of making the "Outward Bound" Edition as full and complete as possible', and he therefore proposed to include in it 'not only *Departmental Ditties* but also two earlier volumes of verse: as well as a large quantity of miscellaneous matter contributed to Indian newspapers.'[13] In 1900 he published the

[12] Charles Scribner's Sons Archive, Box 87, Princeton University Library.
[13] Typescript note of 14 July 1899, with autograph signature, Lilly Library, Indiana University.

volume *Early Verse*, which contained *Schoolboy Lyrics*, *Echoes*, *Departmental Ditties*, and *Other Verses* associated with the last of these. And he acknowledged another reason for including the earlier material: 'I'd never have dug up my early verse & put it in the "Outward bound",' he wrote to Mary Mapes Dodge on 13 July 1902, 'if the pirates hadn't begun that same trick and so deprived me of the (almost) inalienable human (literary) right of decently burying my own dead.'[14] The point is elaborated in a letter of 25 June 1928 to A. S. Watt, of A. P. Watt and Son, his literary agents, on his reasons for refusing to allow such material to be included in a de luxe edition of his poems which was then being planned by Macmillan and Co.:

First—Schoolboy Lyrics was published for private circulation by my people when I was at school. 'Echoes' was work done a little later in which my family took part, as they did in 'Quartette'. I should never have republished them with my own work except for the fact—which you may recall—that U.S. pirates got hold of them and exploited them. That is the reason why in the Scribner 'Outward Bound' there is that volume of 'Early Verse' dated 1900. In the early part of that year Messrs George Haven Putnam, believing that I was at the point of death in New York, ran out an edition of my works, made up of uncopyrighted stuff together with sheets that they had bought from other publishers of copyrighted books in order to take advantage of the market. Hence after the lawsuit Kipling v. Putnam the inclusion of 'Schoolboy Lyrics' and 'Early Verse' [*sic*] in the Scribner's 'Outward Bound' and in Macmillan's first collected edition, which followed the lines of the 'Outward Bound'.[15] I always count 'Departmental Ditties' as the first of my books of verse, since it was the first book that I myself published; and therefore I began my Inclusive Verse with that volume.[16]

In spite of these disclaimers, however, Kipling was to authorize the inclusion of this early material in the Sussex Edition, in his final revision of the canon of his collected works (see below, p. 35).

In providing copy for the *Early Verse* Kipling revised the contents of the constituent volumes. His 'Schoolboy Lyrics' of 1881 are all included with the one exception of 'The Night Before', but they are supplemented by eight poems from the *United Services College Chronicle*, which significantly modify the tone of the original volume. These are 'Donec Gratus Eram', 'The Boar of the Year' ['The Ride of the Schools'], 'The Battle of Assye', 'On Fort Duty', 'Inscribed in a Pres-

---

[14] Donald Dodge Collection of Mary Mapes Dodge, Box 2, Princeton University Library.

[15] i.e. the Edition de Luxe (see p. 34 below).

[16] Macmillan Archive, BL Add. MS 54940, pp. 85–6. (Copy in KP 22/4.)

entation Copy of "Echoes" to the Common Room', 'The Song of the Exiles', 'The Jam-Pot' ['The Worst of It'], and 'Ave Imperatrix'. He includes all thirty-two of his own contributions to *Echoes*, while excluding Trix's seven. To the 'Departmental Ditties' themselves he adds 'Lucifer' from the Second Edition and 'The Man and the Shadow' from the *Week's News*; while to the 'Other Verses' accompanying the 'Ditties' he adds eight further uncollected pieces from Anglo-Indian newspapers. These are 'Carmen Simlaense' ['A Ballad of the Break Up'], 'A Levée in the Plains' ['Levéety in the Plains'], 'Our Lady of Rest', 'The Plaint of the Junior Civilian', 'For the Women', 'A Ballade of Bad Entertainment' ['A Ballade of Dak-Bungalows'], 'O Baal, Hear Us!', and 'New Lamps for Old'. He also revised the text, cutting passages from several poems, making some substantive though minor changes elsewhere, and either initiating or endorsing a more formal, regularized system of punctuation, capitalization, etc. The edition also provides footnote glosses to a number of Indian words or phrases.

The Outward Bound Edition had for many years a special place in his affections. 'The Edition generally strikes me as a wonder and a delight and I am very proud of it', he had written to Scribner's on 4 April 1897;[17] and he was often to bear testimony to the pleasure it had given him. 'I want to assure you that my interest in this edition is unabated', he wrote on 13 May 1920. 'I have never had the same feeling towards any other edition of my work. It was the first collected one formed and my plan for it has always been to make it in its own particular way a perfect edition.'[18] There is every reason to suppose that the 'tidied up' presentation of his early poems in vol. xvii represents his considered view of the form in which he wished to preserve them.

Edition de Luxe

London, Macmillan and Co., 1897–1938, vol. xviii, *Early Verse*, 1900.

The contents of this volume are the same as those of the Outward Bound Edition, vol. xvii. The format and pagination differ in minor respects, but the text is the same apart from the correction of a few typographical slips. The edition would seem to have no independent textual authority.

---

[17] Charles Scribner's Sons Archive, Box 87, Princeton University Library.
[18] Ibid.

Sussex Edition

London, Macmillan and Co., 1937–9, vol. xxxii, *Departmental Ditties: Barrack-Room Ballads*, 1938; vol. xxxv, *Early Verse: The Muse Among the Motors: Miscellaneous*, 1939.

The genesis and development of this great edition can be traced from papers in the Macmillan Archive in the British Library, supplemented by certain of the Kipling Papers at the University of Sussex. Of special relevance are Macmillan and Co.'s copies of correspondence with the Kiplings (Add. MS 54940), and with A. P. Watt and Son from 1928 to 1939 (Add. MSS 54900–4), their Letter-Books for the same period (Add. MSS 55664ff.), their marked proofs mainly for this edition (Add. MSS 55846–76), and the Kiplings' copies of correspondence to and between Macmillan and Co. and A. P. Watt and Son (KP 22/4).

From these it is clear that once the edition had been agreed on in the autumn of 1929 Kipling threw himself with enthusiasm into the task of planning and arranging the contents of each volume, and of reviewing hitherto uncollected material for possible inclusion. A letter of 7 July 1930 from A. P. Watt to Harold Macmillan quotes Mrs Kipling's account of his views on the verse:

I should like to know how Messrs. Macmillan propose to deal with the verse . . . 'Barrack-Room Ballads', 'Seven Seas', 'Five Nations', and 'The Years Between' are to be printed in the order of their original publication. 'Early Verse' can be included in 'Departmental Ditties', as in the Outward Bound, but some arrangement must be made for such uncollected verse as appeared in Macmillan's de luxe edition of last year.[19]

In a reply dated 10 July 1930 Macmillan's suggest that 'as regards the arrangement of the verse, this question could perhaps stand over for the present, as a considerable time will elapse before we shall be able to contemplate beginning work on this section;'[20] but by the time they *were* able to do so, Kipling was dead. He had carefully reviewed the contents of each volume of his prose, initialling lists to signify his approval, and he had given a good deal of attention to the items of 'Uncollected Prose' which constituted vols. xxix and xxx (though after his death Mrs Kipling intervened to insist on the omission of one item which he had approved). The verse, however, which concludes the edition in vols. xxxii–xxxv, had not been reconsidered in the same way, though he had of course reviewed it from time to time for the various

---

[19] Macmillan Archive, BL Add. MS 54901, p. 31. (Copy in KP 22/4.)
[20] KP 22/4.

inclusive editions. It was his widow who authorized the inclusion of additional verse items in the Sussex Edition; and in doing so she relied on what she claimed to know he wanted and did not want of his earliest work[21]. The editor, Mr Mark, paid her a long visit in late April 1937, and she 'was able to give him a great deal that he could not otherwise have got at', but she insisted on hĕr right to decide what Kipling would have wished to be included.[22] *Departmental Ditties and Other Poems* have the same contents as in the Outward Bound Edition, with the addition of 'Diana of Ephesus' (see above, p. 31). The *Early Verse* section has the same contents as the Outward Bound in *Schoolboy Lyrics* and *Echoes*, but three additional items from this early period are admitted to the *Miscellaneous* section of vol. xxxv: 'Two Lives', reprinted from *The World* and misdated 1881; 'The Vision of Hamid Ali', reprinted from the *Calcutta Review*; and 'In Partibus', reprinted from *Abaft the Funnel* (1909) which had reprinted it from the *Civil and Military Gazette*.

Whether Kipling himself would have made a more generous selection had he lived must remain a matter for conjecture; but he had certainly been opposed to the idea in 1928, when he turned down Macmillan's proposal to include hitherto uncollected material in a new de luxe edition of his poems.[23]

As regards work 'not at present accessible to the public', the inclusion of such work makes [*sc.* would make] the new issue more of a collector's book than a considered book of known verse by me offered to the public. Nor, under the circumstances, could it be in any way a complete collection. . . . [*Quite apart from his reluctance to confirm or deny his authorship of many pieces rightly or wrongly attributed to him*] assuming that every item submitted were correct . . . still the collection could not be complete, because there is in existence at least as much again of my ephemeral, private and occasional verse as bibliographers suppose themselves to have traced up to the present. So any attempt to develop this edition on the bibliographical side would be a failure, and might excite the U.S. market to further piratical efforts.[23]

The Sussex Edition was seen through the press by Mr T. Mark of Macmillan's, who had long experience of dealing with Kipling's works. On 6 July 1931 Mrs Kipling had conveyed her husband's thanks to the proof-reader, who was in fact Mark, for his work on *Humorous Tales* (1931): 'He has helped him enormously, and knows his books much

---

[21] Macmillan Archive, BL Add. MS 54903, p. 121.
[22] Ibid., p. 225.
[23] Macmillan Archive, BL Add. MS 54940, pp. 86–7. (Copy in KP 22/4).

better than Mr Kipling knows them himself! He is really very remark-
able in his helpfulness.'[24] Macmillan's began printing the Sussex
Edition in 1930, and from the outset proofs were sent by R. and R.
Clark, the printers, to Mark, who corrected them and forwarded them
to Kipling, often with queries on specific points. Kipling would answer
the queries and correct the proofs further before returning them to
Mark, and these proofs have been preserved, so that the edition can be
shown to have special authority. Verse chapter-headings and poems
included in volumes of prose fiction were treated in the same way, but
the verse volumes were not even set up till after his death. They follow
the text of the Outward Bound and De Luxe Editions of the early
verse, with some minor changes in capitalization and punctuation.
Clearly, these were not authorized by Kipling, though one should
remember that Mark was a sensitive and conscientious editor who was
following conventions established earlier in the edition. In marking the
proofs, for example, Kipling did increase the incidence of capitals for
initial letters: thus 'railway', 'regiment', 'colonel', and 'curator' are all
marked up in this way in his corrections to the opening pages of *Kim*.
Individual examples in the poems are, however, open to query; and I
conclude that as far as the early verses not in the Definitive Edition are
concerned the Outward Bound Edition has more authority.

Burwash Edition

New York, Doubleday, Doran and Co., 1941, vol. xxv, *Departmental
Ditties: Barrack-Room Ballads*; vol. xxviii, *Early Verse: The Muse Among
the Motors: Miscellaneous*.

This edition follows the text of the Sussex Edition and has no inde-
pendent authority.

3 EDITORIAL PRACTICE

Contents

This edition excludes poems which are published in the Definitive
Edition of Kipling's verse or in the collected volumes of his prose fic-
tion.[25] Apart from these, however, it includes all his poems from the

[24] Macmillan Archive, BL Add. MS 54901, p. 180.
[25] In a few cases, where Kipling has used lines from one of the poems included in this
volume as the heading for a chapter or short story, these lines, but not the poem they
come from, figure in the collected prose and sometimes in the Definitive Edition.

USCC, *Schoolboy Lyrics*, *Echoes*, and *Quartette*; all the poems from his four early Notebooks; all the poems in the *CMG*, the *Pioneer*, the *Pioneer Mail*, the *Week's News*, the *Englishman*, and the *Calcutta Review* which can be firmly identified as his (up to December 1889); all the poems of this period from Scrapbooks 1 to 4 and from the Sussex Edition; and all the poems I have been able to assemble from MS sources. This does not mean that the collection is complete. I have not included every line or scrap of verse which occurs in his fiction or journalism. I have excluded some items from Anglo-Indian newspapers which have been attributed to him, but of which his authorship has neither been confirmed nor disproved. And with an author as prolific as Kipling— one so given to improvising occasional verses or scraps of verse—it is never possible to claim the tally is complete. Some works he is known to have written—'a farewell to India', for example, 'after the manner of Walt Whitman'[26]—have never been located. Others—like an early sonnet on 'Ye Fair Griselde'—have been glimpsed only as they passed through salerooms.[27] Others, again, may come to light in collections I have not been able to examine. But readers may take it that they have before them the main corpus of Kipling's verse, apart from items included in the Definitive Edition, up to his début on the London literary scene in 1889. It is arranged in chronological order, in so far as that can be determined. When the date of composition is not accurately known, items are given under their date of first publication. In cases where the dating is speculative, this is made clear in the head-notes to the poems. This edition differs from R. E. Harbord's pioneering attempt in vol. 8 of the *Readers' Guide* (privately printed in a limited edition of one hundred copies) by including many items unknown or unavailable to him, by excluding many items mistakenly or unjustifiably attributed to Kipling, by establishing a more accurate chronology, and by providing more reliable texts, with bibliographical information on sources and locations, and full explanatory annotation.

Titles

Where a poem has appeared under more than one title, the earlier or alternative title is given in square brackets. Where two poems have the same title, the first line of each is also given (e.g. in the list of Contents). Where a poem has no title it is listed under its first line, or

---

[26] Letter to Mrs Hill, 23 Feb. 1889 (KP 16/4).
[27] 'After O.W. the unutterable', catalogue of Sotheby's sale, 8 Dec. 1983, item 110.

under a heading provided by the editor (e.g. 'Inscription in Copy of *Plain Tales from the Hills* Presented to Mrs Hill').

Notes

Bibliographical information is provided in the head-notes to poems, as is biographical and historical material when this is relevant. More detailed glosses on specific terms or topics are provided in the footnotes.

Text

When an unpublished poem exists in only one MS or typed version, that version is used as the copy-text.

When more than one such version exists, holograph versions are preferred to transcriptions by other hands or typed copies (unless these are known to have been approved by Kipling himself). Versions in Notebooks 1 and 3 and *Sundry Phansies* are therefore preferred to those in Notebook 2.

When more than one holograph version exists, later holograph versions are preferred to earlier (but are disregarded if they are merely transcriptions of poems already in print). Versions in Notebook 3 and *Sundry Phansies* are therefore preferred to those in Notebook 1.

In the case of poems common to both Notebook 3 and *Sundry Phansies* the texts seem to be of equal authority, both being deliberate revisions of earlier versions and written at roughly the same time. (Of the twenty-two poems in this category, nineteen are in the first series of poems in Notebook 3, which was begun in the same month as *Sundry Phansies*.) The many minor variants, both substantive and accidental, are attributable not to one version's being earlier and one later, but to the poems still being in a slightly fluid state, liable to minor variation in each authorial transcription. I have taken *Sundry Phansies* as copy-text, since it seems more carefully prepared, but in a few instances, indicated in the head-notes, I have used Notebook 3, and there is a case which I accept for some eclecticism, especially when manifest inadequacy of punctuation in one version can be rectified from the other. It could be argued that in the case of the three poems which occur in *Sundry Phansies* and the second series in Notebook 3, the latter version may well be the later (see above, p. 26–8). This would affect 'Crossing the Rubicon'; but of the other two, 'The Story of Paul Vaugel' is in large part missing from Notebook 3, and 'The Reading of the Will' is superseded by a published version.

When a poem exists only in a single printed version, that version is used as the copy-text.

Published versions for which Kipling himself provided copy are preferred to MS or typed versions, though with due awareness of the possibility of printers' errors, and they are also preferred to published versions the copy for which was provided by others (e.g. *Schoolboy Lyrics*, 1881).

Published versions for which Kipling not only provided copy but read proofs, or approved the final state, are preferred to those seen through the press by others. The Outward Bound Edition of the Early Verse is therefore preferred to the Sussex. Where, however, misprints or errors in the Outward Bound are corrected in the De Luxe or Sussex Editions, these corrections are accepted. Also, where alternative spellings of Indian words occur in these editions, and it is clear from the earlier volumes of the Sussex Edition that Kipling has opted for one of them, that form is adopted even if it differs from the Outward Bound (e.g. 'sais', not 'syce'). This principle is not applied, however, to poems which exist only in MS or newspaper versions, where the original spellings have been retained.

Later published versions known to have been revised by Kipling are preferred to earlier. The Outward Bound versions are therefore preferred to those in the original *Echoes*, *USCC*, etc.

Apparatus

Where such revisions involve major changes such as the exclusion of lines or stanzas, these passages are printed in square brackets in the text or recorded in the head-note to the poem. Where there are other substantive changes of major significance, these too are indicated in the head-notes or footnotes. It is not, however, possible within the confines of this volume to provide a textual apparatus listing all variants, substantive and accidental, between the different MS versions, between MS and published versions, and between the published versions themselves. Such an apparatus would have to be of great bulk and complexity, and it must await the publication of a full-scale critical edition of Kipling's verse.

Regularization

Kipling tried as a matter of policy to have his marked proofs destroyed, but those that survive show his meticulous concern for punctuation and other accidentals. This is reflected in the regularization of accidentals in the presentation of his early poems in the Outward Bound Edition. Other poems, which remained uncollected, were never subjected to this process by the author or his publishers, and there is a case for limited editorial intervention. Many of the poems published in Anglo-Indian newspapers, for example, were proof-read by Kipling in the course of his routine duties, but many, sent to other papers than the one he was working on, were not. In any case, the haste inevitable in the production of a daily newspaper, the slapdash punctuation of the copy itself (because of the pressure under which he wrote), and the propensity to error which he often lamented in native compositors, all suggest the need for minor amendment. There is no virtue in the perpetuation of carelessness, error, or inconsistency. I have not sought to impose the style and conventions of the Outward Bound and Sussex Editions on the uncollected verse; but I have regularized discreetly to provide tidier versions than those first hastily presented in ephemeral publications. I have also rejected, as the collected editions do, the old-fashioned convention of repeating quotation marks at the beginning of each line in passages of direct speech. In semi-dramatic pieces speech ascriptions, which appeared originally and in some cases in collected editions in a variety of types and positions on the page, have been centred as a general rule and printed in small capitals. There has also been some standardizing of the setting of stage directions.

The regularizing of holograph versions is more controversial, since here there is no distorting intermediary, and it is arguable that the idiosyncrasies of the author should be preserved *in toto*. Certainly editorial intervention should be minimal; and I have accordingly accepted punctuation sporadic to a point which Kipling himself would hardly have condoned in print. If a poem is written with no question marks after questions, or indeed no punctuation whatever at the end of many sentences, it is so reproduced, to give the flavour of the MS. When, however, punctuation which is clearly appropriate appears in one version but not in another, when brackets or quotation marks are opened but not closed, when apostrophes are omitted where convention requires them or where they are misplaced, or when the arrangement of line indentations is so arbitrary or so variable as to obscure the intended pattern, there is a case which I accepted for very limited emendation. I have also regularized the use of capitals in the titles of poems.

Here again I have rejected the convention of repeating quotation marks at the beginning of every line of direct speech; I have throughout used single in preference to double quotation marks except for quotations within quotations; and I have throughout reserved square brackets for editorial purposes.

PART ONE

School Years

THE DUSKY CREW

This is the earliest poem of Kipling's which he ever authorized for publication. Its main interest is biographical, demonstrating as it does the importance he attached even at this early date to the special relationship with L. C. Dunsterville ('Stalky') and G. C. Beresford ('M'Turk') which he celebrated long afterwards in 'An English School', *Stalky and Co.*, and *Something of Myself.* Its early history also reveals his eagerness to appear in print: in August 1879, when he was aged thirteen, the poem was offered to but rejected by the *St Nicholas Magazine*, a well-known American periodical for children. (See Catharine Morris Wright, 'How "St Nicholas" Got Rudyard Kipling and What Happened Then', *Princeton University Library Chronicle*, vol. xxxv (1974), pp. 259-89.) It was also contributed, with the signature 'Nickson', to the *Scribbler*, a handwritten magazine produced by the younger members of the Burne-Jones and Morris families between November 1878 and March 1880. (See below pp. 47–8.) First published in *Schoolboy Lyrics*, 1881. Collected in the Outward Bound, De Luxe, Sussex, and Burwash Edns. The capitals at 'the Other Two', which somewhat inflate their importance, appeared for the first time in the Outward Bound and De Luxe Edns. in 1900.

Our heads were rough and our hands were black
    With the ink-stain's midnight hue;
We scouted all, both great and small—
    We were a dusky crew;
And each boy's hand was against us raised—
    'Gainst me and the Other Two.

We chased the hare from her secret lair,
    We roamed the woodlands through;
In parks and grounds far out of bounds
    Wandered our dusky crew;
And the keepers swore to see us pass—
    Me and the Other Two.

And one there was who was light of limb,
    Nimble and wary too.
A spirit grim we made of him
    Unto our dusky crew:
He fetched and carried for all us three—
    For me and the Other Two.

Our secret caves in the cold, dark earth
    The luscious lettuce grew;
We ate the cress in merriness—
    We were a dusky crew;
The radish red gave sweet repast
    To me and the Other Two.

Our lettuces are dead and gone,
    Our plans have fallen through;
We wander free in misery—
    We are a wretched crew:
For a master's wrath has fallen on us—
    On me and the Other Two.

He found our cave in the cold, dark earth,
    He crept the branches through;
He caught us all in our Council-Hall—
    Caught us, a dusky crew;
To punishment he led us all—
    Me and the Other Two.

Our lettuces are dead and gone,
    Our plans have fallen through;
We wander free in misery—
    We are a wretched crew.
Will happiness no more return
    To me and the Other Two?

THE PILLOW-FIGHT

This mock-heroic rendering of an episode of school life was included in the 5 January 1880 number of the *Scribbler* (see above, p. 45), with the signature 'Nickson' (typescript copy BL Add. MS 45337). Published with the signature 'I.N.O.' in the *USCC*, no. 5, 23 July 1881. Uncollected. One line cut from the *Scribbler* version is printed here in square brackets.

The day was ended and a crowd of boys
Raced through the corridor and upward shot
To top-most dormitories, chattering loud
Of the great fray, whilst some their bolsters scan

With anxious eye lest an unnoticed rent
Insidious lurking in the seamy sides
Might in the thick of battle on their heads
Scatter the feathers, others quickly strip
To shirt and trousers; stand expectant all.
The sides are chosen and the 'signal given'.
Rush on the warriors! Then began the din,
The noise of bolsters falling on the floor.
The heavy thud when some well planted blow
Hath brought the strong opponent to his knees.

Now high above the strife was heard the sound
Of earthen pitcher loosened from the stand
And crashing to the earth. The sharper ring
Of myriad glasses breaking swelled the hymn
Of glorious war. Confusion at its height
Raves through the rooms; rattle the windows all,
[Rally the sides, the bolsters thicker fly—]
Fills all the air with dust, dim shadowy forms
Loom through the mist dealing Titanic blows.
Hero meets hero and the gathering roar
Swells like some sea whose murmurs heard at night
Far in the distance grinding hoary stones,
Menace the air.

*　　*　　*　　*　　*

How can I sing of Victory and Defeat?
How can I tell of Battle's awful scenes?
How, least of all, of Vengeance dire and deep?
Vengeance for sleep disturbed and graceless noise,
That echoing loud aroused a master's ire.
The heavy stripes, the long-drawn gasping sob,
Repentant vows wrung from the chastened soul,
The victim's anguish, and the after glow
Let others tell; I only sing the fray.

THE NIGHT BEFORE

A copy of this poem, signed 'Nickson', was found in an editorial portfolio for the *Scribbler* (see above, p. 45), the last completed number of which was dated 8 March 1880. The portfolio contains part of the next projected number,

together with typescript copies of three poems by Kipling, the others being
'The Dusky Crew' and 'Job's Wife' (BL Add. MS 45337). 'The Night Before'
was published in *Schoolboy Lyrics*, 1881, but never collected or reprinted by
Kipling.

I sneered when I heard the old priest complain
That the doomed are voiceless, and dull of brain,
For why should a felon be other than dumb
As he stands at the gate of the world to come?
The tick-tock
Of the great jail clock,
Is more to me than the holiest prayer
That ever was mingled with dungeon air.

Will it never be dawn in the cold, grey skies?
The great, red sun, will he never arise,
Thrusting his rays in my iron-barred cell,
And lighting the city I know so well?
Will the tick-tock
Of the great jail clock,
Beat for ever through brain and heart
Till the tortured soul from the body part?

And now in the gloom of the grated cell
Rises a figure I know full well.
Gashed of throat, and broken of limb,
What do I want today with him?
To the tick-tock
Of the pitiless clock
His body is swaying, slowly and free,
While his shadowy finger points at me.

Will it never be here—the dawn of day,
With the summons to carry my life away?
Nothing to scatter the terrible gloom,
Nothing to herald the hour of doom
But the tick-tock
Of the ceaseless clock,
And the tread of the tired policeman's feet
As he steadily paces the echoing street.

At last the darkness is melting away
In the corpse-like light on the face of day,
   I hear the carts in the street once more
   And the sheriff's step on the stony floor,
      And the tick-tock
      Of the great jail clock,
The whispered words of the warder's round,
And every whisper a thunder-sound!

A mockery! This is the formal demand
In the mighty name of the law of the land,
   For the body of him who is doomed to die
   In the face of men and beneath the sky.
I am safe in your thrall, yet bind me well,
For I might be desperate—who can tell?
As I march to the sound of the clanging bell,
      And the tick-tock
      Of the great jail clock,
And the voice of the priest as he mumbles a prayer,
And the hum of the crowd that awaits me there!

JOB'S WIFE

This poem, another of those found in the Spring 1880 editorial portfolio for the *Scribbler*, was never published by Kipling. It takes as its starting-point Job 2: 9: 'Then said his wife unto him, Dost thou still retain thine integrity? curse God and die.' Signed 'Nickson'. (Typescript copy BL Add. MS 45337; transcribed version Huntington Library MS HM 1698 taken as copy text.)

Curse now thy God and die, for all is done.
Thy bitter cup is filled to the brim.
In all mankind there liveth not a one
That careth for thee. What art thou to him?
There is no need for thee. The world is hard,
And Love is not. Death only standeth by.
Faith is not known. From Hope thou art debarred
Thou canst but choose twixt Death and Misery
O, Life is sad and Death is sweet indeed
To such as thou. If thou believest it

He is a friend to help thee in thy need
And what is Life in that thou leavest it
As though it were a friend? Death's sleep is long
Wilt thou not taste of Lethe[1] and be strong?

THE FLIGHT [HASTE]

This poem exists in two holograph fair copies made in 1882. One in Notebook
3, with the title 'Haste', is dated 25 June 1880. The other, in *Sundry Phansies*,
is entitled 'The Flight'.

So the end came
    In the darkness of night—
There was no flame,
    There was no light
To guide us aright

And I called to her out of the gloom—
    (She was all to me)
    'Flee thou to the sea
Lest they seek for thee
And hale us twain to the doom.'

And she said 'This is woe
    Greater than all—
    In the way that we go
There be many that fall
    And trouble will come to us so'—

But we fled away,
    (Tho' the face of the sea
Was covered with spray,
    And the wave rose angrily)
To 'scape from the God of the Seas—
And we twain were ill at ease

[1] *Lethe*: river of forgetfulness in underworld in classical mythology.

And we came to a weedy shore—
    But when we would have passed
The boat stayed evermore
    In the wrack that held it fast,
Even as Sin that will last,
    Though many years be o'er.

So we waited for God on the sea
    (Silent and hand in hand)
Till there came a wind from the land
    And the deep was stirred with pain,
And she passed with a sigh from me
Into the mist and the rain.[1]—
Yet I pray to the God of the Seas
  That he give me my Love again,
  That he bring[1] my spirit ease.
    But I fear me, my prayers are vain.

MY HAT

Holograph verse letter postmarked 9 August 1880, addressed to 'J. Tavenor
Perry[1] Esq. / 12, The Terrace / Putney'. The address is written within the
crown of a hat drawn on the envelope (Huntington Library MS HM 11877).

Preadmonisheth
ye youth
	A youth but late returned from School,
	    Fourteen, facetious, fat,
	I swear by that I cherish most,—
	    Videlicet[2] 'My Hat'.

And defendeth
his Oath
	Oaths are immoral people say,
	    But still they come so pat
	When one's excited. It's not sin
	    I'm sure, to say My Hat!

Instances when
ye Oath may
be needful
	When nightly slumbers broken are
	    By symphony of cat,
	I think of spring traps, dogs, & death,
	    And vengeful growl 'My Hat!'

---

[1] *rain, bring*: readings from Notebook 3 in place of 'sea' and 'give' in *Sundry Phansies*.

[1] *J. Tavenor Perry*: John Tavenor Perry (1842–1915), an architect and writer on archi-
tectural history.   [2] *Videlicet*: namely.

The *Substance*
of ye Oath
	I have but one,—a bowler 'tis
	    As rough as any mat,
	The felt inside is cocoa-stained,
	    Nathless I love my Hat.

Ye Conscience
that swayeth
ye youth
	Folks say it's seedy, but I stick
	    To it the more for that.
	As Conscience keeps me to my word
	    And lives inside my Hat

The affection
of ye youth
	As student I shall keep it still,
	    Moreover when I mat–
	riculate at seventeen
	    I'll go up in my Hat.

He imagineth
Misfortune
	And if I miss, (which Heaven forbid)
	    Proving myself a flat,[3]
	Then I should find to my disgust,
	    Myself inside my Hat.

And telleth
of his poesie
	When you're at breakfast there will come
	    The postman's rat-tat-tat,
	Bringing your business letters and
	    These verses on my Hat.

THE SONG OF THE SUFFERER
[FOLLICULAR[1] TONSILITIS]

In a letter of 23 August 1880 Alice Kipling wrote to Edith Plowden from 26 Warwick Gardens, Kensington: ' . . . I have Ruddy laid up since Friday last. He has been very ill with Quinsy—but the fever has gone down at length and I hope to have him down stairs tomorrow. He has been patient & cheerful— even amusing, and on Saturday after reading Swinburne wrote the following verses descriptive of his condition. . . . Are they not comic?' (KP 1/10.) The poem was published in *Schoolboy Lyrics*, 1881, and in the *USCC*, no. 12, 11 December 1882, where it bore the title 'Follicular Tonsilitis'. Collected in the

---

[3] *a flat*: fool, greenhorn (slang).

[1] *Follicular*: affecting the glands.

Outward Bound, De Luxe, Sussex, and Burwash Edns. with the heading, which had figured as a note in *Schoolboy Lyrics*, 'Written when ill with fever and sore throat'.

> His drink it is Saline Pyretic,[2]
>   He longs, but he shall not eat,
> His soul is convulsed with emetic,
>   His stomach is empty of meat.
>
> His bowels are stirred by blind motions,
>   His form in the flannel is bound,
> He has gargles, and powders, and potions,
>   And walks as not feeling the ground.
>
> For the doctor has harrowed his being,
>   And of medicine wondrous the might is;
> He suffers in agony, seeing
>   He is prey to acute tonsilitis.

CROSSING THE RUBICON[1]

Holograph versions in Notebook 3 and *Sundry Phansies*. Typescript copy probably of version sent to Edith Macdonald (KP 24/67). In her MS reminiscences *Fond Memory* (Baldwin Papers, 1/19) Edith Plowden recalls that in 1879 John Lockwood Kipling in Lahore received a letter from his son saying 'I am writing a poem it begins like this', and citing the first stanza of this poem. 'Rudyard', she goes on, 'finished the poem in 1880 at my request when we were together at Warwick Gardens.'

> A cry in the silent night,
>   A white face turned to the wall,
> A pang—and then in the minds of men
>   Forgotten—that is all!
>
> For this are we labouring?
>   Red lips that have pulsed and kissed,
> White arms that clasp and cling,
>   Grow cold and are not missed—

---

[2] *Saline Pyretic*: pyretic salts, an effervescing preparation for the relief of fever.

[1] *Crossing the Rubicon*: taking, consciously, an irrevocable step, as Julius Caesar did when he ordered his army to cross the Rubicon, a river separating his own province from Italy, so that he became technically and legally a rebel against the state. The phrase is used here rather oddly to refer to the involuntary process of dying.

The mourners mourn and depart.
   Piece we the broken chain!
The dead one lives awhile in our heart,
   Alas! and is dead again

For as flame that flickers and flies,
   Our memory comes and goes—
Drowned in the light of human eyes,
   And a woe in the time of woes.

CHIVALRY

Holograph version in *Sundry Phansies*, where the title is followed by a question mark in brackets. No date: 1880? A typescript copy probably of the version sent to Edith Macdonald has the readings 'At her foulest she is lovely, at her fairest something more', and 'Hang that woman' in the final line. It also has the concluding note 'If this first instalment hasn't settled you I'll send you some others' (KP 24/67). Edith Plowden, in her typescript for a talk to the Kipling Society in 1938, writes that 'Rudyard could versify on any subject and recited his verses to me as we walked and sat in Kensington Gardens. One "Chivalry" amused me and he dedicated it to me calling me "The Missing Link between Lahore and London". I knew it by heart.' (Baldwin Papers, 1/20.) The context seems to imply that this was in 1880.

Is a woman but man's plaything, fairest woman in her pride?
Should a word be disregarded? Should a whisper be denied?
Should not all things bow before her? And my knightly soul replied,
'Man is born to worship woman, She is man beatified.
At her fairest she is perfect, at her foulest something more—
Serve all women and respect them is my self imposèd law.
For in sooth they all are angels—Who's that knocking at my door?'
'Sir—your Aunt has come to see you—' D—n the woman. What a
   bore!

THE FRONT DOOR

A holograph version of the first three stanzas is dated September 1880 (Baldwin Papers, 2/4). The four-stanza version was published in *Schoolboy Lyrics*, 1881. Collected in the Outward Bound, De Luxe, Sussex, and Burwash Edns.

I stand and guard—such ones as say
   In matter lives no spirit, lie;
The household through me throbs and beats,
The meaning of the crowded streets
   Is plain, and once a year I may
Admit the beings of the sky.

Lost souls revisiting the earth
   To see old loves that they be well,
And find their hold upon the heart,
In life so strong, in death depart;
   Wherefore with peals of soundless mirth
Goes each one to his place in hell.

The curtain on a winter's night
   Struggles and beats as if it fought
In every fold a power of air;
The unseen fills each vacant chair;
   The living lavish not a thought
On those that are not in their sight.

Life and dark death go hand in hand,—
   Believe or disbelieve my tale,—
How Death is Life, how Life is Death,
How that the spirit wandereth,
   How bolts and bars may not prevail
To guard us from the Other Land.

THE LESSON

In a letter of 5 October 1880 John Lockwood Kipling wrote to Edith Plowden from Lahore, saying of Ruddy that 'it would be affectation to ignore his very decided talents and powers. He sends me (or rather Mrs Kipling sends) a copy of verses—"The Lesson" which might be to the address of Miss Flora Gar-rard or possibly to you. In any case they are prettily turned . . . ' (KP 1/10.) The poem was published in *Schoolboy Lyrics*, 1881, which has 'equally' instead of 'utterly' in the fourth line. Collected in the Outward Bound, De Luxe, Sussex, and Burwash Edns.

We two learned the lesson together,
    The oldest of all, yet so new
To myself, and I'm wondering whether
    It was utterly novel to you?

The pages—you seemed to have known them,
    The pictures that changed 'neath our eyes;
Alas! by what hand were you shown them,
    That I find you so womanly wise?

Is it strange that my hand on your shoulder
    In the dusk of the day should be placed?
Did you say to yourself, 'Were he older
    His arm had encircled my waist'?

If it be so, so be it, fair teacher;
    I sit at your feet and am wise,
For each page of the book is a feature,
    And the light of the reading, your eyes.

We have met, and the meeting is over;
    We must part, and the parting is now;
We have played out the game—I, boy-lover,
    In earnest, and you, dearest, how?

THE FIRST DAY BACK

Holograph version written above the title of 'The Eve of St. Agnes' on p. 176
of a copy of *Longer English Poems*, ed. J. W. Hales (London, 1878), which was
used by Kipling as a schoolbook. The half-title page is inscribed 'Kipling,
21.1.80'. (Library of Congress.)

    The first day back, ay bitter cold it was.
    And I tho' rugged and wrappered was a-cold,
    Like boilèd spinach, was the playground grass,
    Yellow our boots, y-clogged with Goosey[1] mould,
    Malarious vapours over *Goosey* rolled.

  [1] *Goosey*: Goosey Pool, in the vicinity of Westward Ho! Cf. L. C. Dunsterville, *Kipling
Journal*, no. 22 (June 1932), p. 49: 'There was a famous pond on the Burrows called
Goosey Pool, famous only to us and probably no more than a dirty pool to the casual
observer.' Cf. also p. 77 below.

Stale bread, bad butter, filled our hungry maw,
Damp were the sheets, huddled in frowsty fold,
Loud forced[2] laughter shook the form room floor
And pale and pinchèd boys peered down the corridor

TOBACCO [UNPUBLISHED SONNET BY KEATS: TO A PIPE]

A holograph version of this 'Unpublished Sonnet by Keats' appears with the subtitle 'To a Pipe' at the end of 'The Eve of St. Agnes' on p. 186 of Kipling's copy of *Longer English Poems*, ed. J. W. Hales. (Library of Congress. See the previous item.) Published with minor revisions in *Echoes*, 1884, under the title 'Tobacco', with 'Burmahs' replacing the 'Cubas' of the original. Collected in the Outward Bound, De Luxe, Sussex, and Burwash Edns.

Sweet is the Rose's scent—Tobacco's smell
  Is sweeter; wherefore let me charge again.
Old blackened meerschaum, I have loved thee well
  From youth, when smoke brought sickness in its train.
Foolish I was: Manillas I disdained,
  And cigarettes to Burmahs did prefer,
And even spurned Havana's fragrant joy;
  But now my mind is pained,
In that my smoking days I did defer,
  Nor knew this pleasure when I was a boy.

UNPUBLISHED FRAGMENT OF POPE: AN AMATEUR

This holograph version appears above the notes on Pope on p. 286 of Kipling's copy of *Longer English Poems*, ed. J. W. Hales. (Library of Congress. See the two previous items.)

Our friend just hears that doggrel writing pays
And sees himself already crowned with bays

    *   *   *   *   *

Borrows whole volumes, burns the midnight oil
And Bores his neighbours with his wordy toil

---

[2] *forced*: reading uncertain.

UNPUBLISHED FRAGMENT OF SHELLEY

Holograph version on p. 201 of Kipling's copy of *Longer English Poems*, ed. J. W. Hales. (Library of Congress. See the previous three items.) Attributed to 'Canto 1, Lament of Xenorial [?], 1. 270'.

> Rather than this should happen, I would see,
> The red sun shaken like an autumn leaf,
> Spin whirling thro the void without a word
> Of fear or wonder, for the gods are not,
> And we thro' our impiety are lost.
> The complex forms that people outer space,
> Rulers of nakéd worlds are paramount,
> In these our scarred hearts. There is no head
> To rule, and have high power. Each is king
> And wallows in his sin, all Hell is here,
> And there is nothing that may turn our fate.

REQUIESCAT IN PACE[1]

This poem and 'Credat Judaeus' (see below, p. 60) were enclosed with a letter from Kipling at Westward Ho! to Edith Macdonald, tentatively dated January 1881: 'Dear Auntie, I promised to send you some more of my scribblings as soon as I had written them. Here is the latest batch. Please give me your opinion on them as soon as possible. I've got one on hand just now and your verdict on *these* will have a great deal to do with it.' (KP 11/10.) Published in *Schoolboy Lyrics*, 1881. Collected in the Outward Bound, De Luxe, Sussex, and Burwash Edns.

> A new-made grave, for the damp earth stood
>   Yellow and miry there at the lips
> Of the pit, where one in her widowhood
>   Waited to witness the coffin's eclipse
> Under the clods, that tumbled and rolled,
> Rattled and thundered o'er clay as cold.
>
> The mother facing the wife—they wept
>   As never I yet saw women weep.

[1] *Requiescat in Pace*: let him rest in peace.

Standing behind them, the watch I kept
   Was a watch that never did mortal keep,
For the thing below that had ceased to be,
With human utterance spoke to me.

'There is knocking at my door, there!—Aspirations long since fled,
High endeavours of my springtime that have lived and perishèd.
Why disquiet me, O phantoms? Wherefore strive to stir the dead?

     Striking on dumb chords, O passion!
      Music comes not. Here below,
    I am of another fashion
      Than the "I" six days ago.

There is knocking at my door, there!—Hopes that fired younger
   blood:
Lust of power, lust of knowledge, fierce desire for the good,
For some truth that might uphold me 'gainst the clamour of Doubt's
   brood.

     Mark ye my closèd mouth well;
      Lines where the strong speech would sit
    Shadowed ere words;—now all Hell
      Stirs not these wrinkles one whit.

There is knocking at my door, there!—as of one that would not wait,
As of one that wished to tear me from my quiet, kingly state.
'Tis some Love that might have saved me, come, alas! too late, too
   late.

     Six days since, around my bed,
      People spake in accents low;
    As a dream half vanishèd
      Were their words six days ago—
    Spake of something that might save,
      Some great power from above,
    Power to open up my grave,
      And I think they called it Love.
    Canst *thou* lift the heavy weight?
      Canst thou help me from the gloom?
    Human love is less than Fate,
      Failing ere it reach the tomb.

There is knocking at my door, there!—Pity calling friends to mind,
Telling loud of those that mourned me, certain ones I left behind.
Surely they may break their shacklings, snap the fleshly chains that
  bind.

Seest thou this hand that would close
  Warm o'er the clasp of a friend?
Tell me the tale of his woes—
  It shall lie still to the end.

There is silence, and I slumber in the narrow, narrow room,
Waiting, waiting, ever waiting, for the judgment and the doom.
Sweet to wearied limbs this resting, sweet to strainèd eyes this gloom.

Cool, and no life to arouse
  Passions that slay and destroy.
Love, and its numberless vows,
  Life, and its manifold joy—
I have quitted them all and for ever:
  Sweep as the tempests at will,
Sure, 'tis an idle endeavour
  Seeking to waken the still.
Beat at my door, O sad mother!
  Wife! rain thy tears on my breast.
I, that was thine, am made other,
  Alien in all; and I rest.'

CREDAT JUDAEUS[1]

Early version, with head-note 'Sketched from life in Lovers Lane Kensington',
and end-note 'and so on till the end of the world', sent to Edith Macdonald
with letter tentatively dated January 1881. (See above p. 58.) Published in
Schoolboy Lyrics, 1881, with end-note 'And so on—for ever'. Collected in the
Outward Bound, De Luxe, Sussex and Burwash Edns.

---

[1] *Credat Judaeus*: See Horace, *Satires*, i. 5: 'credat Judaeus Apella, / non ego'—
'Apella the Jew may believe it, not I' (the general sense being that of 'Tell it to the mar-
ines').

FIRST COUPLE

Three couples were we in the lane,
Keeping our walks and turning again;
 At the point where we meet
 The roar of the street
Like the sound of a beast in pain
 Comes faintly. Here all is sweet.

Who were the others? I did not see.
 Why should I look at the men at all?
Why should their partners interest me?
 I'm sure that I loved mine best of all.

 Perfect in beauty and grace,
 Perfect in figure and face,
She with her eyes divine!
 The present for just us two;
Eternity makes her mine,
 Our love is eternal and true!

SECOND COUPLE

Watch them, dearest, cheek to cheek,
 Arm in arm; when years are past
 Will their love like our love last,
Still so fond, still cheek to cheek?

There is one true love below;
 We have found it! Others kiss
 For a little, part and miss,
Grieve awhile, then lightly go.

These in earnest! I have seen
 Many such; the years will fly,
 Leave us loving, you and I,
While they talk of what has been.

THIRD COUPLE

I wanted them walks so bad
With you, and missus is mad
'Cos she says I gad out at night;
No doubt but what she's right.

Well, I can't stay long, but see,
Promise to 'old to me,
   An I'll 'old to you for hever!
Them people may court a bit—
   They don't love like we two!
   Oh, George! I've got no one but you.
'Old by me! Promise it!
   And I'll never leave you, never!

I, the writer that made them speak,
   Laughed aloud as I passed the three,
Strong in a passion to last a week,
   For Love that is real was given to me!

A LEGEND OF DEVONSHIRE

Published in the *USCC*, no. 4, 30 June 1881, in eleven-stanza version. The
first six stanzas, slightly revised, were republished in *Schoolboy Lyrics*, 1881,
and collected in the Outward Bound, De Luxe, Sussex, and Burwash Edns.
The other five stanzas which appeared in the *USCC* are printed here in square
brackets.

There were three daughters long ago,
   In a lonely house that faced the sea;
They sent their father forth to plough
   The narrow meadow that skirts the sea.

The autumn fogs are drifting by,
   The old man's wits are dull and numb;
He has opened the barn where the young colts lie
   Safe from the biting frosts to come.

He has taken the plough-gear and harnessed three
   Hot young bloods that no lash will bear;
The rain is falling—he cannot see
   If young or old be harnessed there.

He is ploughing the meadow that skirts the sea—
   Old hands a-quivering with the cold;
The furrows are running crookedly,
   And the share is clogged with the clinging mould.

The crow and daw fly fast to eat
    Their food, while afar the sea-gulls scream;
The rain has changed to a stinging sleet;
    He is ploughing as one who ploughs in a dream.

They have swerved from the field; the shingles grate
    Beneath their hooves and the jangling plough;
The day is dying, the hour is late:
    But the salt sea-foam is light to plough.

[The old man smiles, by the handles twain,
    The colts are speeding, the share runs fast;
I plough as tho' 'twere my youth again—
    We'll finish the field and rest at last.

One furrow more, and the thick whip cracks,
    Hot is their blood as the sea is cold;
He has eased the gear from off their backs,
    And stoops to loosen their feet from mould.

He is ploughing again, and the colts go slowly,
    The furrows are filled by the rising sea;
The salt has encrusted the iron wholly,
    And the old man's beard is wet with the sea.

The tide is rising, the shore-spume flees,
    The colts are stamping twixt sea and land,
The gulls are wailing o'er the seas,
    And the forewheel drags in the drifting sand.

The tide is rising, the furrows fill,
    The handles are wet with the flying foam,
The colts are plunging, and over the hill
    They are waiting to welcome the old man home.]

DISAPPOINTMENT

Published in the *USCC*, no. 4, 30 June 1881. Uncollected. This poem may have been written in co-operation with L. C. Dunsterville: see L. H. Chandler's *Summary* (cited p. 31 above), p. 332.

One day whilst full of burning thought,
   I faced the Corridor—
The term was young, and I espied
   A new boy very raw.

His face was pale, his brow was sad,
   His eyes with fearful rolls
Pierced with their dull and leaden glance
   My sympathetic soul.

His attitude of inward pain
   Convulsed each thrilling sense;
Aesthetic souls must leap to him—
   He surely is 'intense'.

What ails thee, gentle boy, I cried,
   Canst thou confide in me,
Is it a mother's care you miss,
   Your home and family?

He turned on me a frenzied glance,
   His eye with passion lights;
'I don't feel quite the thing,' said he,
   'I've just been down to Keyte's.'[1]

THE EXCURSION[1]

Published in the *USCC*, no. 4, 30 June 1881. Uncollected. The mixture of
four and eight-line stanzas results presumably from Kipling's inexperience in
preparing copy for the printer.

A college cap is perched upon my head,
   My stomach fortified with College dinner,
I wander with both hands coat-pocketed,
   A Lower-Third-form sinner,

---

[1] *Keyte*'s: The school tuck-shop at Westward Ho! was run by ex-Sergeant-Major
Keyte, a former cavalryman. (See H. A. Tapp, *United Services College 1874–1911*, Alder-
shot, 1933, p. 10, and *Supplement*, Cheshunt, 1960, p. 1.)

[1] *The Excursion*: the title derives from Wordsworth's nine-book poem *The Excursion*.

Full to the brim of that which boys call cheek,
    (I think the other name is self-assertion)
Out for a desultory stroll to seek
    Some method of diversion.

I chase their stilt-legged offspring from the mares,
    Hurl sundry rocks at sundry wretched ponies,
Disturb some rodents (which were really hares,
    But verse will have them 'conies';)
Beguiled the sheep with scraps of bread and smiling,
    Then scared their simple souls with stones and sticks;—
A sure and certain method of beguiling
    The time from two to six.

Watched in the wind the long reeds shake and quiver,
    Grew cold with watching, therefore watched no more,
Walked till I reached the mud banks on the river,
    Thence into Appledore.[2]

The tide was out, the weeds smelt very strongly,
    And in among the pools the gobies[3] played;
Here asked my way and got directed wrongly
    By a mischievous maid,
Digging for bait in shortest of short dresses,
    A tin to capture and a knife to slay,
An old straw hat strapt over sun-bleached tresses
    With ribbons bleached as they.

I looked sometime and then continued walking,
    And left her limpet-catching on the beach,
She wasn't pretty and she sniffed while talking,
    And mixed the parts of speech.
Turning towards the river bank I strayed there
    For nearly half an hour, found a hut
Some enterprising Colleger had made there,
    Smashed it for fun, and cut.

Retraced my steps, and reached again the houses
    Where people fold their arms and live at ease,
The streets, where every step an echo rouses,
    And children swarm like bees.

[2] *Appledore*: fishing village two miles north-east of Westward Ho!
[3] *gobies*: small fish, gudgeon.

Got nearly strangled by a damsel skipping
    Who threw some tarry oakum round my throat,
Escaped at length and criticised the shipping,—
    Two colliers and one boat.

Felt hungry, turned towards the College slowly,
    Thought of my tea, and hurried up a bit,
Refreshed myself, then wrote in rhyme unholy
    This story:—study it!

DE PROFUNDIS:[1] A BALLADE OF BITTERNESSE

Published in the *USCC*, no. 5, 23 July 1881, with heading 'School Order—
"All cooking is absolutely forbidden in studies henceforth, except in Prefects'
Studies. April, 1881. (Signed) — —." ' Uncollected.

The cup is devoid of its coffee,
    The spoon of its sugary load,
The table-cloth guiltless of toffee,
    And sorrow has seized our abode.
Our tasks they are dry as the sea-sands,
    Our throats they are drier than these,
No cocoa has moistened our weasands.[2]
    We taste not of teas.

We, once that were bloated with brewing,
    We, once that were broad of the beam,
Are utterly changed and eschewing
    All pleasures of junket and cream.
We, once that awakened in sorrow,
    In heaviness, nausea, and night,
Sleep calm through the dark to the morrow,
    Through silence to light.

There be pleasures men take for their pleasing,
    The pleasures of reading and rhyme,

---

[1] *De Profundis*: out of the depths.
[2] *weasands*: windpipes (archaic); hence throats.

That the soul may have comfort and easing,
  And solace and rest for a time.
There be pleasures of palette and painting,
  The pleasures of limb and of length,
Where our spirits stay wearied and fainting
  And lacking in strength.

Let *them* revel in what they require,
  Let them feast upon Beauty and bend
To its passion, its pathos, and fire,
  And follow it up to the end.
Our spirits are simple and placid,
  With principle porcine endued,—
Be it sweetened, or mucous, or acid,
  Our fetish is Food.

The taste on the tongue though it cloyeth,
  The silence unbroken and still,
When the spirit quiescent enjoyeth
  The acidulous down-reaching thrill;
The Joy of the Jaw in its motion,
  The Tooth as it teareth in twain,
These be Gods and they have our devotion
  In pleasure or pain.

The Jampot, the Ginger, the Jelly,
  Meat mortared, enticing in tins,
They are brought as a boon to the Belly,
  What time our instruction begins,
Oleaginous, cramped and confined,
  Sardines as they shimmer in oil,
In the quarter for lunch are designed
  As guerdon of toil.

And therefore this change is a trouble,
  A trouble and wasting of much,
When the kettle hath ceased from its bubble,
  And saucepans are useless as such.
Our tin-ware is turned to derision,
  Our gas-stoves lie grimy and grim.
Our lights like the lights of a vision
  Burn bluely and dim.

RECKONING

Holograph versions in Notebook 3, dated 8 August 1881, and *Sundry Phansies*.

Count we the Cost—the sun is setting fast,
And Love is fading even as the day—
Ere in the silence of a bitter past
Eternally our Passion pass away
Count we the cost—What, when this thinge was new
Gave we for one another? Honour, Truth,
Hope, and the glory of a Maiden's youth,
Worship of all men, was my price for you.
Count we the cost—And was it worth the sin
Oh Dearest! now some halfword lightly spoken,
Breaks that we gave our very souls to win
And all the old sweet intercourse is broken?
The Sun is set—Your face is hid from me,
And darkness comes upon us as a Sea—

THE BALLAD OF THE KING'S DAUGHTER

Holograph versions in Notebook 3, dated 9 August 1881, and *Sundry Phansies*.
Published in *Echoes*, 1884. Collected with subtitle 'Old Ballad' in the Outward
Bound, De Luxe, Sussex, and Burwash Edns.

'If my Love come to me over the water,
    Lowly born, and the King stood by,
How should I greet him, a Monarch's daughter—
    Coldly, strangely, and haughtily?

If my Love come to me over the land,
    Lowly born, and the King stood by,
Should I kiss him, or give him a frozen hand,
    Coldly, strangely, and haughtily?'

Many came to her over the water,
    Princes all, and the King stood by;
But she gave them the scorn of a Monarch's daughter,
    Coldly, strangely and haughtily.

Many came to her over the land,
  Princes all, and the King stood by;
But she gave them to kiss a frozen hand,
  Coldly, strangely, and haughtily.

There came to her one from over the water,
  Lowly born, and the King stood by;
And the warm blood flushed through the Monarch's daughter,
  And lo! she fell on his neck with a cry.

Many there be by land and water,
  (Wait and watch ye patiently)
That gave their love to a Monarch's daughter,
  That bound their heart in the days gone by.

Hope is little by land or water,
  Wait and watch ye patiently.
Gold wins not a Monarch's daughter,
  Neither jewels nor bravery.

Get ye fame by land and water,
  That your name live and do not die,
And ye win the love of a Monarch's daughter . . .
  Little of blessing comes thereby.

WAYTINGE

Holograph versions in Notebook 3, dated 19 August 1881, and *Sundry Phansies*. Not to be confused with another poem of the same title which was published in the *USCC*, no. 7, 5 December 1881. (See below, p. 83.)

Doubte not that Pleasure cometh in the End,—
  And Honor therewithal
When olde Restraints be broken or unbende,
  When olde Disguises fall,
Crampte passions, Pettie Lusts, Desires Small,
  Love's severance, and doubtinges funeral.

Doubte not that Pleasure cometh in the End
   And therewith Perfect Reste,
When Woes be stilled, that scorche and seare and rende,
   When all Things be confeste,
And thou shalt see, (her Hedde upon thy Breste)
How Love of Waytinge born bin Perfectest

TO YOU [A REMINISCENCE]

A holograph version in Notebook 1, with title 'A Reminiscence', gives the original date as August 1881. Another holograph version, with title 'To You', figures as an address, probably to Edith Macdonald, at the end of Notebook 3. In Notebook 1 the third line of the second stanza reads 'God give you comfort as you gave it me', avoiding the simple repetition in Notebook 3. The poem was recycled as an inscription in *Echoes* in 1884. (See pp. 251–2 below.)

A memory of our sojourn by the Sea,
A memory of the talk between us twain
A memory that will not go from me
   Until we meet again.

A boy's wild words beside the summer sea—
A baring of the heart's most secret pain.
A memory that will not go from me
   Until we meet again.

I thank you for I hold you very dear.
I send you these rough first-fruits of my brain.
God keep you safe throughout the waning year
   Until we meet again.

HOW THE GODDESS AWAKENED

Holograph version (incomplete) in Notebook 3, dated 9 September 1881, with note: 'In some village churches of France ancient statues are occasionally unearthed and made to do duty as Virgins and Saints. I have attempted to put down the thoughts of a bedraped Venus on finding herself another goddess.' A complete holograph version in *Sundry Phansies*. Published in *Echoes*, 1884. Collected in the Outward Bound, De Luxe, Sussex, and Burwash Edns.

Where the reveller laid him, drunk with wine,
    At the foot of my marble pedestal,
They are wailing aloud; they call me divine—
    Wherefore is it on me that they call?
    What have I done for the men of this city,
For the pallid folk who bend at the shrine
And call upon me: '*Maid Divine*
    Mother of Sorrows, have thou pity!'

What can I tell of their joy or woe—
I who was fashioned long ago
    By the olive slopes of the marble city,
Where green leaves hid the temple wall?
Wherefore is it on me that they call:
    '*Mother of Jesus, have thou pity!*'

What should I know of sorrow—I?
How should I listen tenderly?
    Sorrow was not in the old white city;
But laughter and love and men and wine
In the temple below me that was mine.
    Who am I, that should give them pity
As, row upon row, they call on my shrine:
    '*Mother of Sorrows, Maid Divine,*
    Spotless Virgin, have thou pity!'

They brought me forth from under the mould
    (For I, too, fell with my city's fall),
They gave my hands a cross to hold,
They cramped my limbs in cloth of gold,
    And set me up to be seen of all.
They came and bowed themselves at my shrine,
    These strange, pale folk of the dreary city,
And called upon me: '*Mother Divine*
    Mother of Sorrows, have thou pity!'

I fain would be where I once have been,
Where the nude limbs flashed through the vine-leaves green,
Where I heard the sound of the summer sea
Far off, and warriors came to me,

And hung their arms the boughs between—
Strong shapes, and I was held their queen.
These men would surely welcome me
With that wild song I knew so well
Before my marble city fell—
Before the foemen took the city
(Before I bowed myself and fell),
Before they brought me here to dwell,
    These men that know not of my city,
And set me in an alien shrine,
And called upon me: '*Maid Divine,*
    Mother of Sorrows, have thou pity!'

And in those days, I saw the sun,
    My brother, greet me in the morn.
But now I see not any one
    Of those I know, while folk forlorn
Flock round me, calling on a name
    I know not, and they give it me.
    I, foam-born, risen from the sea,
    My names were many in the city
Of marble, but *this* is not mine:
    '*Mother of Sorrows, Maid Divine,*
    Spotless Virgin, have thou pity!'

And, in those years, the stars were bright,
    And all the night was full of love;
But now I see not any light,
    Saved what from meagre slits above
Slopes downward on my forehead white.
    I would that I could turn and move
And visit mine own lovèd city,
And hear the laughter as of old,
And see the waters touched with gold
    Far off, and feel against my knees
The boy's warm cheek. Then should I know
    Mine own old happiness and ease.
But here there is no sound save woe:
'*Holy Virgin, Mother Divine,*
Bend we low at thy sacred shrine.
    Mother of Jesus, have thou pity!'

FOR A PICTURE [VENUS MERETRIX][1]

Holograph version in Notebook 3 with title 'Venus Meretrix', dated 30 September 1881, with note '(time 4 A.M.)'. Another holograph version in *Sundry Phansies*, with title 'For a Picture'.

This much am I to you—
    If I departed out of your house
        Coming no more at all—
You would wait a while tis true
    You would lift your voice—You would call—
You would take some Lover into your house
    And be to him all in all.

This much am I to you—
    As I take delight with you in your house—
        And live your love of all.
I do not hold you true—
    I know some day you will fall,—
A horror will come on your gilded house
    Turning delight to gall.

Yet still I hold to you—
    Living with you at ease in your house
I count the gain not small

            *   *   *   *   *

When the years shall come to both of us
    When all old pleasures pall,—
When kisses fail, and we love not thus,
    Nor hold Love all in all—
You will pass away to another house
    Silent and funeral—
You will veil your head in the empty house
    Nor hear me when I call—
Oh woman our Love will go from us,[2]
    Coming no more at all!

[1] *Meretrix*: prostitute, courtesan.
[2] *our Love* . . . : Notebook 3 has reading 'our days will pass from us'.

PRO TEM.[1]

Holograph versions in Notebook 3, dated 13 October 1881, and *Sundry Phan-sies*. Notebook 3 has 'fierce eternal fire' in stanza 8.

> Make we a fire in the dark
>   Numb flesh to warm,
> A little flame, a spark
>   How shall it harm?
>
> There is light on your face and mine—
>   The shades retire—
> Our arms meet and entwine
>   Around the fire,
>   Our flickering wind blown fire.
>
> With store of burr and weed
>   Up-pile it higher!
> What tho' the bared arm bleed,
>   The muscle tire!
>   Feed it—a rising fire!
>
> The night is red with flame—
>   Our lips creep nigher—
> Your eyes have rendered tame
>   The white hot fire,
>   The passionate full fire!
>
> It holds smooth, time-worn stakes
>   Set up to shew
> How far when Tempest wakes
>   The tide shall go—
>   It leaps and lays them low!
>
>   *   *   *   *   *
>
> The light ash smoulders fast,
>   The sparks expire,
> Lo! all the heat is past
>   From out our fire—
>   Our sudden wondrous fire.

---

[1] *Pro Tem.*: for the time being.

The ground lies blistered, bare—
    The starlight dies.
Dawn comes to shew you there
    Against the skies,
        With dull smoke reddened eyes.

Burnt branches—split and charred—
    I place my hand
Upon them—It is hard
    To understand
        That *these* made once our fire,
        Our fierce and driving fire.

Burnt flowers—once white and red
    Dead buds unborn—
The rose's purer head
    With vetch uptorn—
        The lily with the thorn.

The dew damp scarf, the gem
    Set deep in gold—
Your garment's broidered hem
    Sore stained with mould—
        The cup you could not hold.

We gave our hearts' best store,
    Our richest prize—
Remaineth nothing more
    To sacrifice—
        Nought precious in our eyes!

CAVE![1]

Holograph versions in Notebook 3, dated 24 October 1881, and *Sundry Phansies*. (The last line of the former reads 'Lest ye stumble and fall.')

        Lilies be plenty with us,
           Pansies flower for all,
        Take ye heed to the Roses
           Lest they make to fall.

[1] *Cave*: beware.

Violets lie in the meadows—
Take of the Violet—
Who can gather the Roses
And pass away and forget?

Love is sure in the Lily,
Pansie brings us ease.
But he that gathers the Roses
When shall his sorrow cease?

Woodbine clings and decays,
Daffodils blossom and die—
There is no Death in the Roses
Unto Eternity.

Whoso is snared of the Roses
Beareth a brand of Cain—
The fruit of the Tree of Knowledge
Caught from the arms of Pain.

Whoso is snared of the Roses
Hath no peace at all—
Guard your feet from their briers
Lest they make to fall.

INDEX MALORUM[1]

Published in the *USCC*, no. 6, 1 November 1881. Uncollected.

The wild waves beat upon the shore,
The sand is flecked with flying spume,
The cliffs have hid themselves in gloom,
The gas is lit at half past four.

The draughts are flying here and there
All aimless, and our bodies chill;
We plug with wood the window sill
And shiver in the nipping air.

[1] *Index Malorum*: list of evils.

We sit and shiver row on row,
    We wrap ourselves in rug and cloak,
    The chimneys fill the room with smoke,
And we—we wish it were not so.

The rime lies white on Goosey Pool,[2]
    The hoar frost glitters from the sedge,
    We talk of in and outer-edge,
And furbish Skates throughout the School.

Tho' hours be dull and days be cold,
    And spirits, noses, fingers, blue,
    This longest term wears slowly through,
And brings us cates,[3] and Christmas gold—

The gift of those that love us so
    And send us to Devonian strands,
    And sit and rub paternal hands
Behind a yard-broad fire's glow.

They think of us sometimes. Alas,
    Their comforts come before our eyes
    Too vividly whene'er we rise
And hear the ice clink in the glass.

A MISTAKE

Published in the *USCC*, no. 6, 1 November 1881, with subheading 'By R****t
B******g' [Robert Browning]. Uncollected.

Of the two hundred fellows at School
    I'm no fool,
So I flatter myself, yet confess
    My cunning is less
Than a new boy's whose virulent blows
    Brought blood to my nose.

---

[2] *Goosey Pool*: see above, p. 56.
[3] *cates*: choice foods (archaic).

When the term was young at its birth,
   And no dearth
Of money perplexed us, I saw
   Bear-sullen and raw
A new boy uncombed and uncouth,
   An ink-spotted youth.

Whose visage suggestive of woe
   Attracted me so
That I went to him full of good feeling,
   An angel of healing
Self-appointed, and said ' 'Tis relief
   To pour out one's grief

To one whose experience immense
   Has given him sense.'
He drying his eyes on his cuff
   Pluckt heart up, enough
To answer, all snivel and snuffling:
   'Some beggars were scuffling

And hurt him' (I think 'twas his knee
   Suffered most in the spree.)
Then fled. Now it chanced I'd a share
   In that little affair,
Hit some one, who knows? Did I care
   For the how, when or where?

Then I asked him, 'Describe me this youth,
   With spirit and truth;'
He produced a description, full, fervid,
   In speech unservèd,
Of myself as I stood at the time
   Of that Corridor crime:

Wound up his long speech, with a vow,
   (I've forgotten it now—
The words in their fullness and flavour)
   To instruct in behaviour
The person who smote him; then I
   With eagle-grey eye,

In manner most melodramatic
  Transfixed the lunatic
And said, 'I am he, do your worst
  O Urchin accursed!'
And he glared at me hard for a space,
  Then full in my face

Threw himself, laying hold of my throat
  He fixed there and smote.—
Tho' I beat on his head with my fist
  He would not desist;
This continued, not much to my glory.
  To finish my story—

I was pummelled, kicked, scratched, torn, and smitten,
  Bemauled and bebitten,
Till I gave up the field, and departed,
  Upset and downhearted.

With a new boy you don't know, don't quarrel,
Is my long-winded anecdote's moral.

AN AUTO-DA-FÉ[1]

Holograph versions in Notebook 3, dated 3 November 1881, and *Sundry Phansies*.

And did you love me then so much
As you say you did? What made you write
The Love you bore in black and white—
Drop pen—cease loving—end it all,
And give me for greeting the palm's mere touch
In place of a cheek[2] where my kiss should fall?

Now we are sundered, is it strange
That we meet each other and say no word?
Do you think of that time when our hearts were stirred
By less than a murmur? How—once, I kept
Watch and ward o'er the long street's range
Of passionless stucco, while you slept

---

[1] *Auto-da-Fé*: lit.: act of the faith; execution of sentence of the Inquisition, usually by burning.   [2] *cheek*: 'lip' in Notebook 3.

Somewhere, in peace, a maiden's slumber—
And I stood through the night, till morning's glow
Cleared the smoke from the parks below,
And you came with the dawn? How one remembers!
In my heart I have still the name and number—

        *   *   *   *   *

Wherefore I place my pile on the embers.

THE PAGE'S MESSAGE [THE MESSAGE]

Holograph version with title 'The Message' in Notebook 3, dated 21 November 1881. Another holograph version in *Sundry Phansies*, with title 'The Page's Message', subtitle '(Translated from the French of the Garde Ysoude)',[1] and heading: 'Now the Knighte and the Ladye had been long aparte and knew not when they might again meet. So they sent a Message by the Page, sayinge that Love was the same in olde or yonge (for which God shall reste their soules) And the Message was after this sort—'

Spare neither lie, nor deed, nor gold—
    Smite hard, trip not, let no thought stray
    From the purpose set, for short is Day,
And night is moonless, and blank and cold.

If I be dumb for a while—Remain
    Dumb for a season—that none may see
    What is the chain 'twixt thee and me,
And the light loss brings a greater gain.

We have seen the world's most secret woe,
    We have drunk together of bitter springs,
    We fashioned us vain imaginings
That lived and faded long ago

---

[1] *Garde Ysoude*: this seems to be a coinage of Kipling's own, derived presumably from Iseult's name, of which Ysoud(e) is a medieval English form, and Lancelot's castle Joyous Gard where she and her lover found refuge. Cf. Malory's narrative of 'How Sir Tristram and La Beale Isoud came into England, and how Sir Launcelot brought them to Joyous Gard' (*Le Morte D'Arthur*, Caxton Version, Book 10, ch. lii).

Nothing is left but Love alone,
    Binding fast,—as the black frost binds
    When the lake lies dead to the winter winds
And the face of the land is turned to stone—

Spur the Stallion weak and lame,
    (Long it is since his fire past)
    Furbish old armour, come at last
As the perfect knight of my girlhood came—

Ere the night come, come swiftly thou,
    For we are old. Stay not but come.
    Old lips are swiftly smitten dumb
And the lifeblood faileth even now.

TOLD IN THE DORMITORY (i)

Published in the *USCC*, no. 7, 5 December 1881, with subheading 'A****d
T******n' [Alfred Tennyson]. Uncollected. For the continuation of this poem
see below, pp. 128 and 149.

'The merry devil of some idle mood
Prompted me to it, else it had not been—
This tale I tell you of.
                Some years ago
They sent me to a College in the north,
Large, low, and rambling, set in purple moor,
Heather and ling, banked pine-trees thick in front;
Behind, the belted woodland—every shade
Of darkest green—and far away the sea,
A thin grey line—not as we have it here,
Almost beneath the windows. Here, I say,
They sent me, and I liked it well enough
As all things go. The grim preceptors ground
Dry husks of learning hot from many mills
Ere theirs, and forced them down unwilling throats
Agape for something sweeter, drew and proved

Then proved and drew again, how this and that
Were equal or not equal, round or square,
Or else how many bones our bodies bore
Embedded in the flesh they smote upon.
And so the terms passed.
                              Then there came to us
A youth lean-bodied, marvellously spare,
Raw-wristed, angular,—the precious son
Of some thick-headed county squireling,—
Nurtured amid the hedgerows, taught i' the field,
For so he seemed to me—a very clown,
As unsuspecting as the three-weeks lamb
In spring anemones—Fit prey for me
You reckon, therefore—Ay, but there was one
Whose ways were wilder by the half than mine,
Whose brains were quicker at the jest than mine,
Whose laugh was readier on his lips than mine,
And he was my companion—Thus we two
Met him disconsolate one autumn day
And spoke to him. Some pity at the first,
But thrice as much of mischief in our voice:
"And did he know the legends of the place?
And had he heard the customs of the place?
And if he had not, we would shew the place
Ourselves, and tell him." The red gratitude
Flushed through his sallow visage to the hair,—
Then, as we two still queried, wide he ope'd
The stiff portcullis of his rustic speech,
But spoke no word; and thereupon he grinned.
We waited silent, till the silence grew
Oppressive, for his soul was ill at ease.
And lastly we laid hold on him by force
And dragged him with us—laughter and light jest
To soothe him, as one soothes the late-caught colt,
Between the forehead, lest the quick heels fly.
So we—'
              The night-light fading flickered out.
And he that told the story cried 'Let be,
The tale is long and all our eyes are dull,
Sleep therefore'—So we turned away and slept.

To be continued.

WAYTINGE

Published in the *USCC*, no. 7, 5 December 1881. Uncollected. Not to be con-
fused with another poem with the same title in Notebook 3 and *Sundry Phan-
sies* (see above, p. 69).

Waytinge! wearilie waytinge,
   Here by the Fives Court wall,
When the miste comes over the Burrowes,
   And the Daye is beginning to fall,
And the Sea and the Sandes and the Shingles
   Are hid in a shudderinge Pall.

Waytinge! wearilie waytinge,
   While the dead Leaves flutter and flee,
While the Locke-uppe Bell is ringinge,
   And drearilie moanes the Sea.
Has hee eaten the Buns and the Biscuits
   I told him to get for my Tea?

Waitinge! wearilie waytinge!
   Torn of an inward Paine!
While Nighte comes o'er the Hillside
   Borne in a Guste of Raine.
I am wearie at Heart of Waytinge:—
   Robinson, bringe me a Caine.

TWO PLAYERS

Two holograph versions, one in Notebook 3, dated 8 December 1881, with the
odd subtitle 'Or Jay's Mourning Warehouse'; and the other in *Sundry Phansies*.
(The Notebook 3 version has been taken as copy-text in this case.) *Sundry
Phansies* has 'hopelessness' for 'helplessness' in the fourth line, and 'are left'
for 'remain' in the second last line of the poem.

Two Players playing games against the Gods.
   A weary game, and full of strange mischance—
   Of barren shift, and bitter circumstance
Of growing helplessness and dire odds—
What two may hope to strive against the Gods?

Two Players, playing out a losing game—
  A heavy burden—come and see the end
  For they have neither strength, nor stay, nor friend,—
And they are dumb from weariness & shame—
Smitten with sorrow by the wrathful Gods.

Two Players—and they cease not from their game,
  Tho' both be old, and all sweet favour gone
  That made their faces fair to look upon
And nothing but the dice remain the same—
How long shall these two strive against the Gods?

Two Players at the ending of their game—
  Brains weary with long scheming rest at last—
  Now all the struggle of the game is past—
And nothing but the dice remain the same—
The dice, and all the changeless, tireless Gods!

'LO! AS A LITTLE CHILD'

This is the introductory poem to *Schoolboy Lyrics*, 1881. Collected in the Outward Bound, De Luxe, Sussex, and Burwash Edns.

  Lo! as a little child
Looks from its window on a mighty town,
And sees the roofs as far as eye can reach,
But thinks not, knows not—nay, will not believe—
That there are Fathers, Mothers, Sisters, Homes
All like his own, a thousand homely talks,
Manners, and customs—so I saw the world
With millions of my brethren. Then I wrote;
And all my verse sprang fire-new from a brain
That loved it and believed it. But the world
Coldly, in silence, passed my numbers by.
Therefore I sang in fury! When the years
Brought with them coolness, all too late I found
There were ten thousand, thousand thoughts like mine!

TWO SIDES OF THE MEDAL

Published in *Schoolboy Lyrics*, 1881. Collected in the Outward Bound, De Luxe, Sussex, and Burwash Edns.

'I will into the world, I will make me a name,
I will fight for truth, I will fight for fame,
    I will win pure love, and when I die
    The world shall praise me, worthily.'

He entered the world—he fought for fame;
They twined him the thorny wreath of shame.
    I met him once more full suddenly;
    His face was seamed with misery.

'Have you fought for truth? Have you worked in vain?
Have you gained pure love without stain?
    Is your name yet great? Will it ever be?
    Are you praised of all men, worthily?'

He did not answer—he did not speak,
But waited awhile with a reddened cheek,
    Then trembling, faltering, and looking down—
    Good heavens, he asked me for half a crown!

THIS SIDE THE STYX[1]

Published in *Schoolboy Lyrics*, 1881. Collected in the Outward Bound, De Luxe, Sussex, and Burwash Edns.

Naked and shivering, how the oozy tide
Affrights me, waiting! Yonder boatman there
Is dull and moveless as the very stones
That fringe the infernal river. Woe is me!
All that I had, departed, and this state
Of aimless wandering on the farther shore
Is scarcely better than the life of forms
I see around me. Huge, deformèd toads,

---

[1] *Styx*: a river of the underworld in classical mythology.

Yellow and dripping monsters, loathsome plants
Dropping their blotched leaves in the reeking slime.
This is the land of Death in very truth.
The imprisoned air bears not my trembling voice
To shapes, my comrades in the upper life,
To those that sate and laughed with me of old,
Alas, how altered! Tullius Quaestor there
Stands solitary, he that lovèd mirth,
And drank the unmixed[2] wine till morning came
With me, how often! Is that Poetus,
Mine ancient enemy? O Gods! he comes
Beating the dead air with his outstretched palms
In silent supplication. Now his mouth
Is shaping words, and yet there comes no sound;
And now he passes in the drifting mist,
A shadow amid shadows. I alone
Retain a lasting form, or seem to do.
Claudius Herminius, once a trusty friend,
Is fleeting like the others. Is there none
To stay and give me peace? Ixion[3] now
Had eased me, for he beareth greater pain;
But all alone upon these crumbling banks,
False as the world I left, how shall I be,
Or rather cease from being? Could I lose
My soul, sensation, all that makes me I,
Oblivion were thrice blessèd. Lo! the boat
Is moving toward me—now at least is change.
Slowly, oh! slowly parts the stagnant flood,
And slow as is repentance, Charon[4] rows!

READING THE WILL [THE READING OF THE WILL]

Published in *Schoolboy Lyrics*, 1881. Collected in the Outward Bound, De Luxe, Sussex, and Burwash Edns. Holograph versions in Notebook 3 and *Sundry Phansies*, with title 'The Reading of the Will'.

---

[2] *unmixed*: i.e. undiluted by water.
[3] *Ixion*: in punishment for his sins Ixion was bound on a wheel that turned perpetually in the underworld.
[4] *Charon*: the ferryman who conveyed the souls of the dead across the Styx to Hades.

Here we have it, scratched and scored
   By the tides of an impotent human soul;
He that wrote it died abhorred,
   And scarcely the bell had ceased to toll
Ere they crowded together over the cake,
   Ferret-eyed women and keen-faced men,
In the putrid well of his life to slake
   Their viperous throats, and wonder when
The lawyer was coming to give their share—
   Waiting like beasts behind the bars
For the meat apportioned,—and all the air
   Thick with the hissing whisper that mars
Fame of the living and fame of the dead.
   See that woman, her yellow teeth
Pressing the lip's thin line of red;
   Mark the struggle that lies beneath
The outer surface of weepers[1] and veils!
   She was his housekeeper, people muttered
Hints, half-hinting, and half-heard tales,
   Poison tipping each syllable uttered.
Charity, this! And the dead man lies
   Still? Impossible! He must stir,
Slip the bandages, turn and rise,
   Speak, refuting the blot on her!
There is no sign. Does he hear them say
   She has it all, and 'We know how
She wiled it from him, but let us stay
   To hear the reading—it's coming now'?
Slowly, slowly, the red seals break.
   Watch them, marking his ev'ry word—
How in life he had willed to make
   This one wretched, and that preferred.
'I will and I choose that such an one
   Should have my all!' O woe, O woe!
Human potency, what has it done
   To help men's souls in the shades below?
Does he remember his power past,
   How that he made men smile or weep,—
Helpless to hold his riches fast,
   Fighting with blows men strike in sleep?

---

[1] *weepers*: garments symbolic of mourning (e.g. scarf of black crêpe or widow's veil).

AN ECHO

Published in *Schoolboy Lyrics*, 1881. Collected in the Outward Bound, De Luxe, Sussex, and Burwash Edns.

Let the fruit ripen one by one
　　On the sunny wall;
　　　　If it fall
Who is it suffers? What harm is done?
　　　　None at all.

An Eve in the garden am I;
　　Behold, this one
　　　　In the sun
Falls with a touch, and I let it lie,
　　　　My first one.

One fresh from the bough; I break it;
　　The red juice flies
　　　　Into my eyes.
Shall I swallow, leave, or take it,
　　　　Or despise?

Sweet to my taste was that second
　　And I hold it meet
　　　　That I eat;
But ah me! Are the bruised ones reckoned
　　　　At my feet?

CARET[1]

Published in *Schoolboy Lyrics*, 1881. Collected in the Outward Bound, De Luxe, Sussex, and Burwash Edns.

Something wanting in this world—
　　What is it? To each and all
Different desires come,
　　Tides of longing rise and fall.

[1] *Caret*: it is lacking

Hopes of youth still unfulfilled,
    Homes that have an empty chair,
Gulfs that gape and pits that balk;
    Something wanting everywhere.

Can we fill the gap with love,
    Forge the missing link with gold?
Let the heart be ne'er so warm,
    Still one portion blank and cold.

Broken chords are but our share;
    Harmony with discord blends;
Fate's dull web but coarsest cloth,
    Patched with finer odds and ends.

ROSES

Published in *Schoolboy Lyrics*, 1881. Collected in the Outward Bound, De Luxe, Sussex, and Burwash Edns.

Roses by babies' rosier fingers pressed
In wondering amazement. Later, youth,
Attired in knickerbockers, flings them by
Contemptuously. Lovers' offerings then,
Much kissed and withered. Staid and sober age
In snug, suburban villas rears them last:
The world at large is dowered with their thorns!

ARGUMENT OF A PROJECTED POEM TO BE CALLED 'THE SEVEN NIGHTS OF CREATION' [FRAGMENT OF A PROJECTED POEM]

Published in *Schoolboy Lyrics*, 1881, with title 'Fragment of a Projected Poem' and heading 'Argument of a Projected Poem to be called "The Seven Nights of Creation" '. Collected in the Outward Bound, De Luxe, Sussex, and Burwash Edns. The 'Argument' in the heading runs 'The Devil each night of the seven days of Creation works in emulation of the Creator and produces baneful things—fogs, poisonous plants, venomous creatures, etc.—and at last tries

to make a man in imitation of Adam. He fails, recognises his failure, and is
obliged to own that his power cannot rival that of the Creator, and that evil is
less powerful than good.' A much expanded version of the poem, with the title
'The Seven Nights of Creation', was published in the *Calcutta Review* in April
1886, but not collected. (See below, p. 310.)

> Lo! what is this I make! Are these his limbs,
> Bent inward, tottering 'neath the body's weight?
> The body crutched by hairy spider-arms,
> Surmounted by a face as who should say,
> 'Why hast thou made me? wherefore hast thou breathed
> Spirit in this foul body? Let me be!'
> The piteous visage puckers with its woe,
> The strange black lips are working with a cry—
> A cry and protest. Lo! the wrinkled palms
> Are stretched forth helplessly and beat the dark.
> So did not my great foe when he was made.
> I saw his eye glow with the sense of power,
> I saw all wild things crouch beneath that eye;
> God gave him great dominion over all
> And blessed him. Shall I bless my handiwork?
> After thy kind be fruitful, lust, and eat;
> All things I give thee in the earth and air—
> Only depart and hide thee in the trees.
> He rises from the ground to do my will
> And seek a shelter. Can the being speak?
> Stay, thing, and thank me for thy quickening.
> The great eyes roll—my meaning is not there
> Reflected as God's word was in the man's.
> I, maker, bid thee speak, if speak thou canst!
> Lo! what is this? My labour is in vain.
> He plucks the grass-tufts aimlessly, and works
> Palm within palm, then for a moment's space
> Breaks off rough bark and throws it on the ground.
> He hears me not. Oh! would the dawn delay,
> So I might rise and perfect that I make,
> Or rise and build again. Alas! the light
> Is flaming forth to mock me. See, he sits
> Helpless, uprooting grass. While all the world
> Is thick with life renewed that fills my ears,
> My last and greatest work is mockery.
> Depart, O Ape! Depart and leave me foiled.

CONVENTIONALITY

Published in *Schoolboy Lyrics*, 1881. Collected in the Outward Bound, De Luxe, Sussex, and Burwash Edns.

Passion and Fire—bah! are they ever linked with beauty?
Beauty and fairness of face? The devils below can tell
The upper-world folk, if they will,
How it's not the lovely alone that enter the gates of hell.

Heroes and dames of fiction, so wicked, so fair, so accurst,
How we praise their faults and applaud each claptrap speech on the
　　stage!
But red hands may be raised to kill—
The white-mouse eye can sparkle as well as the eagle's with rage.

I knew two people so. Romance! She was nothing at all—
Weak-mouthed and chalky-white, limping, and stuttering too.
He was as dull as ever lead,
Dumb; and we wondered how he had found him words to woo.

Then—God knows how it happened!—there came the crime, and we
　　saw
The two, how they held together through the trial and all the rest
Of the dragging chain of the law;
But alas for Romance! we cut them as though they had been the pest.

ENVY, HATRED, AND MALICE

Published in *Schoolboy Lyrics*, 1881. Collected in the Outward Bound, De Luxe, Sussex, and Burwash Edns.

　　　　Let us praise Such an One,
　　　　　　Give him commendation
　　　　Sincere for labour done—
　　　　　　As honour to the nation.
　　　　　　Such elevation,
　　　　Such perfect taste, was never known before;
　　　　Our ranks admit one poet more,
　　　　　　'Mid universal acclamation.

Such an One is elevated
  To the gods,
  Even to the demi-gods.
Such an One is crownèd king,
  Self and friends
Chew the cud of bitter feeling
      Wondering
  By what ends
These strange vermin come to stealing
  Bay-leaves here and there to make
Forged false wreaths, for sure 'tis odd
  How the world a man may take
      For a god.
      (Even for a demi-god!)

Such an One is gone—there rises
  Such Another:
With old thoughts in newer guises
  Born to smother
Such an One's productions.
Welcomed is he just as loudly,
Trails his mantle just as proudly.
      Whence I draw
      My deductions
That many and many a poet more,
  Ere I lie beneath the sods,
I shall witness swell and soar
  To the gods,
  Even to the demi-gods!

ILLUSION, DISILLUSION, ALLUSION

Published in *Schoolboy Lyrics*, 1881. Collected in the Outward Bound, De Luxe, Sussex, and Burwash Edns.

      Fairest of women is she.
          In all the passion of youth,
          In deed and in word and in truth;
      For time and eternity
      I woo her, so let it be.

Rouge and wrinkles and puff,
Padding and powder enough
    To win a hundred hearts!
    They are welcome. From me departs
    Love for this woman of arts.

Old friend, why discourse of these things?
    Fairest of women *was* she.
    Somewhere in eternity
We may play out the game again;
Here, Time has ended her reign,
    Making her hateful to see.

OVERHEARD

Published in *Schoolboy Lyrics*, 1881. Collected in the Outward Bound, De Luxe, Sussex, and Burwash Edns. with subheading 'Supposed to be after Browning'. A typescript copy of a version (undated) sent to Edith Macdonald, with subheading '(a fact)', has a final passage: 'Well I moved just then / And among the crowds of men / I lost them She with her tale / (Carelessly told[1] indeed) / Of means to supply a need / For bread / Till she's dead / She has my prayers if they're any avail.' (KP 24/67.)

So the day dragged through,
And the afternoon brought the spangles,
    The sawdust smell, the tights,
    The flickering, flashing lights,
        The smile to acknowledge the cheer
As the rider skips and jangles
    The bells. Ye gods!—'twas queer
How the young equestriennes flew.

A programme relished, I lay
    Back in my seat to gaze
On the faces around, to hear what folk say,
While the orchestra rattled and roared,
    Murdering popular lays—
It was hot, too, and I felt bored.

---

[1] *told*: amended from 'cold' in TS reading.

Then a voice from behind, a rustling of dress,
   The step of a man, a silence to settle,
   A babble of children (how they push,
These little ones, making your coat in a mess),
A silence to settle, and after a gush
   Of small talk, I sat and waited,
   Shutting my eyes till the stream abated.
'Twas a tale of trouble, told in a rush.

Who was the speaker? I turned to see—
   A sharp little saucy face,
No whit abashed, gazing at me
With bead-eyes, curiously,
   With a petulant child's grimace,
As I shifted, moving her feet
   From the chair where they'd taken root,
   For the time at least; then again
I listened. Fast and fleet
   She poured out the queer little words to her friend—
   (A sort of an overgrown brute).
   I heard it out to the end—
      A story of pain.
      Here you have it, in fine
         (Her words, not mine):
      'Tried for luck in London—
                   Voilà tout![2]
      Failed, lost money, undone;
      Took to the streets for a life.
                 Entre nous,[3]
      It's a terrible uphill strife,
      Like all professions—too filled.
      And now I'm in lodgings hard by,
      Au quatrième,[4] up in the sky.
      Visit me by and by,
They're furnished, but oh—so cold,
      So cold!'

[2] *Voilà tout*: that's all.
[3] *Entre nous*: between ourselves.
[4] *Au quatrième*: on the fourth floor.

There the queer little voice was stilled;
  She moved to a further chair
  And left me sitting there
    To think on the story told—
  Not to me, but to her friend—
Of a life that had only one end,
  And for burden, 'Oh, so cold!'

Have you ever seen on the face
  Of a child a sort of despair,
  A comical, hopeless air,
When a toy won't work, or a doll won't cry,
Or a cart runs awkwardly?
  Well, I saw it there
  As she moved to a further chair.
She'd broken some toy she had—
Or, was it a life gone bad?

FROM THE WINGS

Published in *Schoolboy Lyrics*, 1881. Collected in the Outward Bound, De Luxe, Sussex, and Burwash Edns.

We are actors at the side-scenes ere the play of life begins,
With the curtain rising on us and the tally of our sins:
You may pace the boards before me while amazed the boxes sit,
I, with all my rant and thunder, may but hardly stir the pit.
You may be a prima donna, winning monarchs with your smile;
What wonder I, your equal, should adore you all the while?
When you stand before the footlights will you do your best to shine
In that part the Fates have cast you? Will you join your part to mine?
Will you mouth your words, or murmur? Will you take me for a friend,
From the shifting of the first scene till the curtain brings the end?
When the act-drop falls upon us, when we've heard the audience
    cheer,
When the people that have watched us leave the stalls and gallery
    clear,
When the lights are near extinguished, when the ghostlike cloths are
    thrown

O'er the purple of the velvet, and the actors stand alone—
Old and wrinkled, grey and toothless, fighting at the other door,
Who shall face the darkness first, and who of them shall go before
To the great unknown that stretches out away there where the lights
Flare and flicker in the darkness of an awful night of nights—
Where French rouge won't cheat the Devil, where pearl-powder never
    lies,
And the belladonna's useless for wide, terror-stricken eyes?
When they're howling in the pit, here, may I claim you for my own?
Face the journey both together—two are better far than one.
We'll rehearse the farce together for a little, little time,
Turn the prose that is our being to a comedy in rhyme.
You be lord, and I'll be lady, and in sufferance take my hand,
Talk of passion never dying (for the woman, understand).
So, we'll play it at the wings here, mind! I've never sworn to be
Constant in the real acting, only in the mimicry!
To your place! Your eyes are wandering! Oh—a girl there in the
    wings.
(Odd that in rehearsing 'tis my jealousy that stings!)
I've been thinking it were better just for once to play it through,
Much in earnest; shall we try it? As the heaven I am true
(Made of blue with tinsel planets!). Well! your oath is real enough;
I believe you—only kiss me! This forced passion's dreary stuff !

SOLUS CUM SOLA[1]

Published in *Schoolboy Lyrics*, 1881. Collected in the Outward Bound, De Luxe, Sussex, and Burwash Edns. Holograph version in *Sundry Phansies*.

> We were alone on the beach,
>   Facing the summer sea,
> Watching the waves on the beach,
>   Watching the moon on the sea.
>
> Words were not many, I ween;
>   Why should we want them, we?
> Two hearts, and nothing between,
>   Facing the summer sea.

[1] *Solus cum Sola*: he alone with her alone.

Silence! such silence is speech.
　　She, with her arm in mine,
Pacing the moonlit beach,
　　Makes it communion divine.

Voice of the world around?
　　Blatant bands on the pier?
We have not heard a sound,
　　And yet you say they were near!

Well, we must go there once more,
　　Hear them play, you and I
Lo! the day's glory is o'er;
　　Until to-morrow, good-bye.

MISSED

Published in *Schoolboy Lyrics*, 1881. Collected in the Outward Bound, De Luxe, Sussex, and Burwash Edns. Holograph version in *Sundry Phansies*. Typescript copy of version sent to Edith Macdonald (KP 24/67).

There is *one* moment when the gods are kind,
　　And, bending down, pour blessings on our head;
It is the moment when all men are blind,
　　And Honour perishèd.

There is *one* moment when the fire flies,
　　God-sent, and flickers; hold it he who may.
It is the moment when on other eyes
　　Our own are turned away.

There is *one* moment when our Love is loving,
　　And would repay our worship. Lo! alas!
It is the moment when the blood is moving
　　Coldly, that these things pass.

There is *one* moment of a high endeavour
　　That stirs our pulse with passion. Be it so;
'Tis but one moment, and is lost for ever;
　　Account this, therefore, woe.

There is one moment only that shall make
    Men equal. For the rest, we strike and strike
The chords all jarringly; no comfort take.
    There are no twain alike.

FAILURE

Holograph versions in Notebook 3, dated 25 December 1881, and *Sundry Phansies*. Transcribed version in Notebook 2, dated 'Winter term 1881'. Published in *Echoes*, 1884. Collected in the Outward Bound, De Luxe, Sussex, and Burwash Edns.

    One brought her Fire from a distant place,
    And She—what should she know of it?—She took
    His offering with the same untroubled look
        Of peace upon her face.

    'And I have brought it of my best,' quoth he,
    'By barren deserts and a frozen land.
    What recompense?' She could not understand,
        But let the bright light be.

    'A kindly gift,' the answer broke at length,
    'A kindly gift. We thank you. What is this
    That fiercer than all household fire is,
        And gathereth in strength?

    Strange fires? Take them hence with you, O sir!
    Presage of coming woe we dimly feel.'
    Sudden She crushed the embers 'neath her heel,—
        And all light went with Her.

A QUESTION [BY THE SEA]

Holograph version in Notebook 3, with title 'A Question', dated 25 December 1881. Transcribed version in Notebook 2, dated 'Xmas Day 1881'. Another holograph version in *Sundry Phansies*, with title 'By the Sea' and first two stanzas transposed.

Bring me a message of hope O sea!
  I am weary of waiting—Goes it well
On the low sand dunes where my heart is set?
I have asked of the winds and they cannot tell
If the Love that was all in all to me
    Passeth, or liveth yet.

Bring me a message of hope O sea!
  I am weary of waiting—the days are long
And there comes to me neither word nor sign
Or in the wind, or the breaker's song,
If the Love that was all in all to me
    Has passed or remaineth mine.

Bring me a message of hope O sea!
  I am weary of waiting, and winter is come
But there comes to me nothing by land or sea
The lake is frozen, the winds are dumb
And the Love that was all in all to me,
    Liveth it yet O sea?

THE PAGE'S SONG

Holograph version in Notebook 3, dated 25 December 1881. Transcribed version of first three stanzas only in Notebook 2, dated 'Winter term 1881'. Another holograph version in *Sundry Phansies*, with subtitle '(Translated from the Romance of the Garde Ysoud)'[1] and heading 'The Page had loste all his wits in Palestine / from a stroke dealte hardily by a Moor / which is a Man alwaie accursed / and coulde say little that might be understanded, and there was one Song which he sang from Dawn to Duske in dolorous wise / and none might stay him from singing. And I have written his song even as I heard it'. Cf. 'The Page's Message' (p. 80 above) which follows this poem in *Sundry Phansies*. In Notebook 3, l. 4 of the second stanza reads 'That sad sword in thy warped wit'.

        Spring-time, shall it bring thee ease
          From the woes the Gods have sent?
        May the leafage of the trees
          Soothe unreste and discontent?
        Can the glory of the fields
        Give what nought in heaven yields?

[1] *the Romance of the Garde Ysoud*: see above, p. 80.

Plucking Hawthorne in the hedge
   Shall a peace be found in it?
Summer's wealth may ne'er disedge
   That sad warp in thy poor wit—
All the hope that being slain,
Turns to venom in the brain.

Gay is spring time, free and bold,
   Summer's blazing pageantry—
Autumn is a lord of gold.
   What can all this profit thee?
Seek thy rest in winter's wind,
King dethroned from one poor mind.

Snow and sleet shall soothe thee best—
   Hail and tinkling icicle
Freeze some comfort in a breast
   Full of fancies terrible—
Seek thy rest in Nature's pain
Oh weak King of one wild brain!

HOW THE DAY BROKE

Holograph versions in Notebook 3, dated 30 December 1881, *Sundry Phansies*,
and Huntington Library MS HM 11886. Transcribed version in Notebook 2,
dated 30 December 1881. Published in *Echoes*, 1884. Collected in the
Outward Bound, De Luxe, Sussex, and Burwash Edns., with subtitle 'Draw-
ing-Room Song'.

The night was very silent, and the moon was going down,
   And the winds of dawn were chilling all the sea.
The full tide turned in silver o'er the ridge's length of brown,
When a little muffled figure left the dim-seen, sleeping town
   By the white road that leadeth to the sea.

The night was very silent, and the tide was falling fast,
   And the dawn was breaking dimly o'er the sea;
The early boats like shadows with their lanterns flitted past,
And the little muffled figure by the sand-hills stayed at last,
   Where the waste land opens on the sea.

The night is well-nigh ended, and the moon has gone to rest
   And the winds of dawn are lashing all the sea.
But the weariness is over and the doubt is all confessed,
And hope is re-arisen and the wrong is all redressed,
As the little muffled figure lays her head upon his breast
    Who has waited for her coming by the sea.

The night is passed and done with, and the day is cold and white
   As the loosed winds riot o'er the sea,
But the woe is passed and done with as a shadow of the night,
And the little muffled figure flitteth, singing, out of sight
    To the fishing-town that faces on the sea.

THE STORY OF PAUL VAUGEL [PAUL VAUGEL]

Holograph versions, incomplete, in Notebooks 1 and 3. Transcribed version in Notebook 2, dated 'Christmas holidays 1881–82', with title 'Paul Vaugel'. Full holograph version in *Sundry Phansies*, with subtitle: 'Shewing how he took to himself an unfortunate, and maintained her, and how she died, and how he buried her in the Pol-Lourdesse and of the evil that came on him'. Similar subtitle in Notebook 3. Notebook 1 has a later comment by Kipling, dating from 1883 or 1884: 'There are over seventy "ands" in this thing but it made Miss Maggie Hooper[1] . . . "weep". Perhaps by reason of its length.'

    This is the story of Paul Vaugel
    Of the Pol-Lourdesse, and how he fell
    From Heaven to that he counted Hell.

    I set for myself one fixed intent—
    (Hope is strong as Love in the Heart)
    As a light to guide me where I went
    (Reckon ye neither burns or smart)

    And I laboured a year with heart and strove
    That out of my Love there should come Love.—

---

[1] *Miss Maggie Hooper*: probably the daughter of Mrs George Hooper, a sister of Miss Winnard who was one of 'the Ladies of Warwick Gardens' (see above, p. 5).

And I laboured a year with heart and brain,
And a Hope as deep as Love in my heart,
But my winter harvesting was pain,
Yet I drew not back for burn or smart—

For the purpose stayed and changed no whit
And I rose again to follow it.

And I laboured that Love should come in the end,
With Hope as deep as Love in the heart,
Alone, in the dark, I had no friend
To comfort a little my bitter smart

And I laboured that Love should come in the end.
And that she I had saved should at length unbend.

And there came no rest by night or day,
And the woman that ruled me passed away

And I, that had worked to gain her bread,
With a hope as deep as Love in the heart
Lifted her up where she lay dead,
And I alone bore pain and smart

For this woman was like to die of pain,
And I—I had given her strength again.

And I swore an oath that by right of sin,
And hope of better in either heart,
The woman should be as my nearest kin,
And I reckoned neither of burn or smart.
And a space I had got her bread to eat
And clothed her body and shod her feet,
And such life as we led² was sweet indeed
With Hope as deep as Love in the heart,
And all her Love for all my meed
And little care for a coming smart,

And our straitened chamber seemed to be
A heaven set apart for me,

---

² *led*: 'lead' in *Sundry Phansies*.

Where she lay still, and white and faint,
But with hope as deep as Love in the heart,
She that to me was very saint,
And I reckoned little of burn or smart.

And the woe of the streets and all their sin,
Beat at the door but came not in.

And then was rest when the day was over,
And hope and Love were high in the heart,
For her white arms closed round me, her lover,
And her kiss was worth all pain and smart

And the heat and toil of a little day,
At the sound of her voice would pass away.

And I thought that this would alway be
And that hope and Love should rule i' the heart,
But God's hand took her love from me
And I alone bore the pain and the smart

For the plague that summer brings to our town
Seized her and held, and threw her down.

And when she died I had lived so,
With the love of one to fill my heart,
There was no friend that could hear my woe,
And comfort a little my bitter smart.

So I raised her up, and combed her hair,
And lifted her down our narrow stair.
And the poor white feet swayed aimlessly,
As I laid the sweet head close to me.
And all the wealth of her hair unbound
Fell o'er my arm to the very ground,
And the pale lips moved as I lifted her,
So that I thought some life did stir;
An hour I chafed her hands and head
(Albeit I knew that she was dead).
And I stood at the foot of our narrow stair
Till the cattle came to the market-square;

So I knew that the noon was passed and over,
And I slid the bolt and bore out my lover.

* * * * *

Where the Pol-Lourdesse runs out by the sea,
Is the burial place for such as we,
Where the green sea poppy flourisheth,
And the dog-fish nuzzles the bones of death.
Where the sand like a sea-mist shifts and moves
Over the bones of our buried Loves,
And the starveling ponies are hardly fed
From the wreaths we poor folk make for our Dead.

* * * * *

The sun was setting angrily
Where the Pol-Lourdesse runs out by the sea,
And the glare of the sunset fell like blood
On the poor pinched face beneath its hood,
As I trod on the shingly sea-ward reach
From the street of the fleshers—out to the beach
And her head on my shoulder rose and fell,
And I thought that her lips framed 'Paul Vaugel'
So I knelt on the road and laid her down,
By the conduit wall of the newer town.
And I chafed her head and called her name
So loud, that the market people came,
And they stood and watched till the sun went down,
And I bore the dead thing out of the town

* * * * *

And I came to the dunes as the sun was hid
By a thick grey bank of clouds that slid
Like blinded beasts round the silent sky,
As our cattle reel before they die

* * * * *

And I found a hillock of bent bound sand,
And I dug her resting place with my hand.
And I lifted her up and lowered her,
And waited to see if she would stir.
(Tho' I knew she was dead)—and then I strove
To put the dry sand over my Love.

And the silver sand in a shower fell
On the feet of the Love of Paul Vaugel
And I covered the waist but could not bear
To lay the filth on her face and hair—
So I sat and waited till night should fall
And I could not see the face at all.
And I plucked sea poppy and wind dried heather,
And wove them into a wreath together
And I set the wreath on her brows as night
Came, and shut them out of my sight—
Then I piled the sand over face and hair
Till I left no whit of the body bare
For I felt in the dark lest foot or hand
Should be uncovered by the sand.
And I stacked up gorze till my fingers bled,
Lest the sheep should pasture over head—
And I weighted the bushes with boulder clay,
And I sat on the Dunes and wept till day.
And a great mist rose from the Dune St Lo,[3]
And an inland wind on the full tide's flow
And all night long the sea-mist passed
In a thousand shapes before the blast
And all our past Life shewed to me
Till morning broke on the sullen sea.

   * * * * *

And I went to my home when the day was white,
And Hope and Love lay dead in the heart,
And I laid her trinkets out of sight,
For Love remembered is bitter smart—
And the cattle came below to the square,
And the street was full of our winter fair
And I went in the street to my booth and stood
(With never a sign of a troubled heart)
As men stand and chaffer in idle mood,
For who could tell of my bitter smart?
But all day long a murmur fell,
'Come thou swiftly O Paul Vaugel'
And the street of the fleshers seemed to ring
With this one cry for my maddening

---

[3] *St Lo*: sc. St.-Lô, market town in north-west France, some 34 mls west of Caen, or more probably the Commune of St.-Lô, west of Coutances. The previous word could be 'Dim'.

And night and day came the bitter cry
'Paul Vaugel, what hope have I?'
And the day and the dawn were full of the same,
And the sunset stamped the words in flame
And the Church bells rang with a weary knell,
'Come thou swiftly O Paul Vaugel!'
And I had no peace by day at all,
And I went to the Dunes at evenfall—
And only there had I any rest
From the thoughts that raged like flame in my breast.
And only there was my spirit still
But then longing came—which was greater ill
And either the cry or the dumb desire
Came to make my life a fire.
And though it is years since my woe was done,
I have found no comfort under the sun—

QUAERITUR[1]

Holograph version in *Sundry Phansies*. No date: 1881–2? Not to be confused
with another poem of the same title in *Echoes*, 1884: see below, p. 241.

Is Life to be measured by grains,
    By hours slow pacing by years,
By cycles of pleasures and pains,
    By laughter and dropping of tears,
By death and the loss of our peers?

Is Life to be fought for as Gold,
    To be struggled for (Well a day!)
By those that were young and are old?
    By those that depart and decay?
Is Life then, so dear to *all* clay?

Is Love to be measured by Life?
    Is Love to be bounded by death?
The End of a fruitless strife
    Cessation—of being and breath.
    I call—who answereth?

[1] *Quaeritur*: lit.: it is sought for; hence yearning.

CONSPIRACY

Holograph version in *Sundry Phansies*. No date: 1881–2? The self-conscious archaisms recall the headings to 'The Page's Message' (21 November 1881) and 'The Page's Song' (25 December 1881). See above, pp. 80 and 99.

> Two that shall plotte together
>   (Craftilie, so craftilie)
> Inn the Dark where no Mann strayeth
> What is it that Each one sayeth
>   Bending lowe?
> (Two heads that plott together)
> Matters it, if Winter weather
> Come upon them suddenlie?
> There is that, within the Twaine
> Making Joy of present Paine
> While long seasons goe
>
> Two—that shall hide together
>   (Secretlie, so secretlie)
> In the wildes that no man knoweth
> To a place that no man knoweth
>   They are gone.
> (Two soules that plotte together)
> Matters it if Winter weather
>   Come upon them where they bee?
> There is that within their breaste
>   Making Peace of all unreste
> While they hide together
>   And the long days goe.

SONG (FOR TWO VOICES)

Holograph version in *Sundry Phansies*. No date: 1881–2? Not to be confused with the 'Song for Two Voices' beginning 'Follow and faint not': see below, p. 152.

SP.[1] or MZ.[2] SOPRANO

I bound his soul by a word and an Oath
(Light Loves pass as the gusts of Spring)—

[1] *Sp.*: soprano.
[2] *mz*: mezzo.

Lo! in a year he had broken both
And I am worn and sorrowing.

CONTRALTO

I bound his soul by my two eyes' might—
My lips' red seal was upon his brow
Between the nightingale's song and the night—
Wherefore I rule his spirit now—

THE SECOND WOOING [A VISITATION]

Holograph version in *Sundry Phansies* with title 'A Visitation'. No date: 1881–2? Published with minor revisions in *Quartette*, 19 December 1885. Uncollected. The last two lines of the published version have no equivalent in *Sundry Phansies*, nor are the pronouns 'He' and 'His' capitalized there. I take 'right' in the last line to be a misprint for 'sight'—one of the many errors Kipling lamented in the printing of *Quartette*. (See above, p. 30).

There came to me One at midnight, on golden pinions, and said:
'Lo! I am Love, and I bring thee a passion back from the dead!'
Then I rose in the darkness and lit the lamp, and there shone in my
   face
The beauty of bygone years and the hope of a bygone grace.
Then I clad myself as of old and sang to myself in joy:
'Shall we change as woman and man who changed not as girl and boy?'
And He entered the room in the midst of my song and we stood apart,
And I raised my eyes to His eyes, and love died out of my heart.
But we kissed each other once on the lips, and His lips were cold;
And hand touched hand for a moment, and then we loosened hold.
And His words were as smooth as mine, but His eyes were as carven
   stone;
And I laid my hand on His wrist, and His pulse was as calm as my
   own.
Yet I strove to talk of our love as a thing that should have no end,
But the words were changed on my tongue—and I talked as the
   merest friend.
And he spoke of His hopes and my beauty, our struggles and hundred
   fears,
As men tell of a dream they have dreamt to their children in after
   years.

And as children parade the cart, the Noah's Ark and the ball,
And set them in rank and order, though delight be passed from all,
As men seek for fire in the embers, and rake them and turn them over,
We paraded old love and we sought for new love, I and my Lover.
And then, when the dawn was approaching, He paled in the coming
    light;
And e'en as He faded from me so Love passed out of my sight.

BRIGHTON BEACH

Holograph version in *Sundry Phansies* with subheading '(After Browning)'. No
date: 1881–2?

A flash in your eye for a minute—
An answering light in mine
What was the mischief in it?
Who but we two could divine—

Before those eyelids droop
Do I read your riddle—Well
I take it an angel may stoop
Sometimes, to the nether Hell.

We'll argue it this way then
Tho' it sound a trifle inhuman—
I am not your man among men,
Nor you my first dearest woman

Each touched some hidden chord
In the other's heart for a minute,
That sprang into light at a word
And pulsed with the music in it—

The veil was torn asunder
As I sighed and pleaded and wooed
And we saw the truth there under
As it stands—uncouth and nude

Now back to the work again—
In the old, blind, tread-mill fashion—
False hope, false joy, false pain,
Rechauffés[1] of by gone passion!

RESOLVE

Holograph version in *Sundry Phansies*. No date: 1881–2?

I said to myself—'I will dream
    As the summer days go by,
    What is my Destiny—'
And I lay and dreamt my dream
    And I woke from it with a cry—

And I said in fear—'I will go,
    Ere the rose's bud be red,
    I will labour for my bread'—
But I knew not whither to go,
And summer passed over my head.

And I said to myself 'I will rise
    Ere the green leaf change to brown,
I will win me great renown
    Ere Autumn chill the skies,
And the laden bough bend down.'

But Winter came and I cried
    From under the sodden trees,
    'Now is the time for Ease'—
And I filled my heart with pride.

L'ENVOI

Holograph version in *Sundry Phansies*, where it forms the last poem in the collection. No date, but another holograph version, inscribed in a copy of *Departmental Ditties* presented to Florence Garrard, has the heading 'written in

---

[1] *Rechauffés*: warmed-up left-over foods.

"81" ' (Berg Collection). The conclusion of that version, corresponding to the
last three lines in *Sundry Phansies*, reads 'One thought to me— / Have I not
thee / As a star and a light for my leading / Through Time & Eternity.'

> Rhymes, or of grief or of sorrow
>   Pass and are not,
> Rhymes of today—tomorrow
>   Lie forgot.
>
> I that am writer of verses—
>   What is my prize?—
> Palm crowns and gold filled purses,
>   Honour that dies
>   As the year flies,
> As the multitude breaks and disperses
>   And the new Generations arise—?
>
> If through these rhymes in their reading
>   Thy blood should be
> Quickened *one moment* conceding
>   Homage to me—
> I have got me a prize far exceeding
>   All prizes that be.

PARTING

Holograph version signed 'J.R.K.',[1] said to be written for Miss Florence Gar-
rard (Berg Collection). No date: 1881–2?

> Hot kisses on red lips that burn—
>   A silence—Then some loving word.—
> Two hearts that parted yearn—
>   A parting long deferred—
>
> Another kiss—What harm is this I do?
>   Another vow of Love that cannot die,—
> Then far asunder thou and I
>   Wait the long blank days thro'.

[1] *J.R.K.*: Kipling's full name was Joseph Rudyard Kipling.

Oh Love, believe me! I have never failed
   In all my passion, for a *moment's* space,
   Oh Love believe me—Years shall ne'er efface
   The memory of thy beauty & thy grace,
      Till Life by Death be veiled

For Time and all Eternity I hold
   Firm fixed to thee—If the strong Powers will
   That thou should'st cease to love me—still
My Love becomes not cold.

One moment longer, ere these lines be thrown
   In fire that is cooler than my soul,—
   Pray thou, that of our sin—*the whole*
Be borne by me alone—

REJECTION

Holograph version in Notebook 3. No date: 1881–2?

    'We will lay this thing here'—
      Thus spake the voice of the sea,
      Murmuring wearily—
    In the rock's ear—

    Then the green laver[1] rose,
      Shook out her folds & cried,
      Before the rising tide
    'Let me repose—

    Stir not my rest O sea,
      With dead things in these silent deeps,
      Surely wave tossed he sleeps
    As heavily'—

    The weedhung chambers then
      Made answer—'O thou sea,
      The beasts that feed[2] in me
    What need they men'—

        [1] *laver*: marine algae.
        [2] *feed*: reading uncertain.

Rock limpets cowering,
   Murmured gloom shaded—'There is meat
   Enough for all to eat
Bear hence this thing—

In thy strong arms O sea,
   Out, even to the quicksands' brink,
   It shall be that he sink—
There, utterly.'

'We will lay this thing here'
   Thus spake the voice of the sea,
   Ever persistently
In the rock's ear.

GIVEN FROM THE CUCKOO'S NEST TO THE BELOVED INFANT—GREETING

Transcription of verse letter to his sister Trix in Notebook 2, dated 28 January 1882. Kipling not infrequently dated letters from his shared study at school as from 'The Cuckoo's Nest'.

I sit in the midst of my study
   With cake crumbs adorning my hair
My boots are confoundedly muddy
   And are leaving wet marks on the chair
That supports the fair feet of your Ruddy
   As he rests with stale cake in his hair

I am full of a sense of importance,
   Of lobster, cream, pilchards and cake
And I feel in my—bosom grim portents
   That herald the course of an ache
I remark I am racked with grim portents
   That usher abdominal ache.

Yet I write you this letter fraternal
   I indite you this brotherly note
Tho' my tortures are waxing infernal
   I write as I ever have wrote
Observe that my tone is fraternal
   And I write as I ever have wrote

Be it known to you fairest of females
    That dulness is dominant here
And there's little to interest we males
    Whose smallness is lesser than beer
I complain that in spite of our three mails
    Per diem[1] there comes nothing here

Moreover the weather is wondrous
    And skies that should rain only shine
We have dry chalk and gravel roads under us
    And the sun is at work before nine
I may state as a fact still more wondrous
    I too am at work before nine

And further to tell you, the Kingsley
    Memorial College[2] is built
And throughout it strange carpenters' things lie
    And paint-pots are lavishly spilt
Id est[3] they are fitting the Kingsley
    With boardings & carvings and gilt.

By a special train chartered at Bristol
    The guilt comes, some two hundred strong
The sons of land-owners who missed all
    Their rents when the Green Isle went wrong[4]
To be plain, all the boys come from Bristol
    By the packets of Vermouth and Long.[5]

We have purchased some tea-pots of delft ware
    We found in a Bideford shop
That crammed on the back of a shelf were
    (Mrs Morten's—she takes things to p–p)[6]
In a shop where a friend & myself were
    Knocking round as we do in a shop.

---

[1] *Per diem*: per day.

[2] *Kingsley Memorial College*: a school for the sons of professional men, opened in 1882 at Westward Ho! quite near the United Services College. It was established there partly in consequence of the troubled state of Ireland, where most of its pupils came from. It had to close down in Dec. 1885.   [3] *Id est*: that is.

[4] *when the Green Isle went wrong*: Ireland ('the Emerald Isle') had been racked by agrarian discontent, and on the imprisonment of Charles Stewart Parnell, the leading advocate of Home Rule, in Oct. 1881 the Land League called on tenants to withhold rents till their leaders were released.

[5] *Vermouth and Long*: presumably a steamship company, but I have found no record of it.   [6] *p–p*:'pop'—slang for 'pawn'.

I have got three most quaintest of glasses
   For Miss Winnard,[7] (I'll send 'em along)
Whose shape all description surpasses
   And I purchased them all for a song
Which means that the price of those glasses
   Was entirely other than long

And now since the sun is descending
   I must finish my brotherly note
I must make of beginning an ending
   I must finish this versified note
Take a picture I've drawn as an ending
   Most fit for a metrical note.

HOW IT SEEMED TO US

Holograph versions in Notebook 1, dated 30 January 1882, Notebook 3, dated 2 February 1882, and *Sundry Phansies*. Transcribed version in Notebook 2, dated 1 February 1882, and typescript copy of version sent to Edith Plowden, dated 1882 (KP 24/30). Notebook 3 has 'served' for 'lived' in the second last line, and 'my heart went out' three lines before.

A grey flat lying out against the sea,
   Where the strait guts are choked with weeded wood
And tangled cordage, moving aimlessly
   Upon the lazy leaden ebb or flood;
A waste of stunted gorze and withered tree,
   Warped by a wind that chills the running blood
And crisps the slime masked puddles in the mud,
   A place of desolation verily—
And yet this place is dearer to us two
   Than any other spot we know on earth—
The North wind ushered in our Passion's birth,
   When by the waste went out my heart to you—
And the blind tide at ebb crawled back again
   To scatter golden spume flakes at our feet
And hail us—who had lived a time of pain
   And being free, had found deliverance sweet.

---

[7] *Miss Winnard*: one of 'the Ladies of Warwick Gardens' (see above, p. 5).

LES AMOURS FACILES[1]

Holograph versions in Notebook 1, dated 2 February 1882, Notebook 3, and *Sundry Phansies*. Transcribed version in Notebook 2, dated 30 January 1882. A later note by Kipling in Notebook 1 reads 'Bad=cribbed/cheap', and he adds the reference ' "Criterion" '.[2]

> A woe that lasts for a little space,
>   A light love passing and soon forgot,
> A little sigh for a vanished grace,
>   For a Love that lives on a lovely face—
>   And the rest—we keep it not.
>
> A fire that burns[3] for a little space,
>   A light smoke rising to mark the spot,
> A ring of black in the fire's place
>   That the soft scraped mould may soon efface—
>   And the rest—we keep it not
>
> Oh! Why have the gods for a little space
>   Bound our lives by a weary lot,
> For each light love leaves some light trace
>   And the heart is seared ere manhood's days,
>   Ere the love that lingers and lights and stays
>   Arrive—and we keep it not.

THE DEDICATION OF THIS BOOK WHICH IS WRITTEN TO A WOMAN [A DEDICATION; DEDICATION]

Holograph version in Notebook 1, with title 'A Dedication', dated 3 February 1882. Other holograph versions in Notebook 3, with title 'The Dedication of this Book which is written to a Woman', dated 3 February 1882, and in *Sundry Phansies*, with title 'Dedication'. (Notebook 1 and *Sundry Phansies* have 'faltering' for 'pitiful' in l. 4; Notebook 3 has been taken as the copy-text.) The poem is presumably addressed to Flo Garrard. On re-reading it in Notebook 1 in his early years in India, Kipling added a marginal gloss attributed to 'Brisbane

---

[1] *Les Amours Faciles*: light loves.
[2] *Criterion*: presumably a reference to the Criterion Theatre, which opened at Piccadilly Circus in 1874.   [3] *burns*: 'lasts' in Notebook 1.

Convict's Song (altered)': 'and she turned me off like a dog my boys / and while I sing this lay-ay-ay / She's a going on the spoon[1] 'neath an English moon / Six thousand miles away.'

What have I more to give thee, who have given thee all my heart?—
Only a faltering verse, and a bungling rhymester's art—
Is it worthy thine acceptation? Is it worthy the light of thine eyes?
Is it worthy thy hand should touch it, this pitiful verse that dies?
Let thy soul's perfect music interpret its harmonies—
The passion that is in a line, and whence that passion had rise,
For my heart is laid bare to thy heart, and my soul in thy hand's hold
  lies.

CHANGE

Holograph version in Notebook 1, dated 10 February 1882. Another in Notebook 3 with the same date, and a third in *Sundry Phansies*. Transcribed version in Notebook 2, with the date 'Feb. 1882'.

A changed life and a changed hope—
  A changed end to our labouring,
From the child's blind wish to the man's fixed scope,
  And a power determinate that shall bring
You to be Queen, and me to be King.

A changed hope in a changed heart—
  A changed end to our labouring—
While we two wait alone and apart,
  Plotting both, for the end that shall bring
You to be Queen and me to be King.

A changed heart and a changed will—
  A changed end to our labouring—
Tho' the hands be bound, is the brain's force still—
  Scheming our last stroke that shall bring
You to be Queen and me to be King?

---

[1] *going on the spoon*: flirting.

A changed will and a changed desire,
   A changed end to our labouring—
While each mouth's breath draws the ending nigher—
   The strange swift ending that shall bring
You to be Queen & me to be King—

A DOMINANT POWER

Holograph version in Notebook 1, dated 16 February 1882. Another in Notebook 3 with the same date. Transcribed version in Notebook 2, dated 23 February.

A strong man pacing over burning sands,
Having no armour, only hard, bare, hands
To hold with and to slay with—Woe betide
If thou shalt meet him in the city! Woe!
If in the fields, or where the salt waves are.
For there be none so strong to lay him low,
And he is swifter than all souls that hide
From him in deserts barren and afar.—
They find no respite—Coming softly shod,
He smites them down, and flees and leaves them there
Unpitied of the people, while with eyes
Hand shaded, turn they on the country bare,
Tracing with wonder and a sad surprise
The golden cloud that hides a fleeting god.

A PROFESSION OF FAITH

Holograph versions in Notebook 1 and Notebook 3, both dated 17 February 1882. Transcribed version in Notebook 2, dated February 1882. In a changed mood Kipling added a later gloss in Notebook 1: 'And how can we pray at an empty shrine? / And how can we call on a goddess that's flown? / Come, come away, sweet mistress mine / And build up a temple all our own.'

Each day watched die together binds us fast,
And each woe of that one black year and all
The waiting and the watching of the past

Bind close and closer, since I first was thrall—
Surely old Love is sweeter far than new,
And old shared sin is lighter through the sharing,
And sin's pain borne together sweet through bearing:
How should I ever turn my heart from you
O Mistress of so long? How should I go,
To some strange woman knowing not my pain
Or night long vigils, or long dumb delays
That were, or hope deferred, or schemings slow
Or the quick lie and plottings of the brain,
That we two knew through those three hundred days?

SIR GALAHAD

Holograph versions in Notebook 1, dated 24 February 1882, and in Notebook
3, with the same date. In Notebook 1 the fourth stanza printed here comes at
the end of the poem and is followed by a note 'But they were disappointed'.
There is a later note 'The usual end', and a final gloss: 'Moral. Never be satiri-
cal on my present resources of rhyme—and reason.'

CHORUS OF ADVENTURERS

'Sharpened sword at saddle bow,
    Strength to wield it well,
Maiden's love where e'er we go—
    We, invincible.
Fighting lust and evil passion
In the old, grim hero fashion.

Who shall stop us as we go
    Down the village road,
Faces, that we love and know,
    In the paths we trod?
We that war with lust and passion
Draw not back thus, woman fashion.

We are rich in hope and blessing,
    Love of all our friends—
Let there be no weak caressing
    Till the journey ends—
Till we vanquish lust and passion
And return in victor fashion.'

CHORUS OF MATERNAL RELATIVES AT THE HALL DOOR
'Who shall tell us where they go!
        Keep them safe O God
    (Little evil do they know)
        In the paths untrod!
Victors over lust and passion.
Bring them back in glorious fashion.'

CHORUS OF ADVENTURERS IN THE DISTANCE
'Who shall tell us where to go
        In the crowded city?
Houses make a royal show
        Sure it were a pity
In this home of Lust and passion
Thus to flee it coward fashion.'

CHORUS OF SURVIVORS SUBSEQUENTLY
'Lo! our swords are bent and rusted.
        Girths are laced with string,
Breastplates scarcely to be trusted
        Casque a ruined thing—
Yielded all to lust and passion
In the very oldest fashion!'

THE QUEST

Holograph versions in Notebook 1, dated 5 March [1882], and in Notebook 3,
dated 5 March 1882. In Notebook 3 the poem figures as the third of a
sequence of four sonnets, the others being 'In the Beginning' [A Creed], 'A
Tryst' ['The Tryst in Summer'], and 'The Attainment' ['Escaped!']. See
below, pp. 139 and 147–8.

In years long past we met a while and vowed
    Light vows we scarcely knew of—she and I—
Made compact sweetly, that if Life allowed,
    I, as true knight should bear her by and bye,
To some strong castle fairy guarded—there
    To be my Queen—and there live out the years[1]

[1] Notebook 3 has 'days', Notebook 1 'years', which the rhyme scheme requires.

Allotted, in all love: but now I bear
    The burden of a thousand hopes and fears
Spring from those words—I knight am old and worn;
    'Tis long time since I saw my Lady's face,
And she perchance is dead, and I am sworn
    To seek her out in whatsoever place
They laid her. Have thou pity on my woe,
And tell me if she be alive or no.

COMMONPLACES

Holograph version in Notebook 1, dated 5 March [1882], with last line 'And there's only a lie to say'. Published in *Echoes*, 1884. Collected in the Outward Bound, De Luxe, Sussex, and Burwash Edns., with subheading '(Heine)'.[1]

    Rain on the face of the sea,
      Rain on the sodden land,
    And the window-pane is blurred with rain
      As I watch it, pen in hand.

    Mist on the face of the sea,
      Mist on the sodden land,
    Filling the vales as daylight fails,
      And blotting the desolate sand.

    Voices from out of the mist,
      Calling to one another:
    'Hath love an end, thou more than friend,
      Thou dearer than ever brother?'

    Voices from out of the mist,
      Calling and passing away;
    But I cannot speak, for my voice is weak,
      And . . . this is the end of my lay.

  [1] *Heine*: Heinrich Heine (1797–1856), famous German poet.

GREETING

Holograph versions in Notebook 1, dated 6 March [1882], Notebook 3, dated 6 March 1882, Baldwin Papers (2/30), and Library of Congress (in a letter of 9 March to Mrs Tavenor Perry, in which he says he has spent some of the time he has been incapacitated in 'hatching out a metrical sentimentality' which he now encloses). Transcribed version in Notebook 2, dated March 1882. The copy in the Baldwin Papers had been sent to Edith Plowden in April 1882, and she considered that it was one of the first of Kipling's poems to show him developing a style of his own.

> What comfort can I send thee sweet,
>   Save that Pain is—we know not why,
>   Save that Pain lives—and will not die?
> What comfort? I can but repeat
>   The old philosophy.
>
> Bear and be patient O my sweet!
>   Pain is—but is our pleasure over?
>   Pain lives—but live I not thy lover,
> Through all the changes we may meet
>   And all new years discover?
>
> What comfort can I send thee sweet?
>   Pain is—and none may flee from it,
>   Pain lives—nor softens any whit—
> A fire with a constant heat
>   Our birth sees firstly lit.
>
> Bear and be patient O my sweet!
>   Pain is—and none can tell us why
>   Pain lives—and dies not till we die,
> Till the heart's pulse has ceased to beat.
>   And after—then come I.

THE TROUBLE OF CURTISS WHO LODGED IN THE BASEMENT

Holograph version in Notebook 1, dated 7 March 1882, with note at end 'A bad case of typhus'. Another holograph version in Notebook 3, with same date; and transcribed version in Notebook 2. A later comment in Notebook 1, dated

4 April 1883, reads 'Thought this perfection when I wrote it—forcible grand and all the rest—In straining after effect I overdid the thing, neglected the woman's life shamefully and shamelessly and mixed my few grains of wheat with so much chaff that the whole affair has been hopelessly spoilt. *Moral* Don't write like that again till I am older—but it *has* one good point.'

Ever so little to shew for it
    And I shouldn't have cared but I haven't a thing
    Excepting her battered turquoise ring
And my finger's so thick it's too small to fit.

Nothing to shew for all the sorrow—
    And I—Good God! I am here by myself
    With those two watch pockets over our shelf
I must take the red one down tomorrow.

I wonder why she went so fast.
    I'm sure she ought to have lived a while,
    For the doctor said, with his sawdust smile,
'She's bound to go—but a week she'll last.'

I shouldn't ha' minded, if only I'd known—
    But it happened so suddenly—first the gasp
    And then—she was holding me tight in her clasp—
The jaw went down, and she fell like a stone.

What came next after the stillness?
    Oh! tea, on a tray, with cups for two—
    (You see *they* thought that she'd pull through,
And we'd always taken it so, in her illness.)

That upset me—Lord knows why:
    When the slavey left and shut the door
    I gulped a bit, and I drop't on the floor
But my throat was so hot I couldn't cry—

And then the business next morning, and all
    The hideous wrangling over the price—
    'For three pun ten, you can do it nice
But there's ten bob more for the use of the pall

And three bob more if you 'as the bell,
    An' then there's the land; *we* manages that,
    And then there's the crape what goes round your 'at
And then there's the parson's fees as well.'

(The worst of it is you can't escape
    The detail after a loved one dies,
    But must quit at once, gird loins & rise
To haggle for feathers and nails and crape)

'We'll manage it all.' God! What did I care
    As he preached in a dreary monotone
    Of the different merits of different stone
And asked when the men should come and where.

A wholesale business—mercantile
    To the gilt-head letter-nails hammered in—
    A matter of money—Who cared a pin
Or thought of my Lottie all the while!

                *   *   *   *   *

Why is it so? What's the good of it all?
I'd ha' kept her alive if they'd let me try—
    And she—what need to make her die?
God of the Pestilence answer my call.

Surely our God is a little blind,—
    Or a little careless maybe—perhaps
    He is out of the reach of those awful taps
On the shell that are driving me out of my mind.

All so horrible! all so strange!
    She can't have altered to this so quickly!
    Her colour was always a little sickly,
But what a change! Oh what a change!

The straight, lax lines by the curve of the lips,
    The stretched wax skin where no colour lingers,
    The blackening tips of her little fingers,
And the hollow under the finger tips

Lottie? The heart of our nomad life?
 Madcap girl with the reckless tongue?
 That her?—Why should she die so young
Scarcely passed from the child to the wife?

Old in the wit that our headrace brings,
 But oh! so sweet, so loving, so ready—
 Younger than I but she kept me steady
Through a year of trouble and buffetings.

And she's somewhere apart and away from me,
 Flown like a wild bird, out of my hand—
 There's the pain—Can you understand
How it feels and what it must be

To think of our councils, her head on my breast
 And the cash book balanced somehow or other,
 With plenty of kisses deficits to smother?
(Foolish of course—but we liked it best)

And then our evening strolls and our talks
 On the benches facing the Serpentine,
 Retold the old story, her hand in mine,
While darkness settled down on the walks,

Went over the year that joined us two
 Step by step—slowly, so slowly—
 Till night hid the lapping waters wholly,
And I felt her ulster damp with the dew.

Now—just nothing and worse than that
 For the room is full of the clothes she wore—
 There's her corset lying about on the floor
With her knowing, brown, little sealskin hat.

But the step, and the laugh and the eye are gone—
 These things proclaim the fact aloud,
 While the sun glares in from the grey smoke cloud,
Lest I miss the bed that she lay upon.—

What days those were—and now they're over—
  I could work like a slave before 'twas light
  All through the day and half the night
But then—I'm Curtiss not Lottie's lover.—

Peace for her, I suppose so—For me
  What peace is there, except the lull
  After a storm has blown to its full
And the sodden corpses come out of the sea,

There's one thought strikes as the worst of it—
  The years will heal the scar they made
  And fix it, a youthful escapade
When I'm older—and wiser a little bit

Nothing is fixed—The newer day
  Smothers the dead one—New interests crowd
  (With little breathing space allowed)
To take the edge of our grief away.—

What have I to keep me out of the pit,
  Now you are gone—What chance for me
  To make my life as it used to be
With you, sole arbitress of it—

Oh girl wife I was the world to you!
  How will it be when we meet again?
  You stamped with my seal, that you remain
For ever as loving, as sweet and true.

And I, with the hand some alien she
  Presses in fire over the first
  Maybe—or else (the last and worst)
My passion frittered utterly

Through a dozen channels of later loves,
  No one single, or perfect or clean—
  How could I face you Oh my Queen
When we meet again if Fate approves.

I think you would put out your arms as of old,
 With that odd, quick gesture—draw my face
 Down on your breast in a strict embrace,
And keep it there till the tale was told.—

And after it all—you would turn your head
 To the bar—'This man was a god to me
 Even as Thou art—set him free
Seeing he stood for a time in thy stead'

What am I raving of? There you lie
 And now you are going—*I* shan't go
 I loved you too much in life, you know
To follow up to the cemetery—

You shall be Lottie, a little worn,
 And very silent, a little pale
 Nothing more—what would it avail
If I walked behind you—where you are borne?

You shall be Lottie—so fast asleep,
 That you will not wake though I kiss you now—
 Once, twice, thrice—lips, eyes, and brow
And give you our marriage lines to keep

Rest in peace—God bless you—Goodnight
 And another kiss before the screw
 Comes to sunder me from you
And the top-board shuts your face from sight

The bitterest wrench of it all is near—
 Up till now it was nothing—but
 God have mercy! It's shut, it's shut
And they're going to take it away from here

Help me someone! Let it bide!
 Open it only once again—
 I'm perfectly well, I can bear the pain,
I'll swear that a camphor bag slipped inside—

   * * * *
    * * *
   * * * *

A great Love spilt, and to shew for it—
   Nothing—the white face there is quiet
   While the first floor children continue their riot,
And my head is aching fit to split

TOLD IN THE DORMITORY (ii)

Published in the *USCC*, no. 8, 20 March 1882. Uncollected. A continuation of
the poem on pp. 81–2 above. See also pp. 149–51 below.

Another day brought on another night
And we were all impatient for the tale,
But when we asked him to continue it
He heaved a lazy arm above his head
And answered shortly 'Let the matter be,
And let me have my rest.' Thereat we raved.
Bolsters and the petitionary howl
Of many tongues subdued him, and he spake
'Ah, where was I?—we took him—each an arm—
We took him, one on this side, one on that,
And let the flood-gates of our fancy loose
In wild imaginings of windy lies:'
(And here he chuckled till the window creaked),
'Yea, I have lied'—And here he chuckled more . . .
'But never as I did to that sweet youth
We hedged between us. Pitiless, three at once,
Came the ten-storied legends swift evolved;—
The history of some strange gargoyle head,
That leered at us above the carven door,
The history of each scratched trowel mark
Where the new playground wall was hardly set,
The meaning of the costumes that we wore,
The why and wherefore of a beaver hat,
And all the inner meaning of a tie.
And he, by all the fools that ever were,
He took them all as articles of faith,
And ever turned a watery blue-grey eye
Fringed with red lashes, up into our face
Most innocently—and we plied him more!

At last we left him—wearied with success—
Until the evening, then a swift thought flashed
Through either mind and so we laid our plans—
And just when all of us were stripping off
The waistcoat from the shoulder, collar-stud
From collar, and the neck-tie from the neck,
And, swinging lightly on the washhandstands,
Discoursed of current matters—then we hemmed
And beckoned with a depth of mystery
That sunk his visage into abject woe.
And so we told him of an ordinance
Most rigorous and binding on us all;
And when he questioned as to what it was,
We, hollowing grimy paws around our lips
Told him with bated breath of one decree
Given to foster manliness in us,
And warts in all our fingers. Every boy
Was owner of a plot of fertile ground
To till and work in till the harvest came
And all the wheat was yellow to its death:
That he—although he knew it not—he owned
A plot of ground to till and labour in,
And it behoved him with all diligence
To labour like the rest—hoe, rake, and dig,
Scratch, graft, bud, foster, harrow—Here we stayed,
Our rich vocabulary all run out
In terms of horticulture—Then there rose
A pleased expression in his vacant face,
And the dropt jaw came upward with a gulp,
For we had touched on a familiar thing,
And things familiar in an alien land
Are pleasant to us all, and he was pleased.'
But now the morning shiver in the pines
Betokened advent of a coming dawn!
And we like wearied sentries slept in peace.

To be continued.

ROMANCE AND REALITY

Published in the *USCC*, no. 8, 20 March 1882. Uncollected. The song referred to in the final stanza has not been identified, but the lover caught in painful or ridiculous circumstances on a garden wall was a commonplace of music-hall song. (I am indebted for this information to Dr J. S. Bratton, author of *The Victorian Popular Ballad*, London, 1975.)

> Was it water in the woodlands,
>   Hidden brooks that sweetly chime
> With the music of the woodlands,
>   Through the golden summer time?
>
> Was it mystic moan of breaker
>   Coming faintly from afar,
> Where the blind sea heaves its shoulder
>   Lazily against the Bar?
>
> Was it sound of loving ringdove,
>   Or innumerable bees,
> Or the great heart of the forest
>   Throbbing through a thousand trees?
>
> It was not what I had fancied,
>   'Twas no Dryad's half-heard note—
> For the Gods are dead and done with,
>   And we learn their names by rote.
>
> It was neither bee or ringdove,
>   Sea, or wood, or brooklet—but
> The voice of Grubbins quartus[1]
>   Chanting softly in his hut.
>
> And I thought my spirit knew it,—
>   That plaintive madrigal
> Of a Lover and his Lady,
>   Of a Garden and its wall.

THE KNIGHT ERRANT

Published in the *USSC*, no. 8, 20 March 1882. Uncollected. In addition to this poem and the two which precede it, this number of the *USCC* included 'Ave Imperatrix', the earliest of Kipling's poems to be included in the Definitive Edition of his verse.

---

[1] *quartus*: the fourth (i.e. the fourth member of that family attending the school).

Ridest a light of chivalry,
Oh young Knight Errant with sparkling eye?
Is it to succour a maid in woe,
That thy gallant beast is hurrying so?

But the young Knight Errant spoke no word,
As he plied the whip and the charger spurred.
The long road clattered beneath his flight,
And he and his steed passed out of sight.

Yet once again did the stranger call—
To the figure that fled in the evenfall,
And the young Knight Errant turned his head,
And faint and few were the words he said:—

'My steed is hired by the hour,
And the clock is chiming from Northam tower.
If I reach not the sea ere the day be done,
I forfeit a shilling to H–nd–rs–n.'[1]

The stranger turned on his heel and said,
'The days of Knighthood be surely dead,
For never heard I of belted lord
That gained his steed with aught save sword.'

Alas for the glamour of chivalry,
And things that are not as they used to be!
For the six-penny hour too quickly passes,
And we drop to the mire from hired asses!

OUR LADY OF MANY DREAMS

Holograph version of six stanzas in Notebook 1, with subheading 'Old Style'
and note 'Paris. Rue de la jolie Mericourt'. Another holograph version, also of
six stanzas, in Notebook 3, dated 20 March 1882. A holograph version of three
stanzas (the first three of the poem as published) is dated simply 1882 (Pem-
broke College Library, Cambridge). Published in *Echoes*, 1884, in four-stanza
version. Collected in the Outward Bound, De Luxe, Sussex, and Burwash
Edns. The second and fourth stanzas in Notebook 1 are printed here in square

[1] *H–nd–rs–n*: Henderson, presumably the keeper of a livery stable in the vicinity.

brackets. In Notebook 3 there is some transposition of lines between these and
stanzas of the poem as published.

We pray to God, and to God it seems
    Our prayers go heavenward;
But She, our Lady of many Dreams,
    Keepeth a secret guard,
And by virtue of every vow we vowed,
    And by every oath we sware,
Is all our worship disallowed,
    And She taketh toll of the prayer.
God is above, but She below,
    Instant and very fair.

[We praye to God, and to God it seemes
    Our prayers goe up on hie.
But Shee—our Ladye of many dreames
    Heareth them presently;
For eache of us guards her secretlie
    And should never question where—
We would lie, till the stars dropt out of the skie
    And the face of Heaven was bare—
God is above and shee below
    Instante & very faire]

And the stroke of the sword is Hers by right,
    And every stroke of the pen,
And the brain and the tongue and the muscles' might,
    For She ruleth divers men;
And the brutal strength is consecrate
    To Her service and Her will,
And the writer labours early and late,
    And the felon doeth ill.
God is above, but She below,
    That we labour, or write, or kill.

[And hers is the hardest houre of strife
    Either by Lande or Sea,
And hers the bitterest houre in life
    And hers, our miserie—
But hers is that houre after the fraye,
    And hers the peace of the dawne

And hers the endinge of the daye,
   And for her is the Noone's heat borne
And for her do we take the ploughe or the pen,
   And for her is the armour worne]

In a secret shrine, far out of sight,
   Seen by no other eyes,
Lieth our Lady day and night
   (Marvellous fair and wise);
For Her shrine is set in a heart's red throne
   By our pulse's fall and rise,
And we pray to Her, and to Her is known
   All good that in us lies.
God is above, but She below
   Compelleth our destinies.

Whether our Lady be gently bred,
   Or sprung of the city's sin;
Whether Her dress be silk or thread,
   Or Her cheeks be full or thin;
Whether Her hair be black or gold,
   Or brown, or blanched, or grey;
Whether our Lady be young or old,
   Is only one that can say—
And he is both Priest and Worshipper
   Whose eyes are turned on my lay!

OUR LADY OF MANY DREAMS (NEW STYLE)

Holograph version in Notebook 1, dated 20 March [1882], with subheading
'New Style' and subtitle 'Under the arches'. It follows immediately on the 'Old
Style' version.

Trees to the very water's edge—
   Pond lilies white and full.
Bulrush & quaking grass and sedge
Where the moor hen clucks, does this seem to you
   Anything more than an hour or two
      Of hot, uneasy pull—?

A waste of mud where the sea scum floats
   Forgotten of the tide,
Gully and gut, and stranded boats
Stretched like carcasses—What do you see
   Just the mud & eternity
     And nothing else beside

The wind—in the bents the hiss of the sand
   Driven along the shore
The sweep of flat alluvial land
In a dozen lines of brown & gray.
How does it strike you—What do you say
   Landscape and nothing more?

A sloping street with a railway arch
     Spanning the end of it
A grey-stone chapel—prim and starch
   Set in its own half acre of green
Railed like a jail and below—half seen
   Red blurs from the lamps just lit

The stillness of dawn—the broad red glow
    Breaking behind the pines
The mist in the valley and far below
   A white smoke puff as the first train flies
Into the open, where serpentwise
    The river curves and shines

Gravel foundation pits half done
    Gaping and deep and dry
Unfinished houses—one by one
   Standing guard over open cellars
To catch unwary inebriate dwellers
   In the thick packed houses by

A voice in the street, some sound unheeded
    By others, a woman's gait
(But that no two women could walk as she did)
And you drift thro' the past on a broken ship
   Derelict ten years—Give me the slip
     While I stand on the shore & wait—

THE LETTER WRITTEN UP IN THE ATTIC

Holograph version in Notebook 1, dated 24 March [1882], with subheading
'Portobello Road 2 A.M.' A subsequent note dated 7 July 1884 reads 'Vile from
first to last and tedious'.

> I bear a mark from your hand my Love,
>   Set red between my brows,
> And the mark is more lasting a mark my Love,
>   Than Love allows
> More lasting a trace it leaves my Love
>   Than all our vows.
>
>
> The mark of that gusty night my Love
>   Scarcely a week ago,
> When you came; mad with your passion my love
>   And dealt the blow
> Struck freely—how could I stop you—my Love
>   Who loved you so!
>
>
> For the lie was stirring your heart my Love,
>   When you struck the blow at me.
> The lie was hot in your brain my love
>   With jealousy
> And I knew of the lie and the liar my love
>   So, let you be
>
>
> And I thought I will try the love of my love,
>   Whether her heart be true—
> And the end of the trial came my love
>   And Love's end too.
> For the mark between my brows my love
>   Cuts me from you.
>
>
> For I have been shamed by a woman my love
>   Struck down by a woman's blow,
> Though my soul was sold for you my love
>   Years past—you know—
> I have too much pride of the body my Love
>   To let this go

A LOCKED WAY [AFTER LONG YEARS]

Holograph version in Notebook 1, with title 'After long years', dated 26 March [1882]. Another holograph version in Notebook 3, with present title, dated 26 March 1882. Transcribed version in Notebook 2, dated March 1882. Published in *Echoes*, 1884. Collected in the Outward Bound, De Luxe, Sussex, and Burwash Edns. (In Notebook 1 a note dated 2 February 1884 reads 'Where did I get the notion from? Reads like a Ros[s]etti-cum-clean Swinburne crib.')

'Open the Gate!
   The dawn is very near at hand.
My eyes are heavy, I have wandered late,
   And trod the white road from a distant land
That stretches 'neath the stars. Open the Gate!'

'What good is it?
   I set the heavy bars up long ago.
The lock is rusted; I have lost the key.
   How should I open to my overthrow?
O Youth's love, what have I to do with thee?'

'Open the Gate!
   The night is passing—thou mayest see it pass.
Behold, the upland hills are tipped with fire!
   The dawn-winds blow across the upland grass.
The cocks crow. Open thou, my heart's desire!'

'That will not I.
   This is no true daybreak my sad eyes see.
How shall I open? Broadens not one whit
   The white light that so often mockèd me.
How shall I open to a lying cry?
   What good is it?'

'Open the Gate!
   The night is truly ended, O my dear!
My feet are bleeding! I am sick to death!
   Open the Gate! God's own red sun is here!
The shadows flee, and the land quickeneth.
   O Love, for Pity, open thou the Gate!'

'Nay, then—for ruth
  I open. I have little love for thee,
And I am sorely changèd since our youth,
  And there is little beauty left in me . . .
For Pity have I opened . . . but, in truth,
  I . . . had . . . not . . . thought . . . with Pity . . . Love might be!'

TWO LIVES

Holograph version in Notebook 1, dated 27 March [1882]. Another holograph version in Notebook 3, dated 27 March 1882. Transcribed version in Notebook 2, dated March 1882. Published in the *World*, 8 November 1882, with signature 'R.K.' Collected in Sussex and Burwash Edns., where it is misdated 1881. A note in Notebook 1, dated 7 June 1883, reads 'Not bad—a direct Shakespeare crib which I thought vastly fine when I wrote it'. See also this passage in 'An English School': 'Later still, money came into the Syndicate honestly, for a London paper that did not know with whom it was dealing, published and paid a whole guinea for some verses that one of the boys had written and sent up under a *nom de plume*, and the Study caroused on chocolate and condensed milk and pilchards and Devonshire cream, and voted poetry a much sounder business than it looks.' (*Land and Sea Tales for Scouts and Guides*, London, 1923, p. 273.)

Two lives, one sweet and one most sad, I lead;
  Two lives—and one is joy, the other woe;
Two lives—one very dear, one loathed indeed;
  Two lives are mine that far asunder flow.
In one I live, in one I do but die;
  In one I am, and in the other seem;
In one I smile, in one I do but sigh;
  In one I toil, and in the other dream.
One life is strange and full of hot red days,
  Strong Love, that checked at naught, wild hope, mad sin;
But in the other there are beaten ways
  I traverse steadfastly nor fail therein,
Yet sometimes wonder, as the long months pass,
That what I am has e'er been that I was.

AFTER THE PROMISE

Holograph versions in Notebook 1, dated 29 March [1882], and Notebook 3, dated 29 March 1882. Transcribed version in Notebook 2, dated 30 March 1882. Never published by Kipling as a complete poem, but the first three stanzas and the last are used, with minor variations, in 'The Finest Story in the World' (*Many Inventions*, 1893), as specimens of the execrably bad love poetry written by the bank clerk Charlie Mears, when he was not inspired by memories of his previous existences.

The day is most fair, the cheery wind
   Halloos behind the hill,
Where he bends the wood as seemeth good
   And the sapling to his will.
Riot O wind! There is that in my blood
   Which would not have you still.

She gave me herself O Earth! O sky!
   Grey Sea! She is mine alone!
Let the sullen boulders hear my cry
   And rejoice though they be but stone!

Mine—I have won her O good brown Earth!
   Make merry, tis hard on Spring—
Make merry, for she is doubly worth
   All worship your fields can bring.
Let the hind that tills you feel your mirth
   At the early harrowing.

Staid beasts of the plough in the river fields
   I have won her, rejoice ye kine!
I have taken the best Creation yields
   O River, the maid is mine!

Poplar, and beech, and thorn, and fir
   Woods where God's altar lies—
Rejoice! I have won the heart of her
   I have got for myself the prize.
The winds shall tell you and ye shall stir
   With human sympathies.

Red cloud of the Sunset tell it abroad—
I am victor. Greet me O Sun.
Dominant master and absolute Lord
Over the heart of one.[1]

IN THE BEGINNING [A CREED]

Holograph version in Notebook 1, with title 'A Creed', dated 2 April 1882.
Transcribed version in Notebook 2 with same title, dated April 1882. Another
holograph version in Notebook 3, with title 'In the Beginning', dated 2 April
1882, figures as the first in a sequence of 'Four Sonnets', the others being 'A
Tryst' ['The Tryst in Summer'], dated 27 May 1882, 'The Quest', dated 5
March 1882, and 'The Attainment' ['Escaped!'], dated 28 May 1882. (See
above, p. 120, and pp. 147–8 below.) The last line does not appear in Note-
books 1 and 2: it is supernumerary, and may be intended as an alternative to
the penultimate line. A later note in Notebook 1 reads 'Commonplace and not
too well put together v. l. 8 and 9 in particular.'

Woe is, and pain, and men grow old thereby,
    And divers lusts bring divers ills to all,
    And through our lusts it is we trip and fall
And through our lusts it is that many die:—
This much of knowledge have I perfectly—
    A hard creed, but believed by every man—
    A true creed, tho' no man dare call it so—
A truth beginning when the world began—
A truth that ends with the world's overthrow:
    And I have learnt it and believe and know.
    But more remaineth for us—This it is
(Or else life were a torment none could cure)
    Oh Brethren! how so long our ills endure
    Be comforted, for after woe is bliss—
Be comforted, 'the end of bale is bliss'

---

[1] *Over the heart of one*: thus in later revision in Notebook 1. Notebook 3 has 'And God
of this life to one', and *Many Inventions* 'Over the soul of one'. In Notebook 1 the last two
lines originally read 'For I am as a God, and a sovereign Lord— / Over the soul of one.'

A PROMISE

Holograph version in Notebook 1, dated 8 April [1882], and another in Notebook 3, dated 8 April 1882. Transcribed version in Notebook 2, dated April 1882.

> Thy woe is mine—for thou hast held my heart
>   So long it is become one pulse with thine,
> Thy woe is mine, though I be far apart
>   From thee and voice of thee thy woe is mine.
> I can but grieve with thee for who may move
> The fates above us, words are all too weak
>   To give the comfort that thy heart would seek.
> Wait but a little and I come to thee,
>   Wait but a little, woman of my Love,
> And more shall be than barren words alone.
>   The comfort of a lover's sympathy
> Where lip is set to lip with no word said,
>   The comfort of my arm about thy head,
> And thy heart beating up against mine own.

WHERE THE SHOE PINCHES

Holograph version in Notebook 3, dated 10 April 1882. Transcribed version in Notebook 2, dated April 1882.

> The pain of parting—once and once again
>   To kiss her pale lips as the hour draws nigh,
> And the black hull steams out into the rain
>   And fades, and fades and fades against the sky.
> The pain of doubting which is very hell,
>   The pain of her pain, when the hands are tied,
> And powerless to comfort, none can tell
>   The pain of this pain save whose Love is tried—
>   The pain of all pain—when we have no right
> To feel the sorrow—It is surely woe
> To suffer openly in all men's sight,
>   But when we suffer and no soul can know,
>   And we must e'en go forward with the care
>   Of daily life, Ah! Woe's own woe is there!

AN ENDING

Holograph version in Notebook 3, dated 11 April 1882. This is the last in the first sequence of poems in that notebook (see above, pp. 26–7), and it is followed by the Index and the poem 'To You' (see above, p. 70).

Oh Dearest! the best I have ever written,
   The best and most perfect of me,
All things good I have ever fashioned
   Are yours and yours only, . . .
The labour of the morning is yours—
   The labour in silence, and alone and in trouble is yours.
   The labour in darkness and the mind's frost is yours,
      Yours and yours only

Have you forgotten—long ago in the fall of the autumn—
In the time of withered leaves and waking tempests,
In the face of a slowly dying year
How once—when the tide was running seaward
And night came to us softly over the flats
   You put your lips to my forehead
And called me—Have you forgotten it—your poet?
Called me, miserable that I was, your poet
By virtue of the few weak rhymes I had written:—
   Unrhymed, and saying nothing

Could you guess how I was consecrate to your service,
By an oath I have never since broken,
By an oath—the only one of my old days, I have held to?
Could you guess in the after years how I was bound to you?—
Could you guess the purpose I set for myself,
The promises, whose first fruits are here for your taking?—
   I think not.

Now that I have accomplished a little,
   Very little truly, but still a little—
Made, painfully some, joyfully others, bitterly many,—
Made, as a boy makes them,—imperfect meaning to be perfect.
Failures many, but telling of what was intended,
They are yours and yours only—
By the power and the dominance that you have over me,
   Yours and yours only.

By the trouble and pains we endured together,
By the council and the help, and the strength which you gave me,
By the influence of your soul over my soul,
By year long vigils watched out together
By the great tie that is between us
   Yours and yours only.

THE WOOING OF THE SWORD

Holograph version in Notebook 3, dated 27 April 1882.

Speaketh THE PRINCESS

'What will ye give me for a heart?
(Gold and jewels gladden the eye)
My three suitors answer apart—
(Standeth Love any more firm thereby)'

Speaketh THE FIRST SUITOR

'You shall be Queen over land and sea,
All my realm to gladden your eye—
You shall have power and sovereignty
And Love shall be assured thereby.'

Speaketh THE SECOND SUITOR

'You shall have that the heart can desire—
Ships and cities to gladden the eye,
And I, on my knee will be your squire,
And Love shall serve and rule thereby—'

Speaketh THE THIRD SUITOR

'I have given up all for the sight of your face
More than gold does it gladden the eye,
I can but give thee an arm's embrace,
And a sword to keep Love sweet thereby—'

Speaketh THE PRINCESS

'Highly oh Men must ye prize my Love,
Paying such price to gladden the eye

That ye have spoken must ye prove
And proving, stand or fall thereby—'

The first one gave her his own gold crown
The second himself to gladden her eye—
But he that had nought smote the two men down,
And Love was won of the sword thereby.

I BELIEVE

Holograph versions in Notebook 1, dated 9 May [1882], and Notebook 3,
dated 9 May 1882. In Notebook 1 the last couplet reads 'Oh Love faint not,
the end is very near, / That makes thy mistress by this woe more dear.'

Oh Love what need is it that thou should'st die?
    Oh Faith what need that thou shouldest wax so cold—
Seeing that good returneth presently—
    And all things are as in that year of old.
Nay—tis a passing cloud that dims the sun
    If Love be for a season full of pain,
A passing woe that swiftly is fordone,
    A passing cloud that melteth in sweet rain.
Have patience for a little, and the end
    Shall pay thy patience and thy hour's dismay
When Woe's remembrance sweets to Joy doth lend,
    And night's black memory brightens the new day.—
Oh Love faint not if she whose slave thou art
Being most maidenlike know not her heart

DISCOVERY

Holograph versions in Notebooks 1 and 3, both dated 10 May 1882. (In Note-
book 1 the last line reads 'And set the dry baked earth above the thing.')
Transcribed version in Notebook 2, erroneously dated February 1882.
Another holograph version was enclosed along with 'Their Consolation' and
'Escaped!' (see below pp. 147 and 148) in a letter of 28 May to Mrs Tavenor
Perry in which he speaks of the ending of his relationship with Flo Garrard
and says of the poems, 'They aren't up to much and perhaps they *might* be
called "reg'lar downright bad", but it's possible that they will interest you:—
wherefore I send them' (Huntington Library MS HM 11882). A letter from

Trix to Rudyard records an argument at Warwick Gardens in which she had maintained that the bird in the poem was 'a kind of allegory—it means dead love—Cupid you know', while the old ladies 'understood that a beloved cage-bird had flown away and been found dead, but the emotion expressed was disproportionate—exaggerated' (cited by Lord Birkenhead, *Rudyard Kipling*, New York, 1978, pp. 53–4). Kipling's later comment on the poem in Notebook 1 reads 'Cheap; Miss Winnard said that the King was a dead canary, for which mistake (a genuine one) I find it hard to forgive her.'

We found him in the woodlands—she and I—
    Dead was our Teacher of the silver tongue,
Dead, whom we thought so strong he could not die,
    Dead, with no arrow loosed,[1] with bow unstrung.
And round the great, grey blade that all men dread
    There crept the waxen white convolvulus,
And the keen edge, that once fell hard on us,
    Was blunt and notched and rusted yellow red.
And he, our Master, the unconquered one,
    Lay in the nettles of the forest place,
With dreadful open eyes and changeless face
    Turned upward—gazing at the noonday sun.
Then we two bent above our old, dead King,
Loosed hands and gave back heart and troth and ring.

MON ACCIDENT!

Holograph versions in Notebooks 1 and 3, both dated 14 May 1882. A later comment in Notebook 1, dated 8 October 1883, reads 'Not a nice subject and inadequately treated—notably the lame fourth verse. Sorry I wrote the thing—almost.' He hints at early sexual experience in a letter of 18 February 1886, to W. C. Crofts: 'I was not innocent in some respects, as the fish girls of Appledore could have testified had they chosen' (Kipling Collection, Dalhousie University Library).

Child of sin, and a broken vow,
    Weakling—sad indeed was the plight of thee—
Crying wearily camest thou—
    There was wailing at the sight of thee—

---

[1] Later revision in Notebook 1, replacing 'used', which also figures in Notebook 3. The Huntington MS has 'loosed', as does Notebook 2.

Roseleaf fingers, stretched in appeal,
 Broken and low, the sound of thy weeping—
She, thy mother it was could feel
 Thy sorrow and take thee into her keeping.

Yea, for she yearned to thee at the sound,
 The joy of a mother filled the heart of her—
When her soft arms clasped thy body round
 And thy lip at her breast soothed the soul's smart of her.

There be only three of us little one—
 Three of us and there is none other—
To hold together till Life is done—
 Thou, and I, and She thy mother.

HIS CONSOLATION

Holograph version of five stanzas in Notebook 1, dated 21 May 1882. Published in four-stanza version in *Echoes*, 1884. Collected, with subheading 'Browning', in the Outward Bound, De Luxe, Sussex, and Burwash Edns. In Notebook 1 the third stanza reads 'Know this—I should be doubly beast— / If I turned from the purpose set / Years back—And now when Love is least / Toward me, I can linger yet / While others share the feast'. A later comment reads 'A good echo of Browning if I had left out the 3rd verse'; and it is in fact cut from the published versions.

So be it; you give me my release,
 And let me go. Yes, I am free.
But think you that a love will cease
 By bidding merely? Can yon sea
  Stop at the tide's increase?

You hold the matter ended, then?
 Are right if you begin anew?
You turn your eyes on other men.
 Can that fact cut my love from you,
  If you win one or ten?

Your words count nothing, since your soul
 Is mine—as you will find at last,

When you have finished out the whole
Of life, and stare at me aghast,
Waiting you at the goal.

You cannot, *cannot* understand?
Go forward, then. The time will be
When, lip to lip and hand to hand,
By some far-distant planet's sea
We meet—and *I* command.

AFTER THE FEVER

Holograph version, undated, of the first of these verses in Notebook 1, follow-
ing 'His Consolation' ('So be it—you gave me my release') which is dated 21
May 1882, and preceding 'His Consolation' ('Alas! Alas! it is a tale so old'),
which is dated 26 May. It has the subheading '2 A.M.' The second verse, with-
out date or title, appears in a holograph version in the same notebook, between
'The Tryst in Summer', dated 27 May, and 'Escaped!', dated 28 May. It
appears to be a continuation of the same poem: the first stanza is written at the
foot of a right-hand page, the second at the top of the next left-hand page but
one, suggesting that Kipling turned over two pages by mistake. Not to be con-
fused with 'After the Fever, or Natural Philosophy in a Doolie': see below,
p. 266.

Let the worst come now, and I shall not fear,
I won one woman and you are she—
Won her myself—for good and all,
And shall keep her throughout Eternity
Though the end of this world's Love is near
And your day begins to fall

I ask God one thing and it is this,—
That I am with you when you die,—
That you die with your head at peace on my breast,
And that *my* mouth takes your last Life's kiss—
For who has a better claim than I,
To this, for I loved you best

HIS CONSOLATION [THEIR CONSOLATION]

Holograph version in Notebook 1, with title 'His Consolation', dated 26 May [1882]. A second holograph version in Notebook 3, with the same title, dated 26 May 1882. A third version, with title 'Their Consolation', enclosed with letter to Mrs Tavenor Perry dated 28 May 1882. Transcribed version with the same title in Notebook 2, which has 'strong limbs and warm hearts' in l. 4.

Alas! Alas! it is a tale so old—
   Alas! Alas! its pain is very new;
   It is a strange, hard thought for me and you—
That warm limbs and strong hearts should ere wax cold,
That ever Life should cease within our eyes,
   And silence for a season fall on each,
   And for a season, Loving ended be.—
Ah! Sweet, what need to follow phantasies
When Love's best fruit lies hard within our reach—
   And nought disturbs immutability—
Trust me—when weak the heart and faint the hand,
And Death, the master, little tarrieth—
Then, through Death's own blow shall we understand,
   How Love is stronger than all earthly Death.

A TRYST [THE TRYST IN SUMMER]

Holograph version in Notebook 1 with title 'The Tryst in Summer', dated 27 May [1882], with later note 'Torrington Woods'. Another holograph version in Notebook 3, with title 'A Tryst', dated 27 May 1882. (This figures as the second in a series of 'Four Sonnets', the others being 'In the Beginning' ['A Creed'], 'The Quest', and 'The Attainment' ['Escaped!']: see above pp. 120 and 139, and p. 148 below.) Transcribed version in Notebook 2.

The night comes down in rain, grey garmented—
   The night winds rise and wander listlessly
Across the dun slopes, downward to the sea—
   Or murmur sadly in the pines o'erhead.
The air is thick with whispers of the night,
   The hedgerows murmur, half articulate,

The secret of the woodlands, heard aright—
    And I—I listen for my Love and wait
The white road fades as, layer on layer the shade
    Draws denser, and the ceaseless, warm rain falls.
The stars burn faintly—it is very late—
The woods are still, save, where far down the glade
A hare limps, or the wakeful white owl calls,
    And I—I listen for my Love and wait.

THE ATTAINMENT [ESCAPED!]

Holograph version in Notebook 1 with title 'Escaped!', dated 28 May [1882]. Another holograph copy with the same title was one of three sonnets sent to Mrs Tavenor Perry in a letter dated 28 May 1882, the other two being 'Their Consolation' ('Alas! Alas! it is a tale so old') and 'Discovery': see above, pp. 147 and 143 (Huntington Library MS HM 11882). A third holograph version is included in Notebook 3, dated 28 May 1882, with title 'The Attainment' and the cryptic subtitle 'known to the initiated as "The Angry Baker" '. This would seem to refer to a shared joke, based presumably on a misreading of l. 7 of the poem. The poem figures here as the fourth of a group of four sonnets (see above p. 120). A revised version was published as 'Concerning a Jawàb: After', in the *CMG*, 6 August 1887: see below p. 383. Uncollected.

Peace for a season—in the heart of me,
    The peace which springs from very weariness.
As one wave rescued looketh on the sea,
    So look I on the time of my distress,
A powerless power stretching forth weak hands
    To seize me who am fled from out its reach—
An angry breaker beating on the beach,
    To die in spume streaks on the level sands—
Yea, peace is come to me, and I am free,—
    And all the past is dead & will not rise—
And that which shall be stretcheth fair, untrod—
    As one wave rescued turneth from the sea,
    Landward to rest him—so I turn my eyes
From past things to the future, thanking God.

TOLD IN THE DORMITORY (iii)

Published in the *USCC*, no. 9, 3 June 1882. Uncollected. The conclusion of the poem begun in the *USCC*, no. 7, 5 December 1881, and continued in no. 8, 20 March 1882. See above, pp. 81–2 and 128–9.

An ending comes to all things, and his tale
Drew slowly to an ending likewise—thus.
The third night of the three came down in rain,
And through the rattle of the rain he spoke:—
'I am sore wearied and will tell the tale
Now, hastily, attend ye or I cease!
I said we touched on a familiar thing,
I said that he was pleased—alas, too pleased!
The fountains of his speech were broken up
And spouted verbal torrents—Scarce, I think,
Adam the gardener could have said so much
When springtime bloomed o'er Eden. Straight he gave
The long, long story of his sister Joan,
And all her tulips, Grissel's hollyhocks,
Blossom, the one-eyed cart horse and her feats
At rural ploughing-bouts—Patient we stood,
Nodding a careless Yes or No to stem
The pent-up torrent of his eloquence,
But all to no avail—I almost think
We should have spared him for his innocence
And utter earnestness, but that he bored,—
Yea, was too long, so pity faded out
Into sheer weariness, and he was lost . . .
My friend spoke curtly: "Do you wish to see
The ground allotted for your labour? Look!"
And so flung up the casement: far and near
The full moon lit the garden beds below,
And faced with silver all the aspen leaves;
The night winds wandered listlessly, their feet
Stirring a few cast roses on the grass;
Or else they murmured promise of the dawn
Among the folded flowers, that they bowed
In dreams to greet the tidings and were still.
Ay, all was lovely, but our minds were set
And so relented nowise—Fair and smooth
In all the glory of close-tended turf

And gleaming white chalk lines and boundaries,
An emerald in the rose beds, lay that court
Sacred to Masters only, for the game
Of tense-strung net, and swift alternate strokes
To toss the ball in air and keep it there,
Flying from bat to bat. Most precious this,
The very hearts' heart of the Commonroom:
The grizzled Dean would come and muse by it,
The sprightly, younger masters played on it,
And all the tennis-players sighed for it.
My friend, one finger pointed on the green,
Turning upon the victim made him look
(How should *he* ever know a tennis court,
To whom all verdure was as grass or plough,
And all creation one great farm-stead, split
By follies that made other men than hinds?
And told him it was his, whereat we strove
To keep him back from climbing down thereto
And delving in the moonlight—and such gear
As men in summer use for night—one shirt
Made of the thinnest. So the venom worked!
We pacified him and he dropt asleep
To babble of green fields, while each of us
Vowed solemnly to tell him in the morn
And undeceive him, lest in some wild fit   ı
He should turn gardener on the tennis ground.—
We slept and vowed to tell him in the dawn—

              *   *   *   *   *

How shall I tell you further? Ye can guess.
The imp that rules men's minor destinies
Battled against us. When the grey dawn broke
His bed was empty, he had scaled the wall,
Some ill-fate furnished him with fork and spade,
And in his night-gear he began his work!
We saw him and he waved a grimy hand
And called with rustic clamour. "Lo! my work,
See what I did or ever it was light."
We shuddered and we saw, my friend and I.
The court—the court—the court was stripped of turf,
And neatly broken into cole-wort beds
Or some such like abomination—Rich

And loamy was the soil I make no doubt,
And very fit for planting cole-wort too,
Most fit for colewort—but for Tennis, no!
Why should I keep you longer? it was done—
And the limp feeling after daring deeds,
Or jokes miscarried came upon us both
And loosed the sinews of the knees—'twas done
Ay, well done, for the brute had told no lie
In saying he could break land with the best!
What was there left to do? We called him in
Heart brokenly, and told him of his crime,
Or rather, *tried* to tell him, for his soul
Was full of uncouth happiness withal.
"I rose," quoth he, "I rose before the dawn.
I wished to give you pleasure so I delved,
And *did* I give you pleasure? I can dig;
They tell me so at home: did I dig well?'
It is an evil game to jest with fools,
We saw our folly, as the dawn drew near,
Sitting disconsolately upon our beds,
Full of imagined tinglings in the back,
When he—the Dean should see the colewort court
And hale us twain to judgment'—
                                        Here his voice
Brake chokedly, perchance with weariness,
Belike through many memories of the time,—
We did not question—save the least of us
Piped suddenly: 'The End—Tell us the end!
Have you forgotten?'—In the utter gloom
There flashed a boot-heel swiftly through the air,
And hit the questioner—'The end was pain—
The end of all is pain—Be still and sleep.'

THE JAM-POT [THE WORST OF IT]

Published in the *USCC*, no. 9, 3 June 1882, with title 'The Worst of It' and subheading 'R****t B******g' [Robert Browning]. Collected in the Outward Bound, De Luxe, Sussex, and Burwash Edns. with title 'The Jam-Pot' and subheading '(In the Manner of Robert Browning)'. 'The Worst of It' is the title of a poem by Browning.

The Jam-pot—tender thought!
    I grabbed it—so did you.
'What wonder while we fought
    Together that it flew
In shivers?' you retort.

You should have loosed your hold
    One moment—checked your fist.
But, as it was, too bold
    You grappled and you missed.
More plainly—you were sold.

'Well, neither of us shared
    The dainty.' That your plea?
'Well, neither of us cared',
    I answer. . . Let me see,
How have your trousers fared?

SONG FOR TWO VOICES [SONG (FOR MUSIC)]

Holograph version in Notebook 1, with title 'Song for Two Voices', dated 11
June 1882. Transcribed version in Notebook 2 with title 'Song (For Music)',
dated June 1882. Not to be confused with the 'Song (for two voices)' in *Sundry
Phansies* ('I bound his soul by a word and an Oath'): see above, p. 107.

Follow and faint not, if the road be long
    The pathway desolate,
No day so sad but reacheth even song
    Be still and wait
Through good report and ill, through joy and sorrow.
Surely thy Lady comes to thee tomorrow—

I followed tho' the way was long indeed
    The pathway desolate,
Night came not to me in my dire need
    Where lost, I sate.
Through good report and ill, through joy and sorrow
I waited, but there came not any morrow
    Surely who waits on woman waits on sorrow. . . .

LAND-BOUND [ΘΑΛΑΣΣΑ, ΘΑΛΑΣΣΑ¹]

Holograph version in Notebook 1 with title 'Θάλασσα! Θάλασσα', dated 12 June [1882]. Another holograph version in Notebook 3 with same title, (with comma after first word) undated. Transcribed version without title in Notebook 2, dated June 1882. Published in *Echoes*, 1884, with minor revisions and title 'Land Bound'. Collected under title 'Land-Bound' in the Outward Bound, De Luxe, Sussex, and Burwash Edns.

> Run down to the sea, O River,
>   Haste thee down to the sea—
> To the foaming strife at the Bar
>   Where the grey breakwaters are,
> And the buoys roll merrily
> In the dip and heave of the sea
>   Coming over the Bar.
>
> Bear me with thee, O River—
>   On the rush of thy flood to the sea—
> I am sick of this smooth, green land;
>   I long for the breeze off the sand.
> Take me away with thee
> To the shifting face of the sea,
>   And the low, wind-bitten strand.
>
> Bear me swiftly, O River,
>   My heart is athirst for the sea,—
> To the dotted herring-floats
>   And the brown, tar-fragrant boats,
> And the little wave-washed quay—
> I am sick of hedgerow and tree,
>   And the hills in their stifling coats.

PARTING [IN THE HALL]

Holograph version in Notebook 1, with title 'Parting' and subheading 'St Katharine's Dock. 5 A.M.', dated 13 June [1882]. Another holograph version with same title, undated, in Notebook 3. Transcribed version in Notebook 2

---

¹ ΘΑΛΑΣΣΑ, ΘΑΛΑΣΣΑ: 'The sea! The sea!' The cry of the Greek army, as reported by their leader Xenophon, when they came in sight of the coast after a prolonged and ill-fated expedition into Asia Minor in 401 BC (*Anabasis*, iv. 7).

with title 'In the Hall', dated June 1882. Not to be confused with the poem
'Parting' written for Florence Garrard ('Hot kisses on red lips that burn'): see
above, p. 111.

The last five minutes were worth the price—
    The lies and the petty shifts to get them—
They sent for the cab—by my advice
    Not from the stand but the place where they let them

Bonnetted, gloved and ready to start
    My darling stands—and here we count
By each beat of heart against beating heart—
    How much is slipped from the whole amount
Allotted yet—and what a reward
    Shall come in the end to all our trouble
When the year flies over and she is restored—
    Once, for ever to me her Lord
    Who would pay for her sake his past pains double—

And a gorgeous web is spread before us,
    Flashing in crimson & stiff with gold,
Before our life's dark days come o'er us,
    Before we turn again to the cold—
Her lip leaves my lip, her hand my hold
    And below in the streets comes the waking chorus
    Of a world on its wheel in torment rolled:—

                        'Love is no prize,
                        Fame is a lie,
                        Love's mysteries
                        Are set to buy.
                        Honour is dead,
                        Truth is all told,
                        Only a goodlihead
                        Resteth in gold—
                        Masters make haste
                        To gather in gold'—

        Out on the doubt and the ghostly pain,
            Let the world's lying in at the door—
        Her lip is put to my lip again,
            I hold her hand for a moment more

I have learnt my lesson, the truth is plain—
   Love is the only perfect gain—
The worst is done with—my night is o'er

      *   *   *   *   *

Darling be quick or you'll miss the train

THE REAPING

Holograph versions in Notebook 1, dated 19 June [1882], and Notebook 3, undated.

Hush—What appeal
  From inexorable Fate?
The gods can feel
  Nor Love nor hate.
They strike blindly for our evil and as blindly for our good—
Caring not if Honour follow on the sword blow or our blood.

What good to rave?
  They are stronger e'en than Jove—
If we can save
  Our store of Love,
From this world's wrack and chaos, ere we wander lone to Hell—
Bear the precious burden with us where the weary shadows dwell—
Life has not been wholly barren tho' for aye we say 'farewell'—

A CRAVEN

Holograph versions in Notebook 1, dated 20 June [1882], and Notebook 3, undated.

I who was crownèd King am now bereft
  Of crown and treasure.
I, who was Monarch, have no good thing left
  To give me pleasure.

I had my treasure guarded faithfully,
  By one sure heart—

My crown seemed mine to all eternity
   But both depart.
I am discrownèd and my treasure flies
Out of these arms, away from these sad eyes.

   I faced the world and proved myself a man,
     In word & deed.
I knew my treasure safe and foremost ran
     To others' need.
What comfort can I give thee now O friend—
Seeing both crown & treasure are at end?

   Oh give me back my old life's crown again,
     My old life's treasure—
I have been tested and I shrank the pain
     Let me taste pleasure—
O give me back my treasure in my breast—
Only for this life—God shall judge the rest—

UNDERSTANDING

Holograph version in Notebook 1, dated 21 June [1882].

   One time when ashen clouds received the sun
     And the sea rose beneath us, clamouring
At the wind's wrath, and day was almost done
     We met upon the levels, and heard sing
A little mother lark—and found her nest
     Among the sodden sedges, while above,
She poured us from the treasury of her breast
     Hiatus of long standing[1]
And for an instant both our hearts were stirred
     To the same music, and our souls were one
And to her lips my own hot lips were set—
     Then close behind us dropped the mother bird,
And either heart drew back to dwell alone—
And bitterly each soul cried out 'Not Yet'—

---

[1] *Hiatus* . . . : *sic*, but italics mine; followed by two illegible words.

A VOYAGE

Holograph versions in Notebook 1, dated 6 July [1882], and Notebook 3, undated.

Our galley chafes against the Quay,
   The full tide calls us from the beach,
While far away across the sea
    Is set the isle that we would reach
      The haven where we fain would be.

Let us go forward—doubting not—
   Into the grey waste flecked with foam—
Adventurers that have no spot
    So dear that they should call it home—
      Lone men, of all men most forgot.

Grim men, with some deep hidden sin,
   About their bosom, haggard eyes
That shew the bitter soul within
    Warped by a thousand miseries
      Pale men, with drawn white lips and thin.

Old men, that lose their faith in good,
   And so take service recklessly
In any strife by land or flood,
    Wherever evil chance to be,
      Prodigal of their life's last blood.

Young faces, very old with woe,
   Strong men, in evil stronger still
These make our crew and so we go
    Climbing each shifting waterhill
      That heaves us upward from below.

Our galley lamps are bright with hope,
   Our voices ring across the sea—
In other lands is wider scope
    For all our virile energy
Let be the past, leave we the quay
    With firm hands on the tiller rope

SEVERANCE [WOKING NECROPOLIS]

Holograph version in Notebook 1 with title 'Woking Necropolis', dated 7 June [1882]. (This is presumably a slip of the pen for '7 July', since the poem follows 'A Voyage', dated 6 July, and is followed immediately by 'What the Young Man's Heart said to Him', dated 9 July.) Another holograph version, undated, in Notebook 3, with title 'Severance'. Notebook 1 does not have 'Love' at the end of ll. 5, 6, and 7 in the first and second stanzas.

Plight my troth to the dead, Love?
   How can that be?
Youth is swift to wed love,
   What does it matter to thee,
With the banked earth over head Love,
   Whither our hopes are fled Love,
Where are the words we said Love,
   By the grey wind troubled sea?

Lying so silent there Love,
   Silent, alone,
Forget the oaths we sware Love,
   Forget that thou wast mine own,
When Life was very fair Love,
   And soul to soul lay bare Love,
Forget that these things were Love
   Rest calm beneath the stone

Forget the life we led Love,
   Life's hope, Life's pain—
Our time together is fled Love,
   And only regrets remain—
Hear me from that chill bed Love,
   Now all is finishèd Love,
If prayer be allowed to the dead Love,
   Pray that we meet again—

WHAT THE YOUNG MAN'S HEART SAID TO HIM

Holograph version in Notebook 1, dated 9 July [1882]. The whole poem is crossed out, indicating its rejection, but there is no indication of when this was done.

Break, ah Break!
What pleasure more in Life have I
Seeing, that sleeping or awake,
   I am distraught with misery
         I take no pleasure in the sun,
            Would that my Life's sad course were done
Aye, would that I might straightway die—
         Break ah break!
   For the best of my life is gone by,
   And no good thing is nigh.

'I am the heart in thee,
   And my throbbings never cease,
   Till God lays hands on me.
         And I bring the lusty blood
   Be thou happy or ill at ease—
Look up, the world is good
   And thou art too young for release
From an over happy lot—
   And every stroke of mine
   Is cheering thy soul like wine
Although thou knowest not
   And soon, as the months fly over,
So shall thy trouble fade,
   Thou shalt go again as a lover
         To woo another maid—
And be thou ill at ease
   Or full of happiness
My labours never cease—
   Till God command me to rest,
   I give thee strength in thy breast,—
         In woe or weal no less'

SATIETY

Holograph versions in Notebook 1, dated 19 July [1882], and Notebook 3, undated. L. 8 of the first stanza does not appear in Notebook 1.

   Last year's wreath upon our brow
      Withereth;

What good thing is left us now
        After Death?
That sad Death we all must die,
        Once at least—
Pass from Love, aye utterly,
    That we gave so much to buy
    Leave it—since in verity
        It hath ceased.

Last year's words are wearying
        Touch us not.
Last year's songs are ill to sing
        Half forgot,
Half remembered—profitless
        Let them be.
Twelve short months since, who could guess
    That we openly confess—
    'We two, in our bitterness,
        Would be free.'

DONEC GRATUS ERAM[1]

Published in the *USCC*, no. 10, 24 July 1882, with subheading '(Devonshire dialect)'. Collected in the Outward Bound, De Luxe, Sussex, and Burwash Edns. with same subheading. Kipling gives an account of the occasion of the poem in 'An English School': 'There was one boy . . . to whom every Latin quantity was an arbitrary mystery, and he wound up his crimes by suggesting that he could do better if Latin verse rhymed as decent verse should. He was given an afternoon's reflection to purge himself of his contempt; and feeling certain that he was in for something rather warm, he turned "Donec gratus eram" into pure Devonshire dialect, rhymed, and showed it up as his contribution to the study of Horace. He was let off, and his master gave him the run of a big library, where he found as much verse and prose as he wanted; but that ruined his Latin verses and made him write verses of his own . . . ' (*Land and Sea Tales for Scouts and Guides*, London, 1923, p. 268.) The original publication experimented even more boldly with spelling to render dialect pronunciation.

---

[1] *Donec gratus eram [tibi]*: while I was dear [to thee]. See Horace, *Odes*, III. ix.

HE

So long as 'twuz me alone
　An' there wasn't no other chaps,
I was praoud as a King on 'is throne—
　Happier tu, per'aps.

SHE

So long as 'twuz only I
　An' there wasn't no other she
Yeou cared for so much—sure*ly*
　I was glad as could be.

HE

But now I'm in lovv with Jane Pritt—
　She can play the piano, she can;
An' if dyin' 'ud 'elp 'er a bit
　I'd die laike a man.

SHE

Yeou'm like me. I'm in lovv with young Frye—
　Him as lives out tu Appledore Quay;
An' if dyin' 'ud 'elp 'im I'd die—
　Twice ovver for he.

HE

But s'posin' I threwed up Jane
　An' niver went walkin' with she—
And come back to yeou again—
　How 'ud that be?

SHE

Frye's sober. Yeou've allus done badly—
　An' yeou shifts like cut net-floats, yeou du:
But—I'd throw that young Frye ovver gladly
　An' lovv 'ee right thru!

THE BATTLE OF ASSAYE[1]

Published in the *USCC*, no. 28, 2 July 1886, with title 'The Battle of Assye'. Collected in the Outward Bound and De Luxe Edns. under same title, and in the Sussex and Burwash Edns. under title 'The Battle of Assaye'. The poem was composed while Kipling was still at school, though his use of the terms *jhil* and *ghat* or *gaut* suggests that it may have been revised in India. See *Something of Myself*, p. 37: 'Many of us loved the Head for what he had done for us, but I owed him more than all of them put together . . . There came a day when he told me that a fortnight after the close of the summer holidays of '82, I would go to India to work on a paper in Lahore, where my parents lived, and would get one hundred silver rupees a month! At term-end he most unjustly devised a prize poem—subject "The Battle of Assaye" which, there being no competition, I won in what I conceived was the metre of my latest "infection"—Joaquin Miller.[2] And when I took the prize-book, Trevelyan's[3] *Competition Wallah*, Crom Price said that if I went on I might be heard of again.'

> *Save where our huge sea-castles from afar*
> > *Beat down, in scorn, some weak Egyptian wall,*[4]
> *We are too slothful to give heed to war.*

> *As a gorged Lion will not stir at all,*
> > *Although the hunter mock him openly,*
> *So we are moveless when the trumpets call.*

> *A soldier's letter, written long ago*
> > *(The ink lies yellow on the tattered page),*
> *Telling of war, with rugged overflow*
> *Of epithet, and bursts of uncouth rage;*
> > *And as I find the letter—so I write*
> *My record of brave deeds in a dead age.*

---

[1] *Assaye*: a village in South India, the scene of a major victory by Arthur Wellesley, later the Duke of Wellington, over a Mahratta army in 1803. The library of the ladies of Warwick Gardens (see above, p. 5) had included 'all Wellington's Indian Despatches', which had fascinated Kipling in his boyhood (*Something of Myself*, p. 22).

[2] *Joaquin Miller*: Cincinnatus Hiner Miller (1841?–1913), who adopted the name 'Joaquin', was a minor American poet, author of *Songs of the Sierras* (1871), etc.

[3] *Trevelyan*: Sir George Otto Trevelyan (1838–1928), author of *The Competition Wallah* (1864), an account of life in India in the post-Mutiny years.

[4] *Save where . . . .*: a reference to the bombardment of Alexandria by a British fleet on 11 July 1882.

3. Kipling *c*.1882.

'The man was a man you could follow to death,
And dying, thank with your latest breath
For the honour granted—and he had led
From the sea to the scorching plains inland,
Where the soil would flay the skin from your hand
If you let it rest for a moment there;
And the sun at noonday strikes you dead,
And the breeze is a blast of furnace air;
Where the Jungle stands in an inland sea,
When the hills send down their floods to the plain,
And the waters drown the coiled tree-snake,
And the reed-thatched hamlets by *jhil*[5] and lake
Are swamped and demolished utterly.

How can I tell of the months of fight?—
The whole thing slid like an evil dream,
With the same tired halt at camping-time,
When the hot day sank into hotter night,
A broken sleep and a dream of home;
Then grain for each lowing bullock-team;
And then the sun in the parched blue dome—
The dusty march like an endless rhyme,
And the weary, broken sleep again.

But one thing stays in my mind, and will stay
Stamped in fire till the day I die:—
How the wild Mahratta ranks gave way
From a poor four thousand of Englishmen,[6]
By the little village they call Assaye—
For we were one where they numbered ten;
How we fought the through hot September day
In the face of their cannon, and how we slew;
How the horsemen galloped down on us,
And we broke their ranks and fought anew,
In the midst of a fire so murderous
That it seems a wonder that I am alive;
And, last of all, how we chased the crew,
Drove them like bullocks our peasants drive,
Footsore and bleeding. It happened thus:

[5] *jhil*: swamp (Sussex Edn.).
[6] *Englishmen*: a Scottish editor may be pardoned for drawing attention to the fact that Wellesley's infantry consisted of two Highland regiments and several battalions of Madras Native Infantry.

Three armies were met together to crush
The whole of our little force—and we
(Thanks to the tale of a lying scout)
Had come on their camp so suddenly,
Where the Kaitua River curves about
In the steep clay reaches of Bokerdun,
That we knew we must either fight or die,
Since no succour could come by land or sea,
And we knew that retreat was worse than defeat;
And we thought this over, there in the bush,
As we faced their masses of cavalry,
And counted each point-blank, grinning gun,
While the turbid river rolled between;
And far away from the plains' burnt green
The still ghats[7] watched us against the sky.

We found a ford, and the word was given,
And over we went as glad as might be—
Seeing, for months past, we had striven
With a foe who fled like a dusky cloud,
And we thirsted to meet them in open field,
With no quarter asked or grace allowed,
And fight till one of us two should yield,
So, a splash through the stream with arms held high,
A rattle of stones when the horses passed,
And we found ourselves on the farther side,
And we only feared lest the foe should fly—
Cheating us out of our fight at the last.
For we saw their ranks fall back and divide,
And we watched their faces horrified
That our handful should dare to strive with them.
And then the view was hid from us wholly—
Like a fleecy fringe on a garment's hem,
The whole of the front of their line outbroke
In a dense, white bank of blinding smoke,
That rose against the blue sky slowly,
While the red death flickered in spirts of fire
As each cannon opened its lips and spoke
A deep-mouthed warning to bid us retire.

---

[7] *ghats*: mountain ranges parallel to the eastern and western coasts of India.

On the left the Kaitua hemmed us in,
On the right a rushing watercourse;
In front their masses of infantry,
Their surging waves of Mahratta horse,
Came down on us like a winter sea;
And we fought as they fight who fight for life—
Each one as though the army's fate
Hung on the strength of his own right wrist
When he warded away the cold curved knife,
And the wiry devil that wielded it
Recoiled from the bayonet—just too late—
And the steel came out with a wrench and a twist.
So we fought and slew in the midst of the din
Till their line was broken—till man and horse
Fled over the rushing watercourse,
And the greatest fight of the world was our own!
And now my face is scarred to the bone,
And I'm lame maybe from a musket-ball—
Yet I thank God always (and ever shall)
That I fought in a fight the world will applaud;
For the new generations by and bye
Shall be proud of that long September day,
When ten men fled from the face of one,
And the river ran red on its seaward way,
As it flowed through the village of Bokerdun—
Red with the blood that was spilt at Assaye!'

CONFESSION

Holograph copy in Notebook 1, dated 10 August [1882], with later note 'being
verses for a picture'.

Is not the dawning very slow to rise—
    Set both your arms about my weary head,
        Let me lean back a moment & confess
    My great misdeed—lest when that I am dead,
        You, knowing nothing of my wickedness
Should say 'my darling is in Paradise'

Is not the dawning very slow to rise?
    Come closer to me for my voice is weak,

And my soul loathes the words I have to say—
   Open the windows it is surely day
But that my eyes are darkened. Kiss my cheek,
   Once loving, ere you spurn me for my lies

'LO! I AM CROWNED'

Holograph version of this verse fragment in Notebook 1. Undated, but it follows 'Confession', dated 10 August, and precedes 'El Dorado', dated 16 August. The fragment is crossed out, but it is not clear when this was done.

Lo! I am crowned,
A King among men,
Coming among men,
From a new world,
Rich in my Kingdom
Having no fear
In Earth or in Heaven,
Confident, Masterless
Through my heart's power,
Through the magnificence
Of my Love's dower,
A King among men.

Whence have you wandered?
Surely we knew thee,
Well in the old days,
Sullen were you
Profitless always
Scantily gaining
Thy daily bread,
Moody and mute,

[incomplete]

EL DORADO[1]

Holograph version in Notebook 1, dated 16 August [1882]. Another holograph version in Notebook 3, with same title but also with facetious subtitle 'Or "He Done His Level Best" '.

> A golden place—whose portals shine
>   So far across Life's dead-flat level,
> That they have drawn this heart of mine
>   To question if the tale be true
>   That says—'Here rest shall come to you'—
> Or whether leasing of the Devil.
>
> Bring me my horse for far away—
>   Across our Life's most dreary level
> The golden city lies, they say—
>   That city of eternal ease,
>   With firmly-founded palaces
> Strong fenced against each earthly devil
>
> A mile beyond our city wall—
>   But one scant mile along the level
> I wandered, and at even fall
>   Returned, for I had gotten grace
>   To dwell forever in that place
> Which is not scaled of any devil.
>
> 'And what good lay beyond the wall?
>   What profit in the outer levels?
> Why wander wide at evenfall
>   Seeing that none of us ere went
>   A furlong from the Battlement
> But found thy country full of devils
>
> That rend and tear us limb from limb
>   That roam in droves along the levels
> When first the daylight draweth dim
>   Perplexing us in heart and mind,
>   No certain rest a man may find
> Who wanders out among these devils

[1] *El Dorado*: lit. the gilded one; originally the name given to the supposed King of a fabulous city of gold sought by both Spaniards and English in South America; hence the city itself.

How got you grace to dwell therein?
　How came you scatheless o'er the levels?
Is there a city, we may win
　　Builded of gold such as they say,
　　If only we shall dare to stray
Alone, among the shadowy devils?'

Nay 'twas a little place indeed—
　A little place along the levels—
But large enough to serve my need
　　And built so firmly, it will last
　　Until our city's life be past
Our town and its besieging devils

Its walls are sweeter far to see
　Than my dream city's in the levels
Two weak white arms that cling to me
　　A pure mouth with a bridge of red
　　Two eyes that struck a light heart dead
And drew it from the lewd loose devils.

Two dark grey eyes that have more light
　Than lurid meteors on the levels—
And they have kept my soul aright
　　This was the golden place I found
　　Thus am I strong through being bound
Stronger than all the restless devils

And if another man may win
　A golden city in the levels—
And if he wish to dwell therein
　　It must be that he go alone—
　　Into the desert: which is grown
A habitation for all Devils—
　A dwelling place of lust & sin—
And there take harness—fight or fall
　A furlong from our city wall—
For so it was—I crossed the levels.

THE SIGN OF THE FLOWER
[THE SIGN OF THE WITHERED VIOLET]

Holograph version in Notebook 1, with title 'The Sign of the Withered Violet',
dated 16 August [1882]. Another holograph version in Notebook 3, with title
'The Sign of the Flower', undated. Years afterwards Trix commented on the
possible significance for this poem of the fact that Florence Garrard's middle
name was Violet (KP 32/24).

'Wait for a little—and if my woe
   Be greater than I can bear alone,
By the sign of the flower shall you know—
   By the sign of the withered violet,
When the time is come to reseek your own'
   So spake she, as parting our two mouths met.

And the grey sea sighed 'She is sick to death—
   Go swiftly and comfort the heart of her'—
'Go swiftly' I heard in the breeze's breath.
   But without the sign I dared not stir,
For I waited the withered violet.

And the grey cloud hurried low to the land,
   And he called—'go swiftly'—but I was still
Waiting the sign of the withered flower,
   That I might be certain & understand,
Lest I missed the fortunate day and hour,
   And thro' too much Love, Love came to ill

And the night came down and cried aloud,
   Whenever the night winds 'gan to blow
'Go swiftly, while time remaineth yet'
   But I listened neither to night or cloud,
For I waited the sign of the violet
   And without the sign, I dared not go

PART TWO

India and After

AMOUR DE VOYAGE[1]

Holograph version in Notebook 1, as first of a group of poems entitled '*Les Amours de Voyage*' and headed 'S. S. Brindisi / Sept 20th to October 20'. These dates probably refer to the duration of the voyage rather then the period of composition. (The *Brindisi* sailed from England on 20 September and arrived at Bombay on 18 October.) Probable dating October–November 1882. This one poem from the group was published in *Echoes*, 1884, and collected in the Outward Bound, De Luxe, Sussex, and Burwash Edns.

And I was a man who could write you rhyme
    (Just so much for you—nothing more),
And you were the woman I loved for a time—
    Loved for a little, and nothing more.
We shall go our ways when the voyage is o'er,
    You with your beauty and I with my rhymes,
With a dim remembrance rising at times
    (Only a memory, nothing more)
Of a lovely face and some worthless rhymes.

Meantime till our comedy reaches its end
    (Its comic ending, and nothing more)
I shall live as your lover who loved as a friend—
    Shall swear true love till Life be o'er.
And you, you must make believe and attend,
    As the steamer throbs from shore to shore.

And so, we shall pass the time for a little
    (Pass it in pleasure, and nothing more),
For vows, alas! are sadly brittle;
    And each may forget the oaths that we swore.
And have we not loved for an age, an age?
    And was I not yours from shore to shore?
From landing-stage to landing-stage
    Did I not worship and kneel and adore?
And what is a month in love but an age?
    And who in their senses would wish for more?

[1] *Amour de Voyage*: shipboard romance. The title derives from Arthur Hugh Clough's *Amours de Voyage* (1858).

LES AMOURS DE VOYAGE[1]

Holograph version in Notebook 1. (See above, p. 173.) The first poem in the group, 'And I was a man who could write you rhyme', is numbered '1'. Then comes the figure '2', followed by the two stanzas beginning 'When the decks were very silent'. They are followed by the figure '3', a note which reads 'Too much waste of time to continue; the subject being a flabby not to say unwholesome one', and a third stanza ('But it may be—Since at first') which may have been intended as a draft conclusion or a separate item. The final stanza ('For the devil that was in your heart') is clearly a separate poem (stigmatized by Kipling in a subsequent note as 'mighty fine but cheap withal').

> When the decks were very silent
>   And the lights along the beach
> Flared and flickered in the nightwinds
>   Blowing down the open reach—
> When the blazing fires[2] before us
>   Shewed the toilers on their ships
> Then it was my heart found utterance
>   Thro' the channel of my lips
> Then it was I told you all things
>   In the pallid moon's eclipse
> While the harbour breeze sighed softly
>   In the rigging of the ships
>
> From the cynical half speeches,
>   In the sunlight on the Bay ,
> To the whispers in the Harbour
>   What a gulf between them lay.
> From the time I met you lightly
>   Half in pleasure, half in scorn
> To the time we watched the night-jar
>   And I knew my love was born.
> I have merited derision
>   You were right to give me scorn.
>
> But it may be—Since at first
>   Love was not but rather scorn,
> Since we knew the best and worst
>   Of each other truthfully

---

[1] *Les Amours de Voyage*: see note to previous poem.
[2] *fires*: reading uncertain.

Long before our Love was born
It may be that for a year
   We shall hold each other dear,
Till remembrance grows less clear
   Till our idyl of the sea
   Is a misty memory
And we murmur—Was it so
   We two loved so long ago.

For the devil that was in your heart—called out to the devil in mine
And the stars were silent above, as the steamers furrowed the sea—
And the sound of our voices was drowned in the noise of the troubled
   brine
And our faces were shrouded from sight by the night's obscurity

A MORNING RIDE

Holograph version in Notebook 1, as first of the Indian series, preceding 'Les
Amours de Voyage'. Undated: probably October–November 1882. A later note
of Kipling's reads 'Published in the Englishman with one howling misprint. A
better poem than the old rag had published for some time wh. isn't saying
much'; but this printing has not been located. Uncollected.

In the hush of the cool, dim dawn when the shades begin to retreat,
And the jackal bolts to his lair at the sound of your horse's feet;
When the great kite preens his wings and calls to his mate on the tree
And the lilac opens her buds ere the sun shall be up to see;
When the trailing rosebush thrills with the sparrows' pent up strife,
Oh! a ride in an Indian dawn, there's no such pleasure in life.

'There's a bend on the (Ravee)[1] river' by the ruined temple gate
There's a halt in the flowering millet; some twenty minutes to wait
There's a glimpse of a dark blue habit—a ripple of laughter sweet
And . . . only the mynas[2] are witness how the Sahib and the Miss Sahib
   meet —
There's a whispered sentence of greeting as we canter over the
   grass—
Where the river runs to the sea like a river of molten glass

   [1] Ravee: the Ravi, one of the great rivers of the Punjab, flows past Lahore.
   [2] mynas: starlings.

Ah! well it is to be living when hands and heart are good
To fetter a pulling horse or to love as a youngster should
When pay and the ponies prosper, and the *bunniah*[3] cheaps his gram,[4]
And the munshi[5] swears by the prophet, that the Sahib will pass his
    exam.[6]
What matter if life has its sorrows while the Present sufficeth for me,
And I live a life in an hour by the bend of the blue Ravee!

OUT OF SIGHT

Holograph version in Notebook 1, dated 13 November [1882]. In this item and
the next Kipling returns to the theme of separation from the love he has left in
England: they are virtually the last of his introspective love poems.

    Out of thy sight—away from thy lips' smiling—
    Out of thy sight—away from thy pure eyes
I spend the weary moments in reviling
    The fate that ruleth all men's destinies
Whereby we two—being one—are far apart
Whereby we two—being one—are two indeed
When longing heart calls out to longing heart
    And hands outstretched help not each lover's need—
Out of thy sight—what good is it complaining?—
    Since neither sees the other where we stand—
    Surely the sunshine cometh after raining,
And after tempest—peace is in the land;
The Gods are not so hard they shall deny
    Some recompense for sorrow—bye and bye.

'AS FAR AS THE EAST IS SET FROM THE WEST'

Holograph version in Notebook 1, untitled and undated: probably November
1882. A note at the end reads 'Probandum est'[1]—and the onus probandi[2] lies
on my shoulders'.

---

[3] *bunniah*: corn-merchant.   [4] *gram*: pulse crop used for feeding horses.
[5] *munshi*: native teacher of languages.
[6] *his exam*: i.e. in one of the Indian languages, in which a young Indian Civil Servant
had to prove his competence.

---

[1] *Probandum est*: it needs to be proved.   [2] *onus probandi*: onus of proof.

As far as the East is set from the West,
 As far as the North from the South,
So far is my breast set from thy breast
 And my mouth from thy mouth.
I in the East and thou in the West
And nought between us but deep unrest

In the East there liveth unresting pain,
 And pain in the sullen West,
And the sea keeps peace between us twain,
 And the sea is never at rest
For the winds that torture a barren main,
Are full of the messages twixt us twain

Bound hands stretched from the sullen West,
 To fettered hands in the East;
And Love, a troubled and wearied guest
 And Love, a hopeless priest
Building his altar in east and west,
And two hearts hoping aye for the best

Shall my eyes always turn to the west
 As thine toward the east
Can a love that found its spring in the west
 Die in the glaring east,
Shall we each find comfort where we be,
With never a thought for over the sea.

 Shade that lieth equally,
 On Western sea and Eastern sea,
 Who can tell what the end can be

THE PIOUS SUB'S CREED

Holograph version in Notebook 1, dated 26 January 1883. The 'sub' of the title is a sub-editor, not a subaltern, and the poem gives a light-hearted view of Kipling's work on the *CMG*. A later marginal comment reads 'Skittles[1] but catchy'.

---

[1] *Skittles*: nonsense.

I *do* believe in Afghan wars
    (As far away as Peshin[2] is)
I love to stick them in because
    Deception most refreshin' is.
And thirteen hundred copies mean,
    Just thirteen hundred lies you see,
And other papers think we've been
    No end informed and wise you see.

I do believe in 'frontier news'
    At least *cum grano sălis*,[3]
As giving scope to Wheeler's[4] views
    Who my eternal pal is
And anything conducive to
    A 'scrap'[5] with 'frontier gup'[6] in it
Would make us most abusive to
    All papers less well up in it.

I do believe the C.M.G.
    The type of all perfection
And other papers mostly be
    In need of much correction
I do believe the native press
    A sink of all that vicious is,
And each 'babu'[7] in English dress
    A 'darn side'[8] too officious is.

I do believe the British Press
    Are censors of morality
Collectively, but none the less
    Imply their deep rascality,
I do believe commandments ten
    To keep one should endeavour
At least, all unofficial men
    But viceroys—hardly ever.

---

[2] *Peshin*: one of the furthest forward posts retained by Britain on the North-West Frontier after the 2nd Afghan War of 1878–81.

[3] *cum grano sălis*: with a grain of salt.

[4] *Wheeler*: Stephen Wheeler, editor of the *CMG*, was a hard taskmaster and no 'eternal pal' of Kipling's. (See above, p. 13.)

[5] *scrap*: short item contributed to the paper by the editor or sub-editor.

[6] *gup*: gossip.

[7] *babu*: educated Bengali; sometimes used in the more restricted sense of Bengali clerk.   [8] *side*: pun on 'sight' (as in 'darn sight') and 'side' meaning conceit.

I do believe in Earthquake shakes
    And tickets compliment'ry
The one at least a column makes
    The other free-seat entry.
If any foolish Briton du'st[9]
    Loose captives from captivity
I do believe each journal must
    Incontinently give it he.

I do believe in tiger skins
    From fourteen feet to twenty
At least when for my many sins
    Mail items aren't in plenty.
I do believe in 'monster' leaps
    By 'liliputian' horses
And dig out 'flying shots' in heaps
From 'most authentic sources'

I do believe the scissors are
    The world's most sure foundation
And pasting paragraphs by far
    The finest occupation,
I do believe that naught too low
    Or high for daily grist is—
I think the Bible's true—I know
    The Indian Civil List[10] *is*

SAINT VALENTINE HIS DAY

Holograph version, unsigned, with subtitle 'To You', sent as a valentine to Evelyn Welford, whom Kipling described in 1889 as 'an ally of mine seven years ago' (entry for 12 November 1889 in diary-letter to Mrs Hill: KP 16/5). She was the daughter of the London representative of Charles Scribner's Sons. The valentine is undated, but a later note by a member of her family says it was sent 'before 1884' (Pierpont Morgan Library). February 1883?

  [9] *If any foolish Briton du'st*: perhaps a reference to adverse comments on the decision by the Viceroy in Council in Jan. 1883 to free the surviving Wahabis (members of a fanatical Muslim sect) who had been sentenced to transportation for life in 1864 for 'abetting the waging of war against the State'; or to the decision of the Madras High Court in Jan. 1883 to quash the convictions of a number of the alleged ringleaders in religious riots which had taken place in Salem in South India in 1882.
  [10] *The Indian Civil List*: an official publication which listed Government personnel and the positions which they held.

Shall I sing you a festive and flippant lay?
   Send you a sonnet across the sea?
Chaunt you a ditty of Valentine's day?
Write you a rollicking roundelay
   Of 'Loves' and 'Doves' and 'Eternity'?

Verily, rhymes be hard to write,
   Verily hearts be not seldom sad—
After the sunshine cometh the night—
After Pleasure, is Pleasure's flight
   After the good, look out for the bad.

Moral Sentiments these I wis,
   Highly improper the ones below
After torment expect we bliss,
Videlicet[1]—after the quarrel the kiss
   And an arm to embrace that gave the blow.

Faithfullest friend of all my friends
   Dearest of Evelyns, doleful am I,
For the Lord he knows when my waiting ends
While the hot winds blow, or the palm tree bends,
   Or the little white cloud scuds over the sky.

Nevertheless, from over the sea,
   I wish good wishes to you and yours
(Tho' you haven't written for weeks. N.B.
This is a hint.) and am faithfullee
   Yours to command while life endures.

Wishes for happiness, wealth and peace
   (While the hot wind blows or the palm tree sighs)
Length of living and infinite ease,
So long as the leaf shall bud on the trees,
   So long as the sun looks out of the skies.

'By Moonlight or Starlight—by water or wold'
   (The old curse runs—which I alter to bless)
So long as the lamb shall bleat in the fold,
While summer is hot, or winter is cold
   So long may the Gods send happiness.

       [1] *Videlicet*: namely.

So long as a woman shall lean to a lie,
   So long as a man shall weary and wait,
So long as the wild geese northward fly,
So long as the flitting swallows cry,
   So long as the wrack comes down with the spate.

And if ever you send a thought this way,
   (Vagrant fancies across the sea)
Think of a youngster whose lavish pay
Leaves him as wretched a whelp today
   As ever a body might hope to be.

THE SUDDER[1] BAZAR

Holograph version in Notebook 1, dated March 1883. Published in *Echoes*, 1884. Collected in the Outward Bound, De Luxe, Sussex, and Burwash Edns. The Notebook version has two additional stanzas, printed here in square brackets, and some variants like 'vakil's' for 'pleader's' in l. 24.

The motive that calls for my ditty
   Is to tell you how many things are
To be found on the road to the City,
   Which we call it the Sudder Bazar.

When the Mission bell's tinkling insistence
   Has ceased, through the dust-laden air
Comes the call from the Mosque in the distance—
   The call of the Faithful to prayer.

Unmoved, though the world fall asunder,
   The voice of the *muezzin*[2] you hear,
While our guns, in the citadel under,
   Are booming for Tel-el-Kebir.[3]

With an eye to where offal and meat lie,
   The kite circles near and afar,
And the pie-dog sleeps calmly and sweetly
   In the dust of the Sudder Bazar.

[1] *Sudder*: chief.
[2] *muezzin*: Muslim crier who proclaims the hours of prayer from the minaret of a mosque.
[3] *Tel-el-Kebir*: victory by British forces under Sir Garnet Wolseley over those of Arabi Pasha in Egypt, 13 Sept. 1882.

And the wrinkled old sweet-seller squats there,
   With his daughters (two two-year-old houris),
And his sweetmeats in baskets and pots there,
   And his bank, a fat bag full of cowries.[4]

There the Kabuli horse-dealers swagger
   In sheepskins—the skinny side out
And jostle the Deccan quail-bagger
   And the pleader's ubiquitous tout.

Staid bulls, much beloved of the Brahmin,[5]
   Stroll round, taking food as they go;
And the cat shares its meal with that 'varmin',
   The bottomless-pit-coloured crow;

[Comes the *jât*[6] from slush[7] canefields suburban
   And the Sikh hating white men like swine,
With his beard fastened under his turban
   And the gowala[8] goading his kine.

Serene and most learned of manner
   By the drainpipe the stamp vendor sits
With his stock in trade—value one anna
   Translating our *Khitmâgar's*[9] chits[10]]

While the *ekka*[11] (a tea-tray on wheels, dear)
   Flies past, as the occupants sit,
(Since a pony, you know, never feels, dear),
   All five tugging hard at the bit;

And the wicked wee tats[12] with a coat of
   Fluffed wool (brought down south in the hope
Of a sale), like the man Swinburne wrote of,[13]
   'Kick heels with their neck in a rope';

---

   [4] *cowries*: small white shells then used as currency in parts of South Asia.
   [5] *Brahmin*: member of the highest (priestly) caste among the Hindus. A Brahminee bull was one which was regarded as sacred and allowed to wander freely, helping itself to such food as it could find.
   [6] *jât (Jat)*: member of one of the main races of north and north-west India.
   [7] *slush*: for Kipling's use of this as an adjective, cf. p. 193 below, l. 2 of poem.
   [8] *gowala*: cattle-driver.   [9] *Khitmâgar*: table servant.   [10] *chits*: notes.
   [11] *ekka*: small one-horse carriage, much used by natives.
   [12] *tats*: country-bred ponies.
   [13] *the man Swinburne wrote of*: a reference to his 'Song in Time of Order': 'We shall see Buonaparte the bastard / Kick heels with his throat in a rope'.

Disturbing the marriage procession
   And its cohort of tom-tomming men,
And the bridegroom's sublime self-possession—
   That dusky young husband of ten.

In the midst of this turmoil pell-mell met,
   You may catch from the spot where you stand
Some glimpse of T. Atkins's[14] helmet—
   The power that governs the land.

And these are a few of the faces
   Of strangers come in from afar,
Of the *olla podrida*[15] of races
   That seethes in the Sudder Bazar;

Some notes from the gamut of face-tints,
   That ranges through yellow to tar[16]—
The pavement mosaic of race-tints,
   That mottles the Sudder Bazar.

But what do I care for their faces,
   For the Jat, the *fakir*[17], or the Sikh,
When here, in these populous places,
   I meet ninety thousand a week?

Oh, give me the wet walks of London,
   And a tramp with my sweetheart as well,
And our 'Power in the East' may be undone,
   And the Sudder Bazar go to[18] . . . Well,

So this is the reason, my dearest,
   When I walk where those infidels are,
That I bang the small boy who stands nearest,
   And flee from the Sudder Bazar.

[14] *T. Atkins*: Tommy (originally Thomas) Atkins—i.e. a private soldier, from the name used in the 19th cent. to represent a typical private in specimen Army forms.

[15] *olla podrida*: Spanish dish of meat, beans, sausages, etc.; hence a mixture.

[16] *That ranges . . .*: 'From yellow, through smoke hue, to tar' in Notebook 1.

[17] *fakir*: '*gosain*' (religious mendicant) in Notebook 1 and *Echoes*.

[18] *go to*: a facetious note of Kipling's in Notebook 1 reads ' "Go to" is a Shakespearian phrase not to be confounded with any other term of abuse'.

A NEW DEPARTURE

Published in the *CMG* for 29 March 1883, as reprint of item in the *Saturday Evening Englishman*, signed 'The Other Player'. Uncollected, but included in Scrapbook 1. Lord Ripon, who had been appointed Viceroy by Gladstone in 1880, had pursued a determinedly Liberal, pro-Indian policy which offended much Anglo-Indian opinion. Opposition came to a head in the Ilbert Bill controversy. C. P. Ilbert, Legal Member of Council, brought forward proposals for an amendment to the Criminal Procedure Code with a view to 'removing the present bar upon the investment of native Magistrates, in the interior, with power over British subjects.' This sought to abolish the anomaly of native magistrates in general having lesser powers than their British equivalents or than native magistrates in the Presidency towns of Calcutta, Bombay, and Madras (where, however, they were subject to closer oversight by higher courts). Opposition was intense and prolonged: it was particularly violent in Calcutta, among the expatriate commercial community, but feeling ran high throughout Anglo-India. Particular objections were urged to the subjection of Englishwomen to the jurisdiction of Hindus or Muslims, because of the low position accorded to women in their societies; and also to the miscarriages of justice likely to occur in cases involving planters in outlying areas, in disputes arising from labour relations. The heart of the matter was, however, Anglo-Indian distrust, twenty-five years after the suppression of the Mutiny, of what was seen as an erosion of British hegemony. Indicating that he would wish to consider all views before reaching a decision, Ripon left Calcutta for Simla in late March, while controversy continued to rage. This was the occasion of Kipling's verses.

> He had said, in a Viceregal homily,
> (Alas for the sternness of rhyme!)
> 'I surmise British law's an anom*i*ly,
> Give place to Bengal for a time.'
> These words were the pith of his homily
> And Calcutta considered them crime.
>
> From the City of Baboos[1] and *bustees*,[2]
> From that sorrowing City of Drains,
> Came the cry:—'Oh my friend, let us trust he's
> But mad, through long stay in the plains;
> Perplexed with the stench of our *bustees*,
> His reason has reeled in the plains.'

[1] *Baboos*: educated, English-speaking Bengalis.

[2] *bustees*: a word 'applied in Calcutta to the separate groups of huts in the humbler native quarters, the sanitary state of which has often been held up to reprobation' (*Hobson-Jobson*). The sanitation of Calcutta as a whole was a recurrent matter of complaint.

And the Planters who plant the Mofussil,[3]
  With Indigo, Coffee, and Tea,
Cried out, when they heard:—'Blow that cuss he'll
  Come down on such folk as we be,
Our coolies will "boss" the Mofussil,
  With his pestilent A.C.P.C.'[4]

But the Baboos that browsed in each office
  Of Subordinate Civil Employ
Cried 'Hurrah for our Viceregal novice!
  Hurrah for the Brahminee boy!
Let the "mean white" be silent, and doff his
  Pith hat to Brahminee boy!'

And the papers they print in Calcutta,
  And the journals men read in Madras,
Were known in their pages to utter
  Some hints that he might be an · · · !
And this spread, from the sinks of Calcutta,
  And the swamps of benighted Madras,
Till the thought set the land in a flutter—
  'Ye Gods! *was* His Lordship an · · · ?'

For his notions of natives *were* curious,
  So India objected, and rose,
And, when India was properly furious,
  He remarked. 'This discussion I close,
The heat to my health is injurious,
  I hie to Himalayan snows.'

With the tact that belonged to his station,
  With a suavity solely his own,
He had set by the ears half a nation
  And left it—to simmer alone.
With his maudlin *ma-bap*[5] legislation,
  He had played merry Hades and—*flown*.

---

  [3] *Mofussil*: country districts.
  [4] *A.C.P.C.*: Amendment to the Criminal Procedure Code.
  [5] *ma-bap*: from the phrase 'Āp mā-bāp hai khudawand' ('You, my Lord, are my mother and father'), used by natives seeking assistance, begging release from a penalty, or reluctant to obey an order (*Hobson-Jobson*); hence 'ingratiating'.

WITH A LOCKET

Holograph version of verse-letter to his sister Trix, in Notebook 1. Undated: probably March–April 1883.

What can I send to a sweet little sister
  Kisses, on paper, are lukewarm stuff—
She knows, too well, how much I have missed her
  To tell it again would be stupid enough.
Love, I have long ago sent to my sister
  There's little left over. Isn't it rough.

Let me then think of a gift to my sister
  I've a notion she wouldn't like cheroots,
Black & knotty, her face to blister
  And a gentleman's saddle scarcely suits
The figure and style of a female sister
  Any more than Manilla cheroots

Would she care for an army revolver my sister—
  Bore 450,[1] weight not small,
Many a time have its bullets missed a
  Six inch mark on the stable wall
'Tis an unsafe gift to give to a sister
  Who shuts her eyes when she fires at all.

Would she care for a grass-green parrot my sister?
  Hundreds harry our gardens now,
Plucking our loquats just as they list, a
  Band of Brigands whose fort is the bough—
I am rather afraid one would reach my sister
  As the French of the school says:——*Tray no gow*[2]

Io triumphe![3] Eureka,[4] my sister
  Bueno! Bahut accha![5] ver guten! tres bon(g)

---

[1] *Bore 450*: i.e. .45 of an inch.
[2] *Tray no gow*: schoolboy slang—'*Très* (very) no go'.
[3] *Io triumphe!*: cry of triumph uttered by Roman soldiers in triumphal procession—'Hurrah, victory!' [4] *Eureka*: I have found it.
[5] *Bahut accha*: very good (each phrase in this line having a similar sense).

I will send Trinchinopoly gold[6] to my sister
And finish my terribly tedious song
A goddess in gold shall be sent to my sister
May she think of her 'Brer' and be pleased with it long.

A MURDER IN THE COMPOUND

Holograph version in Notebook 1. Undated: probably April 1883. Occasioned by an incident reported in the *CMG* for 3 April 1883, in an item dated 2 April: 'A native woman was found, this afternoon, lying with her throat cut, in the compound of the *Civil and Military Gazette* Office. The police are endeavouring to find some clue to the murder.' Published in *Echoes*, 1884 (with reading 'The crows hold conclave high' in l. 11). Collected in the Outward Bound, De Luxe, Sussex, and Burwash Edns.

At the wall's foot a smear of fly-flecked red—
    Discoloured grass wherefrom the wild bees flee.
Across the pathway to the flower-bed,
    The dark stream struggles forward, lazily,
Blackened by that fierce fervour overhead
She does not heed, to whom the noontide glare
    And the flies' turmoil round her livid lips
Are less account than that green puddle where,
Just out of reach, the turbid water slips
Between the corn-ridge and the *siris*[1] trees . . .
    The crows are gathered now, and peer and glance
Athwart the branches, and no passer sees,
    When Life's last flicker leaves her countenance,
How, merrily[2], they drop down, one by one,
To that gay-tinted bundle in the sun.

DUET FROM THE 'PINAFORE'

Published in the *CMG*, 17 April 1883, with signature 'The Other Player' (see above, p. 184), and with subheading '(As lately sung at Calcutta)'. Uncollected. A report on a debate in the Legislative Council on the Ilbert Bill (see

---

[6] *Trinchinopoly gold*: *sic*; the gold- and silversmiths of Trichinopoly in South India were well known for their filigree work.

[1] *siris*: acacia (Sussex Edn.).   [2] *merrily*: 'silently' in Notebook 1.

above, p. 184) had appeared in the London Press under the heading 'Reuter's Telegrams', but it was in fact based on an official telegram from the Government of India sent through Reuters. This led to accusations in the Anglo-Indian press of sharp practice by the Government, firstly by giving a biased account of the debate, emphasizing the views of the Viceroy and his supporters but not those of the opponents of the Bill, and secondly, by seeking to pass the communication off as an independent Reuters report. The poem parodies the duet between the Captain and Dick Deadeye in Act II of *HMS Pinafore*.

REUTER'S YOUNG MAN

Kind public, I've important information,
　　Sing hey, the trusting public that you are!
About a certain intimate relation,
　　Between our liberal Viceroy and a *tar*[1].
Our *much* too liberal Viceroy and a *tar*.

PUBLIC

Good fellow, in conundrums you are speaking,
　　Sing hey, the mystic Reuter that you are!
The answer to them vainly we are seeking,
　　Sing hey, our truthful Viceroy and the *tar*!
Our *very* truthful Viceroy and the *tar*!

REUTER'S YOUNG MAN

Kind public, that sly Viceroy's been a trying,
　　Sing hey, the guileless public that you are!
A garbled tale by Reuter to send flying,
　　Sing hey, the truthful Viceroy and the *tar*!
Our *very* truthful Viceroy and the *tar*!

PUBLIC

Good Reuter, why not give us timely warning?
　　Sing hey, the downy Reuter that you are!
We'll talk to that sly Viceroy in the morning,
　　Sing hey, the scornful papers and the *tar*!
The angry public feeling and the *tar*!

[1] *tar*: telegram.

FROM THE HILLS ['WHAT MAKES MY HEART TO THROB & GLOW?'[1] (NORTH INDIA VERSION)]

Holograph version in Notebook 1 with title "What makes my heart to throb & glow?' (North India version)'. Undated: probably April–June 1883. Published in *Quartette*, 1885, with title 'From the Hills'. Uncollected. The Notebook version has a number of variant readings, such as 'singing' in l. 2, 'Sorely' in l. 5, 'the pi dog' for 'Creation' in l. 19, 'miss' for 'mull' in l. 23, and 'civilians' for 'big bosses' in l. 27.

ORION GOLIGHTLY B.C.S.,[2] *sings*:

Skin may be scorching, and brain may be batter;
   Head may be swimming, and tongue may be white;
Liver uneasy—but what does it matter?
   The mail brings Her into the station tonight!

Sadly the heat from July to September
   Has soddened and shaken a fever-racked frame:
Complexions may change but She will remember
   That, even in India, the Heart is the same.

Scant time indeed have I had to be merry,
   Little of leave and less of delight,
Stewing all day in that frowsy *Kutcherry*;[3]
   What do I care?—She is coming tonight!

Tennis be hanged! I am off to the Station,
   '*Tum-tum men tattu hamara rukho!*'[4]
Ages it seems since in deep tribulation
   I watched Her departure, just five months ago.

Back from Olympus[5] to damp-laden, steamy
   Plains, and her lover who longs for the sight,
My Darling returns; and Creation may see me
   The happiest man in the Province tonight.

---

[1] *What makes my heart . . .* : unidentified.
[2] *B.C.S*: Bengal Civil Service. (Golightly does not figure in the Notebook version.)
[3] *Kutcherry*: court-house.
[4] *Tum-tum men . . .* : Put our pony in the dog-cart.
[5] *Olympus*: Anglo-Indian slang for Simla, from Mount Olympus, the abode of the gods in Greek mythology.

My bearer's a drunkard; my *sais*[6] cribs the gram;[7]
   My one polo-pony's as lame as a post:
I *know* I shall mull[8] my next Persian exam.;[9]
   My pay is a scanty five-fifty[10] at most.

I'm only a Stunt[11]-sahib employed in the 'Revenue';
   But yet I am dearer in Somebody's sight
Than all the big bosses at Simla She ever knew;
   And I'm off to the Station to meet Her tonight.

               (*Climbs into tum-tum*[12] *and exit tumultuously.*)

'DEAR AUNTIE, YOUR PARBOILED NEPHEW'

Holograph verse-letter to Edith Macdonald, dated 12 June 1883 (Library of Congress). It includes some lines from 'A Morning Ride' (see above, p. 175).

Dear Auntie, your parboiled nephew reclines with his feet on a
    chair,
Watching the punkah swing through the red-hot fly-full air;
For, when work is nearly at end and the telephone ceases to ring,
Then the soul of the poet awakes and the 'Stunt'[1] begins to sing.
Sings, as Sterne's starling[2] wailed, watching the blazing sun
'I can't get out'—at least, till after the sunset gun;
For the heavens are red hot iron and the earth is burning brass,
And the river glares in the sun like a torrent of molten glass,
And the quivering heat haze rises, the pitiless sunlight glows
Till my cart reins blister my fingers as my spectacles blisters my
    nose.
Heat, like a baker's oven that sweats one down to the bone
Never such heat, and such health, has your parboiled nephew
    known.

---

[6] *sais* (*syce*): groom.
[7] *gram*: a pulse crop used to feed horses.   [8] *mull*: fail, make a mess of (slang).
[9] *Persian exam*: Persian was the official language of administration under the Mogul Empire, and it continued to be used for some purposes in the British Raj.
[10] *five-fifty*: £550 p.a.   [11] *Stunt*: Assistant (slang).   [12] *tum-tum*: dog-cart.

[1] *Stunt*: see n. 11 above.
[2] *Sterne's starling*: see 'The Hotel at Paris' in *A Sentimental Journey*.

May the Gods forgive my boasting, but nearly a year has fled
And I haven't been seedy once in liver or stomach or head.
An inference thence I draw that, given a daily fill
Of work, I've no time to waste in loafing and 'feeling ill'.
But what are my liver and lights and other organs to you?
We've all of us got 'em, I know and some of us badly too,
Let me off to another subject—that joy of my youthful heart
A varnished dream of delight, my *beautiful* bamboo cart,
With a *real live* horse attached, and whip with no end of a lash
And a groom to sit behind, in *case* I should meet with a smash,
A fearful and wonderful way is the fashion wherein I drive,
But the Pater's been driven by me—and the pater is yet alive.
And after the cart comes the Club—I am honorary member:
Waiting for pukka[3] election by ballot in next September.
And this is a pleasant thing and pleasant it is to stray,
Down to the gossip and 'coolth' at the end of a busy day
Pleasant to breakfast or dine there, pleasant to chat there—and that
    recalls
A fact to my mind, I'm engaged, just now, on some station
    theatricals
This is exciting work and calculated to slump any
Man in the world, to deal with an amateur acting company.
Everyone wants 'best part', every one slurs the fact,
That unless we rehearse at times we shall never be able to act
Nobody comes to rehearsal—everyone says 'all right
We're a wee bit shaky now but we'll struggle through on "the
    night" '
Wednesday; I went for a ride this morning, before it was light
Down to my office to see the 'weekly edition' put right
In the hush of the dim, dark, dawn as the night began to retreat
And the jackal dashed to lair, at the sound of my horse's feet;
When the great kite preened its wings, and called to its mate
    from the tree,
And the lilac opened its buds 'ere the sun should be up to see;
And the trailing rose clumps thrilled with the sparrows' pent up
    strife
Oh! a ride in an Indian dawn there's no such pleasure in life!
(Solemn and sober my trot (for I haven't a jockey's hold)
But the freshness woke up Joe, who frisked like a two-year-old

---

[3] *pukka*: regular, proper, permanent.

Snorting and stamping and neighing, as he thought of the decade or
two
Since he ran by his mother's side at Wazirabad or Bunnôo)[4]
But the sun rose only too soon, and at seven I came back, yet
My saddle was (saving your presence) as black as my boots with
sweat
And my face was a dripping horror and Joe a reeking offence—
When I gave him his slice of bread, in the garden, and staggered
thence
To my room for a *tunda ghuzul*[5] (which means a refreshing tub)
Then went to my proofs till nine, and at nine o'clock went to my
grub—
Verily, this is a rough written, empty aimless screed . . .
I can only ask you Aunt Edie to take the will for the deed
Had I time, as inclination, I would send you a twenty page budget
But the needs of the paper are many and therefore this letter I
fudge it.
The sound of our thundering presses comes up like the surge
on that shore
We sat by and talked together six thousand miles from Lahore—
If I shut my eyes and the parrots were hushed in the palms outside,
I might fancy myself for a time by some wholesome English tide
But the hot air puffs in my face, and you are away from me
While the punkah puddles the heat of an office at ninety three
White, limewashed glaring walls are *not* like a white chalk cliff
And only my daily work and never a breeze is stiff.
So I end my dolorous ditty with a howl of wild despair
As I write in my sodden shirtsleeves, with feet put up on a chair
Oh, what is 'two hundred[6] a month', and half-year 'rises' to come
To a fellow with hairs in his pen, and lizard-tails in his gum;
His ink putrescent and loathsome, a paste of corrupting flies
His spectacles dimmed and steamy, and goggles over his eyes.
'Oh give me a London *trottoir*,[7] some byewalk damp and muddy.
In place of this wholesome heat' is the cry of your washed out
                                                        Ruddy

[4] *Wasirabad or Bunnôo* (sc. Bannu): areas of the Punjab.
[5] *tunda ghuzul*: cold bath.
[6] *two hundred*: i.e. rupees, not pounds.
[7] *trottoir*: pavement.

THE SONG OF AN OUTSIDER

Holograph version of ten stanzas, signed 'R.K.'; undated, probably summer 1883 (Houghton Library, Harvard University, MS Eng 1267.2). Another version, also undated, which was sent to the Padre at Westward Ho!, had more use of school slang—'spidger' for 'sparrow' and 'tweaker' for catapult—a number of variant readings, and an additional stanza after stanza 4: 'E'en now, that heavy College 'crock' / Brings round the College tea: / E'en now, the hungry first form mock / J. Short's economy'.[1] (*Kipling Journal*, no. 54, July 1940, pp. 30–1.) One effect of the revisions in the Harvard version is to make the poem more accessible to readers who had not themselves been at the school.

E'en now the heron treads the wet
    Slush swamps of Goosey pool,[2]
Now proses vex my Latin set
    That first set upper school.

E'en now, across the summer air,
    The call bell's clamour floats,
Down to the weed hung rock pools where
    The Juniors sail their boats

E'en now the gorze is out in bloom
    Along the Torridge valley,
E'en now the sparrow meets his doom
    From catapult & 'Sally'[3]

E'en now to Corey's bath they flock
    Old comrades, after three.
E'en now the lower schoolboys 'rock'[4]
    The Bideford bargee

For me no call bell rings alas!
    For me, no proses are,
No lounging on the playground grass
    No sails across the Bar.

[1] *J. Short's economy*: John Short was one of the College servants, referred to by his own name in *Stalky and Co.* (London, 1899, p. 40.) The reference to his economy is obscure, some school joke being involved.

[2] *Goosey pool*: cf. 'The first day back', p. 56 above.

[3] *Sally*: saloon pistol (Kipling): i.e. a pistol adapted for short-range practice.

[4] *rock*: stone (Kipling).

The hot winds blow, the punkah flaps
   Incessant, to and fro.
Ah well for those most lucky chaps
   Who lark at Westward Ho!

The sunlight thro' the palm tree falls,
   Full on the whitewashed roof,
And worse than any college 'calls'
   Are printers' calls for proof

More dread than any sudden squall
   A careless prose could raise,
Are people who drop in to call,
   And take my busiest days.

Grimmer than any 'thousand lines',
   The lines that I must read
More crabbed than Euclid's worst designs[5]
   A correspondent's screed

What wonder, while the punkah flaps,
   And hell like hot winds blow,[6]
I envy those too lucky chaps
   Who *work* at Westward Ho!

DIVIDED ALLEGIANCE

Holograph version in Notebook 1, dated 15 June 1883. Published in *Quartette*, 1885. Uncollected.

My Love is beautiful as day—
   My Love is very fair:
The gold gleam of the sunset ray
   Has nestled in Her hair.
The gold that in the Sun is set
Is all the gold that She will get;
I love Her well. But yet . . . but yet . . .

[5] *More crabbed* . . . : the Padre's copy reads 'More mystic than C——t's list of fines', referring to W. C. Crofts (see above, p. 7).
[6] *And hell like* . . . : the Padre's copy reads 'And coolies puff and blow'.

My Round Rupee is greasy, dim—
    More light than He should be;
Some *bunnia*[1] must have 'sweated'[2] Him
    Before He came to me.
All things that 'neath the Sun are set
I know my round Rupee can get;
I love Him well. But yet . . . but yet . . .

IN MEMORIAM JULY–AUGUST 1883

Holograph version, undated: probably autumn 1883 (Pierpont Morgan Library). Kipling's first hill leave was in the summer of 1883, when he spent a month at Simla as the guest of James Walker, one of the proprietors of the *CMG*. 'The Walkers, with whom I was staying are angels without wings and did their level best to make things comfortable for their guests', he wrote afterward to Edith Macdonald. 'The month was a round of picnics, dances, theatricals and so on—and I flirted with the bottled up energy of a year on my lips . . . ' (letter of 14 August 1883, Library of Congress). This poem forms the main part of a belated thank-you letter to Mrs Walker.

    If I have held my peace so long
        Here, in the bosom of the plains
        Trust me—'t was but because my brains
    Would yield no echo of a song

    A peaceful lot is mine to sing;
        In dullness deep my lines are laid
        Save when—to please some sporting maid,
    I tilt (and tumble) at the Ring

    Three black cheroots the day beguile;
        Week follows week—the long month goes,
        And Adlard[1] sends his bill for 'close'
    Which I receive and promptly—file.

---

[1] *bunnia*: [corn] merchant.
[2] *sweated*: lightened (by illicit means).

[1] *Adlard*: W. Adlard and Co., Civil and Military Tailors, Lahore and Dalhousie.

No longer flies the fiery steed
    Ramping (on two rupees per diem,
    To be refunded if you buy 'em)
Across the Annandyllic² meads.

No longer by the Jhampan's³ side
    I frisk along the crowded Mall
    From half past four till evenfall,
Or by Peliti's⁴ take my ride.

No longer through the stately pines
    The soft Hill breezes come and go,
    No longer, in the dusk below
The merry 'Rickshaw's lantern shines.

For Jakko's⁵ woods are far away
    And, in the place of Combermere,⁶
    Across the muddy *chick*⁷ I hear
The rain that 'raineth every day'.⁸

Unharrowed is my tender soul
    By M–ss O'M––ʀ–ᴀ's⁹ bold black eye—
    For, far from any passer by
I hear the sullen presses roll

The foul *chaprassi*¹⁰ in his lair
    Sits silent as a turban'd Sphinx;
    And all the city's million stinks
Float inward on the frowzy air,

And so I rest a graceful boot
    Upon the table's inky baize,
    And think of other—happier days
And sob above my cheap cheroot

---

² *Annandyllic*: a pun on 'idyllic' and 'Annandale'—the race-course and wooded glen near Simla.   ³ *Jhampan*: a kind of sedan-chair, for use by ladies.
⁴ *Peliti's*: a famous café and confectioner's in Simla.
⁵ *Jakko*: mountain at Simla, encircled by a road which made a favourite evening ride.
⁶ *Combermere*: Combermere Bridge connected Simla with the area known as Chota-Simla.   ⁷ *chick*: a window or door screen.
⁸ *that 'raineth every day'*: see Feste's song in *Twelfth Night*, echoed in *King Lear*.
⁹ *M–ss O'M––ʀ–ᴀ*: a Miss O'Meara is mentioned in a report of a fancy-dress ball at Simla in the *CMG* for 18 Sept. 1883.   ¹⁰ *chaprassi*: office messenger.

I dream of lotos eating days,
    Of pleasant rides in pleasant places,
    Of half a hundred pretty faces,
Of Solan beer[11] and Henry Clays[12]—

'A change' like that which Byron wrote,[13]
    Comes 'o'er the spirit of my dream;'
    I hear the restless parrot scream
And watch the gay thermantidote;[14]

Too moved for words, its wings I study,—
    Wipe well each glass protected eye
    And, ere I throw the inkstand by
Subscribe myself your truly,
                Ruddy.

'WAY DOWN THE RAVI[1] RIVER'

Holograph version in Notebook 1, dated September 1883. Published in *Echoes*, 1884. Collected in the Outward Bound, De Luxe, Sussex, and Burwash Edns.

I wandered by the riverside,
    To gaze upon the view,
And watched the Alligator glide
    After the dead Hindu,[2]
Who stank and sank beneath the tide,
    Then rose and stank anew.

The evening dews were falling fast,
    The damp, unwholesome dew;
The river rippled 'neath the blast,
    The black crow roostward flew;
And swift the Alligator passed
    In chase of his Hindu.

---

[11] *Solan beer*: there was a brewery at Solan, 30 mls. from Simla.
[12] *Henry Clays*: a brand of cigars.
[13] *Which Byron wrote*: see his poem 'The Dream', which is quoted here.
[14] *thermantidote*: a device to cool rooms in hot weather by driving a current of air through wet screens fixed over the windows.

---

[1] *Ravi (Ravee)*: one of the great rivers of the Punjab, which flows past Lahore.
[2] *the dead Hindu*: partially burned bodies often floated down-river after being placed on their pyres at the river's edge.

And, from the margin of the tide,
   I watched the twain that fled—
The Alligator, scaly-thighed,
   Close pressed the flying dead,
Who gazed, with eyeballs opened wide,
   Upward, but nothing said.

And many a time at eventide,
   As night comes on anew,
I think upon the riverside
   Where, gazing on the view,
I watched the Alligator glide
   After the dead Hindu.

THE SONG OF THE EXILES

Published in the *USCC*, no. 16, 15 October 1883, with subheading '(As sung by one of them)', signature 'Gigs'[1], and an additional seventh stanza: '*Sunt quos curriculo*[2] (translate / *Curriculo* by *tat*)[3] / The dust of Simla Mall in state / *Collegisse juvat*'. Also extant in thirteen-stanza holograph version dated 3 November 1883, signed 'R.K.', on the back of a photograph of Kipling and his father sent to L. C. Dunsterville ('Stalky') in 1884 (Library of Congress; cf. KP 14/51). This version includes the stanza just cited, excludes the ninth stanza in the poem as printed below, and has a twelfth stanza which reads 'Scarce healed from prefectorial stripes / For "powers to flog"[4] we beg; / And lips, yet moist from College "swipes"[5] / Drain deep the whisky-peg'. It also has some minor variants such as 'blank old barrack' in stanza 1, 'the Punjab dust-storms' in stanza 5, 'awful steeds' and 'Simla' for 'Murree' in stanza 10, and 'Exiles indeed', 'city's tumult', and 'surge of Northam tide' in the last stanza. Collected in present form in the Outward Bound, De Luxe, Sussex, and Burwash Edns.

That long white Barrack[6] by the Sea
   Stares blankly seaward still,
But other grimy paws make free
   With pignuts on 'The Hill'.

---

  [1] *Gigs*: see above, p. 5.
  [2] *sunt quos* . . . : an adaptation of Horace, *Odes*, I. i. 3–4. 'Sunt quos curriculo pulverem Olympicum / Collegisse iuvat' (There are some whom it delights to gather Olympic dust upon the racing chariot).   [3] *tat*: country pony (Kipling).
  [4] *powers to flog*: one of the first privileges of a young police-officer (Kipling).
  [5] *swipes*: very weak beer.   [6] *long white Barrack*: the United Services College.

4. Kipling and his father, 1883. Dunsterville's copy of 'The Song of the Exiles' was written by Kipling on the back of a copy of this portrait.

Fresh faces in the Gym appear,
   New knives cut other names;
Fresh sinners carry on, I fear,
   Our very same old games.

Terms come and go, scenes shift and fade,
   The young moustache progresses;
In place of call-over, 'parade',
   Instead of dinner, 'messes'.

By some mysterious law of fate
   I cannot understand,
Most College fledgelings gravitate
   To 'India's coral strand'.[7]

In steamy mists of moist Bombay,
   Or dreary Dum-Dum 'lines'.
Or where Karachi dust-storms play,
   An O.U.S.C.[8] pines.

Some watch the tender tea-plant grow
   In gardens of Cachar;
Some wait at Quetta for the slow
   Sure-coming Frontier war.

By Naga Hills our feet are set,
   Or swamps of North Bengal;
Some spend their leave in far Tibet,
   Some get no leave at all.

Some lead the R.A.[9] guns afield
   (At least upon parade),
Some watch lest *kutcha*[10] dams may yield
   To rifts the rains have made.

Some write voluminous reports
   On 'forest land increase',
Some work at survey in the Ghats,[11]
   And some in the Police.

---

[7] *India's coral strand*: see Bishop Heber's hymn, 'From Greenland's icy mountains'.
[8] *O.U.S.C.*: an old member of the United Services College.
[9] *R.A.*: Royal Artillery.   [10] *kutcha*: temporary (Kipling).
[11] *Ghats*: the mountain ranges parallel to the eastern and western coasts of India.

Some prance beside their *gorah-log*[12]
    On bony beasts and strange,
Some test, at Murree or Jutogh,
    The flashing signal's range.

A scattered brotherhood, in truth,
    By mount, and stream, and sea,
We chase, with all the zeal of youth,
    Her Majesty's Rupee.

Exiles are we—yet, through our dreams
    Old scenes and faces glide,
So that the city's murmur seems
    The voice of Northam tide.

PREADMONISHETH YE GHOSTE OF DESMARETS [SPEAKETH YE GHOST OF DESMARETS]

Holograph version dated 20 December, with title 'Preadmonisheth ye Ghoste of Desmarets', grotesque drawings, and end-note 'Here shall end ye preadmonishment of ye ghoste', as part of handwritten programme for *Plot and Passion*. The list of dramatis personae includes Rudyard Kipling as Desmarets (Library of Congress). Another holograph version, with title 'Speaketh ye Ghost of Desmarets', has only the first five stanzas but at some points it is more fully punctuated. (KP 2/1). *Plot and Passion*, a play by T. P. Taylor and John Lang, was performed by the Lahore Amateurs on 20 and 22 December 1883, in the Railway Theatre, Lahore. The play is set in Paris in 1810, one of the principal characters being Maximilian Desmarets, Head of the Secret Department of Police. The *CMG* for 22 December carried an enthusiastic review of the opening performance, commenting that 'Desmarets is played by Mr R. Kipling, who has evidently a talent for acting, and played a very complicated part with much success.' Even warmer praise was given on 25 December for the performance on the 22nd, it being noted that 'Desmarets seemed to be the hero of the evening, and, at the end of the second act, was loudly recalled.' The poem, with the programme note, was obviously intended as a souvenir of this occasion, both versions being written neatly on small gilt-edged programme cards.

---

[12] *gorah-log*: European soldiers (Kipling).

In the Paris of the Empire, in the days of long ago,
Moves the drama they are acting, move the puppets of their
    show.—
Those were days when life went briskly; when the stakes were
    hearts and brains;
And the rattle of the dicebox hid the clink of Fouché's[1] chains—
But those days are past and done with, and you've changed the tune
    (I know)
From the tune we played in Paris—in the days of long ago

Ere Hausmann's[2] streets were builded—ere the *coup d'état*[3] was
    tried—
How we lived like Gods at Paris! How we gambled, loved and lied!
Ere we lost the Quartier Latin—when the Rue La Harpe[4] was
    new;
Ere the bugles blew to battle through the wheat of Waterloo—
Ah! Life was worth the living (if you 'scaped the Headsman's blow)
In the Paris of the Empire—in the days of long ago.

I was member of 'the Force' there—what you'd call a D. S. P.[5]—
Half the secrets of our Paris—Lordly Paris—passed through me.
I was plotter, lover, liar, with the best of all my friends—
I was foiled, refused, detected (so this moral drama ends)
I betrayed my love and lost her, lost the love I strove for so—
(Hearts were true *sometimes* in Paris, in the days of long ago.)

Now, the lights are all extinguished in the rooms I knew so well;
Never sound of Royal laughter wakes the Hall where Fouché
    fell—
I, a shadow scorned of shadows, linger by the gilded ball
Of the great Hôtel we guarded in the days of Cadoudal;[6]

[1] *Fouché*: Joseph Fouché (1759–1820), politician, Minister of Police and then Minister of the Interior under Napoleon. He was dismissed from office for suspected treason in 1810.
  [2] *Hausmann*: Georges Eugène Haussmann (1809–91), the French administrator responsible for the modernization of the street system of Paris in the third quarter of the 19th cent.
  [3] *the coup d'état*: Napoleon III was elected president of the French Republic in 1848, seized power by a *coup d'état*, and was proclaimed emperor in 1852.
  [4] *Rue La Harpe*: Haussmann's plans drastically changed the old *Quartier Latin*, and the Rue de la Harpe was reduced to a mere side-street, but it was not 'new' in the days of the Empire as 18th cent. gazetteers make plain.
  [5] *D.S.P.*: Deputy Superintendent of Police.
  [6] *Cadoudal*: Georges Cadoudal (1771–1804), Royalist conspirator involved in resistance to the Revolution and to Napoleon; executed in Paris in 1804, after an abortive plot to depose or assassinate Napoleon.

For we murdered ladies sometimes ('twas *affaire d'état* you know)
In our Paris of the Empire, in the days of long ago.

What know *ye* of 'plot and passion'—as we took their meaning then?
When our Goddesses were women, and our men were more than
    men;
When Life and Death were counters, and we staked them boldly
    both—
And the guillotine might follow on a lover's broken oath;
When the 'ladies from the Fauberg' broke the bank of Petiot[7]
At Paris of the Empire in the days of long ago

Yet I linger for a moment—mark the progress of your play;
Watch some guileless little *gamin* act the part of Desmarets.
But your words have lost their passion, and your speech is strange &
    cold,—
You can neither love nor hate Sires, as we did in days of old.
Ah me for faded glories of 'Le Petit Denisot'![8]
Where I schemed and died at Paris, in the days of long ago.

A COUSIN'S CHRISTMAS CARD

Holograph version sent to Margaret Burne-Jones with signature 'W.O.P.' (see below, p. 253) and subtitle 'a demi-official communication compiled at the office of the C.M.G. for the benefit of other Cousins.[1] With marginal notes and official translations.' The Indian words used are glossed in the margin. There are two illustrations, one of which, opposite stanza 2, shows the sun rising, with the couplet 'And the day shall have a sun, / That shall make thee wish it done' (KP 11/6). At the end Kipling writes, 'And he hadn't time to finish an otherwise perfect epic'; and on the reverse, 'Shew this to Miss Plowden and she will find out one or two mistakes.' Undated, but his awareness of possible errors suggests an early date. Christmas 1883?

---

[7] *Petiot*: reference unidentified. Perhaps a garbled allusion to Pétion (Jérôme Pétion de Villeneuve, 1756–94), a moderate Revolutionary, elected Mayor of Paris in 1791, who committed suicide after the overthrow of his party by the Jacobins. In this case the 'ladies from the Fauberg' were presumably the women of the revolutionary quarter, the Faubourg St-Antoine.

[8] *Le Petit Denisot*: reference unidentified: perhaps a café named after its proprietor.

---

[1] *other Cousins*: members of the Burne-Jones, Poynter, and Baldwin families (see p. 7 above).

As coming from an Eastern Land,
I'd have the cousins understand,
'Tis absolutely stiff with speeches,
An Eastern printing office teaches,
And rich with Hindu mystery
In Tamil, Urdu and Hindi

The cousin
premises of the
beauty of his poem,

For instance—when the loathsome '*tár*'[2]
Calls the '*chuprassi*'[3] from afar
And at your '*hookum*'[4] swift he goes
A '*tunda moorghie*'[5]—minus clothes
Across the '*maidan's*'[6] icy space
With '*kummels*'[7] clouted round his face
    This to the English mind—I'm sure—
    Might seem a little bit obscure
    But to *this* Anglo-Indian one
    It shows his labour is begun.

and of its extreme
subtilty in parts

Moreover, when the '*admís*'[8] sit
With Rook-ud-din's[9] most greasy '*chit*'[10]
And to your '*Kia hai*'[11] some grunter
Growls '*Gurebpurwar Jawab Munta*',[12]
    This to the cousins might indeed
    Appear a jabberwocky screed:—
    But to the tortured Rudyard's soul
    It shows his foreman's in a hole.

and continues
his tale yet
further
in mystic wise

---

[2] *tár*: telegram (Kipling).
[3] *chuprassi*: messenger (Kipling).
[4] *hookum*: order (Kipling).
[5] *tunda moorghie*: cold fowl (Kipling).
[6] *maidan*: heath (Kipling). Sc. open space.
[7] *kummels*: heavy clothes (Kipling).
[8] *admís*: men (Kipling).
[9] *Rook-ud-din*: Mian Rukn Din (see above, p. 15).
[10] *chit*: note (Kipling).
[11] *Kia hai*: what is it (Kipling).
[12] *Gurebpurwar Jawab Munta*: Protector of the poor, an answer is wanted (Kipling).

And further—when all work is '*chúck*'[13]
And boss and '*stunt*'[14] sit round & '*buck*'[15]
And through the '*chics*'[16] the *tattoos*'[17] neigh
Comes clearly from the near '*Serai*',[18]
Then rising cry we '*Syce bolow*'[19]
Snatch up '*terais*'[20] and *Juldee Jao*.[21]

and
with a
display of
great wisdom
in his poesie

      This *may* appear—but I'm resolved
      It shall not seem the *least* involved
      And so I tell you, for your knowing
      These six lines show the staff when going

Yet once more—by the '*chíllag's*[22] light
When '*wallahs*'[23] wake you in the night
With '*Hakim Sahib ke gher khan hai*?[24]
Memsahib bemar'[25]—and you reply
Half wakened '*Memsahib bahut bemar*?[26]
Tomara pahs nehai sowar?'[27]

      This in a London city read
      Would prove the poet off his head
      But in an Anglo Indian station
      It means—increase of population

A BALLAD OF BITTERNESS

Holograph version dated December 1883, with subheading 'Dedicated (without permission) to my Mater' (Rudyard Kipling Collection, George Arents Research Library, Syracuse University). Alice Kipling had gone to England

---

[13] *chúck*: done with (Kipling).
[14] *stunt*: Assistant (Kipling).
[15] *buck*: talk (Kipling).
[16] *chics*: blinds (Kipling).
[17] *tattoos*: ponies (Kipling).
[18] *Serai*: stable (Kipling).
[19] *Syce bolow*: call the groom (Kipling).
[20] *terais*: sun hats (Kipling).
[21] *Juldee Jao*: go quickly (Kipling).
[22] *chíllag*: wick in oil (Kipling).
[23] *wallahs*: men (Kipling).
[24] *Hakim Sahib ke gher khan hai*?: Where is the Doctor's House? (Kipling).
[25] *Memsahib bemar*: the Memsahib is ill (Kipling).
[26] *Memsahib bahut bemar*?: Is the lady very ill? (Kipling)
[27] *Tomara pahs nehai sowar*?: Haven't you a mounted messenger to send? (Kipling)

some months previously to bring Trix out to India; and Rudyard was on his own at Lahore, since his father was preparing a display for the Calcutta Exhibition. The poem is, however, addressed not to Alice Kipling but to Mrs Tavenor Perry, a kind of substitute mother whom he had been in the habit of addressing as 'Mater' when he was at school. (Cf. p. 12 above, and p. 250 below.)

How shall he sing of Christmas fun,
    Or Christmas holiday,
A youth beneath an Eastern sun,
    Six thousand miles away?

No holidays are his to take,
    No theatres to see;
His Christmas songs the Presses make
    That drive the C.M.G.

Beneath the palms, the dusty palms,
    That shade his office roof,
He takes the telephone's alarms,
    And wades through piles of 'proof'.

Along the course, the dusty course,
    (Fresh from his morning tub)
He steers the 'bucking' waler[1] horse
    Or hunts the jackal cub.

From nine to five his scissors gleam
    Mid fifty-seven papers—
He tries by 'piling on the steam'
    To drive away the 'vapours'

Yet—spite of office din and noise
    Intrusive thoughts will come
And life, perhaps, has higher joys
    Than scissors, proofs or gum.

Unhitched from paper leading strings
    A vagrant thought will rove,
To where the Brompton smoke fog clings
    O'er 'Twenty five, The Grove'[2]

---

[1] *waler*: Australian horse, imported from New South Wales.
[2] *Twenty five, The Grove*: Mrs Tavenor Perry's address at this time was 25 The Grove, The Boltons, Kensington, which was near Brompton Road.

It spoils the taste of his cheroots,
   With telegraphic quickness
As, through his weary head, there shoots
   A pang of—well, homesickness!

He wonders if you'll understand
   How much this child can miss you;
And what he'd give to take your hand,—
   And what he'd give to kiss you.

He wonders if, in years to come,
   He'll save enough to go,
And take a first class ticket home,
   Aboard the P and O.[3]

He dreams of half a hundred things
   Above the table's baize;
Of redhot months, with leaden wings,
   And fever stricken days.

Of weary nights when, half the year,
   The punkah creaked and swung
And, shrilling in his sleepless ear,
   The foul mosquito sung.

But now the year begins to die
   And Christmas is at hand—
What gift to greet you worthily
   Can reach you from his hand?

He has no Christmas card to send—
   No scented *billet doux*,
And so he forwards, dearest friend,
   His heart's best love to you.

And if, on old ball programmes writ,
   The speech looks poor and mean,
Believe him—half the truth of it
   Lies deeper than is seen

[3] *P and O*: vessel of the Peninsular and Oriental Steamship Company.

He asks:—'In midst of Christmas fun
    And all your new year joy
Think of him 'neath an Eastern sun
    Your always loving
                    Boy.'

AT THE END OF A YEAR

Holograph verse letter to Edith Macdonald, signed 'Ruddy' (Library of Congress). Undated: December 1883.

This is the end of a Year
        Auntie dear;
        Drear—
    (Horridly, hopelessly drear)
        As I write
        In the night;
    (From the depths of a frosty night)
I've little to show for the year,
        I fear,
In the book of the Bank or the Heart.
    (In cash or Flo's heart.)[1]
I'm twelve months older its true—
        Entre nous,[2]
That's all I can truthfully write
        Tonight—
Painful, but painfully true.

I'm drawing three hundred a year
        Out here,
    But it's queer
I'd barter the 'bloomin' lot'
        On the spot,
        (If I could)
        For the wood
Pavement of Kensington High-
    Street, and a London sky,

---

[1] *Flo*: Florence Garrard.   [2] *Entre nous*: between ourselves.

And the noise of the local trains,
   (Those merry city trains)
And the flashing theatre lights,
     In the Strand,
   And the bustle and stir o' nights—
   And 'the touch of a vanished hand'[2]

(Do you think you could understand
   What it is to live in the plains,
   (The doleful dusty plains)
     Alone, like a hermit crab,
  Where gas is never seen
     And there's half the world between
     Yourself and a hansom cab?)

So I dream of a thousand things,
  (As I scribble & smoke and think)
Of months with leaden wings,
   Bedraggled with printers' ink,
Of chalky Sussex cliffs,
   And how—were it not for the 'ifs'—
(Those pestilent practical 'ifs')
   I would pack up my traps and go
  By the bounding P and O;[3]
     And quit Lahore tonight
  But that is impossible *quite*.

For the facts of the case are this
   (The prose of my being is this)
  On the table beneath my hand,
   (In a neat little tape-bound row)
  Are the proofs which the printers expect
  (The proofs which this child must correct)
   For tomorrow's issue you know.
  And, in case I should be remiss,
   This legend is writ for a guide:—
   (On their fat little backs for a guide)
   'Sir. Bearer is waiting outside

---

[2] *the touch of a vanished hand*: quotation from Tennyson's 'Break, Break, Break'.
[3] *P and O*: vessel of Peninsular and Oriental Steamship Company.

Please arrange. Sir,—Yours to command
Badshee Shah'—So you *see* I am tied
Verily, tight am I tied
To the land.

And the moral hereof is plain
I maintain
I've lost my first love and the heat
Of much primal conceit
(*Nota Bene* [4], There's lots of it yet
You bet).
I've lost all the fun of the college,
And half my school knowledge,
I've lost my first trust in all men,
From Colombo[5] to Quetta[6],
I've lost (shall I find her again?)
My Love from the place where I set her.

I've gained what is called a 'good start'
A horse and a cart
A gun and a few suits of clothes
And a stock of 'strange oaths'[7],
A place at the Club
And my grub.
That is—if I face all the ills
Of fevers and chills,
And, once in two years, take a tolera-
Ble chance of a spasm of cholera.
In view of which facts I may safely assert
That I'm bound to Lahore till—I turns to its dirt.
And some fifteen years hence may be gaily employed
In spreading the germs of malignant typhoid.
Or, with cowdung and straw, duly plastered and set,
I may guard my successor's young head from the wet

A BELEAGUERED CITY

Published in the *CMG*, 28 January 1884, with heading ' "The reader must
understand that the rifle range of the 1st Punjab Volunteers is hard by the

---

[4] *Nota Bene*: note well.   [5] *Colombo*: port in Ceylon.
[6] *Quetta*: military station in Baluchistan on North-West Frontier.
[7] *strange oaths*: see Jaques' speech on the seven ages of man in *As You Like It*.

Lawrence Hall Gardens; and that people, walking or driving in the Gardens or along the Mall, are likely to find a bullet inside them at any moment."—*C. & M. Gazette*.' Signed 'Blank Cartridge'. Uncollected. The quotation is from an item which appeared on 26 January denouncing the hazards of having a rifle range sited in the heart of the station at Lahore. 'I need only explain', Kipling wrote to Edith Macdonald, 'that I too was once nearly shot while riding down the Mall, and the "Poet's mind"[1] was, consequently, vexed by the "shallow wit" of volunteers who could miss a mark at two hundred yards and nearly hit a man at two thousand . . . The 1st P.V.R.[2] are seeking the blood of the person who wrote the verses.' (Library of Congress.) The newspaper's protests led to official reconsideration of the use of this range. The poem, a parody of 'The Walrus and the Carpenter', derives its title from Mrs Oliphant's novel, *The Beleaguered City* (1880), which is read by Beetle in *Stalky and Co.* (London, 1899, p. 123).

The Stranger and the Resident
   Were strolling down the Mall;
The former jumped at times to see
   The merry bullets fall,
'If this goes on for long,' he said,
   'Expect a funeral.'

'If twenty men, with twenty guns,
   Blaze at the Bull, his eye,
Do you suppose they hit it once?—
   Do you suppose they try?'
'I doubt it,' said the Resident,
   'They fire rather high.'

'Oh seek the culvert's shade, my friend,'
   The Stranger then besought,
'For death may be the pleasant end
   Of this peculiar sport'—
The Resident said nothing but:—
   'They *really* didn't ought.'

'A coat of mail', the Stranger said,
   'Is what we chiefly need,
A half inch steel revetment plate
   Would be a boon indeed,
I trust I'm not obtrusive, but
   My head begins to bleed.'

[1] *the "Poet's mind"* . . . : 'Vex not thou the poet's mind / With thy shallow wit' (Tennyson, 'The Poet's Mind').   [2] *P.V.R.*: Punjab Volunteer Rifles.

Then other bullets whistled up,
    By ones and twos and threes—
Came frisking through the aloe hedge,
    Or hurried through the trees,
Which wasn't odd because, you know,
    We know the P.R.V.s.

'Oh Stranger,' said the Resident,
    'There goes the mid-day gun,
Shall we be trotting home again,
    The squad have almost done?
You mustn't mind their play because'—
    But answer came there none,
Which wasn't odd, considering
    The risks that man had run.

AU REVOIR [A VALENTINE ; A SONG OF ST. VALENTINE]

Holograph version in Notebook 1 with title 'A Valentine'. Another holograph version with title 'A Song of St. Valentine', subheading 'To A.E.W.', and end-note 'With the Compliments of the Printer's Devil', is dated 14 February 1884 and seems to have been sent as a valentine to a friend as yet unidentified (Huntington Library MS HM 11884). Published in the *CMG*, 12 August 1887, under title 'Au Revoir'. Uncollected. The MS versions of the fourth stanza begin 'There is one greeting for all— / One salutation', and there are other minor variants such as 'promise' or 'triumphs' for 'Pageant' in l. 6, and 'errant' for 'blue-eyed' in l. 19.

What Song shall we sing to the Swallow,
    In Spring?—
To the restless, roving Swallow
    That heralds an English Spring?
Surely, sad Autumn must follow
    The Pageant of Spring;
And, what Time the Winds blow hollow,
    Where is the Swallow?

What song to the Flowers of May,
    In Summer?—
To the Buds and the Blossoms of May
    That jewel an English Summer?

Surely, These pass away
  With the waning Summer,
And, what Time the Woods decay,
Where are the Flowers of May?

What Song to an English Maid
  'Neath our Sun?—
To a blue-eyed English Maid
  Who braves for a Season our Sun?
Surely, the Lilacs fade
  Ere the Season is done;
And, what Time June burneth the Blade,
Where is the Maid?

There is one Message to All,
  One Invitation,—
When Birds flit or Flowers fall,
  Or the Maid quits the Station:—
'Come back with the cooler Spring Wind,
  For the Land lieth lonely!
Come back, for Ye leave Us behind
Sweet Memories only!'

MAX DESMARETS[1] HIS VALENTINE

Holograph version on small gilt-edged card, dated 14 February 1884, with
grotesque illustrations and end-note 'The ende of the Valentine'. Original in
possession of Miss M. E. Macdonald; photocopy in Baldwin Papers, 2/6.

How shall a ghost from the *Père-la-Chaise*[2]
  Greeting send to a vanished love?
  How shall he struggle the sods above
And merrily chatter of by-gone days?
Woe is me! Through the matted grass
  That grows by my head (where the gamin plays
  In the silent alleys of *Père-la-Chaise*)
Never a soul like mine can pass.
      Madame, if spark of life be thine,
      List to a ghostly Valentine.

[1] *Max Desmarets*: see above, p. 201.
[2] *Père-la-Chaise*: famous cemetery in Paris.

Seventy years in a coffin pent
   Little of beauty have I to show,
   Seventy years will alter one so
With a coffin lid for a firmament
  And the inky darkness night and day;
    With the murmur of all the restless dead
    With the hum of Paris overhead,
What wonder, then, if I fall away . . .
In place of a heart my white ribs shine . . .
   Pity a skeleton Valentine

Bony palms on your hand would close,
   Words of love from a fleshless jaw,
   Might trouble the bravest soul with awe,
  Madame if once again I rose.
I am *not* pleasant to look upon,—
   (Never a thing on the Earth today
   Is fouler favoured than Desmarets)
For, verily, most of my 'padding' is gone.
   Nerveless trunk and a fleshless chine
   Make me a loathely Valentine

  How can I greet a ghostly love
    Knowing not where her soul is fled
    In the Courts that confine the myriad dead?
  How can I follow her flight and discover?
Here, from behind my dungeon bars,
Goeth my question up to the stars:—
    'Moon in the sky,
     Suns as ye roll,
    Meteors that fly
     Search for her soul.
    Bring me her greeting
     Spirits of grace
    Planets swift fleeting
     Through infinite space.
    Waste worlds that, fireless,
     Wander destroyed;
    Comets that, tireless,
     Whirl through the void
    By the gateways of Hades,
     Of pale Proserpine
    Oh! tell her this shade is
     Her true Valentine.'

ON FORT DUTY

Beginning of holograph draft in Notebook 1, dated February 1884. Full holograph version, undated, with heading 'I ween my Lords of Admiralty / Would rather send than come', subheading 'O.U.S.C. singeth sorrowfully', and signature 'Z. 54.[1] R.A.'[2] (Pierpont Morgan Library.) Sent to Cormell Price (see above, pp. 7–8) with letter of 19 February 1884, and published in the *USCC*, no. 18, 28 March 1884, with subheading 'An O.U.S.C. singeth sorrowfully', and signature 'Z. 54. R.A.' Collected in the Outward Bound, De Luxe, Sussex, and Burwash Edns. The first stanza of the draft in Notebook 1 corresponds to the first in the published versions, but the second looked at Frontier news from the viewpoint of a journalist, not an artillery subaltern: 'And the news came in from Northward / Came from Northward on the wire / Of wild Waziri risings— / Of plunder, loot and fire / Came pouring into office / On the flimsies of the wire.' In his covering letter to Price Kipling indicates that this poem, like 'The Song of the Exiles', is 'written at the parents rather more than the boys' (Library of Congress).

> There's tumult in the Khyber,
>   There's feud at Ali Kheyl;
> For the *Maliks*[3] of the Khyber
>   Are at it tooth and nail—
> With the stolen British carbine
>   And the long Kohat *jezail*.[4]
>
> And I look across the ramparts
>   To the northward and the snow—
> To the far Cherat[5] cantonments;
>   But alas! I cannot go
> From the dusty, dreary ramparts
>   Where the cannons grin arow!
>
> There's fighting in the Khyber,
>   But it isn't meant for me,
> Who am sent upon 'Fort-duty'
>   By this pestilent Ravi,[6]
> With just one other subaltern,
>   And not a soul to see.

---

[1] *Z. 54*: cf. Thackeray's 'Pleaceman X. 54', in his 'Ballads of Policeman X' in *Contributions to 'Punch'*.   [2] *R.A.*: Royal Artillery.

[3] *Maliks*: head-men (Kipling, collected edns.)

[4] *Kohat*: town on Afghan border; *jezail*: matchlock (Kipling, collected edns.)

[5] *Cherat*: military station near Peshawur on the North-West Frontier.

[6] *Ravi (Ravee)*: one of the great rivers of the Punjab, flowing past Lahore.

Oh! it's everlasting gun-drill
   And eight-o'clock parades,
It's cleaning-up of mortars
   (Likewise of carronades),
While the passes ring with rifles
   And the noise of Afghan raids.

And I look across the ramparts
   To the river broad and grey,
And I think of merry England
   Where the festive Horse Guards[7] play.
Oh! take the senior grades for this
   And spare the young R.A.!

THE ORNAMENTAL BEASTS

Published in the *CMG*, 26 April 1884, with signature 'Dan Dindigul', and heading ' "A grant of Rs. [rupees] 700 was sanctioned towards the purchase of two tiger cubs from Delhi for the [Zoological] Gardens".—*Proceedings of Lahore Municipality*, April 23rd, 1884.' Uncollected. The same issue of the *CMG* has a leader commenting adversely on the Municipal Committee's action: 'Considering that the incidence of Municipal taxation is rather higher in Lahore than in Umritsar and Delhi, and a good deal higher than the incidence of taxation in Lucknow, Allahabad, Cawnpore, or Agra, and considering, too, that the state of the roads and drains in Lahore shows evident traces of parsimony in these respects, it may well be urged that the Municipal Commissioners might have found something better to spend their money on than tiger cubs.' Kipling acknowledges authorship of this poem in a letter to Edith Macdonald dated 28 April 1884: 'This "Poet's mind"[1] has been vexed by the "shallow wit" of the Lahore Municipality and the result, as you will see, is duly enclosed. Maybe it will amuse you. The Municipality are fairly wrath, the more so as most of the other Indian journals are copying the doggerel.' (Library of Congress.)

Our drains may reek—we do not care—
   Our wells be full of crawly things,
What matters typhoid in the air?
   We want those merry tigerlings.
And having these our hearts will steel
'Gainst death rates what you please per mille.

---

[7] *Horse Guards*: Army Headquarters, from the fact that the Commander-in-Chief and other senior personnel had their offices in the Horse Guards Building in Whitehall.

[1] *'Poet's mind'*: see p. 211 above, n. 1.

Their hides are yellow, striped with black,
  They eat with joy their daily ration,
And this consoles us for the lack
  Of what some fools call 'sanitation'.
À bas les² drains! les morning tubs!
Give us those Delhi tiger cubs!

Shut up the water works—dispense
  With culverts or conservancy,
Drive every useless *bhisti*³ hence,
  And let the dust-cloud wander free.
But, in the name of all things thrifty
More tigers at rupees three-fifty.

We do not yearn for cleanliness,
  Oh wise Municipality;
And, *entre nous*,⁴ let us confess
  We'd very much prefer to die,
If, by our death, the local Zoo
Were dowered with a kangaroo.

Ho! burgesses of Donald Town,⁵
  Ho! householders of fair Mozung,⁵
Weave, weave for them the laurel crown,
  And loudly let their praise be sung,
Who, knowing all our wants, determine
To saddle us with high-priced vermin.

THE MAY VOYAGE

Published in the *CMG*, 23 May 1884, with signature 'E.M.' Uncollected.

Mariners we
Where the hot winds be,
  Caught in the Doldrums one and all;
This is our song
When the breeze blows strong
  From the wooden hatchway cut in the wall:—

---

² *À bas les*: down with the.
³ *bhisti*: water-carrier.
⁴ *entre nous*: between ourselves.
⁵ *Donald Town, Mozung*: areas of Lahore.

'Oh! a *kus-kus* tatty[1] shall be our sail,
And in place of the ocean a brimming pail,
And the throb of the screw that drives our boat
Is the throb of the gay thermantidote;[2]
While the surge of the sea in the good ship's wake
Is the surge that a two-foot *nand*[3] may make.'

Gallant and free
Sons of the Sea,
   Sailing along on the steadiest keel
What though the wind
Cease?—never mind,
   We can admonish the 'man at the wheel'.

For our brown Tom Bowlings[4] are staunch and true
And we'll merrily sail the long months through,
With a '*juldee kinch*'[5] and a 'yo heave ho!'
Keeping our hot weather 'watch below'.

Dibden may rave[6]
Of the wind and the wave—
   Barring a dust-storm who cares for a squall?
Join then our song
As the breeze blows strong
   From the wooden hatchway cut in the wall.

---

[1] *kus-kus tatty*: kus-kus or cuscus were grass roots used to make screens or *tatties* to cover door or window openings in the hot season. 'The screens being kept wet, their fragrant evaporation as the dry winds blow upon them cools and freshens the house greatly.' (*Hobson-Jobson*.)

[2] *thermantidote*: a kind of winnowing machine, operated by hand, and used to drive a continual current of air through the wet *tatties* to counteract the heat.

[3] *nand*: earthenware vessel.

[4] *Tom Bowlings*: sailors. The name derives from a character in Smollett's *Roderick Random*, but it was made famous by Charles Dibdin (1745–1814) in his song 'Tom Bowling'.

[5] *juldee kinch*: pull quickly.

[6] *Dibden* [sic] *may rave*: Dibdin was famous for his nautical songs.

'FAIR MISTRESS, TO MY LASTING SORROW'

Verse-letter to Miss Coxen, dated from 'My Stables', 20 June [1884], and pur-porting to be from Kipling's pony Joe[1] (Library of Congress). W. S. Gilbert's play *The Palace of Truth* was performed by the Lahore Amateurs in the Railway Theatre on 14 and 15 April 1884. It was advertised for several days previously in the *CMG* with a cast list showing that Palmis was to be played by 'Miss Coxen' and Chrysal by Rudyard Kipling. Reviews on 16 and 18 April indicate, however, that he was prevented from taking part by a sudden illness. Several letters of May–June 1884, one of them signed 'Chrysal', refer to his lending Miss Coxen his pony. He was to write again on 2 September enclosing a copy of *Echoes* and telling her of Joe's death at Dalhousie: the pony had fallen over the *khud*[2] and broken his back as a result of carelessness on the part of his groom (Library of Congress).

> Fair Mistress,
>   To my lasting sorrow,
> I learn you leave Lahore tomorrow.
> Conceive my grief! (*Experto crĕde*)[3]
> I've smashed my master's cart already—
> I've bit my *syce*.[4] Poor consolation,
> For your approaching emigration!
> And, in my stall, I think with fury
> Of lucky 'tats'[5] in far Mussoorie.
> Thrice happy beasts, who have the power
> To bear you out to cool Landour.[6]
> But, lest their lot should be *too* pleasant,
> Accept, I pray, my little present.
> Spare not to use it when they shirk
> (As I have shirked) their daily work
> Their ways shall bring you back, may be,
> Some memories of your rides on me:—
> Your evening canters down the drear,
> White road that leads to Mian Mir[7],

---

[1] *Joe*: cf. pp. 191–2 above.
[2] *khud*: precipitous mountainside.
[3] *Experto crede*: believe one with experience.
[4] *syce*: groom.
[5] *tats*: country-bred ponies.
[6] *Landour*: Landaur, a convalescent depot for British troops near the hill-station of Mussoorie.
[7] *Mian Mir*: the cantonment six miles from Lahore.

When, hat in hand, with loosened rein,
You 'bucketted' along the plain—
Remember, if a pony rears,
Don't bring the butt down on his ears;
And when he shies (as I have shied),
A stiff 'rib-bender' on his side
Will keep him straight—These few last lines
End up my letter—So I signs
Myself, as long as I can go,
From heel to headstall, Yours,

'Old Joe'

MUSIC FOR THE MIDDLE-AGED (extract)

The *CMG* for 21 June 1884 contained a spoofing letter by Kipling, under the
pseudonym 'Jacob Cavendish, M.A.', on the inappropriateness of English
drawing-room ballads to life in India, and on the need to devise alternatives.
Uncollected, except for the item 'I had a little husband' (see below, p. 231).
Included in Scrapbook 1.

. . . In the name of common sense, let the mothers of our families—
they are . . . the greatest offenders—sing songs that may be 'under-
standed of the people', ditties dealing with the conditions under which
we of the East live and work. Here is my scheme, imperfect as yet, for
the regeneration of after-dinner music.

I propose to publish, by subscription, a series of Songs entitled
'Music for the Middle-aged' . . . I would not, at first, turn our mature
warblers too suddenly from the beaten paths wherein they are wont to
travel. The Form of their songs shall be respected, but the Spirit
altered, and I flatter myself improved in the altering, to perfect har-
mony with our every-day life.

Take for instance Tennyson's 'Maud' referred to above. Give her
the true local colour, and behold the result:—

Come under the Punkah, Maud,
    For the air is devoid of ozone,
And the scent of the brick-kilns is wafted abroad,
    And the germs of infection are blown,
Are daily dispersed o'er our bed and our board,
    From the huts that our *nauker-log*[1] own.

---
[1] *nauker-log*: servants.

Here is something which we can all understand and appreciate. 'Twickenham Ferry'[2] again, adapted to Eastern exigencies, would obviously run:—

Juldee Ao![3] *Juldee Ao!* To the Simla dâk gharri,[4]
 The fever's about, and the glass going up.
So send in for leave, and no longer we'll tarry,
 And by eight in the even at Simla we'll sup.
       Juldee Ao! (ad lib.)

No one will be prepared to deny that the open vowels of this refrain are infinitely preferable to the senseless 'Yo-ho-o' of the original, inasmuch as they convey a meaning patent to any griffin[5] who has been in the country twenty minutes.

Once more, I submit that all the pathos of parting, experienced by the older members of the community, is compressed into the following lines:—

  In the spring time,[6] Oh my husband,
   When the heat is rising fast,
  When the coolie softly pulling
   Puddles but a burning blast,
  When the skies are lurid yellow,
   When our rooms are 'ninety-three',
  It were best to leave you, ducky,—
   Rough on you, but best for me.

When the world come to admit—as it will—the excellence of my system, I make no doubt that there will arise a race of virile poets, owning no allegiance to, drawing no inspiration from, Western thought, who will weave for the drawing-room of the future, songs as distinctly *sui generis*[7] as an overland trunk or a *solah topee*,[8] and breathing in every word the luxuriant imagery and abundant wealth of expression peculiar to the East.

---

 [2] *Twickenham Ferry*: song by Theo Marzials with refrain 'O-hoi-ye-ho! Ho-ye-ho! Who's for the ferry? / (The briar's in bud, the sun's going down) / It's late as it is and I haven't a penny, / And how shall I get me to Twickenham town?'

 [3] *Juldee Ao*: come quickly.   [4] *dâk gharri*: posting carriage.

 [5] *griffin*: Anglo-Indian slang for a newcomer to India.

 [6] *In the spring time*: parody of an extremely popular drawing-room ballad of the 1880s, by Lady Arthur Hill: 'In the gloaming, oh my darling, / When the lights are dim and low, / And the quiet shadows falling / Softly come and softly go; / When the winds are sobbing faintly / With a gentle unknown woe, / Will you think of me and love me / As you did once long ago?'

 [7] *sui generis*: of their own kind.   [8] *solah topee*: pith helmet.

To ensure this, however, our children must be trained from their cradles to discard the nursery rhymes of an effete civilization . . . I for one, hope to hear the nursing mothers of Anglo-India instructing their babes in infantine lispings such as these:—

I had a little husband

[*see below, p.* 231]

'A WEED, ONE WEED AND ONLY ONE HAD I '[1]

In a letter to Edith Macdonald, begun on 11 July 1884, Kipling tells her about the projected volume *Echoes* and mentions his own parodies of Tennyson and Browning (Library of Congress). 'Tennyson', he goes on, 'lends himself to parody only too quickly:—[*gives text below.*] But this is frivol and drivel and my letter must come to an end.'

> A weed, one weed and only one had I,
>   One weed the weediest one of all my store
> One weed, with but one match to light it by
>   A weed was mine that now is mine no more.
>
> A weed, a weedy weed was mine to smoke
>   Oh ay! ay oh! the match that burns and dies
> My true love garmented in russet cloak
>   Ay oh! oh ay! the flickering flame that flies.
>
> And one went out and one refused to burn
>   And one expired, and 't other would not draw.
> And both have failed me—Whither shall I turn
>   For withered weeds that shall be mine no more.

EPIGRAPH TO ECHOES

Published in *Echoes*, 1884. Collected in the Outward Bound, De Luxe, Sussex, and Burwash Edns. By collecting it, Kipling seems to acknowledge this item as

---

[1] *A weed . . .* : Cf. Tennyson's *Pelleas and Ettarre*, ll. 391–400 ('A rose, but one, none other rose had I'); *The Last Tournament*, ll. 724–32 ('Ay, ay, O ay—the winds that bend the brier!'); and 'Tears, idle tears' (' . . . the days that are no more').

his own; but the initials 'J.L.K.' in the copy sent to his Aunt Louie (Mrs Alfred Baldwin) suggest that the lines may have been written by his father (Baldwin Papers, 2/39).

> THE DUKE. *A new song, sirrah?*
> FIRST MINSTREL. *New as is new bread,*
> *Baked with the corn of yester-year, my lord:*
> *These fledgelings of the nest will try their pipes,*
> *And shrill it boldly in the same old tunes*
> *You hear on every woodland bough.*
>
> OLD PLAY.

A VISION OF INDIA

Parody of Tennyson's 'Vision of Sin', published in *Echoes*, 1884. Collected in the Outward Bound, De Luxe, Sussex, and Burwash Edns., with subheading '(Tennyson)'. *Echoes* has 'Slay' for 'Kill' in l. 4.

> Mother India, wan and thin,
>   Here is forage come your way;
> Take the young Civilian[1] in,
>   Kill him swiftly as you may.
>
> Smite him with the deadly breath
>   From your crowded cities sped;
> Still the heart that beats beneath
>   That girl's picture o'er his bed.
>
> Brains that thought and lips that kissed,
>   Mouldering under alien clay,
> Stir a stagnant Civil List,[2]
>   Help us on our upward way.
>
> (Ice the amber whisky-peg!
>   Every man that yields to thee
> Gives his juniors each a leg,
>   Shakes the sere Pagoda-Tree.)[3]

[1] *Civilian*: member of the Civil Service.

[2] *Civil List*: the *Indian Civil List* was an official publication listing all Government officials and their appointments.

[3] *Pagoda-Tree*: a pagoda was a coin long current in South India; 'shaking the pagoda tree' was a slang phrase for growing rich quickly in the East.

Well indeed we know your power,
   Goddess of our deep devotion,
Who can grant us in an hour
   Steps of rapidest promotion.

Lurking in our daily grub,
   Where the untinned[4] *degchies*[5] lie;
Smiting gaily at the Club,
   O'er the card-room's revelry.

Chaperon to many a maid,
   Calling, when the music dies,
To a stiller, deeper shade
   Than the dim-lit balconies.

(Fill the long-necked glass with whisky!
   Every man that owns thy sway
Leaves a widow, mostly frisky,
   Makes the gossip of a day.)

Brown and Jones and Smith shall die;
   We succeed to all their places,
Bear the badge of slavery,
   Sunken eyes and pallid faces.

Laughter that is worse than tears
   Is our portion in the land,
And the tombstones of our peers
   Make the steps whereon we stand.

THE CITY OF THE HEART

Parody of Longfellow, published in *Echoes*, 1884. Collected in the Outward
Bound, De Luxe, Sussex, and Burwash Edns., with subheading '(Longfel-
low)'. *Echoes* has 'alley' for 'gully' in l. 11 and 'things' for 'beasts' in l. 14.

---

[4] *untinned*: brass cooking vessels were coated with a thin layer of tin to avoid the taste
of brass.   [5] *degchies*: cooking pots (Kipling, collected edns.).

I passed through the lonely Indian town,
    Deep sunk 'twixt the walls of wheat,
And the dogs that lived in the land came down
    And bayed at me in the street.

But I struck with my dog-whip o'er nose and back
    Of the yelping, yellow crew,
Till I cleared a pathway athwart the pack,
    And I and my horse went through.

I passed through the streets of my haunted heart,
    In the hush of a hopeless night;
And from every gully a dog would start
    And bay my soul with affright.

But I smote with the dog-whip of Work and Fact
    These evil beasts on the head,
Till I made of my heart a wholesome tract,
    Empty and garnishèd.

THE INDIAN FARMER AT HOME [THE RAIYAT[1] AT HOME]

Parody of Burns, published in *Echoes*, 1884, under title 'The Raiyat at Home'. Collected under present title in the Outward Bound, De Luxe, Sussex, and Burwash Edns., with subheading '(Burns)'.

Hoots! toots! ayont, ahint, afore,
The bleth'rin' blast may blathe an blaw
    An' shak' my *dhoti*[2];
But I am canty, crouse, and full,
An' aiblins at my pipe I pull,
    Safe in my *khoti*[3].

I bang the gudewife wi' my loof,
And shak' the dung-cakes fra' the roof
    To feed the low;

[1] *Raiyat* (*ryot*): tenant farmer, peasant.
[2] *dhoti*: loincloth (Kipling, collected edns.).
[3] *khoti*: house (Kipling, collected edns.).

An' gin my dinner crowds my *pét*[4],
My wee bit bairnies stamp it straight
   Wi' joyous crow.

What mair, I ask, could man desire
Beyont his bit of bread an' fire,
   An' safe inves'ment
O' bawbees in a silver chain
To guard against a day of rain
   Or raised assessment[5]?

THE FLIGHT OF THE BUCKET

Parody of Browning, published in *Echoes*, 1884. 'I have written a psychological poem on Jack and Jill, in Browning's vein', Kipling wrote to Edith Macdonald that July (Library of Congress). Collected in the Outward Bound, De Luxe, Sussex, and Burwash Edns. with subheading '(Browning)'. The title recalls that of Browning's 'The Flight of the Duchess', the opening that of 'The Heretic's Tragedy' ('Preadmonisheth the Abbot Deodaet') and the final exclamation the close of 'Soliloquy of the Spanish Cloister'.

Pre-admonisheth THE WRITER:

 H'm, for a subject it is well enough!
Who wrote 'Sordello'[1] finds no subject tough.

Well, Jack and Jill—God knows the life they led
(The poet never told us, more's the pity)
Pent up in some damp kennel of their own,
Beneath the hillside; but it once befell
That Jack or Jill, niece, cousin, uncle, aunt
(Some one of all the brood) would wash or scour—
Rinse out a cess-pit, swab the kennel floor,
And water (*liquor vitae*,[2] Lawson[3] calls,
But I—I hold by whisky. Never mind;

---

[4] *pét*: stomach (Kipling, collected edns.).
[5] *assessment*: for tax payable on land.

---

[1] *Sordello*: Browning's poem *Sordello* (1840) was notoriously difficult.
[2] *liquor vitae*: the fluid of life.
[3] *Lawson*: Sir Wilfrid Lawson (1829–1906), Liberal politician of Radical persuasion, life-long advocate of temperance, and exponent of local-option right to prohibition.

I didn't mean to hurt your feelings, sir,
And missed the scrap o' blue at buttonhole—)⁴
Spring water was the needful at the time,
So they must climb the hill for't. Well and good.
We all climb hills, I take it, on some quest,
Maybe for less than stinking (I forgot!
I mean than wholesome) water . . . Ferret out
The rotten bucket from the lumber-shed,
Weave ropes and splice the handle—off they go
To where the cold spring bubbles up i' the cleft,
And sink the bucket brimful in the spate.
Then downwards—hanging back? (You bet your life
The girl's share fell upon Jack's shoulders.) Down,
Down to the bottom—all but—trip, slip, squelch!
And guggle-guggle goes the bucketful
Back to the earth, and Jack's a broken head,
And swears amid the heather does our Jack.
(A man would swear who watched both blood and bucket,
One dripping down his forehead, t'other fled,
Clinkety-tinkle, to the stones below,
A good half-hour's trudge to get it back.)
Jack, therefore, as I said, exploded straight
In brimstone-flavoured language. You, of course,
Maintain he bore it calmly—not a bit.
A good bucolic curse that rent the cliffs
And frightened for a moment quaking Jill
Out of the limp, unmeaning girl's tee-hee
That womankind delight in. . . . Here we end
The first verse—there's a deal to study in't.

.   .   .   .

 So much for Jack—but here's a Fate above,
A cosmic force that blunders into right,
Just when the strained sense hints at revolution
Because the world's great fly-wheel runs aslant—
And up go Jill's red kibes. (You think I'm wrong;
And Fate was napping at the time; perhaps
You're right.) We'll call it Devil's agency
That sent the shrieking sister on her head,
And knocked the tangled locks against the stones.

⁴ *the scrap o' blue at buttonhole*: blue ribbon worn as badge of temperance.

Well, down went Jill, but wasn't hurt. Oh, no!
The Devil pads the world to suit his own,
And packs the cards according. Down went Jill
Unhurt. And Jack trots off to bed, poor brute,
Fist welted into eyeball, mouth agape
For yelling,—your bucolic always yells,—
And out of his domestic pharmacy
Rips forth the cruet-stand, upsets the cat,
And ravages the store-room for his balm.
Eureka!—but he didn't use that word—
A pound of candles, corpse-like, side by side,
Wrapped up in his medicament. Out, knife!
Cut string, and strip the shrouding from the lot!
Steep swift and jam it on the gaping cut;
Then bedward[5]—cursing man and fiends alike.

      ·   ·   ·   ·   ·   ·   ·   ·   ·

  Now back to Jill. She wasn't hurt, I said,
And all the woman's spite was up in arms.
So Jack's abed. She slips, peeks through the door,
And sees the split head like a luggage-label,
Halved, quartered, on the pillow. 'Ee-ki-ree,
Tee-hee-hee-hee', she giggles through the crack,
Much as the Roman ladies grinned—don't smile—
To see the dabbled bodies in the sand
Appealing to their benches for a sign.
Down thumbs, and giggle louder—so did Jill.
But mark now! Comes the mother round the door,
Red-hot from climbing up the hill herself,
And caught the graceless giggler. Whack! flack! whack!
Here's Nemesis whichever way you like!
She didn't stop to argue. Given a head
Broken, a woman chuckling at the door,
And here's your circumstantial evidence complete.
Whack! while Jack sniffs and sniggers from the bed.
I like that horny-handed mother o' Jill.
The world's best women died, sir, long ago.
Well, Jack's avenged; as for the other, *gr-r-r-r!*

---

[5] *Then bedward* . . . : in *Echoes* this line is followed by 'Blindly (your true bucolic always swears).'

LAOCOÖN[1]

Parody of Arnold, published in Echoes, 1884. Collected in the Outward
Bound, De Luxe, Sussex, and Burwash Edns. with subheading '(M. Arnold)'
or '(Matthew Arnold)'.

Under the shadow of Death,
Under the stroke of the sword,
Gain we our daily bread.
Exile that hath no end,
And the heaping up of our woes,
Are given into our hand
As the gifts of the Gods to men.

Lo! in a leaguered town,
Compassed by many foes,
Weary citizens wait,
Neither joyed nor afraid,
The unseen doom of the shot—
Only, at times, when a friend
Falls from their side and is lost
Out of his place on the wall,
Lift they their hands aloft,
Crying aloud to the Gods,
The pitiless, far-off Gods:
'Spare us this last for a space—
Not for ourselves, indeed,
Seeing that this is our right,
But for our children and wives!'

So, under Indian skies,
Compassed by many ills,
Weary workers abide,
Neither joyed nor afraid,
Waiting the unseen doom.
Only, at times, when a friend
Falls at their side and is lost

---

[1] *Laocoön*: a priest of Apollo who warned the Trojans against bringing the wooden
horse into Troy. When he was offering a sacrifice to Poseidon, god of the sea, two great
serpents emerged from the waves and attacked his sons. When he went to their defence,
the serpents coiled around all three and crushed them.

Out of his place in their life,
Lift they their hearts aloft,
Crying aloud: 'If a God
Govern the ways of men,
Spare us this last for a space—
Not for ourselves, indeed,
Seeing that this is our right,
But for our children and wives!'

Neither joyed nor afraid
Of the snakes of circumstance,—
The marble snakes of mishap
That girdle our fleshly limbs,—
We of the East abide:
But if at times our souls,
Being broken by ills,
Blench and are sorely disturbed,—
Not for ourselves, indeed
(Seeing that this is our right),
But for our children and wives,—
Shall we be judged as afraid
By our complaining, O God?

NURSERY RHYMES FOR LITTLE ANGLO-INDIANS

These parodies were published in *Echoes*, 1884, 'I had a little husband' having already appeared in 'Music for the Middle-Aged' (see above, p. 220) Collected in the Outward Bound, De Luxe, Sussex, and Burwash Edns. *Echoes* contained one additional item, printed here in square brackets.

Hush-a-by, Baby,
    In the verandah!
When the sun drops
    Baby may wander.

When the hot weather comes
    Baby will die—
With a fine *pukka*[1] tomb
    In the ce-me-te-ry.

[1] *pukka*: permanent (Kipling, collected edns.).

I had a little husband
   Who gave me all his pay.
I left him for Mussoorie,[2]
   A hundred miles away.

I dragged my little husband's name
   Through heaps of social mire,
And joined him in October,
   As good as you'd desire.

['Ba-Ba-Babu[3], have you got your will?'
  'Yes Sar, Yes Sar, thanks to the Bill.[4]
Four-anna witnesses—plenty telling cram,
And *bless* the Barra-Lat-Sahib,[5] who says how good I am.']

See-saw, Justice and Law,
   The *Raiyats*[6] shall have a new master.
And the Zemindar[7] ain't allowed to distraint
   Because they can't pay any faster.

Sing a Song of Sixpence,
   Purchased by our lives—
Decent English Gentlemen
   Roasting with their wives

In the plains of India
   Where like flies they die.
Isn't that a wholesome risk
   To get our living by?

The fever's in the Jungle,
   The typhoid's in the tank,
And men may catch the cholera
   Apart from social rank;

---

[2] *Mussoorie*: a hill-station in the lower Himalayas.

[3] *Babu*: English-speaking educated Bengali.

[4] *the Bill*: the Ilbert Bill (see above p. 184).

[5] *the Barra-Lat-Sahib*: the great Lord Sahib; i.e. the Viceroy.

[6] *Raiyats*: tenant farmers, peasants.

[7] *Zemindar*: landowner or proprietor holding land directly from the Government. There is an allusion in this poem to the projected Bengal Tenancy Bill, which was thought to favour tenants against landlords.

And Death is in the Garden,
  A-waiting till we pass,
For the *Krait*[8] is in the drain-pipe,
  The Cobra in the grass!

With a lady flirt a little—
  'Tis *manners* so to do.
Of a lady speak but little—
  'Tis *safest* so to do.

Jack's own Jill goes up to the Hill
  Of Murree or Chakrata.[9]
Jack remains, and dies in the plains,
  And Jill remarries soon arter.

Mary, Mary, quite contrary,
  Where do your subalterns go?
For love is brief and the next 'relief '
  Will scatter them all like snow.

APPROPRIATE VERSES ON AN ELEGANT LANDSCAPE

Parody of Cowper, published in *Echoes*, 1884. Collected in the Outward Bound, De Luxe, Sussex, and Burwash Edns. with subheading '(Cowper)'.

The fields were upholstered with poppies so red,
  And black as my hat was each rook;
And the hedges were bordered, like quilts on a bed,
  With the bombazine braid of the brook.

And I thought to myself, with an auctioneer's smirk,
  As I gazed on the freehold so rare:
'O Lord, if on Earth these chaste shows are thy work,
  Of what is the Kingdom up there?'

[8] *Krait*: a kind of poisonous snake.
[9] *Murree, Chakrata*: hill-stations.

THE CURSING OF STEPHEN

Parody of Tennyson, published in *Echoes*, 1884. Collected in the Outward Bound, De Luxe, Sussex, and Burwash Edns. with subheading '(Tennyson)'. 'I have . . . made an idyll of the King, out of the rhyme of King Stephen', he told Edith Macdonald in July 1884 (Library of Congress). The rhyme in question was a stanza in a folk-song recorded in Percy's *Reliques*, which had earlier figured in *Othello*, II. ii, and which had presumably been transferred to collections of nursery rhymes: 'King Stephen was a worthy peer, / His breeches cost him but a crown; / He held them sixpence all too dear, / With that he called the tailor lown.'[1] The opening lines of the poem are modelled on those of Tennyson's 'Godiva'.

> I turned the pages of the baby's book,
> I hung with children on the rocking-horse,
> And shook the rattle till it rang again;
> And, while I gambolled 'mid these buds of youth,
> I shaped the nursery legend into this:
>
> King Stephen, o'er the castled battlement
> That frowned above the fir-copse and the lake,
> Looked downward on his people and beheld
> The many-mouthèd nation call on him
> Who was a worthy peer. The pine-woods rang,
> In slumb'rous thunder to the girdling sea,
> With 'Worthy peer'; and, down the long white street,
> Green-shuttered cots re-echoed; 'Worthy peer.'
> But in the great king's bosom pain was lord,
> And 'neath his brows the royal eyeball burnt,
> As dying brands burn on the wasted hearth
> When those that tend them slumber. Slowly first
> The hot words brake beneath the bearded lips,
> And the mailed hand slid backward to the throne
> Whereon the king was seated. As some dam
> In spring bursts down the wall and whelms the vale,
> So broke the king's 'Damn' o'er the silent Court,
> And stilled the Jester into utter peace,
> And all the courtiers wondered where they sate
> 'What ails King Stephen!' Then the great king spoke,
> As Saul had spoken in the shrouded tent,

[1] *lown*: rogue, worthless fellow.

Before the Son of Jesse[2] soothed his soul
With sackbut and with psaltery: 'Woe is me!
Sin creeps upon our servants at the board,
And in my royal palace find we sin—
At first among the lowest; being low,
They sin as brutes, in brutal, bestial wise.
But ever upward curls the flame of sin,
Infecting e'en the highest. Lust of gain,
That spareth not the person of the king,
Hath fallen upon us, and behold I go
To fight corruption, though I lose my life;
Not loving life, but rather fearing death
With life's corruption on my parting soul.
Pray for me, O my courtiers!' And they wailed,
Those bearded rulers of the fosse and field,
Great princes of the Plough-tail, for the king;
And sorrow hung about the sobbing Court,
And that great charger squealed like any she.
So, in the twilight, passed the king away
Adown the long white street, all armed and mailed,
Past dune and wind-swept hedgerow, till he reached
A low-built cottage by the roaring sea,
Wherein one sat for ever at a board,
Cross-legged, and drave the needle to and fro,
Through silk and samite, minever and lawn,
As swine in autumn pierce the fallen mast
For forage with their keen, white, curvèd tusks;
And evermore the singer sang his song,
And through the windows Stephen heard the strain:

'A Devil and a Tailor, fiend and man,
That were at strife since first the world began—
Read me my riddle's reading an you can.

A Tailor and a Devil—man and sprite.
Black as black thread was one—the other white
As cloth that clothes the great king's limbs at night.

The Devil and the Tailor. Silk and thread,
O primrose minever! O samite red,
That drapes the curtains of the great king's bed!

---

[2] *the Son of Jesse*: David (see 1 Sam. 16: 23).

For men must clothe their nakedness, and I,
For credit or for cash, give swift supply
Of woven gauds and broidered bravery.'

And then the voice ceased suddenly within,
Because the charger whinnied through the dusk,
And shook the windows of the crazy cot.
Whereon, with eyelids shaded, and huge shears
Slung swordwise at his side, the churl advanced,
And saw the great king's shadow on the door,
But made no reverence, as befits a churl
In royal presence, only, from his breast,
Dragged forth a store of papers, tape, and thread,
And murmured: 'Credit is the thief of time!
My gold, King Stephen, for the doublet gay,
For hose and baldric, now some three months old,
And for the broidered cloak upon thy back—
My gold, King Stephen!' But the blameless king
Drew swiftly from his scabbard that which pays
All debts in one; and at the great blade's light
The churl fled backward to the cottage door,
And Stephen spake in this wise to the churl:
'I, being king, an I had cleft thy form
From chin to chine, had sullied my good sword
With useless slaughter of a ninth-part man;[3]
And I am come in sorrow, not in wrath,
To judge thee for thy treason 'gainst the king;
Our noble order has no thought of guile
To me or mine—my menials know no sin,
And all my people are a sinless folk,
Content with little save the gifts of God
And my exceeding glory. Only thou,
Misled by lust of gold, hast fallen in sin—
The deadlier, being self-conceived: for sin
Caught by contagion (as the dove's red foot
Is soiled by mire) is a lesser fault
Than crime self-centred in a single breast
And bred in isolation. I, thy king,
Have worn the garments of a spotless life,
And also (since the world desires more

---

[3] *a ninth-part man*: from the proverb 'Nine tailors make a man.'

For human limbs) some garments made by thee;
And these were hose and doublet, as thou sayest,
And also breeches for my lower limbs,
And in these breeches lieth all thy sin:
Rapine and greed, and interest sought on bills,
And monthly increment of silver coin
Charged for the lapse of time—which is God's act,
Nor any handiwork of thine, O churl;
And thou, being void of shame, hast written down
The cost of these same breeches that I wear
At usury and interest, sinful churl,
And I adjudge the cost exorbitant
By six round pence. Behold!' and here his hand
Slid backward to the cantle of his selle,
And grasped the spacious garment that he wore
In kingly wrath. 'Behold the size of it!
The airy effluence of fold on fold,
And mazy complications of the seat,
Between the saddle and my royal flesh,
Chafed to a gall thereby. This is thy work—
Large and ill-fitting as the wrinkled buds
That hide the larches' children in the spring.
Thank, therefore, such vile stars as saw thy birth
That silver and not steel discharge the debt. . . .
Yet Lancelot falls to his own love again,
And tailors reel into the ninth-part beast
And wholly vermin—and my speech, I fear,
Falls deadly on dull ears that can but catch
The clink of shears and silver. Wherefore, churl,
I am resolved to curse thee—not in wrath,
For wrath is alien to the minds of kings,
But for remembrance' sake, and, ere I go,
I call thee—out of sorrow, not in wrath—
I, Stephen, call thee *Lown*.' And all the weald
Shuddered at Stephen's curse, and far at sea
The fishes shivered, though they knew not why;
And homeward-flying crows forgot to call
At sound of the king's curse. And he, the churl,
Shrank as the beetle shrinks beneath the pin
When village children stab him in their sport,
And, logwise, rolled before the charger's feet;
And Stephen came to his own Court again.

JANE SMITH

Parody of Wordsworth, published in *Echoes*, 1884. Collected in the Outward
Bound, De Luxe, Sussex, and Burwash Edns. with subheading '(Words-
worth)'. On the controversy over authorship, see above. pp. 29–30.

> I journeyed, on a winter's day,
>   Across the lonely wold;
> No bird did sing upon the spray,
>   And it was very cold.
>
> I had a coach with horses four,
>   Three white (though one was black),
> And on they went the common o'er,
>   Nor swiftness did they lack.
>
> A little girl ran by the side,
>   And she was pinched and thin.
> 'Oh, please, sir, *do* give me a ride!
>   I'm fetching mother's gin.'
>
> 'Enter my coach, sweet child,' said I;
>   'For you shall ride with me,
> And I will get you your supply
>   Of mother's eau-de-vie.'
>
> The publican was stern and cold,
>   And said: 'Her mother's score
> Is writ, as you shall soon behold,
>   Behind the bar-room door!'
>
> I blotted out the score with tears,
>   And paid the money down,
> And took the maid of thirteen years
>   Back to her mother's town;
>
> And though the past with surges wild
>   Fond memories may sever,
> The vision of that happy child
>   Will leave my spirit never!

NURSERY IDYLS

Parodies of poems from Christina Rossetti's 'Sing-Song', published in *Echoes*, 1884. Collected in the Outward Bound, De Luxe, Sussex, and Burwash Edns. with subheading '(Christina Rossetti's 'Sing-Song')'. *Echoes* has the reading 'Malli's[1] mate' in the first line of the last poem.

A little sigh, a little shiver—
And that means liver.
A little liver when June is nigh,
And then we die.

Daffodils in English fields
   And breezes in the clover;
But here's a sun would strike you dead
   Seven times over!

Cook's tourist comes and goes—
   He is but a rover,
While *I* watch the burning sun
   Turn over and over.

And I dream of daffodils
   And the breezy clover;
Turning on my little bed,
   Over and over.

In England elm-leaves fall
   When winter winds blow keen,
But the Indian *pipâl*[2]
   Is always gay and green.

Ne'er in rain or sunshine
   Leaf or blossom dies—
But I'd give the world for an English elm
   Under English skies!

---

[1] *Malli*: gardener.
[2] *pipâl*: fig-tree (Sussex Edn.).

Here's a mongoose
Dead in the sluice
Of the bath-room drain.
How was he slain?
He must have lain
Days, it is plain . . .
Stopper your nose,
Throw him out to the crows.

Tara Chand is the gardener's mate,
   And labours late and early;
But Dunni is my pony's *sais*,[3]
   And steals the golden barley.

Golden barley, roses red,
   Rejoice in your morning beauty!
For I have broken Tara's head,
   And given Dunni *chuti*.[4]

SONNET

ON BEING REJECTED OF ONE'S HORSE

Parody of Wilfrid Scawen Blunt, author of *The Love Sonnets of Proteus* (1880).
Published in *Echoes*, 1884. Collected in the Outward Bound, De Luxe, Sussex,
and Burwash Edns. with subheading '(Wilfrid Blunt)'.

Give me my rein, my *sais*![1] Give me my rein!
   I have a need of it, an absolute need,
To climb upon that bounding back again
   And curb the bad, mad gambols of my steed.
'Tis strange we are thus parted—by no lust
   Of mine, but rather blind, unwearied force
   That worked upon the sinews of my horse,
And drove me from him, howling in the dust.

---

[3] *sais* (or *syce*): groom (Kipling, collected edns.).
[4] *chuti*: his dismissal (Kipling, collected edns.).

---

[1] *sais*: see n.3 above.

Now he is neither gentle, kind, nor quiet,
   And strives (though vainly) to outleap his girth,
While right and left the armèd hooves are hurled.
O Destrier! bethink thee that this riot
   Shall, in the end, bring neither rest nor mirth. . . .
Only the heaviest bit in all the world!

KOPRA-BRAHM

Parody of Emerson, published in *Echoes*, 1884. Collected in the Outward Bound, De Luxe, Sussex, and Burwash. Edns. with subheading '(Emerson)'. *Kapra* or *Kappra* means 'clothes'; and Brahm was the supreme god in Hindu mythology, an impersonal spiritual being pervading everything. Hence Kopra-Brahm is the Supreme (Clothes) Deity. The poem makes fun of Emerson's sense of the oneness of the universe, and the interpenetration of Spirit and Nature.

Cosmic force and Cawnpore leather
Hold my walking-boots together.
All the gnomes of Under-earth
Travailed at my tie-pin's birth.
Myriad dryads, nude and quick,
Brake for me my walking-stick,
Breathing still in every knot
Of the Javan bamboo-plot.
Brotherly, where'er I go,
Sheep regard my paletot,[1]
And the silkworm thrills to note
How his fathers warm my throat.
Atropos,[2] with iron shears,
Cut the cap that guards my ears.
Thus Alphonso's[3] mind can see
In each garment Deity.
And though loose the trousers' fit,
Nature's forces fashioned it.
Wherefore, steads it not to see
Tailor's work cri*ti*cally,

---

[1] *paletot*: cloak.
[2] *Atropos*: the Fate who in Greek mythology cut the thread of man's life.
[3] *Alphonso*: a reference to Emerson's poem 'Alphonso of Castille'.

But, with wide-embracing mind,
Gaze at them before, behind.
Since, beyond his needful clothes,
Something more each man-soul owes,
Brahma[4] shall endue thy shirt,
(With thy belt is Zeus engirt),
And the tread of either sole
Waken echoes round the Pole!

QUAERITUR[1]

Parody of Swinburne in *Echoes*, 1884. Collected in the Outward Bound, De
Luxe, Sussex, and Burwash Edns. with subheading '(Swinburne)'.

Dawn that disheartens the desolate dunes,
    Dulness of day as it bursts on the beach,
Sea-wind that shrillest the thinnest of tunes,
    What is the wisdom thy wailings would teach?
Far, far away, down the foam-frescoed reach,
    Where ravening rocks cleave the crest of the seas,
Sigheth the sound of thy sonorous speech,
    As grey gull and guillemot gather their fees;
    Taking toll of the beasts that are bred in the seas.

Foam-flakes fly farther than faint eyes can follow—
    Drop down the desolate dunes and are done;
Fleeter than foam-flowers flitteth the Swallow,
Sheer for the sweets of the South and the Sun.
What is thy tale, O thou treacherous Swallow?
    Sing me thy secret, Beloved of the Skies,
That I may gather my garments and follow—
    Flee on the path of thy pinions and rise
    Where strong storms cease and the weary wind dies.

Lo! I am bound with the chains of my sorrow;
    Swallow, swift Swallow, ah, wait for a while!
Stay but a moment—it may be to-morrow
    Chains shall be severed and sad souls shall smile!

---

[4] *Brahma*: the Creator, one of the manifestations of Brahm.

[1] *Quaeritur*: lit.: it is sought; hence yearning.

Only a moment—a mere minute's measure—
    How shall it hurt such a swift one as thou?
Pitiless Swallow, full flushed for thy pleasure,
    Canst thou not even one instant allow
    To weaker-winged wanderers? Wait for me now!

LONDON TOWN

Published in *Echoes*, 1884. Collected in the Outward Bound, De Luxe, Sussex,
and Burwash Edns.

There's no God in London,
    Weary, wicked London.
For, look you, I've lost my friend—
    Lost her in London.
My heart's best friend
    Is astray in London,
        Your terrible London!

You've miles of granite streets
    In stony London;
And millions toiling in London,
    Crowded London;
But I cannot find my friend,
    My poor lost friend,
For the tumult and traffic of London,
        Pitiless London!

It's cruel seeking in London,
    Boundless London,
For a face that'll never come—
    For the face of a friend,
The face of my lost, lost friend,
    Lost in London.
There's no God in London,
        Your terrible London!

HIMALAYAN

Parody of Joaquin Miller (see above, p. 162), published in *Echoes*, 1884. Collected in the Outward Bound, De Luxe, Sussex, and Burwash Edns. with sub-heading '(Joaquin Miller)'. The third stanza was used as a heading to the story 'At the End of the Passage' in *Life's Handicap*, and included in the Definitive Edition of Kipling's verse as a 'Chapter Heading' (p. 569).

Now the land is ringed with a circle of fire,
    Burnt with the fire and dead with drouth,
    And the bare, brown fields hold the heat of Hell—
Wherefore, I tell you, once and for all,
    Fly with the speed of a hot desire;
    Fly from the land that is parched and dead,
To Simla or Murree or Naini Tal,[1]
    With a limber *lunkah*[2] thrust in your mouth,
    And a *solah topee*[3] to guard your head,
    And a tat[4] beneath you can trust to *chel*.[5]

For the hills look down on the burnt plains under,
    And the great green mountains are good to see—
    Fair to behold and sweet to gain;
    They are capped with the snow and cooled with the rain,
Cooled with the tears of the wailing thunder.
Wherefore, I tell you, mount and ride,
    Till the spurs are red and the whip-hand tires,
    And the saddle is broken across the tree—
Till your spurs are red in your horse's side—
    Fly from the heat of our summer fires!

The sky is lead and our faces are red,
    And the winds of Hell are loosened and driven,
    And the gates of Hell are opened and riven,
    And the dust flies up in the face of Heaven,
And the clouds come down in a fiery sheet,
    Heavy to raise and hard to be borne.

[1] *Simla, Murree, Naini Tal*: well-known hill-stations in North India.
[2] *lunkah*: cheroot (Kipling, collected edns.).
[3] *solah topee*: pith helmet.
[4] *tat*: country-bred pony.
[5] *chel*: go (Kipling, collected edns.).

And the mind of man is turned from his meat—
   Turned from the trifles for which he has striven,
     Sick in his body, and heavy-hearted;
And his soul flies up like the dust in the street—
   Flies from his flesh and is gone and departed,
     As the blast that they blow on the cholera-horn.[6]

Wherefore, I say, while life remains,
   While the knees can grip and the right hand flog,
     Fly with the speed of a parted lover
     From the heated heavens that cloak and cover
The burning heat of the bare, brown plains.
   Flee to the mountains, once and for all—
To the calm, cool rains and the drifting fog,
     To the rains that cool and the clouds that hover
     O'er Simla, Murree, or Naini Tal!

THE MAID OF THE MEERSCHAUM

Parody of Swinburne, published in *Echoes*, 1884. Collected in the Outward
Bound, De Luxe, Sussex, and Burwash Edns. with subheading '(Swinburne)'.

Nude nymph, when from Neuberg's[1] I led her
   In velvet enshrined and encased,
When with rarest Virginia I fed her,
   And pampered each maidenly taste
On 'Old Judge' and 'Lone Jack' and brown 'Bird's-eye,'
   The best that a mortal might get—
Did she know how, from whiteness of curds, I
   Should turn her to jet?

She was blond and impassive and stately
   When first our acquaintance began,
When she smiled from the pipe-bowl sedately
   On the 'Stunt'[2] who was scarcely a man.

---

[6] *cholera-horn*: corruption of 'collery horn' (from the name given to a non-Aryan
people living east of Madura)—'a long brass horn of hideous sound often used at native
funerals' (*Hobson-Jobson*).

[1] *Neuberg's*: J. Neuberg, Meadows Street, Bombay—an emporium famous for cigars,
cheroots, etc.   [2] *Stunt*: Assistant (slang).

But *labuntur anni fugaces*,[3]
    And changed in due season were we,
For *she* wears the blackest of faces,
    And I'm a D.C.[4]

Unfailing the comfort she gave me
    In the days when I owned to a heart,
When the charmers that used to enslave me
    For Home or the Hills would depart.
She was Polly or Agnes or Kitty
    (Whoever *pro tem.*[5] was my flame),
And I found her most ready to pity,
    And—always the same.

At dawn, when the pig broke from cover,
    At noon, when the pleaders were met,
She clung to the lips of her lover
    As never live maiden did yet;
At the Bund,[6] when I waited the far light
    That brought me my mails o'er the main—
At night, when the tents, in the starlight,
    Showed white on the plain.

And now, though each finely cut feature
    Is flattened and polished away,
I hold her the loveliest creature
    That ever was fashioned from clay.
Let an epitaph thus, then, be wrought for
    Her tomb, when the smash shall arrive:
'Hic jacet[7] the life's love I bought for
    Rupees twenty-five.'

ESTUNT[1] THE GRIFF[2]

Parody of William Morris, published in *Echoes*, 1884. Collected in the Outward Bound, De Luxe, Sussex, and Burwash Edns. with subheading '(Morris)' or '(William Morris)'.

  [3] *labuntur anni fugaces*: the fleeting years slip away. (An adaptation of the opening lines of Horace, *Odes*, II. xiv.)

  [4] *D.C.*: Deputy Commissioner (Kipling, collected edns.).

  [5] *pro tem*: for the time being.

  [6] *Bund*: embankment.   [7] *Hic jacet*: here lies.

  [1] *Estunt*: native pronunciation of 'stunt' (i.e. Assistant).

  [2] *Griff or Griffin*: Anglo-Indian slang for a newcomer to India.

ARGUMENT: *Showing how a man of England, hearing from certain Easterlings of the glories of their land, sets sail to rule it.*

And so unto the End of Graves[3] came he,
Where nigh the staging, ready for the sea,
Oarless and sailless lay the galley's bulk,
Albeit smoke did issue from the hulk
And fell away, across the marshes dun,
Into the visage of the wan-white sun.
And seaward ran the river, cold and grey,
Bearing the brown-sailed Eastland boats away
'Twixt the low shore and shallow sandy spit.
Yet he, being sad, took little heed of it,
But straightly fled toward the misty beach,
And hailed in choked and swiftly spoken speech
A shallop, that for men's conveyance lay
Hard by the margin of that watery way.
Then many that were in like evil plight—
Sad folk, with drawn, dumb lips and faces white,
That writhed themselves into a hopeless smile—
Crowded the shallop, making feint the while
Of merriment and pleasure at that tide,
Though oft upon the laughers' lips there died
The jest, and in its place there came a sigh,
So that men gat but little good thereby,
And shivering, clad themselves about with furs.
Strange faces of the swarthy outlanders
Looked down upon the shallop as she threw
The sullen waters backward from her screw
And, running forward for some little space,
Stayed featly at the galley's mounting-place,
Where slowly these sad-facèd landsmen went
Crab-wise and evil-mouthed with discontent,
Holding to sodden rope and rusty chain
And bulwark that was wetted with the rain:
For 'neath their feet the black bows rose and fell,
Nor might a man walk steadfastly or well
Who had not hand upon a rail or rope;
And Estunt turned him landward, and wanhope

---

[3] *the End of Graves*: 'the burgh of Graves' in *Echoes*; i.e. Gravesend, off which the P. &
O. liners moored in the Thames, passengers being ferried out by tender.

Grew on his spirit as an evil mist,
Thinking of loving lips his lips had kissed
An hour since, and how those lips were sweet
An hour since, far off in Fenchurch Street.[4]
Then, with a deep-drawn breath most like a sigh,
He watched the empty shallop shoreward hie;
Then turned him round the driving rain to face,
And saw men heave the anchor from its place,
Whereat, when by the river-mouth, the ship
Began, amid the waters' strife, to dip.
His soul was heaved between his jaws that day,
And to the East the good ship took her way.

CAVALIERE SERVENTE[1]

Parody of Dante Gabriel Rossetti's poem 'Alas for me, who loved a falcon well'. Published in *Echoes*, 1884, with subheading 'A Lady laments the loss of her Lover under the similitude of a Lapdog.' Collected in the Outward Bound, De Luxe, Sussex, and Burwash Edns.

Alas for me, who loved my bow-wow[2] well!
    So well I loved him that methought his heart
    Would never from my beauty's rule depart,
And so, grown certain, grew insatiable.
Now hillward he has fled. I cannot tell
    Whether Mussoorie's[3] maids have fettered him,
    Or whether Tara Devi,[4] cloaked and dim,
Hears his devotions to another belle,
    And other lips that answer tenderly.
Ah me, my bow-wow! I had taught thee skill;
    With lore of ladies' hearts I dowered thee,
Whereon thou hast returned my favours ill,
    And, breaking from my woven chain, art free,
Armed, at my hands, with all the darts that kill.

---

[4] *Fenchurch Street*: railway terminus from which trains ran to Tilbury, opposite Gravesend.

---

[1] *Cavaliere Servente*: a cavalier in attendance on a married woman.
[2] *bow-wow*: Anglo-Indian slang for a lover or hanger-on. (Cf. 'poodle-faker'.)
[3] *Mussoorie*: a Himalayan hill-station.
[4] *Tara Devi*: a mountain near Simla.

THE BOAR OF THE YEAR [THE RIDE OF THE SCHOOLS]

Enclosed with letter of 10 August 1884 to Cormell Price (Library of Congress). Published under title 'The Ride of the Schools' in the *USCC*, no. 21, 30 October 1884, with signature 'N.W.P.'[1] Collected with minor revisions in the Outward Bound, De Luxe, Sussex, and Burwash Edns. (In the *USCC* the second and third stanzas were transposed.) The pigsticking activities of the Lahore and Mian Mir Tent Club were regularly reported in the *CMG*. There is no record of Kipling's having taken part in them, though he implies as much by a note in the *USCC*. In that version l. 2 of the third stanza ended 'and we marked Him for "thirty-three good" ', on which Kipling comments 'Thirty three inches at the Shoulder. On measurement he wasn't much more than two inches under our estimate, though, as I have said, he looked as big as a bullock.' In his letter to Cormell Price he says that 'a Crofts House boy took "first spear" off a 30 inch boar at one of our Tent club meetings—to my intense disgust and I have recorded the fact in verse of the Whyte Melville[2] order.'

In the shade of the trees by the lunch-tent the Old Haileyburian sat,—
A full fourteen-stone in the saddle, and the best of hard riders at
    that,—
And he shouted aloud as we passed him: 'I'll wait till the claret-cup
    cools.
There's a sounder[3] broke loose in the open! Ride, boys, for the love of
    your Schools!'

Bull-huge in the mists of the morn at the head of his sounder he
    stood—
Our quarry—and watched us awhile, and we thirsted aloud for his
    blood;
Then over the brawn of his shoulder looked back as we galloped more
    near—
Then fled for the far-away cover; and we followed the Boar of the
    Year!

There was Cheltenham perched on an Arab—so rich are these thrice-
    born[4] R.E.'s;[5]
And Rugby—his mount was a Waler;[6] and a couple of O.U.S.C.'s;[7]

---

[1] *N.W.P.*: North-West Provinces.

[2] *Whyte Melville*: George John Whyte-Melville (1821–78), soldier, fox-hunter, novelist, and poet, who wrote especially about sporting life.

[3] *sounder*: herd of pig (Kipling, *USCC*).

[4] *thrice-born*: very high caste (ironic). A Hindu was 'twice-born' when he had been initiated into his caste.   [5] *R.E.'s*: Royal Engineers.

[6] *Waler*: Australian horse (Kipling, *USCC*).

[7] *O.U.S.C.'s*: old boys of the United Services College.

And the rest of the field followed after. They were older and wiser,
    perhaps—
For we flew over tats[8] at the nullahs,[9] but they scrambled through by
    the gaps.

Away like a bird went the Arab—head and tail in the air, which is
    wrong:
For a pig-sticker worthy his salt looks down as he gallops along;
And the Arab was new to the business. What wonder that Cheltenham
    fell
In the grip of a buffalo-wallow, and sat down to rest him a spell?
Then Rugby shot forward the first of us three, for to reason it stands
That a coachy Artillery charger has the legs of a mere fourteen-hands.

But he jinked, and the Waler went wide; but the country-breeds
    wheeled and we flew
O'er the treacherous black-cotton furrows—spears up, riding all that
    we knew.
Now, a beast with a mouth like a brickbat can't turn to a turn of the
    wrist—
And the Waler took furlongs to turn in; and the rest of the run Rugby
    missed.
So we shed him and spread him and left him, after manifold jinkings
    and chouses,[10]
And the issue was narrowed to this: 'Ride, boys, for the love of your
    Houses!'

Dull-white on the slate of his hide ran a spear-scar from shoulder to
    chine:
And a pig that is marked by the spear is seldom the sweetest of swine.
When he stopped in the shade of the reh[11]-grass that fringes the
    river-bed's marge,
The lift of his rust-red back-bristles had warned us: Look out for the
    charge!

And we got it! Right-wheel, best foot foremost—with a quick sickle-
    sweep of the head
That missed the off-hock of my pony and tore through a tussock
    instead,

---

[8] *tats*: country-bred ponies.
[9] *nullahs*: beds of watercourses, dry all summer (Kipling, *USCC*); ravines (Kipling, collected edns.).   [10] *chouses*: tricks.   [11] *reh*: salty, barren soil.

He made for the next horse's belly—the jungle-pig's deadliest trick—
And he caught the spear full in the shoulder, and the bamboo broke
    short at the nick:
Then the prettiest mare in the Province let out with her ever-quick
    heels,
And the sound of the Ancient his death-grunt was drowned in her
    feminine squeals!

And which of the Houses got first-spear?[12] With sorrow unfeigned be
    it said,
I jabbed at his quarters and missed, and—I rode for the Black and the
    Red;[13]
And he for the Black and the Yellow, and his was the first and last
    spear
That ended the hunt by the river, and won you the Boar of the Year.

So we drank in the shade of the lunch-tent to the Barrack that stands
    by the Sea—
We drank to the health of its fellows—to all who have been and may
    be.
And Cheltenham joined in the chorus and Rugby re-echoed the cheer
On the day that we rode for the College, and won you the Boar of the
    Year!

INSCRIPTIONS IN PRESENTATION
COPIES OF *ECHOES*

(*a*) In copy sent to Mrs Tavenor Perry, with inscription 'The Mater / From Ruddy. / August 22nd 1884' (Rudyard Kipling Collection, George Arents Research Library, Syracuse University). Kipling's mother was not in fact in England at this time, but with Trix at the hill station of Dalhousie, where Kipling joined them in August. For this mode of address to Mrs Tavenor Perry (cf. pp. 205–6 above).

Who is the Public I write for?
Men 'neath an Indian sky
Cynical, seedy and dry,
Are these then the people I write for?
No, not I.

---

[12] *got first-spear*: drew first blood.

[13] *the Black and the Red*: the colours presumably of Pugh's House of which Kipling had been a member at Westward Ho!, and the Black and Yellow must be the colours of Crofts' House (see head-note).

How should they know whom I write for
   Papers that Praise me or scoff?—
   More than six thousand miles off
Lives the dear Public *I* write for,
     Under an English sky.

Will she look at the rhymes I have written?
   Send me a long letter back,
   Telling in plain white and black
All that she thinks of the rhymes I have written?
     Let her reply.

(*b*) In copy sent to Edith Macdonald, who thought the verse must have been
intended for Flo Garrard (Baldwin Papers, 2/40).

   Though the '*Englishman*' deride it,
   Though the captious '*Statesman*' chide it,
   Your dear judgment shall decide it
      Yours alone.
   For the good that in each line is,
   From the title page to Finis,
      Is your own.

(*c*) In copy sent to Flo Garrard, with inscription 'F.G. from R.K. Sept. 1884'
(reprinted here from L. L. Cornell, *Kipling in India*, London, 1966, p.69).

    I wrote you verses two years syne
    When I was yours and you were mine
    Will you accept these rhymes I send
    If I but call myself your friend
    And should my foolish songs discover
    Some traces of your girlhood's lover
    Forgive me—two long years apart
    Still leaves me[1] mistress of my heart.

(*d*) In copy sent to Evelyn Welford (see above, p. 179), with inscription 'Eve-
lyn from R.K. Sept. 1884' (facsimile in Kipling Collection, Dalhousie Univer-
sity Library). Cf. 'To You' [A Reminiscence], p. 70 above.

[1] *me: sic*; sc. you.

The memory of a maiden's sympathy,
    The memory of the talk between us twain—
A memory that will not go from me
        Until we meet again.

Now Love's first triumph turns to mockery,
    And Love's own homage alters to disdain—
God give you comfort, as you gave it me
        Until we meet again

I thank you—for I hold you very dear,
    I send you these rough first-fruits of my brain.
God keep you safe throughout the waning year
        Until we meet again

(*e*) In copy sent to Miss Winnard and the Miss Craiks (see above, p. 5), with inscription 'To / The Ladies of Warwick Gardens' and signatures 'Ruddy & Trix' (Berg Collection).

To our first critics send we these
    In memory of two years ago
    When, in the 'Children's Room' below,
We laboured at our poesies.

And often after supper time,
    Miss Georgie laid her work aside
    (Kindest of critics) to decide
The merits of some halting rhyme.

Then by the Syndicate of Three
    The red-hot verse was duly tried—
    This thing or that was set aside,
Or shaped to perfecter degree.

And far into the night we sate,—
    (With ink and thoughts that gaily flowed)
    Dashed from the lyric to the ode
Nor e'en an epic seemed too great.

The morn brought council—ever wise,
   And ever kind and freely given,
   As though the writers twain had striven
In verse that should outlive the skies.

And you shall find, if you will look,
   How much your words have stayed with us,
   When verse was written thus and thus
Among the pages of 'Our Book'

For even now, as then, we feel
   The rhyming brochure we submit
   Will reach, when you have studied it,
Our Court of Ultimate Appeal.

(*f*) In copy sent to Margaret Burne-Jones, Kipling's cousin (Kipling Collection, Dalhousie University Library). She was later to explain that 'Ruddy and I called each other Wop in our teens, and for long after. Some laughing talk and slip of the tongue produced the word. And then in Dickens's Letters we found one signed "The Sparkler of Albion", and so when Ruddy went to India, he became The Wop of Asia and I The Wop of Albion.' (*Readers' Guide, p. 5060.*) The page is headed with the inscription 'Margaret Burne-Jones / from Ruddy and Trix'.

The Wop of Asia—that lordly Beast—
Writes from His Lair in the burning East
To the Wop of Europe:—'Peace and Rest,
From Allah who giveth Them be in your Breast.

Behold it was writ on our Brows at Birth
We should sing in the East of the Sons of Earth:
(And how shall a Man, be He ne'er so wise
Escape that Sentence between his Eyes?)
Wherefore We sang, and the Songs We send
May serve to amuse You in far North-End[2]

[2] *Far North-End*: the Burne-Jones family lived at The Grange, North End Lane, Fulham.

Now the Gnat sings gaily at Eventide,
And the Bullfrog sings by the Waterside,
And the Wind of the Desert across the Sands
Singeth what no Man understands—
But whether We sing as These or worse,
Behold it is written here in our Verse.'

(g) In copy presented to the Common Room of the United Services College, with inscription 'To / "My very noble and approved good Masters" ', and cartoon of Kipling as a schoolboy handing in 'lines' done as a punishment (Kipling Collection, Dalhousie University Library). Published in the *USCC*, no. 41, 27 March 1889. Collected in the Outward Bound, De Luxe, Sussex, and Burwash Edns., with title 'Inscribed in a Presentation Copy of "Echoes" to the Common-Room', and subheading 'My very noble and approved good masters'.

Placetne, Domini?[3]—in far Lahore
   I wait your verdict, 'mid the palms and roses,
Much as I did those judgments writ of yore
   Upon my 'proses'.

Blue-pencil X's when constructions queer
   Ran riot down the inky, thumb-marked page;
And wondrous words that moved too oft, I fear,
   Your righteous rage.

Red-pencil marks when half a dozen rules,
   Smashed at one stroke, broke down your patience, too,
And left me, in the silence of the Schools,
   With 'lines to do'.

These were your judgments—well deserved enough
   By one who daily scorned his Latin Primer.
What is your verdict on the latest stuff
   Sent by this rhymer?

Placetne, Domini?—'neath India's sky
   I wait your answer, laymen and divines;
And, as of old, upon your table I
   'Show up my lines'.

    [3] *Placetne, Domini?*: Does it please you, Masters?

(*h*) Printed broadside headed *"ECHOES" BY TWO WRITERS* with subheading '(A.M. D.-D.[4] R.K., OCT. 1884)'. Obviously intended to accompany a presentation copy. The recipient 'A.M.' was A. Macdonald, assistant-editor of the *Pioneer*, who had been acting as editor of the *CMG* while Wheeler was on leave. (Kipling Collection, Dalhousie University Library.)

> Between the gum-pot and the shears,[5]
>   The awful emblems of my trade—
> First-fruits of two hot Indian years—
>   These rhymes were made.
>
> Will he who left with passing years
>   The weapons of his accolade,
> The gum-pot and the office shears
>   For labour staid
>
> At leaders on the inner leaf
>   Finance, War, Famine, Trade or Crimes,
> Past Master of my Craft in brief
>   Accept those rhymes?

LORD RIPON'S REVERIE

Published in *CMG*, 15 September 1884, with signature 'E.M.' Uncollected, but included in Scrapbook 1. Lord Ripon, whose credibility had been undermined by the prolonged controversy over the Ilbert Bill (see above, pp. 184 and 187) and the Government's eventual capitulation, resigned from his viceregal appointment before his five years were up. In a letter to Edith Macdonald, written on 17 September, Kipling commented with satisfaction on this 'parody of [Tennyson's] Locksley Hall, which . . . has disturbed the Pioneer who wanted to say something nasty about Lord Ripon's retirement but only came out with a ponderous leader no one read.' (Library of Congress.)

> I shall leave it in a little—leave it ere my term has run.
> Of the millions that I govern, who will wish me back? Not one.
> Curse the land and all within it. As of old, the papers scoff—
> Dreary columns of invective, read by stealth at Peterhoff.[1]

---

[4] D.D.: dono dedit (gave as a gift).
[5] *gum-pot and the shears*: scissors and paste. Cf. p. 396 below.

[1] *Peterhoff*: the viceregal residence at Simla prior to the building of the more ambitious Viceregal Lodge on Observatory Hill by Lord Dufferin, Ripon's successor.

Peterhoff, that through the pine-trees overlooks the Simla hills,
And the City of Calcutta where they rave against my Bills.
There I sketched my swart Utopia, nourishing the Babu's[2] pride
On the fairy-tales of Justice—with a leaning to his side.
Many a morn at *Chota Hazri*[3] have I read Britanni*cus*[4]
In the merry, merry spring-time when we'd Ilbert's child at 'nuss'.
There, at more than one *tamasha*,[5] have I heard the rowdies hiss,
And the whisper filled my pulses with a more than mule-like *vis*.[6]
So I pushed my measures forward, moulding words and facts like clay,
And I *think* I raised a dust storm in my 'cycle of Cathay'.[7]
Praise be blessed! *I* 'cut my lucky'[8]—too delighted to resign
All the God-forsaken *sub chiz*[9] to a clearer head than mine.
As the Country, so the Satrap. I was set to rule a land
Where the dullness of its people stayed my philanthropic hand.
And I held them, when they halted,' spite of legislative prog,
Something slower than a snail, a trifle denser than a log.
So *you*'ve got it now, dear Duffy.[10] Don't imagine East is West.
Come and rule it ('tis your duty); try to kick it from its rest.
It will answer:—'*Sahib jo hookum*'[11], and when pressed to clean its
        drains:—
'We don't want to play at *mehters*.[12] Give us crops and steady rains.'
(For my 'Lokil Sluff's'[13] a failure, and I'll whisper, *entre nous*,[14]
There's a limp, unhappy Rent Bill[15] that you've got to carry through.)
Yes! I see you old and soured (as you will be in a year),
Playing skittles, just as I did, with the rights men hold most dear.

---

  [2] *Babu*: English-speaking educated Bengali.
  [3] *Chota Hazri*: little breakfast, taken in the early morning.
  [4] *Britannicus*: pen-name of one of the most strident opponents of the Ilbert Bill in the columns of the *Englishman*.
  [5] *tamasha*: entertainment, big occasion.
  [6] *vis*: vigour, force.
  [7] '*cycle of Cathay*': quotation from 'Locksley Hall'.
  [8] *cut my lucky*: decamped (Cockney slang).
  [9] *sub chiz*: outfit.
  [10] *Duffy*: Lord Dufferin, the incoming Viceroy.
  [11] *Sahib jo hookum*: what the Sahib orders (sc. will be done).
  [12] *mehters*: sweepers.
  [13] *Lokil Sluff*: a derisive reference, mocking native pronunciation, to Ripon's policy of fostering political education through Local Self-Government, with elected Municipal Committees which had responsibility for sanitation among other things.
  [14] *entre nous*: between ourselves.
  [15] *Rent Bill*: a reference to the Bengal Tenancy Bill (see above, p. 231).

As for me. Well—read the *Mirror*.[16] Chatterjee[17] becomes my foe.
I am but a simple Viceroy. Where is it that I shall go?
Where there dwells no Secretariat—nor the myriad caller flocks—
Never comes the red *chaprassee* with the clinking office box.
Stay! I have it! O'er the ocean, man and climate both are kind.
I will fly to Studley Royal[19]—that shall soothe my wearied mind.
Clad in tweed of heather-mixture will I turn to rod and gun—
Catch the salmon with the gaff, and 'pot' the rabbits as they run.
I would wish you joy, dear Duffy, you've your work cut out, I know.
But the special train is waiting at Umballa,[20] and I go.

THE STORY OF TOMMY

Published in the *CMG*, 29 September 1884, with subtitle 'A Story without a
Moral' and signature 'E.M.' Uncollected, but included in Scrapbook 1. There
were frequent reports in the Anglo-Indian press of shooting incidents involv-
ing British soldiers. On 26 September, for example, the *CMG* carried a report
of an outrage at Mooltan, in which three soldiers of the Manchester Regiment
had wandered out with rifles and ammunition and shot at various natives, kill-
ing one: 'It seems that the men were mad with drink at the time. . . . ' Other
cases involved the murder of fellow-soldiers. In 1887, in an attempt to check
such incidents, the Commander-in-Chief (India) ended the practice of requir-
ing soldiers always to be in possession of ball cartridges.

This is the story of Tommy, aged twenty and drunk in his cot;
Marvellous drunk was Tommy, and the night was marvellous hot;
And the fever had held him all day, till Tommy was told by his 'chum'
That the worst of fevers would yield to a couple of 'goes' of rum.—
So he drank till the bare plain rocked 'neath his regulation boots,
And kept the liquor in place with a dozen *bazar* cheroots.

---

[16] *Mirror*: the *Indian Mirror* was the principal Indian (as opposed to Anglo-Indian)
English-language newspaper. The issue for 12 Sept. 1884 carried an article on 'The
Coming Viceroy' which expressed misgivings about the appointment of Lord Dufferin,
but also deep disappointment over Lord Ripon's inadequacies: 'Since the *fiasco* over the
Ilbert Bill, Lord Ripon seems to have sunk into perfect quiescence, showing little or no
sign of official vitality from his retreat at Simla.'

[17] *Chatterjee*: common Bengali name, used here for the whole genus of Babus.

[18] *red chaprassee*: red-uniformed office messenger.

[19] *Studley Royal*: Lord Ripon's Yorkshire seat.

[20] *Umballa*: the railhead for Simla in the 1880s.

Marvellous hot was the night (hot as they make 'em in June),
Merrily came the mosquito and cheered his soul with a tune,
Over the nose of Tommy softly the punkah swept,
But coolies are only human, and somehow that coolie slept.—
Sweating and swearing profusely, dizzy and dazed with his smoke—
Mad with the drink and the fever, Tommy, aged twenty, awoke.

'*Zor se kencho* you *soor!*'[1] Never an answering wrench,
Peacefully slumbered the coolie, '*Kencho* you *budzart, kench!*'[2]
Three times Tommy had called him; gaily he slumbered on.
In at the barrack-room windows softly the moonbeams shone.
Gleamed on a polished belt-jag—gleamed on a barrel brown,
Stuck in a rack, and inviting Tommy to take 'em down.

Only an arm's length away, swaddled in paper and twine,
Ten regulation 'pickets'[3]—if you subtract one, nine.
Tommy has settled that question as 'Little Jack Horner' of yore,
Clutches the smooth brown barrel, staggers across the floor.
Only a tug at the lever, only a jerk of the thumb,
Now for the last temptation. Query. Will Tommy succumb?

Mistily muses Tommy—finger laid on the trigger:—
'Ain't it a bloomin' lark to frighten a blasted nigger?
Now for to wake up the *soor!*' Never a sign from the coolie.
Tommy has shouldered the rifle—strives to present it duly.
Little night-owls are chuckling. Loudly the coolie respires,
Laughing aloud as he does so, Tommy, aged twenty, fires.

Merrily hiccupped Tommy when they locked him up in the dark.
Tried to explain to the Guard how it was only a 'lark'.
Didn't remember at trial aught that he did or said,
Wherefore was justly ordained to be 'hanged by the neck till dead'.
Waited a couple of weeks, while the *padris* came and harangued,
Then, in the Central Jail, Tommy, aged twenty, was hanged.

---

[1] *Zor se kencho you soor*: pull hard, you pig.
[2] *Kencho you budzart, kench*: pull, you blackguard, pull.
[3] *pickets*: cartridges, rifle bullets.

THE DESCENT OF THE PUNKAH

Published in the *CMG*, 10 October 1884, with signature 'E.M.'. This poem celebrates the end of the hot season, as 'The May Voyage' did its beginning. (See above, p. 217.)

Yes, lay the *jharun*[1] coats aside,
Likewise my snow-white trews,
And bring me forth my sober tweeds
More fit for Autumn use.
And ope for me the bottled beer
That once I used to shun.
Who dares to hint at 'liver' now
The summer days are done?

Within the deep verandah's shade
There lurks a form I know,
It is the punkah-pulling fiend
Hi! *Juldee chuti do!*[2]
Noor Ahmed! chase him from my sight,
That evil form and brown.
And recollect, ere I return,
Have all the *punkahs* down.

A necessary evil he,
And somnolent withal,
Who snored through fifty steamy nights,
Nor wakened at my call.
But stay—my soul is filled with peace,
E'en towards my Aryan neighbours—
Eight annas[3] shall be his beyond
The pittance of his labours.

Fresh faces at the Band appear—
Apace the station fills—
And half a hundred friends return
From half a hundred hills.

---

[1] *jharun*: a duster material with loud colourful checks, much affected for summer suits or jackets, especially by military men.

[2] *Juldee chuti do*: dismiss him quickly.

[3] *annas*: there were sixteen annas to a rupee.

Yea, straightway to the Club will I,
(Though worldly prudence frown)
And drink in driest Monopole[4]
My toast:—'The punkah's down.'

LAID LOW

Published in the *CMG*, 20 November 1884, with signature 'E.M.' Uncollected. The occasion was a spoofing letter to the Editor, headed 'Laid Low' and signed 'A. Radical', in the *CMG* for 17 November: 'SIR,—It is most pleasing to persons of my convictions to see how thoroughly the precepts of my school are being carried out in Lahore, at any rate, in small things as in great. There were, a few days ago, in the Lawrence Gardens, two old trees, situated in a position where their offensive antiquity was especially provoking—placed as they were, right in front of the Montgomery Hall. In this region of recent vegetation they could not fail to attract the attention of the most careless passers-by. I have reason to believe that they were much admired by that benighted section of the community who consider that antiquity is its claim to admiration in timber, and who maintain that it is far easier to cut a tree down than to grow one. I write to express my profound admiration of the exhibition of the spirit of the times which has been shown by the Lawrence Hall Department, in nipping this ridiculous doctrine in the bud, and proving its absurdity, by planting a fine bed of chrysanthemums in the place of the useless old trees. There is a Terminalea, on the left of the Bandstand which looks quite antique already, and the Eucalyptus by its side, with the two which form an arch over the road way, are also beginning to be offensive. Let them be laid low without much delay. Our principles are infallible, and can be applied to horticulture with quite as much benefit as to politics.'

He wandered by the L—wr—nce H—ll
        (An axe upon his shoulders laid)
Quoth He:—'I do not like at all
        An upstart tree that casts a shade;
Besides, it's bigger than the rest,
Which rankles in my Liberal breast.

It took some twenty years to grow.
        It is a *most* offensive tree;
And shall I pass without a blow,
        Arboreal aristocracy?
Jamais—nevaire! So down it comes.—
Bed out some neat chrysanthemums.'

---

[4] *Monopole*: champagne. Heidsieck Dry Monopole was a well-known brand.

The long weeks came; the long weeks passed;
    The neat chrysanthemums were bedded;
But some grew slow, while some grew fast,
    And some were long, and some short headed,
He watched their nodding ranks with tears,—
And fetched a *malli*[1] and the shears.

'*Dekho!*[2] Look here. *Ye burra hai,*[3]
    And this is *chota*[4] don't you see?
And Priest of that dread creed am I
    Which worships Uniformity.
Iswasti, baito[5] by the beds
And cut *kurro*[6] the *lumbar*[7] heads.'

The *malli* lopt for many years,
    (He came and viewed the work with pride)
Until, beneath official shears,
    Those unresponsive flowers died.
'We'll supersede the lot' He said,
'Make the whole place one *kunkur*[8]-bed.'

DEKHO![1] LOOK HERE!

This parody of Walt Whitman, with its prose preamble, was published in the *CMG*, 6 January 1885, as part of the regular feature 'A Week in Lahore', with signature 'Esau Mull'. Uncollected.

It is seldom that an American poet condescends to interest himself in so remote a land as India; and I am proportionately glad, therefore, to be able to record this week a great kindness on the part of no less distinguished a singer than Walt Whitman. Once upon a time, indeed, the bard was styled—not by his admirers—the 'Inspired Auctioneer of the Universe', but he has long outlived the reproach which the elaborate detail of his workmanship drew down upon him; and the swing of his half rhythmic, half declamatory, wholly musical lines has now drawn

---

[1] *malli*: gardener.   [2] *Dekho*: look, look here.   [3] *Ye burra hai*: this is big.
[4] *chota*: small.   [5] *Iswasti, baito*: for this reason, sit.
[6] *cut kurro*: do a cutting (caricaturing ignorant attempts at Hindustani).
[7] *lumbar*: tall.   [8] *kunkur*: gravel.

---

[1] *Dekho*: see n.2 above.

round him a delighted and admiring school of followers. What the great poet's views of an Indian New Year are may be seen from the following reply to a modest request for 'something seasonable':—

'Dekho! Look here!
From the pines of the Alleghannies I, Walt Whitman—colossal, pyramidal, immense—send salutation.
I project myself into your personality—I become an integral part of you.
I am the Junior Civilian horribly *dikked*[2] by the Superior Being, and squabbling with a tactless, factless Municipal Committee;[3] and I too pray for a happy new year.
I am also the Superior Being, impassive, and waltzing on the toes of all within reach. I too pray, without prejudice, for a happy new year.
I am the European loafer, drunk in the bazaar on country spirits, with blue lips and a green rat crawling down my neck. I too, out of the gutter pray for a happy new year.
I am the gay, the joyous subaltern, with six ponies in my stables and a shroff[4] in the background. And I too pray for a happy new year.
I am the "joy of wild asses"[5] with my husband absent in the Soudan[6] and a ten-strong following at my high silk heels. And I too pray for a happy new year.
I am in Sirsa, Jhang or Montgomery,[7] separated from Dicky, Emmy or Baby, living in a tent with my husband who is seedy and overworked. I read the smudgy, round-hand home-letters, and I too pray for a happy new year.
Oh! Civilian, Superior Being, Loafer, Subaltern, Grass-Widow and Grass-Mother of many conflicting domesticities, I salute you.
In the name of our great ruler Humanity I too wish you all individually and collectively, somehow or any how—a Happy New Year.'

---

[2] *dikked*: troubled.
[3] *Municipal Committee*: a committee elected under Lord Ripon's Local Self Government schemes (see above, p 256).　　　　[4] *shroff*: money-lender.
[5] *joy of wild asses*: a married woman attractive to predatory males. See Job 24: 5: 'Behold, as wild asses in the desert go they forth to their work; rising betimes for a prey', and Jer. 2: 24: 'A wild ass used to the wilderness, that snuffeth up the wind at her pleasure, in her occasion who can turn her away? all they that seek her will not weary themselves; in her month they shall find her.'
[6] *absent in the Soudan*: units from the Indian Army were serving in the campaign to relieve Gordon at Khartoum.　　　　[7] *Sirsa, Jhang, Montgomery*: districts in the Punjab.

ON A RECENT MEMORIAL

Parody of Browning's 'A Toccata of Galuppi's', published in the *Englishman*, 9 January 1885, with subtitle 'An Unofficial Reply' and signature 'E.M.' Uncollected, but included in Scrapbook 1. The occasion was an item reported in the *CMG*, 31 December 1884: 'The Indian Association,[1] in their recently presented Address to Lord Dufferin, complain that "their countrymen find themselves practically excluded from the commissioned ranks of the Army, and from the privilege of serving as Volunteers. . . . " Why Bengal, of all peoples in the land, should raise the cry, it is hard to conceive; for there is but little affinity between the spoiled children of the Government and military employ. But an "invidious race distinction" was a safe find under our late lamented Viceroy's[2] regime; and the Association naturally expected that Lord Ripon's successor would be equally ready to right imaginary wrongs.' Kipling's diary entry for 6 January 1885 includes the item 'Sent Englishman set of verses on the Indian Associations memorial.' (Houghton Library, Harvard University.)

Verbum sap.[3]— Oh, wise Bengalis, it is very sad to find
We cannot mistake your meaning; it would prove us worse than blind,
So forgive us if our answer be unwelcome or unkind.

Truth, that nasty, nude old beldame, lives (thank Heaven)
        underground,
But alas! upon occasion speaks with no uncertain sound.—
Though your ring–fence be a large one, yet the iron runs all round.

You may bush it up with laurels—academic if you please,
Hide it neath the brick and mortar of a hundred colleges,
In the centre (do *we* stop you?) print sedition at your ease.

Strip the laurels, raze the buildings? more's the pity. They were fair,
(Served to shield your budding fancies from the nipping outer air)
Rises Private Thomas Atkins to attention,—'As you were.'[4]

---

[1] *Indian Association*: founded in 1876 to help express the aspirations of Indians in politics and government. Its plea for Indians to be allowed to enlist in Volunteer Corps was indeed made largely by the educated and unmilitary: for some it was simply a stick to beat the Government with; for others it symbolized an important claim to trust and recognition.   [2] *our late lamented Viceroy*: Lord Ripon.

[3] *Verbum sap.*: a word to the wise.

[4] *As you were*: a parade-ground word of command.

For we love not to obtrude him. See! the fence is lost to view,
Greener grow the verdant laurels; rise the colleges anew,
But the laurels men call martial are not meant for such as you.

'Tis a brutal truth and ancient—but Time's verdict on your race—
Be content with mere sedition; rise to high judicial place;
Point to 'galling race distinctions' with your smooth Bengali grace.

Yet forget not, Holy Russia would have hanged you for one word
Of the deftly put Memorial lately printed and preferred—
Will you pardon then our laughter when we call the thing—absurd?

L—D D–FF–R—N'S CLÔTURE[1]

Published in the *CMG*, 6 March 1885, with heading: ' "The debate on the Bengal Tenancy Bill was continued yesterday. During the debate the Viceroy made a protest against written speeches and thought that the members would do better to trust to their natural powers of eloquence." *Vide* today's telegram.' No signature. Uncollected, but included in Scrapbook 2. This bill had been under discussion for some years (see above, pp. 231 and 256) and had now reached the stage of being debated at length in the Viceroy's Legislative Council. The *CMG*'s Telegraphic Intelligence in the issue of 6 March contains the item quoted here, which is dated 'Calcutta, March 5', and which continues 'The Maharaja of Durbungah withdrew a large number of the amendments standing in his name. The amendments standing on the agenda paper were then proceeded with, as far as Section 22; and with one or two exceptions all were thrown out. The Council then adjourned until today.' Kipling's diary for 5 March records the fact that the poem was written by noon on a telegram received at 10.40 a.m.

> 'Oh drop your notes' the Viceroy said,
>   'Let be the script and scrawl;
> No longer shall debates be read
>   In Legislative Hall.

---

[1] *Clôture*: technical term for the closing of a debate in the French Assembly by the will of a majority; applied to mechanism for closing debate in the House of Commons when this was introduced in 1882.

By unassisted verbal skill
Into the Act shall bud the Bill.'

The fiat passed. The notes were dropped;
   The script was laid aside.
Incontinent the speakers stopped,
   The long discussion died.
D–rb–ngha drooped, and, so 'tis sung,
E'en fluent Ilbert[2] held his tongue.

With 'hems' and 'haws' and 'ahs' and 'ohs',
   And 'wells' and 'buts' and 'thens'
The torrent trickled to its close;
   The stenographic pens
Ceased from their penning—ceased no less
Reports throughout the Indian Press.

The Senior Member winked one eye,
   In Legislative style;
And o'er his visage crept, forebye,
   A Legislative smile:—
'Habent'[3], he murmured. 'Oh my friends
Methinks the Rent Bill struggle ends.'

And so it did. With break and pause,
   With gasp and groan and snort,
They shovelled off each weighty clause,
   (Mnemonics weren't their forte).
The ghost was laid. The Members wept;
And like a child our V–c–r–y slept.

'AS ONE WHO THROWS EARTH'S GOLD AWAY IN SCORN '

Holograph version dated 'Simla—June 2nd, 1885' and signed 'Rudyard Kipling'. Original in possession of Miss M. E. Macdonald; photocopy in Baldwin Papers, 2/2.

  [2] *Ilbert*: the Legislative Member of Council: see above, p. 184.
  [3] *Habent*: lit.: they have it. The singular form 'habet' was used when a gladiator received a fatal blow in the arena.

As one who throws Earth's gold away in scorn,
    Holding Tomorrow shall refill his purse,
So he who spurns his brain's light offspring, born
    In prose or verse.

Behold the night is certain when our hand
    Shall fail from labour and our eye from sight.—
Thrice mad who has no treasure at command
    Against that night.

Wherefore, while each new day brings some new thought
    And Life's chain sparkles, golden link by link
Write quickly; good or evil, all is fraught
    More deeply than you think.

AFTER THE FEVER
OR
NATURAL THEOLOGY[1] IN A DOOLIE[2]

This imitation of Browning was published in the *Pioneer*, 22 June 1885, with
signature 'R.K.', and reprinted in the *Pioneer Mail*, 28 June. The text here is
from a revised and corrected version preserved in Scrapbook 2, but its source
has not been located. Uncollected. (In the *Pioneer* and *Pioneer Mail* the
speaker's name is given as 'Browne', not 'Jones'.)

JONES, B.C.S.,[3] *soliloquises*:

'Let us begin[4] and carry up this corpse,
Singing together.' So their song to me
Sounds all the day long, racking, restless climb
Past cactus hedge and scrub-oak of the down,
And here at noon the wind-swept mountain path,
And rock and pine a thousand feet below.
Out of the jaws of Death they tell me. Lost
So nearly that they thought me dead indeed
Only two days ago. Now Lazarus,

---

[1] *Natural Theology*: theology based on the facts provided by nature and experience,
without the benefit of revelation. ('Natural Theology on an Island' is the subtitle of
Browning's 'Caliban upon Setebos'.)   [2] *Doolie*: covered litter.

[3] *B.C.S.*: Bengal Civil Service.

[4] *'Let us begin'* . . . : the opening of Browning's poem 'A Grammarian's Funeral'.

Uncertain 'mid his fellow-ghosts, who hears
The 'Rise! come forth!' And wonders:—'Am I called?'
Aye. *Am* I called? The call is faint at least.
The wind across the snows comes to my cheek
And murmurs some half fragment of it—'Rise!
Stand up! be healed!' Who knows I hear aright?
Another fancy of the fever left
To mock me. It may be so. After all
What if I found my answer otherwise
Six miles ahead? Crawled to the naked ridge,
And so met God there, just in front the snows?
Met God there—That's another word for Death.
Three weeks ago, with all my life alight
And blazing into work, thought, deed and fact,
I should have shuddered at it. Edith's hand
Behind my pillow; my report half done;
The bay mare's whinny in the stable; Smith
Who hates me as I hate him (so we love
In some inverted fashion) would have held
Me back to life, half mad with fear at Death.
And now! Why Death's upon me, so they said—
My one-half chance hill breezes. Not one hope
Or fear to play with. Edith, Smith, the rest,—
Reports, Love, horseflesh, work, position, pay—
All shadows. I'm the only flesh and blood
This side the grave—and I'm more ghost than flesh.
No credit then for coolness. Life or Death!
A hair may turn the balance. Just one shower,
(That cloud may bring it) ten short minutes' rain
(They said a chill would kill me). Then Smith's step,[5]
And something longer than a step for me. . . .
Whether the black cloud bursts or quits the pine
To drench the *bajra*[6] northward I'm content.
I *cannot* care. The flesh must back the brain
To make it cling to life so. Up or down
The beam goes, and I watch it 'neath my wraps—
Life, Death, the Judgment, and the rest of it
All swaddled in the cloud there.   God is good.

[5] *step*: promotion.   [6] *bajra*: millet.

I couldn't face Death living. Flesh and blood
Would back the brain, and I should tremble. Death
Is good. He takes me gently, by degrees,
Not the full cess at once. Remission, rest,
The half crop ere the whole one. Power first
To act, to write, to think, to hope, to pray;
And then the aftermath. But that's unfair.
Men aren't let off for ever. Brain and heart
Come back again, or where's the world to be?
And after Judgment? What's my creed again?
I'm a Materialist and, after Death
I judge myself in space, alone, unchecked—
And yet the record past my own control;
And self-condemned pass on to my new life
Higher or lower as the record runs.
That isn't Darwin's notion. Buddhism,
Mixed up with half-a-dozen old beliefs,
And love for Edith. . . . Here's my thought returned
And Terror with it. Face to face with Death!
Those six black swine to help me through the gate,
'I judge myself alone, unchecked.' No help!—
'And yet the record past my own control'—
'Higher or lower as the record runs.'
My God! I *knew* men couldn't die like beasts!
Thought, Memory and Reason all at once;
And no one near me. Edith's firm white hand
Might ease me some few inches down the pit,
As Hers will push me deeper, and Her eyes
Shrivel me quicker than the flames below.
Hers—No, not Edith's. Edith would have helped—
Saved may be . . . Six black swine! . . . Men don't die drugged!

*   *   *   *   *

'*Siste viator*'.[7] Here's the doolie still
And no one spoke; at least in Latin. Death
Gone from me when he had me by the throat—
The black cloud northward. It was Life, then, back
More terrible than Death. . . . Thought, Memory
And Reason. . . . and the pains of Hell. . . . but Life—
Life after all. No God in front the snows.
My case postponed! God's law is much like ours.

---

[7] *Siste viator*: stop, traveller (a common inscription on Roman tombstones.)

THE LETTER OF HALIM THE POTTER

Holograph verse letter from Kipling to his father for the latter's birthday on 6
July (KP 11/6). Probably 1885, though 1888 has been suggested as another
possibility. Full title: 'The Letter of Halim the Potter to Yusuf His Father and
Master Craftsman in the walled city of Lahore; written on the fifth day of the
month of the Scales.'[1]

> Halim the Potter from the rainy Hills,—
> Under the diamond coronetted pines,
> The dun, rain sodden clouds that jewel them,
> The snake plants hooded tongued and venemous
> The briers and the orchids—sends his word.
> His Greeting to the Father whence he gained
> First, Life and then such Knowledge of The Craft
> As is his portion.
>   For a double gift
> A double greeting. Though alas! the Reed[2]
> But bears the message coldly, and no gift
> From Halim's hand to yours accompanies.
> Yet he, being set about with many thoughts
> Because the Day is lucky (So they hold
> Who say Man's Day of Trouble is a thing
> Not to be disregarded lightly, kept
> Year after year, whenas the Day returns,
> With such observance as the Life demands—
> To the great Life great Joy, the Little less.
> The work alone is worthy—not the Day
> Or Birth or Death or—Softly. Who am I
> Halim, to hold a fancy thus?) He searched
> For gifts but after saw the thought was vain
> Knowing fit weapons of The Craft were thine,
> And the Sage Councillor that burns and dies
> Within the *chillam*[3] Phoenix fashion, born
> Anew in greater labours fresher power
> Than the unholpen brain could hope for—this
> Was also thine; and so he held his hand
> Knowing there were no other gifts. He writes
> Instead his letter to the man who made

---

[1] *the Scales*: Libra, the 7th sign of the Zodiac, which Kipling seems to associate with
the 7th month, though this runs counter to astrological theory.
[2] *the Reed*: the pen.   [3] *chillam*: hookah.

Him and his knowledge—so the gift returns
In some poor fashion to the giver.
                                                    First
Behind the *Purdah*[4] (since I write to thee
Thee only, and the Munshi[5] at my side,
My thumb and two first fingers, cannot blab)
The Mother and the Child—which last e'en now
Toils at her fancies in the lower room,
Weaving a mighty empire out of ghosts[6]
As I red armies from the coarser clay—
Are fain of Thee because they know and feel
How daily upwards runs the silver thread[7]
Up from the silver pellet—which the men
Beyond the seas have impiously set
As record of Gehenna's[8] torments. Ay,
The Prophet (blessed in Allah) writes;—'Take heed
Because ye are the Chosen, yet all skill
Concentres not in Islam. Swine and dogs
Have knowledge of the weather more than ye—
Learn from them, praising Allah.' So they learn
Your torment, written in the accursed tongue
That babbles daily and is past my power
To riddle—for my work is otherwise—
Than Munshis babes and Babus. So they learn
Your daily torment and would have you here,
Save that the old distemper of the Hills
When clouds are lowest, holds The Mother fast
A little space. I doubt not that the drugs
Of them who know not Islam (—Read again
The Prophet's sentence, though thou knewest it
Before I knew the platter from the cup—)
Will heal her shortly—all three sides are well
Of our small square but that they lack the fourth.
I mostly O my Father! for what e'er
The Women wish, my loss is most of all
Seeing that it is double and I lose
My Master Craftsman with my Father. Look!

---

[4] *Purdah*: curtain screening women from the sight of strangers.
[5] *Munshi*: language teacher or, as here, clerk.
[6] *ghosts*: perhaps a reference to Trix's story 'The Haunted Cabin', published in *Quartette* in Dec. 1885.   [7] *the silver thread*: mercury in a thermometer.
[8] *Gehenna*: hell.

Thou knowest (no man better) how the clay
Bends inward on the wheel, bends breaks and falls
If my hand run the pitcher lip too high.
Yea, one nail's breadth beyond the guide—Thou knowest
How the raw clay—removed the potter's hand—
Falls inward also—whether formed or not
(I can but choose the similes I know)
(And know thou seest the meaning ere I write.)
As with the clay so with the potter—Close
Too close the likeness—thus my young mind thinks—
Two months ago I held my skill was mine
Admitting hastily a certain hint
A council here and there. Perhaps one touch
On spout or belly ere we fired the kiln
Thy hint, *thy* council and *thy* Touch. No more
Than just so much as made (Why blink the truth?)
The bad thing good; the drunken pitcher straight
A thing desirable in the front of the stall.
My workmanship thou saidst—and I believed
It was so small a touch, so slight a word.
I threw the wet clay—marred it. *Now* I see!
The hand went and the clay thereafter fell
Uncouthly. These two months[9] have shown the Truth.
It may be that thou knewest it before.
I learnt it lately, toiling at a vase
To do me credit. For myself alone.
(Was this the cause of failure . . . It may be)
Because I loved the labour and no gold
Should draw it from me. 'Twas a noble vase.
(I recollect *you* gave the first design
A clean and noble fashioning thereto)
The thing has failed—not wholly failed. I learnt
Much that I should have learnt before alas!
The fair lip sprouted into useless length
(Who said I needed mud–banks for *chirags*?)[10]
And all the belly blistered 'neath my hands
With shapes of *Afrits, Shaitans, Djinns* and *ghouls*[11]
'I could not help it' so I told myself
And knew I lied—Thou knowest more than I.

---

[9] *two months*: in July 1885 Kipling had been at Simla for approximately this period.
[10] *chirags*: lamps made of clay.
[11] *Afrits* . . . : varieties of demons in Islamic mythology.

But the distorted vessel still remains
Against your coming. Does not Yusuf say
'Even the marred and unclean clay keep thou
As record of past error. Hand and brain
May both take warning?' I have kept my work
For judgment. I can only see the faults
The Remedy is hidden. It may be
My pitcher lip exceeds the nail's breadth. This
At least is certain that the raw clay bends
Into ignoble shapes without thy hand
The vase has taught me. O! make haste and come,
I can but mar the good, grey, clay till then
And know I mar it, and would mar it more
But for past councils.
Halim Yusuf's Son.

THE VISION OF HAMID ALI

Published in the *Calcutta Review* for October 1885 (vol. lxxxi, no. clxii, pp. 419–20). By permission of the BL. Signed 'Rudyard Kipling'. Collected in the Sussex and Burwash Edns. Mentioned in a letter to Edith Macdonald, 30 July 1885, where he says that 'the *Calcutta Review* has written very sweetly about a poem of mine—in blank verse—which appears in the August number' (Library of Congress).

This came to him by night—the *ganja*[1] burnt
To powder, and the City sunk in sleep.

Azizun of the Dauri Bagh; the Pearl;
And Hamid Ali of the Delhi Gate
Were present, when the Muezzin called to prayer
At midnight from the Mosque of Wuzeer Khan,[2]
Drinking the *ganja*, drowsy with its fumes
Above the dying *chillam*.[3] I, the Scribe,
Was with them and the words I write are true;
(Albeit Hamid spoke against the Twelve,[4]
And Islam and the Prophet. God is judge
Whether the *ganja* moved him or his soul.)

[1] *ganja*: hemp dried for smoking (Sussex Edn.)
[2] *Mosque of Wuzeer* [or Vazír] *Khan*: one of the sights of Lahore, near the Delhi Gate.
[3] *chillam*: hookah (Sussex Edn.)
[4] *the Twelve*: the twelve Imams (religious leaders) of the Shia branch of Islam.

Azizun's anklets tinkled when she turned
In slumber; and the Pearl of Courtezans
Laughed softly at some fancy of her brain,
Born of the *ganja*. Hamid Ali lay
As dead upon the cushions by the door
For half a watch; and then he cried to me:—
'The thing is hopeless and an idle dream!
I saw it even now. O Moulvie![5] write!'
(Before the Perfect Flower had dulled our brains,
Azizun; Hamid Ali; I; the Pearl,
Spoke of the Prophet and the other, Christ
Our rulers worship; and men's minds in Roum;[6]
And whether Islam shall arise again
And drive the Christ across the Western sea
As people hold shall be in two more years,
When from the North the Armies of the North
Pour like the Indus and our rulers fly,
And Islam and the Sword make all things clean.)
     I wrote—my brain was heavy with the drug:—
'The Mosque has fallen. Hamid Ali saw
The *khashi*[7] on the gateways peel and flake;
The domes sink inwards and the minarets
Break at the base and crumble like the dust
The wind uplifts in Sind and leaves again
No bigger than an ant-hill. It has fallen.
I, Hamid, saw and knew the meaning. Turn,
Turn ye to slumber. Fold your hands and sleep.
Ours was an idle dream.' The Pearl laughed low:—
'*I* dreamt no dream but ye. My breasts are real;
My lips; my love, O Hamid! Nothing else,
Nor Islam nor the Prophet nor the Twelve.
Turn ye to slumber. Fold your hands and sleep.'
     And Hamid answered:—'Fold your hands and sleep
Not yet till ye have heard the vision. Write!'
(I wrote and marvelled, as the Muezzin called.)
'Nor Islam, nor the Prophet, nor the Twelve,
Nor Christ, nor Buddha, nor the other gods
Avail us. Lo! The Mosque fell into dust;
And with it fell the Prophet and the Twelve;

---

[5] *Moulvie*: title given to a learned man.
[6] *Roum*: originally Rome, meaning the Eastern Roman Empire centered on Byzantium: hence Christendom.   [7] *khashi*: fresco (Sussex Edn.).

The Banner[8] and the Crescent[9] rang below,
And with them fell the Cross, the Wheel,[10] the Flowers;[11]
Parvati[12] broken at the waist, and He,
The calm-eyed Buddha, handless, crushed and maimed.
The Priests with these. I, Hamid, saw them fall
And knew our dream was hopeless. Never more
The Banner or the Cross will lift themselves.
(Write, Moulvie) Underneath the Seven Stars,
Blood red and golden, to the dark plain's verge
There swept the sharp edge of a monstrous sword
That lit the firmament as does the sun;
And blood was falling from the haft and point;
And where it fell the Mosques of all the lands
Fell also, burnt with fire; and the Priests
Cried to the Heavens that their gods were dead,
And none remained to feed their ministers
Or tend the altars; and the great sword fell
Above Mahomet and the other men,
And broke into ten thousand drops of blood
Before it faded and I woke to you,
Azizun and the Pearl. I, Hamid, saw
And read the meaning of the vision!'
　　　　　　　　　　　　　　　　Soft
The anklets tinkled as Azizun woke.
Then Hamid hollow-eyed rose from the couch
And staggered doorward—but the Pearl withstood
And only laughed:—'Oh, Hamid, will you take
Me for your Prophet if I read the dream?'
And Hamid answered:—'Surely. It is writ'—
Whereat the Pearl laughed louder:—'Is it writ?
Who wrote, and wherefore? Let the vision go,
For I at least am real.'
　　　　　　　　　　　　　Then the dawn . . .
Swept like a sea into the gully. I,
Still heavy with the *ganja*, held my peace
And marvelled that a man should so blaspheme. . . .
God grant it was the *ganja*. Otherwise
Hamid is lost for ever, with the Pearl.

[8] *The Banner*: Shiite banner carried in procession in the Mohurrum festival.
[9] *the Crescent*: emblematic of Islam as the Cross of Christianity.
[10] *the Wheel*: the Buddhist emblem of the Wheel of Life.
[11] *the Flowers*: probably flowers used in Hindu temple ceremonies.
[12] *Parvati*: goddess of beauty, wife of Siva the Destroyer in Hindu mythology.

THE TALE OF TWO SUITS

Published in the *Pioneer*, 15 August 1885, under general heading of 'BUNGA-LOW BALLADS': the first of this series, which Kipling published anonymously. Reprinted in the *Pioneer Mail*, 27 August. No signature. Uncollected, but included in Scrapbook 2.

These are the ballads, tender and meek,
Sung by a bard with his tongue in his cheek.
Sung by a poet, well a day!
Who doesn't believe a word of his lay.

Rattleton Traplegh was pretty and pink;
Rattleton Traplegh was (only think!)
Sadly addicted to flirting with
Mrs. Saphira Wallabie Smith.

List to a legend wholly untrue!
Mrs. Saphira's men wore blue
Coats with a chevron of crimson-lake,
Just where one feels a stomach-ache.

(They pulled her *rickshaw* in storm or shine
When she went round J—ko[1] or went to dine.)
Was it an accident? Was it a game?
Mrs. Y. Canterby's men wore the same!

Mrs. Y. Canterby wasn't a *belle*—
Mrs. Y. Canterby's age was—well
More than thirty! and Mrs. Y.C.
Was 'down' like a vulture on Rattleton T.

(Needless to state what you all must guess,—
Mrs. Y. Canterby *loathed* Mrs. S.)

List to a legend wholly untrue!
The clock in the steeple was striking two;
The dance was ended, and, filled with hope,
Rattleton rattled down B————e[2] slope.

---

[1] *J—ko*: Jakko, a mountain at Simla, encircled by a road which made a favourite evening ride.

[2] *B————e*: Boileaugunge, the western area of Simla.

Blue were the coats by the *rickshaw* shaft;
Red were the chevrons fore and aft.
Closed was the hood; but, nevertheless,
Under the hood sat Saphira S.

So thought Traplegh. Her voice was gruff.
He never noticed, but whispered stuff
To the hooded *rickshaw* he 'hadn't orter.'
(Rattleton's drink was *never* water.)

Rattleton Traplegh's tongue was stilled;
Rattleton Traplegh's blood was chilled
(Fill the *hiatus* yourself. Not I.)
When the lamplight showed Mrs. Canterby.

Was there a 'ruction'? Who can say?
Rattleton Traplegh bolted away
To a place in the plains (which are rather warm)
Left Mrs. Smith in the thick of the storm.

Now for the moral. Never walk
By night with a *rickshaw*, and never talk
In a way you shouldn't. At least, take care
To look in the *rickshaw* and *see who's there.*

A TALE OF YESTERDAY'S TEN THOUSAND YEARS

Published in the *Pioneer*, 27 August 1885, under general heading of 'BUNGA-LOW BALLADS'. Reprinted in the *Pioneer Mail*, 30 August. No signature. Uncollected, but included in Scrapbook 2.

Oh! come along ye tuneful 'spins',[1] Melpomene & Co.,[2]
And help to twang this poet's lyre and draw his long, long bow,
While he retails a 'corker' of ten thousand years ago!

Ten times ten weary centuries ago
(The world runs round in circles) from below
We came to Simla. Same old game you know!

[1] *spins*: Anglo-Indian slang for unmarried women (spinsters).
[2] *Melpomene & Co.*: the Muses.

And I was I, and You were You, and They
Were They, and We were We, and pay was pay;
And Hearts were trumps, as at the present day.

Ten times ten wicked centuries gone by
One Hakim[3] Khan, astrologer, nati-
vity, and fortune-teller, came to my

Hotel with leaden dice; and broke my peace
With prophecies of Marriage and Decease,
And Wealth and Wisdom—all for five rupees.

Quoth he:—'Four months from now ('twas April then)
Oh *Sahib*! esteem yourself most blessed of men,
At Goldsteen's[4] *khotee*[5] when the clock strikes ten.

When'—here he paused, and murmured,—'Who am I?
Oh Sahib! to force the hand of Destiny?
Look for the maiden with the azure tie.'

I answered:—'Hakim, this is fraud confest:
I know no maiden epicenely dressed.
Fly Hakim'—and he fled . . . For it was best.

Three months rolled on—ten thousand years ago—
I loved (how passionately none can know)
And went to 'Goldsteen's' when the moon was low.

In the verandah, as the clock struck ten
(The dance had barely started), blessed of men
Was I, oh worthy Hakim! Edith Venn

(That was her name ten times ten centuries
Ago) bare on her breast, to my surprise,
A three-inch riband azure as her eyes.

---

[3] *Hakim*: physician.
[4] *Goldsteen*: Herr Felix von Goldstein was a professional musician and Bandmaster to the Viceroy. In 1869 he purchased 'Benmore', a well-known Simla residence, added a ballroom and skating rink, and made it for years a centre of social activity in Simla. When a new Town Hall was built in 1885, incorporating a ballroom and other facilities, Goldstein sold 'Benmore' to the Punjab Government for use as office accommodation. (See Kipling's poem 'The Plea of the Simla Dancers' in *Departmental Ditties*.)
[5] *khotee*: house, building.

We married. Then I asked her—'Was it fate?'
She told me Hakim Khan had bade her wait
In April for a man with sword-scarred pate.

'Wear then this riband.' On her breast she wore—
We met at 'Goldsteen's'—married—for a score
Of years she lived. Then died. I lived ten more.

Died also. Died the Hakim. Died all men.
The world spun round. My old wife, Edith Venn,
I wait at 'Goldsteen's' when the clock strikes ten

Tonight . . . the riband on her breast . . . and she
May haply, at that hour remember me . . .
At all events, I'll 'pop'[6] to her and see.

A LOST LEADER

Published in the *CMG*, 31 August 1885, with heading: 'London, 25th. The Marquis of Ripon, in a speech made at Bolton yesterday, appealed to the people of India to vindicate his administration, &c.—*Reuter's Telegram.*' The quotation is from an item of Telegraphic Intelligence in the *CMG* for 26 August. The occasion of Ripon's appeal was a severe attack on his record as Viceroy by Lord Randolph Churchill, when presenting the Indian Budget to the House of Commons. No signature. Uncollected, but included in Scrapbooks 1 and 2.

George Samuel, Marquis of Ripon, is sadly in need of a *chit*.[1]
Chatterjees, Bannerjees, Mookerjees,[2] rise ye and fashion it!
What did His Lordship do for the land that ye live in? Write,
This was his 'policy',—turmoil and babble and causeless strife.
Seeds of dissension to sprout when the sower's name is forgot:
Pedantry set on the throne, preaching the thing which is not.
What has he done for the land? Look ye. From North to South,
Have ye a nobler gift than the word of His Lordship's mouth?

---

[6] *pop*: propose.

[1] *chit*: letter of recommendation given to a servant.

[2] *Chatterjees, Bannerjees, Mookerjees*: common Bengali names, used here collectively for Babus in general, though there were also individuals of these names active in the Indian Association (see p. 263 above) and the Indian Press.

Infinite torrent of speech—and he clamours in England yet;
Crying aloud to the East, lest the East forgive and forget.
Forgive him the lust for a name that led to his pitiful toil—
Forget what he sowed 'twixt the black and the white—the brawl and
    the broil.
He was 'greatest of all our rulers'. Are ye better thereby or worse?
Did he charm black want from your fields, or silver into your purse?
Did he sharpen the sword at the threshold that the house might be
    free from the foe?[3]
Has he given you aught save words that ye worship His Lordship so?
Ay! Fittest of rulers was he for a loud-mouthed, cackling land.
For ye live by words where *men* live by the work of their head and their
    hand—
As *He* lived, and shall live, by words who has fashioned him ropes of
    sand.

REVENGE—A BALLAD OF THE FLEETER

Published in the *Pioneer*, 31 August 1885, under general heading of 'BUNGA-
LOW BALLADS'. Reprinted in the *Pioneer Mail*, 6 September. Unsigned and
uncollected. The title is a distortion of Tennyson's 'The Revenge. A Ballad of
the Fleet'. (Cf. p. 24 above.)

Two lovers to one maid. Aye! It was so.
    O aye! Aye O! Two knights to one ladye.
Two lovers—for the world is managed so
    On principles of curst economy:
And sometimes it is two and sometimes three,
Four, five, six, seven, as the case may be.

Number ONE ne'er told his passion,
    But it simmered in his breast:
Number TWO (whom she most favoured)
    Both with brass and brass[1] was blessed;
And they *bukhed*[2] in friendly fashion as the sun sank down to rest.

---

[3] *Did he sharpen the sword* . . . : Ripon was accused by Lord Randolph Churchill of
lack of foresight and military unpreparedness in the face of Russian advances in Afgha-
nistan.

---

[1] *brass and brass*: money and effrontery.   [2] *bukhed*: talked.

For they talked of station scandal,
　　And they touched on woman's guile,
And they puffed the acrid Burma,
　　And they sipped a 'peg' meanwhile;
And they beamed on one another with a Damon–Pythias[3] smile.

Rose the Second from his chair then,
　　As they raved of Lola Hawke,
Of her merits and her beauties,
　　Cutting short the friendly talk:—
'By the way I think her house lies hence a scant ten minutes walk.

I propose *ek dum*,[4] or sooner—
　　Thanks, no, *not* another weed.'
Came a sudden inspiration
　　To the First One in his need:
'Seek her hand in dusty highlows![5] Never!
　　Mount my bounding steed!'

Now there stood an old grey stallion
　　That had come from Krab Bokhar
(Five miles off) within ONE's compound,
　　'Neath the Colonel Sahib's *sowar*; [6]
And ONE knew the old grey stallion was a beast of wrath and war.

Ah me! my pen to sully
　　With breach of faith so black;
But ONE slipped an English saddle
　　On the gallant grey his back,
And murmured, 'Dear old chappie, take this most superior hack.

Scarce two minutes easy amble
　　Lies her threshold from this door,
And the gallant grey will bear you
　　As you ne'er were borne before,
You have raised my bluff (I loved her) and the hand is yours
　　　　therefore.'

---

　　[3] *Damon–Pythias*: Damon and Pythias (from Damon and Phintias of classical legend)
became emblematic of devoted friendship.
　　[4] *ek dum*: immediately; in an instant.
　　[5] *highlows*: laced shoes or boots reaching to the ankle.
　　[6] *sowar*: mounted orderly.

Full five miles off the stables
  Where lived the gallant grey;
What wonder for those stables
  The hungry beast made play,
As sweeps the gale cyclonic across Bengala's bay?

Oh! 'tis rattle o'er the *pukka*,[7]
  And 'tis lope along the plain,
With a double-actioned buck-jump,
  When the Rider pulled the rein . . .
ONE went forth, proposed, and won her, with a conscience free
  from stain.

          *   *   *   *   *

Men say that in the evening
  They heard the stallion neigh;
They heard the troopers snigger
  As the Rider drove away
From the Krab Bokhar Cantonments in a sober *ticca* 'shay'.[8]

Love came down that night in glory
  To the City of Minars;[9]
While the Rider cursed the Rival
  Underneath the silent stars,
And patched his tattered raiment, and coldly creamed his scars.

AN INDIGNANT PROTEST

Published in the *CMG*, 4 September 1885, with heading: 'The Ootacamund[1] paper states that "during the stay of the Commander-in-Chief and party at Arconum several of them were seized with choleraic symptoms. They had been advised to use bromide of soda for some days previous to embarkation for England, to ward off sea sickness. The chief and family commenced the three days' course of the treatment at Arconum. The two Aides-de-Camp did not take it, nor did the governess, and they were not ill." ' No signature. Uncollected, but included in Scrapbook 2. The Commander-in-Chief (Madras) at

---

[7] *pukka*: permanent (roadway).
[8] *ticca* 'shay': hired chaise or carriage.
[9] *Minars*: minarets (the City of Minars being Lahore).

---

[1] *Ootacamund*: hill-station in South India, the summer headquarters of the Government of Madras.

this time was Sir Frederick (later Lord) Roberts,[2] who was going home on leave to England prior to taking up the post of Commander-in-Chief (India).

> The journalists of Southern Ind
>   Must be a *most* abandoned crew;
> For (kindly look above) I find
>   A tale which, even were it true,
> Should ne'er have met the public eye;
>   And is a breach of privacy.
>
> The Story of Sir Frederick R———
>   Is briefly this. The Bounding Sea
> Has terrors for the Man of War
>   (Exactly as it has for Me).
> He . . . suffers when he is afloat,
> And wants some soothing antidote.
>
> Of thousands, He selected one,
>   Bromide of Soda, for his need;
> And, long before His voyage begun,
>   Was very, very, ill indeed.
> (Bromide of Soda, draught or pill,
> In overdoses *makes* you ill.)
>
> Not He alone was smit with pain;
>   The C.-in-Chief his family
> Fell also. Of that noble train
>   Escaped, in fact, a scanty three—
> Two A.D.C.'s, one Governess—
> Declined, with thanks, that awful mess.
>
> The papers talked of cholera;
>   And afterwards of poison. Then
> Debated whether Frederick R—
>   Imbibed the grim medicamen-
> t on full or empty stomach. Hence
> My strictures on impertinence.

---

[2] *Sir Frederick Roberts* (1832–1914): Won VC in Indian Mutiny and had many years of distinguished service in India, culminating in his victories in the 2nd Afghan War, 1878–80; Commander-in-Chief, India, 1885–93. Later appointed Field Marshal, and was in supreme command in South Africa in 1899–1900, when he inflicted several major defeats on the Boers. Received earldom 1900 in recognition of his services.

Suffice it that a C.-in-C.
  Is, in his fleshly fashioning,
Remarkably like you and me.
  And sorrow, such as that I sing,
Is *not* exactly fitting grist
For the Abandoned Journalist.

P.S.

They *might* have told him that elixir
Invariably makes one sick, Sir.

THE LEGEND OF THE PILL

Published without individual title in the *Pioneer*, 5 September 1885, under general heading of 'BUNGALOW BALLADS'. Reprinted in the *Pioneer Mail*, 6 September. No signature. Uncollected, but included in Scrapbook 2. The *CMG* for 9 July 1885 had carried an item by Kipling (unsigned) on a Dr Jager of Vienna and his ' "anthropine" pills, the sublimated psychical essence of individuals, by him prepared, boxed and sold', productive of complete personality change in the consumer. 'His preparations', wrote Kipling, 'open out the most unpleasant possibilities of wholesale demoralization as well as benefaction. Conceive . . . the disastrous effect that a box of assorted psychical pills-
. . . would produce in this country, if administered by unscrupulous hands. His Excellency the Commander in Chief might imbibe the harmless whisky peg and be straightway transmuted in soul to one John Bright[1] . . . '; and he goes on to multiply examples.

One final—Oh my Muse Mendacity!
One crowning 'crammer'[2] ere the Bard descends
From 'trailing clouds of glory'[3] in the sky
(*Anglice*[4] from the Hills) to baser ends,
To rain-logged reeking plains that 'neath him lie,
To his belongings—children, wives, and friends,
More briefly, ere he leaves his hotel bill
Unpaid, help out the Legend of the Pill!

---

[1] *John Bright*: Radical statesman and orator, and opponent of militarism (1811–89).
[2] *crammer*: lie (slang).
[3] *'trailing clouds of glory'*: quotation from Wordsworth's 'Immortality Ode'.
[4] *Anglice*: in English.

'The pills are psychological', the worthy vendor wrote
(He wrote low German, and his name sticks in my tuneful throat):
'I send a mixed assortment (see the labels on the boxes)—
Superior kinds—"St. Ursulas",[5] "Brights", "Bradlaughs",[6] "Pitts",
    and "Foxes",[7]
And others, still more powerful, consult the invoice, please,
And kindly send per P.M.O.[8] two fifty-nine rupees.'

The pills *were* psychological—ten-grainers, capsuled. They
Stirred up the moral system in a very curious way;
For the soul that they were made from (Do you follow?) changed *your*
    soul
Into his or hers for ever—which was pleasant on the whole,
If you took a highly moral pill in water after dinner,
And woke some mediaeval saint and not a modern sinner.

I had my plan, cut, stacked, and dried, for making S—— a[9] nice.
But *Jimp*, my Skye, upset the pills while hunting after mice;
And Hussein Buksh, who picked them up, *he* couldn't understand
That 'Bradlaughs' and 'St Ursulas' are of a different brand;
He *oolta-pooltaed*[10] everything and mixed the labels too—
That's how I did a lot of things I never meant to do.

There *were* some 'Hortense Schneiders',[11] I—I really cannot tell;
I meant to give 'St Ursulas' at Paradise Hotel;[12]
I fancy though these latter were administered by me
In the whiskies and the sodas of the Simla U.S.C.,[13]
For they spoilt a pleasant dinner and a lot of rare *bons mots*,
And Rattley Trapton (sub of 'ours') tried singing through his nose.

---

   [5] *St. Ursula*: saint and martyr who, according to legend, was put to death with 11,000 other virgins near Cologne.

   [6] *Bradlaugh*: Charles Bradlaugh (1833–91), a free-thinker who refused to take the customary oath on entering Parliament.

   [7] *Pitt and Fox*: William Pitt the Younger (1759–1806) and Charles James Fox (1749–1806), the two leading politicians of their day.

   [8] *P.M.O.*: Postal Money Order.

   [9] *S——a*: Simla.   [10] *oolta-pooltaed*: confused, mixed up.

   [11] *Hortense Schneider*: French actress and singer (1838–1920), particularly known for her performances in Offenbach. She starred in *La Vie parisienne*, etc.

   [12] *Paradise Hotel*: a fashionable hotel in Simla.

   [13] *U.S.C.*: United Services Club.

I *had* a Julius Caesar—I can only hope all's right—
But it seemed as if the C. in C. was very much John Bright.
He sent the Goorkha Guard away; called fighting 'red d—nation';
And I fancy must, by this time, have resigned his situation;
I meant that five-grain 'Bright' for H—e[14] or C——n,[15] but it's queer
That C——n yearns for Egypt[16] and that H—e's a volunteer.

Our V——y[17] I'd have made a Machiavelli, but for *Jimp*,
(As sure as there's a fresh mistake I'll shoot the little imp!)
It must have been a 'Simsly Sant,'[18] or something of the sort,
For H–s E————y[19] carolled to the grand pianoforte
Instead of circumventing Giers.[20] Where *did* my 'Garrick'[21] go?
A—h D——n M.'s[22] last lecture was a grand success, you know.

'Relations of the Pulpit and Proscenium.' I guess
That those capsules from Vienna will hatch out some ghastly mess.
The're six 'Bradlaughs' round Elysium[23], 'Adah Isaks Menken'[24]
      (three)
In an ice plate at Peliti's;[25] and a 'W.E.G.'[26]
Somewhere at the back of Jakko.[27] Hunt,[28] Savonarola,[29] Lowe,[30]

---

[14] *H—e*: probably Allan Octavian Hume (1829–1912), ex-Indian Civil Servant, member of the Theosophical Society, and founder member of the Indian National Congress.

[15] *C——n*: Sir Auckland Colvin (1838–1908), the Financial Member of Council.

[16] *Egypt*: hostilities were still in progress in the Sudan.   [17] *V——y*: Viceroy.

[18] *Simsly Sant*: unidentified; perhaps derived from the names of two famous singers, John Sims Reeves (1818–1900), and Sir Charles Santley (1834–1922).

[19] *H–s E————y*: His Excellency.

[20] *Giers*: the Comte de Giers, the Russian Foreign Minister.

[21] *Garrick*: David Garrick (1717–79), the famous actor.

[22] *A—h D——n M.*: Arch-Deacon the Venerable Henry James Matthew from the See of Lahore.   [23] *Elysium*: another well-known Simla hotel.

[24] *Ada Isaks* [sc. Isaacs] *Menken*: an actress (1835–68), who achieved considerable notoriety for her appearance 'in a state of virtual nudity' when bound to the back of a horse in a dramatization of Byron's *Mazeppa*. She had many husbands and lovers, and many literary friends.   [25] *Peliti's*: famous café and confectioner's at Simla.

[26] *W.E.G.*: William Ewart Gladstone.

[27] *Jakko*: mountain on the side of which Simla was situated. The road round it was a favourite ride.

[28] *Hunt*: probably 'Orator' (Henry) Hunt (1773–1835), a demagogic politician.

[29] *Savonarola*: Fra Girolamo Savonarola (1452–98), Dominican monk and famous preacher who played a leading role in Florentine affairs after the expulsion of the Medici.

[30] *Lowe*: probably Robert Lowe, Viscount Sherbrooke (1811–92), a well-known political figure.

Kant,[31] Schopenhauer,[32] Bismarck,[33] Keats, and Harriet Beecher
    Stowe;[34]

Swinburne, Richter,[35] Poe, Grimaldi,[36] Wainwright,[37] Burke and
    Hare,[38] and Reynolds,[39]
And half a dozen others which nor memory nor pen holds
In suspension. These are missing! *Jimp* has swallowed three or four;
And his canine soul seems torn between Von Bulow[40] and Cavour.[41]

It's a very, very awful 'hat'[42] and this is how you see
That none of you are you at all, nor even I am me.
Before *Jimp* mixed the pills I took a 'Shakespeare' and a 'Dante'.
That is why my verse is perfect. See this ballad *seq. et ante*![43]

TRIAL BY JUDGE

Published in the *CMG*, 16 September 1885, with signature 'R.K.' and sub-
heading '(*As recently performed with qualified success at Simla*)'. Uncollected, but
included in Scrapbook 2 and mentioned in Kipling's Diary for 1885. This par-
ody of Gilbert & Sullivan (cf. their title *Trial by Jury*) was occasioned by the
appointment of a native barrister, Pundit Ram Narain, to be a Judge of the
Chief Court of the Punjab. The *CMG* had argued editorially not against the
individual and not against the appointment of an Indian as such, but against
the positive discrimination involved in the Lieutenant-Governor's preferring a

---

[31] *Kant*: Immanuel Kant (1724–1804), famous German philosopher.

[32] *Schopenhauer*: Arthur Schopenhauer (1788–1860), philosopher best known for his pessimism.

[33] *Bismarck*: (1815–98), the first Chancellor of a united Germany.

[34] *Harriet Beecher Stowe*: (1811–96), best known as the author of *Uncle Tom's Cabin*.

[35] *Richter*: Johann Paul Friedrich Richter (1763–1825), German novelist and humor-ist who wrote under the name of Jean Paul.

[36] *Grimaldi*: Joseph Grimaldi (1779–1837), a famous clown whose memoirs were edited by Dickens.

[37] *Wainwright*: Thomas Griffiths Wainewright (1794–1852), a well-known art-critic and notorious poisoner.

[38] *Burke and Hare*: notorious Edinburgh body-snatchers who killed their victims in order to sell their bodies for dissection. Burke was executed in 1829.

[39] *Reynolds*: Sir Joshua Reynolds (1723–92), portrait-painter and first President of the Royal Academy.

[40] *Von Bulow*: Count Friedrich Wilhelm von Bulow (1755–1816), a Prussian general.

[41] *Cavour*: Camillo Bensi, Count di Cavour (1810–61), Sardinian prime minister who played a large part in the unification of Italy.

[42] *hat*: difficulty (slang).   [43] *seq. et ante*: before and after.

native candidate over better qualified Europeans. The appointment was announced at Simla on 9 September and reported in the *CMG* on the 10th.

Scene: *A rugged mountain pass near B*————*e.*[1]

Enter P——T R–M N————N (R)[2] *singing and dancing.*

SONG: P——T R–M N————N.

I am convinced my merits rare,
  And powers of legal disputation,
Indubitably levers were
  To this exalted situation.
He marked me with His eagle eye,
  When, lowly pleading, oft I pleaded;
And, e'en ten weary years gone by
  I *knew* I did not toil unheeded.
In Cap.[3] and Code, both Civ. and Crim.
  I have no rival. *Hushiar*[4]
Beyond all pleaders, I to Him
  Appeared a legal Avatar:

For I am an Aryan[5] judge! Hurrah!
  I am an Aryan judge!
(*pp con molt. exp.*) And it's not half bad sport, if you are the right sort,
  To be an Aryan judge!

Pas Legislatif. Crosses R to L[6] *and comes down.*

Enter Full B–N C H P——B[7] *also singing and dancing (R), with attar, pán*[8]
and garlands.

CHORUS: B–N C H (*fortissimo*).

He's an affable Aryan judge—
  A star and a light to our leading—
Though the vulgar may snigger and nudge
  We will pass by their comments unheeding,

---

[1] *B*————*e*: Boileaugunge, the western area of Simla.
[2] *R*: right.   [3] *Cap.*: chapter (Latin *caput*).   [4] *Hushiar*: clever, intelligent.
[5] *Aryan*: term applied to the Indo-European group of languages, but used in the 19th cent. to refer to users of the original Aryan language or their descendants, and more specifically to the Asiatic portion of these, since the Indians and Persians had called themselves Arya (from Sanscrit *ārya*: noble, of good family). Hence applied to the inhabitants of North India.   [6] *R to L*: right to left.
[7] *B–nch P*——*b*: Bench of the Punjab.   [8] *pán*: betel leaf chewed by Indians.

For who in his senses would grudge
A seat on the B–nch to this judge?
This
Indigenous, affable, eloquent, erudite, excellent, Aryan judge?

Pas Legislatif. The P——T *skipping over garlands.*
Exit (R) wreathed with smiles and roses. B–NCH *sit down (C)[9] and sing*
pianissimo: looking warily at the B————e lights.

CHORUS: B–NCH

We *know* we aren't exactly strong
Hush! Hush! Hush!
In weighty matters of the law.
Hist! Hist! Hist!
We think Sir C——s[10] *extremely* wrong
Hush! Hush! Hush!
We watch his latest step with awe.
Hist! Hist! Hist!
We know we aren't *exactly* strong
In weighty matters of the law
But,
If We *are* incompetent, which *We* of course deny,
Why not new importations of *Our* nationality?
And,
If We *aren't* incompetent, Oh why insult the trus-
ty band of *ticca*[11] j–dges with a course of action thus?

Da Capo Pianissimo. Practicable window opens in B————e
R.U.E.[12] *discloses Sir C——s with P——b G——tte[13] in his hand,*
which he waves in time to the music.

BASS SOLO: SIR C——S

Rash men of Law and bold!
Restrain yourselves! Be still!
Yet shall the truth be told—
It was the Princi*pil*.

[9] *C*: centre.
[10] *Sir C——s*: Sir Charles Umpherston Aitchison, Lieutenant-Governor of the
Punjab 1882–7; author of important works on *The Native States of India* and *A Collection
of Treaties . . . Relating to India and Neighbouring Countries*. 'He was a staunch advocate of
the policy of advancing natives of India in the public service as they proved their fitness
for higher posts and for more responsible duties.' (*Dictionary of National Biography*.)
[11] *ticca*: on contract.   [12] *R.U.E.*: right upper entrance.
[13] *P——b G——tte*: *Punjab Gazette* (in which official appointments were announced).

B–NCH, *seriatim, in state of nervous collapse.*

JUSTICE A.—Bai Jove!
JUSTICE B.—Yes! yes! yes! yes!
JUSTICE C.—Indeed!
(ALL) The Princi*pil*!
The Princi*pil*! The Princi*pil*!

SIR C.	The only moral	
B–NCH	That gruesome fraud the	princi*pil*!

SIR C.	That truly perfect	
B–NCH	That most mysterious	princi*pil*!

SIR C.	The perfectly unshirkable	
B–NCH	The utterly unworkable	princi*pil*!

SIR C.	Perfectly lawful	
B–NCH	Thoroughly awful	princi*pil*!

ENSEMBLE. Princi*pil*!

BASS RECITATIVE: SIR C. (*leaning out of the window*)

I am the proud owner, trainer and head jockey of a hobby-horse which
it would be wholly absurd to expect you either to appreciate or
understand;
For the simple reason that you cannot bring yourselves to look at it in
a sufficiently abstract and Liberal light.
Therefore, being a 'strong' man (at least, that's what I pride myself
upon) I have, literally, taken the law into my own hand;
And, at the cost of making you worthy gentlemen a trifle indignant, I
have played my political trump and set a monstrous injustice
right.
I had not the faintest intention of inquiring into the merits of the
various *munsiffs*,[14] pleaders, and court thistle-whippers[15] of every
kind,
(Because I believe that a pleader of fifteen years' standing is fully
equal, under certain circumstances, to a Bengal Civilian[16] of
thirty, *plus* an expensive English education),
But, with a Law list in one hand, and a pencil in the other, and closing
my eyes, in order that (like Cupid and Justice) I might be blind,

[14] *munsiffs*: native civil judges of lowest grade.
[15] *thistle-whippers*: hare hunters (contemptuous).
[16] *Bengal Civilian*: member of the Bengal Civil Service.

I brought down the pencil sharply and at random on the page; thus
    largely simplifying an arduous process of provincial legislation.
In this particular instance my pencil struck the name of the (doubtless
    very able and respectable) P——t R–m N——n;
And I have, in consequence, put him over your heads. Possibly to your
    extreme disgust, which I may tell you doesn't affect me at all.
Because, as soon as I find a fitting opportunity, I shall most certainly
    go through this identical performance again;
Since to the truly enlightened Liberal mind, Principles are everything,
    and the interest of mere Provinces and men (especially English
    gentlemen who can be trusted not to make themselves
    unpleasant) extremely small.

    Shuts down window, while B–nch faint in the order of their seniority; and
        are removed one by one by the P——t. (R)

           CHORUS OF NATIVE EDITORS *under Window (C)*

                Hear our unanimous cry.
                Mulk-i-Lat Sahib ke Jai![17]
                Strengthen your soul with the thought
                You have our warmest support.
                How shall your Honour take harm
                Backed by the *Akhbar-i-Aam?*[18]
                Friend of the great *Koh-i-Noor,*
                Widely perused in L——e?[19]

(*ffff*)   In short every journal of native persuasion
                That boasts a two hundred per week circulation,
                That's bought by a *bunnia,*[20] or read by a *reis,*[21]
                That's lithoed in gullies, or sold for a *pice,*[22]
                That's worked by a schoolboy on thirty rupees,
                That serves as a wrap for *mussalas* and *ghis,*[23]
                Shall, *nemine contradicente,*[24] proclaim
                Your Honour's just dealing and wisdom and fame,
                Shall hold you on high to the World's admiration:—
(*fff fff*)   And this is the voice of the Indian Nation!

---

[17] *Mulk-i-Lat Sahib ke Jai!*: Hail to the Lord Governor!
[18] *Akhbar-i-Aam and Koh-i-Noor*: Indian vernacular newspapers with strong political
slant, published in Lahore.   [19] *L——e*: Lahore.
  [20] *bunnia*: corn merchant.   [21] *reis*: native gentleman.
  [22] *pice*: copper coin of very small value.
  [23] *mussalas and ghis*: curries and boiled butter.
  [24] *nemine contradicente*: with no one saying the contrary.

SIR C——S *bowing his acknowledgments from window, and*
    accompanying himself on a mandolin:

Yes! yes! 'Tis the voice of the Indian Nation.

SONG: SIR C——S

Oh! he shall try the gay Ghilzai,[25]
    The wild Pathan shall bow before him;
The Khyberee shall quake to see
    The thunders of dark justice o'er him;
And Thomas A.,[26] whose lavish pay
    Leads him to gross intoxication,
With pallid cheek, shall watch that 'Beak'
    Ordain him due incarceration.

CHORUS *rapturously*:

Aye! Thomas A., whose lavish pay
    Leads him to gross intoxication,
(*Lat Sahib ke Jai*),[27] our worthy *bhai*[28]
    Shall doom to instant strangulation.

SOLO: SIR C——S

By measures such as these I much
    Delight the teeming land;
And closer bind my fellow-kind
    In amicable band.
And in a few more decades, to
    United India we,
With one consent, our Government
    Resign and homeward flee.
Oh! This is Government by Love,
    And Truth, and bound to come,
And I anticipate from this
    The new Millenium.

CHORUS *still more rapturously*:

Yes *this* is Government by Love,
    And Right, and *bound to come.*

---

[25] *Ghilzai, Pathan, Khyberee*: tribesmen of the North-West Frontier.
[26] *Thomas A.*: Tommy Atkins (cf. p. 183 above).
[27] *Lat Sahib ke Jai*: Hail to the Lord Sahib.
[28] *bhai*: brother, cousin.

Be this our cry:—'Sir C—s; our *bhai*;
And the Millen*ium*!'

Blue, red and green fire, Bengali lights; showers of roses and
tumultuous cheering.

CURTAIN

CARMEN SIMLAENSE [A BALLAD OF THE BREAK UP]

Published in the *CMG*, 20 October 1885, with title 'A Ballad of the Break Up',
subtitle '*Carmen Simlaense*' (a Simla Song), and date 17 October. No signature.
Collected in the Outward Bound, De Luxe, Sussex, and Burwash Edns. as
'Carmen Simlaense'. Newspaper reports from Simla often adopted an elegiac
tone as the Season came to an end: thus in the *CMG* for 14 October a corre-
spondent writes that 'the signs of the passing of the Simla season of 1885, have
saddened me into all sorts of bewildering reflections.' The *CMG* version had
an additional stanza, printed here in square brackets, and ' "dibs" ' for 'cash'
in l. 5 of the third stanza:

I've danced till my shoes are outworn
From ten till the hours called small;
I've cantered with Beauty at morn—
At even made love at the ball.
Light Loves for five months were my lot,
Heavy bills and long 'ticks' that appal
Me when counting the cost of the shot.
Lord! What was the good of it all?

Good-bye to the Annandale[1] roses—
Sweet talks in the dusk on the Mall;
Adieu to a season that closes—
Peliti's,[2] the Club, and the call!
To the pines that moaned over our playtime,
The deodars[3] sombre and tall—
Diversions of night and of daytime.
Lord! What was the good of it all?

[1] *Annandale*: wooden glen near Simla; also the site of the racecourse.
[2] *Peliti's*: famous café and confectioner's in Simla.
[3] *deodars*: Himalayan cedars.

I sit on my bulgy portmanteau
　　(As once in his tent-gloom lay Saul),[4]
And I write me this cynical canto,
　　In the ink of derision and gall,
As I think of the cash I must borrow
　　From that excellent *shroff*[5] Bunsee Lal,
And the tonga[6] I've booked for to-morrow.
　　Lord! What was the good of it all?

Of tuppenny passions and small,
　　Of Levée and function and feast,
Of charmers that used to enthral
　　For a month, or a fortnight at least,
From October to April I'm clear—
　　From Olympus to Hades I fall.
By the bills on my file, ye were dear!
　　But what was the good of it all?

　　　　　　[L'ENVOI

Princess! It was pleasant to meet;
　　(Loves fade, and Leave ends, and snows fall)
And I turn to the Plains at our feet
　　From the racket, the ride and the ball;
From a season that comes to a stop,
　　From flirtations that weary and pall,
And I wonder, as downward I drop:
　　Lord! What was the good of it all?]

THE INDIAN DELEGATES

Published in the *CMG*, 21 November 1885, with subheading '(*A farcical com-
edietta now running, with enormous success, in London*)'. No signature. Uncol-
lected, but clearly by the same hand as 'Trial by Judge'. In 1885 a number of
the most important Indian Associations concerned with political reform
decided to send three delegates to England, to bring Indian aspirations and
grievances to the attention of the British public in the run-up to a forthcoming
General Election. One was selected from each of the Presidencies: Narayan

---

[4] *Saul*: see Sam. 1: 16.　　　　[5] *shroff*: money-lender.
[6] *tonga*: light two-wheeled vehicle, drawn by two ponies, much used on the roads to
Simla and other hill-stations.

Ganesh Chandavarkar, editor of a moderate Bombay newspaper and an attorney in Bombay High Court; Man Mohan Ghose, a well-known barrister and journalist from Calcutta; and S. Ramaswami Mudeliar, a wealthy land-owner and attorney from Madras. Their mission achieved little, partly because of their error of judgement in aligning themselves openly with the Radical Liberals, after which they were pilloried by the Tories as unrepresentative of the Indian public as a whole.

Scene, a spacious public hall in England. Trio of Indian Delegates discovered singing softly to music of vina and sitar.[1] *Great British Public in foreground*:

TRIO. DELEGATES

Delegates we
From over the sea
From the teeming millions of down-trod Ind;
With an education
The British nation
Supplies for the use of the Indian mind.

RECITATIVE. DELEGATES

(Con molt. exp.; to obligato accompaniment of their own trumpets)

We have mastered in decades five or six
The whole of your system of politics;
Assimilated the centuries
As we took your trousers, your boots and ties.
We have learnt to print the folly we write,
We worship Kaye and Blunt and Bright.[2]
By the knowledge we've gained in the schools they built,
We accuse our rulers of crime and guilt;
By right of the learning we've swallowed raw
We are fit to administer rule and law;
By virtue of what you have taught us, we
At the end of one century claim to be free;
And appeal in Equality's sacred name
For the land misgoverned from whence we came.

They speak, from divers platforms on many subjects. G.B.P. *generalizes hastily after its fashion*:

[1] *vina and sitar*: Indian musical instruments akin to the lyre and the guitar.
[2] *Kaye and Blunt and Bright*: Joseph Kay (1821-78), liberal economist; Wilfred Scawen Blunt (1840-1922), traveller, politician, poet (see above, p. 239), and critic of British imperialism; John Bright (1811-89), Radical orator and statesman.

CHORUS. G.B.P.

The facts which we deduce
From the language that they use
And the excellent impressions they convey,
Is that natives, all and each,
Are as fluent in their speech
As the gentlemen we've listened to today;
(*Crescendo*) That the millions of Ind
Are enlightened and refined,
That they study Mill and Kant[3] (without the C)
And in every single way
The nation 'neath our sway
Is rather more intelligent than we.
(*Crescendissimo Impetuoso*) And these things being so
We should greatly like to know
Why a bureaucratic, autocratic crew
(Civilians and such)
Oppress our friends so much
As these gentlemen of colour say they do.

They proceed to make enquiries at the British Museum and elsewhere. Interval of twenty minutes allowed for enquiries. Re-enter G. B. P. *with books of reference in their hands, and wet towels round their foreheads. They generalize hastily*:

CHORUS. G.B.P.

The facts are simply thus,
They are not homogen*us*;
And Babus and Pathans[4] will never mix;
And the ryots[5] when they rest,
Do *not* study with a zest
The course of Indo-British politics,
(*Cres. Queruloso*) Which we thought, from our friends' oration,
Was their principal occupation.

Gurmukhi and Tamil!
Bullock cart and camel!
Bhils and Ghonds! Punjabi and Marattha!

---

[3] *Mill and Kant*: cited as examples of European philosophy.
[4] *Babus and Pathans*: educated, English-speaking Bengalis and tribesmen of the North-West Frontier.   [5] *ryots*: tenant farmers, peasants.

Indo-Mussulmanic shindies!
Parsees, Assamese, and Sindees!
Our notion of 'United India' shatter!

(*Crescendo as above. With trombone accompaniment.*)

And we thought at the very least,
These gentlemen of the East,
Stood man by man as ally and as brother;
But we find it is not the case,
And one half of that civilized race
Objects to eating dinner with the other.

Wedlocks precocious!
Customs atrocious!
Think of *our* girls in the grip of the *purdah*![6]
Babe-widowed wives[7]
Leading such lives
As drive them perforce to abortion and murder.

(*Crescendo as above*)—

And we fancied these excellent men
Did *not* marry wives of ten;
But they *do*, and we think it very beastly!
The 'pressing reforms' that they want
Are not in our power to grant;
But wholly in their houses in the East lie!

They continue to make enquiries; and sing pianissimo to one another:

We are a simple public we
And blind;
But this much we can plainly see—
The kind
Of gentlemen we've met to-day
Do not
Stand for, in any single way,
That lot
Of ill-conditioned peoples who
Would fight

---

[6] *purdah*: system of the seclusion of women.

[7] *Babe-widowed wives*: the wretched lot of Hindu widows, especially those who had been married in childhood, was a matter of frequent comment in the Anglo-Indian press.

At once like wolves if we withdrew
Our right
Of interference; and we find,
If these
Were *really* gentlemen of Ind,
Deep peace
(Marred maybe by sedition cheap)
Would fall,
Upon the Empire that we keep . . .
That's all!

CHORUS OF A BORED AND BRUTAL PROLETARIAT

Hi! You! Bring forward if yer can
A 'orny 'anded workin' man!
A Hinjian workin' man!

TRIO. DELEGATES.—(*Largendo imperioso*)

We wholly fail to understand
How our requirements are affected
By low-caste brutes with horny hand;
Or how a link can be detected
Between ourselves, who really are
High caste, and *mistri*[8] or *chumar*.[9]
Extended life political—

Alarms and interruptions. G.B.P. *generalizes afresh from information received*:

CHORUS. G.B.P.

The Indian artizan
Lies not within your plan,
Nor for trader, nor for tiller do you care!
That you fight for your own hand
We can fully understand,
But to pose as British India isn't fair!
Oh eloquent orators, swarthy and sweet!
Have you heard of the Tailors of Tooley Street?[10]
Of Too-oo-oo-oo-oo-oo-oo-oo-ooo-ley Street (*Da capo*[11] *ad lib*)

---

[8] *mistri*: artisan.   [9] *chumar*: a low caste which included leather-workers.
[10] *the Tailors of Tooley Street*: three tailors of Tooley Street, Southwark, were said to
have addressed a petition of grievances to Parliament beginning 'We, the people of Eng-
land . . .'   [11] *Da capo*: from the beginning.

Two thousand strong at most
Is the 'nation' that you boast
(A 'nation' of M.A.'s and LL.D's)
And, in every single point,
Its ideas are out of joint
With the peoples' of our Empire overseas.
Oh! silver-tongued Trio, again we repeat,
Have you heard of the Tailors of Tooley Street?

RECITATIVE. G.B.P.

Urgent reforms you need—See that you get 'em.
Make *women* of your wives; don't cuff and pet 'em.
Doctor them when they're ill—they die like flies.
Reform corrupt Municipalities.
We worked our freedom out through thirty reigns—
Show your own power to manage your own drains.
Don't howl for Government when things look black.
Grow moral backbone in your moral back.
Try to speak truth—you've years before you plenty—
And marry on the other side of twenty!

GRAND FINALE. FULL ORCHESTRA

When you and yours shall eat with us—
Your wives as equals meet with us—
Then comes the time to treat with us—
Not now oh fluent Three!
When sterner-knit your morals are—
When sunk sectarian quarrels are—
For you our brightest laurels are,
To wear them worthily—

Bass-viol solo on the lower D—And when shall these things be?

CURTAIN

EXCHANGE

Published in the *CMG*, 18 December 1885, with signature 'R.K.', subtitle '(A Personal View of a Public Question)', and heading ' "Exchange is now quoted at 1-5⅞" *C & M Gazette*, December 17th.' Uncollected, but included in Scrapbook 1. The falling value of the rupee against the pound sterling was a matter

of great concern to Anglo-Indians in the middle and late 1880s. The pound
was on the gold standard, the rupee depended on the value of silver; and there
was no fixed value between them.

> I am a man of culture small
>   With seven mouths to fill,
> And do not understand at all
>   Why money can't keep still;
> Bi-metallism[1] is to me
> A grim unfathomed mystery.

> Years back—ere Mrs Smith was fat
>   Or I an ardent lover,
> The fraudulent Rupee stood at
>   Two 'bob'[2] and something over.
> I led her to the altar—then
> It altered too, to one and ten.

> Years passed, and children came with years
>   Demanding food and drink,
> And raiment oft—we watched with tears
>   The vengeful token sink—
> Sink with each new born innocent—
> Nine, eight and seven—down it went!

> We sent them overseas to flee
>   The fate that dogged their path,
> And fed with all economy
>   Our babe-denuded hearth.
> A fourth was born. Next day with pain
> I read—'Exchange is down again.'

> That was two weary years ago
>   No other child succeeding,
> I hoped 'twould take the hint—but no,
>   Exchange dropped down unheeding,
> To fractions past my counting—Yet
> *Another* filled the bassinette.

[1] *Bi-metallism*: the use of two metals, especially gold and silver, at fixed relative values
as the basis of currency.   [2] *bob*: the old shilling of twelve pence.

Sudden and swift the vengeance came;
    I learnt but yesterday,
I lose in this most losing game
    Three-eighths my annual pay.
While all the little Smiths out-grow
Their garments twice a year or so.

Oh tell me not of wedded bliss—
    Its joys are gall to me,
Who've struggled thirteen years with this
    Malthusian[3] Rupee.
For sure as Death, or Birth, unkind
It drops when Mrs Smith's confined.

I am a man of culture small
    And intellect obtuse,
Facts, tracts and explanations—all,
    I answer with abuse.
Whate'er you others say or write
I think it's just a piece of spite.

AT THE DISTANCE

Published in *Quartette*, 19 December 1885, with heading ' "5TH RACE. Ladies'
Nomination. For all *bona-fide* polo ponies, owners up. 13-2[1] to carry 10-7;
4 lbs. allowed for every $\frac{1}{4}$ inch under. Distance, $\frac{3}{4}$ mile on the flat. Prize, a gold
locket."—*Any Gymkhana Prospectus.*' Uncollected. The technicalities on
handicapping, etc. are of the kind regularly used in advertising and reporting
race-meetings in India.

GREEN, *on Jezebel, g.c.b.m.,*[2] *13-2, to himself, excitedly*:

Can she stay? Here's the chestnut behind us—he's trying to pass to the
    right;
And I daren't pull her out from the railings! Daren't touch her! Can
    only sit tight,

---

[3] *Malthusian*: discouraging propagation (from Thomas Malthus's *Essay on the Principle of Population*, 1798).

[1] *13-2*: thirteen hands, two inches was the maximum height allowed for a mount to be classified as a pony under Calcutta Turf Club Rules.

[2] *g.c.b.m.*: grey, country-bred, mare.

Hands low on the withers, head forward, and watch with the tail of my
    eye
The chestnut's blue brow-band creep nearer. By Jove! How the
    beggar can fly!
He's fit to the minute—I know it,—and *Jezebel's* not running steady.
(And I want that gold locket for Kitty) I fancy she tires already!
There's his fiddle-head up to our throat-latch. I *can't* suffer longer—
    Here goes!
One welt for you, close to the girth, dear! You won't shut up *now*, I
    suppose?
You will! Swaine and Adeney,[3] help me! Another—and over my boot
The chestnut's red nostrils are snorting. I wish I could shake off the
    brute!
If *only* old Brown wasn't on him—he gives me three good on the flat—
But I'm racing for love and for Kitty, and don't care two pice[4] for my
    tat.[5]
If cat-gut and spurring can do it we're landed. Go on then you jade!
Go on, if I cut you to ribbons! No good! *Her* bolt's shot I'm afraid.
Where the deuce have we got to?—I'm blinded and dusty and sweating
    and done,
With a mouth like the roof of a lime-kiln—Who's shouting behind us?
    I've won!
Queer—Brown dying off at the finish—his chestnut's the best of the
    two—
Suppose 'twas my riding that did it—I squeezed the last ounce from
    my screw.
She's strained a back-sinew, I'm certain! Poor beast, how I've cut
    her!—Who cares?
I've won the gold locket for Kitty. Who-a up, there, you sweetest of
    mares!

    BROWN, *confidentially to his mount, Robin, ch.c.b.p.,*[6] 13-2:

I can romp in alone when I please. I can leave him behind when I will.
I could give him a furlong with ease; and I'm three times his equal in
    skill!
But I'm rolling about in my seat, (They'll think that I'm out o' my wits)
And I'm working my hands and my feet like a Cabuli dealer in fits.

    [3] *Swaine and Adeney*: well-known firm supplying saddlery, riding kit, etc.
    [4] *pice*: copper coin of very small value.
    [5] *tat*: country-bred pony.
    [6] *ch.c.b.p.*: chestnut, country-bred, pony.

No, Robin; you mustn't get nearer. This wasn't our form I admit,
When we fluttered the dovecots at Dehra,[7] and won by two lengths
and a bit.
I don't care a rap how it goes. *His* heart is one stake in the race,
(Miss Black's in the Stand, I suppose) and he'd slaughter his mare for
a place.
I'll save the old screw all I can, though my arms are nigh wrenched
from their socket—
Was ever a race since Gymkhanas began yet 'pulled'[8] for the sake of a
locket?
Well, I've got a wife of my own, and I rode for her once in our wooing
With a man who could give me a stone, and who—did pretty much
what I'm doing.
Come back, Rob! You're pulling like sin! (Poor tat, how he's making
her bleed!)
Come back!—It's an eight-anna[9] 'spin',[10] to be finished at twelve-
anna speed.
You leather-mouthed son of a caster![11] I daren't pull you more than
I've done!
My faith! but we'd very near passed her—All right! Go ahead then!
He's won.
You know your own business too well, Sir? Put it all down to wicked
Miss Black!
I ran you to lose. Don't you tell, Sir! *He's* ruined a second-rate hack.

A TRAGEDY OF TEETH

Published in *Quartette* on 19 December 1885. Uncollected. Kipling's father,
writing to Margaret Burne-Jones on 31 January 1886 about Rudyard's reluc-
tance to accept criticism, deplored the 'coarseness' of this item (KP 1/1).

> Lucretia Sempavee Riddens McWhone
> Was loveliest of the Daughters of the Hills,
> And therefore made an idol of by Those
> Who should have been at school, but drew instead

---

[7] *Dehra*: capital of the Dehra Dun district in the North-West Provinces.
[8] *pulled*: deliberately lost, by the rider holding his horse back.
[9] *anna*: the sixteenth part of a rupee.   [10] *spin*: gallop, spurt.
[11] *caster*: horse considered no longer fit for service (e.g. in the cavalry or artillery), and
therefore sold by public auction.

Rupees two hundred, ten, and some odd pice[1]
For serving an ungrateful Government.
And L.S.R.McW. enjoyed
Herself exceedingly, and made to fly
The pay of Angus, who was fat and red,
And, at some early period of his life,
Had been her husband. Angus didn't care,
And L.S.R.McW. drove on.

*   *   *   *   *

She had a Skeleton. Who hasn't? Two
In fact. The one she kept beneath her stays
And dressed with clothes from Europe. T'other one
She generally hid inside her mouth
Because it wasn't hers, except by right
Of purchase—gold paid down for pearls and gold.
Two were the molars of a Communist
Young lady, pistolled on the barricades;
The canines came from some grim Plevna[2] fosse;
And one bicuspid from the Schipka[2] pass;
The rest from Javanese rhinoceri;
But all were lovely and had cost much gold,
And had a lot of little pegs and plates
And springs and wires. And she loved them much.
And no one knew of it or only guessed;
And thus our naughty little world goes round.

*   *   *   *   *

He was *Macacus Rhesus*,[3] Sterndale[4] says—
I call him *Bandar*[5]—and at half past six
One summer morning through the open door
He ambled, searching for an early meal,
His Simian *chota hazri*.[6] L.S.R.
(I really can't repeat her name again)
Was sleeping. Angus was at Bogglybad,

[1] *pice*: copper coins of very small value.
[2] *Plevna and Schipka*: scenes of a seige and a battle respectively in the Russo-Turkish war of 1877-8 (cf. p. 9 above).   [3] *Macacus Rhesus*: rhesus monkey.
[4] *Sterndale*: Robert Armitage Sterndale, author of *Natural History of the Mammalia of India and Ceylon*, Calcutta and London, 1884.
[5] *Bandar*: monkey.   [6] *chota hazri*; little breakfast.

And Something Else was in a tooth glass.—This
Macacus Rhesus bolted with and chewed
It on a pine tree half way down the *khud*,[7]
And spat It out, and put It in his pouch
To please his babes with. Then he let It drop
At Mrs. Duvvlegh's bedroom door-sill. Thus
Our naughty, naughty little world goes round.
Then L.S.R. McW. awoke,
And slapped her *ayah*,[8] called the *Khitmutgar*,[9]
The *mehter*,[10] *bhisti*,[11] *sais*,[12] *massalchi*,[13] cook,
And from the safe side of her bedroom door
Addressed those menials in a wobbly voice
That thrilled their dusky marrows. Then she wept,
And then she lifted up that voice again
Da capo, piano, prestissimo,
Fortissimo, ad lib. till ten o'clock;
Then she *darwaza banded*[14] up the house,
And wept in the verandah. Mrs. D.
Woke also; found It at her bedroom door;
And since she wore an article herself
Of plates and springs and pegs and pearls and gold;
And since she was a rival, hating much
Lucretia Sempavee Riddens; and since
She understood that memsahib was *bemar*,[15]
She guessed, and wrote a pretty little *chit*[16]
On pink and perfumed paper; sent her *sais*
And went to call on ten dear female friends
With Something in a satchel on her arm,
And looked extremely pretty. So did not
Lucretia when the *sais* produced the *chit*,
But mumbled naughty epithets like 'Wretch',
'Thing', 'Vixen', 'Hussy', 'Beast', *et cœtera.*
Yet wrote a gushing little answer back
And sat and 'grizzled' in her dressing-gown.

*   *   *   *   *

---

[7] *khud*: deep valley or precipitous hillside.   [8] *ayah*: lady's maid.
[9] *Khitmutgar*: waiter.   [10] *mehter*: sweeper.   [11] *bhisti*: water-carrier.
[12] *sais*: groom.   [13] *massalchi*: dish-washer.
[14] *darwaza banded*: indicated she was 'not at home'.
[15] *bemar*: ill.   [16] *chit*: note.

At half-past four she got It, smashed and spoilt,
The Communistic molars upside down
And marks of other molars on the plates,
(*Macacus Rhesus* had a lovely set)
And all the pretty little springs and wires
Like tempest-tossed umbrella ribs. 'Tis thus
Our naughty, naughty little world goes round.

*   *   *   *   *

They laughed at Mrs. L.S.R. McWhone;
She sent It to Calcutta for a week,
And then she left the Station for the Plains.
And this is how the Gods afflict our lives
Sometimes, somehow, for nothing. . . . Which is hard.

OVER THE KHUD[1]

Printed version from newspaper, with subtitle 'A Mountain Morality', in Scrapbooks 1 and 2, with signature 'The Other Player' (cf. pp 184 and 187 above). Source unlocated. 1885-6? Riding accidents were not uncommon in the Simla region: the 1883 edn. of Murray's *Handbook to the Punjab* urged caution, noting that 'up to 1875 at least 22 ladies and gentlemen were killed by falling over precipices at this station, and many more have had narrow escapes . . . ' (p. 174.)

That's where he fell;
Mark the spot well.
See the smashed saddle and lower his blood.
Count then, my friends,
On your ten finger ends,
People you know who've gone 'over the *khud* '.

Pretty Blue Eyes
Ask with surprise—
'How *could* he fall from a path broad as this?'
What would she do
If we said—'You
Dance all *too near* to the *khud* as it is'?

[1] *Khud*: deep valley or precipitous hillside beside road in lower Himalayas.

Given a hack
Ready to back,
Crash through the railings and down with a thud;
You'll find it *so* easy
When roadways are greasy,
To slip from the level and 'over the *khud* '.

Far, far below
Men we 'don't know',
Stare at us hopelessly out of the mud.
We're on the Mall,
Safe side the Wall;
They were the fools to go 'over the *khud* '.

People look down,
'Cut' them or frown,
Lighthearted picnickers merrily stone 'em;
And strong in the sense,
Of propriety's fence,
Mount on the very same hack that has thrown 'em.

Horses are strong,
Apt to go wrong,
We are reluctant the curb to apply.
Only a stumble
And we too may tumble
Down, down the cliffs where those poor devils lie.

Look at the stones
White with their bones,
Look at the rocks that are dark with their blood.
Thank the Lord all
You're safe on the Mall
So far, and pity poor souls '*down the Khud* '.

THE COMPLIMENTS OF THE SEASON

Published in the *CMG*, 1 January 1886, with signature 'K'. Uncollected, but
included in Scrapbook 2.

He came in the winter midnight—
   Our Ruler—Time's youngest boy,
And we murdered his predecessor,
   With revel and riot and joy.

'*Te morituri salutant!*'
   Oh! what are your measures?' we cried.
'And what is your policy usward?'
   And our baby King replied:—

'My people! Some chairs will empty;
   And sundry cradles will fill;
And divers passions will vanish;
   And hopes and hearts will chill

Ere I quit you in next December.'
   (Our Ruler paused and smiled,
And the eyes of the terrible Father
   Looked out from the face of the Child.)

'Some vows will be plighted and broken
   And women and men will lie;
And envy and hatred and malice
   Will thrive apace till I die.

And Loves Eternal will perish,
   Ere half of my reign be done,
And a thousand good resolutions
   Will melt like snow in the sun.'

Then we spread the tables for feasting
   And made the great bells swing;
And clamoured aloud for largesse
   At the hands of our generous King.

Rich nuts to the toothless gave he;
   Strong meats to the aged and weak—
The gift of a fading eyesight—
   The gift of a withered cheek.

---

[1] *Te morituri salutant*: those about to die salute thee (the traditional greeting to the Emperor by gladiators entering the arena).

High hopes, brave aspirations,
   That sank us deep in the mire;
Fair visions of long-lost chances;
   The gifts of a vain desire.

He dowered us richly with knowledge,
   The sins of our youth to mourn,
And gave us the gift of loving,
   When the time for loving was gone.

So we hugged his gifts to our bosoms,
   And feasted and made good cheer;
And we grasped the hands of our neighbours,
   And wished them:—'A Happy New Year'.

THE QUID PRO QUO[1]

Published in the *CMG*, 16 January 1886, with signature 'R.K.' and heading:
' "He was aware how heavily the least addition of pressure must fall on
Englishmen in India struggling to maintain a position here, and educate their
children at home, with the depreciated rupee; but his Lordship's words of
sympathy, last Monday, no doubt, had gone to their heart."—*Report of the
Hon'ble W. W. Hunter's*[2] *speech in the Legislative Council, Jan. 11th.*' Reprinted in
the *Pioneer*, 18 January, and *Pioneer Mail*, 20 January 1886. Uncollected, but
included in Scrapbook 2. The *CMG* for 6 January 1886 contained a news item
on the meeting of the Legislative Council in Calcutta on 4 January. It reported
a policy statement by the Viceroy and a financial statement by Sir Auckland
Colvin, the Financial Member, the burden of which was that increased
revenue was required to balance the falling value of the rupee and to meet the
increased cost of expenditure incurred by strengthening defences on the
North-West Frontier and pursuing the war in Burma. The restoration of the
cut in duties on salt made in 1882 or the reimposition of import duties had
been rejected as options, since their effect would have been 'to increase the
burdens of the poorest classes in the community': instead it was proposed to
introduce an Income Tax of 5 pice in the rupee (approximately 2 per cent) for
incomes above 2,000 rupees per annum. This would produce revenue from

---

[1] *Quid Pro Quo*: a return given as good as was received, with a pun on 'quid' as a slang
term for pound.
[2] *W. W. Hunter*: William Wilson Hunter (1840-1900), an eminent Anglo-Indian
administrator; also an historian, and compiler of the *Imperial Gazetteer*, a statistical sur-
vey of the Indian Empire; member of the Viceroy's Council; knighted in 1887. See also
pp. 315 and 404 below.

'the classes in this country who derive the greatest security and benefit from the British Government' [i.e. the professional and mercantile classes] but who 'contribute the least towards it'. The tax would also apply to British officials. This is the subject of Kipling's better-known poem 'The Rupaiyat of Omar Kal'vin', published in the *CMG*, 30 January 1886, and collected in *Departmental Ditties*.

'He was aware'—Oh great and good
 And virtuous Doctor Hunter!—He
Observed in sympathetic mood,
 My struggles with the base Rupee.
Yea—he could feel for others, who
By *thousands* counts his monthly 'screw'!

'He was aware' my Jimmy's bills
 For schooling annually grow.
He found the balm for all my ills—
 The panacea as below:—
'Five pie *per* hardly earned rupee
Secures His Lordship's sympathy.'

'He was aware' my wife desired
 A homeward journey in the spring;
'He was aware' my son required
 A final College polishing . . .
My son will be a clerk—but I—
I have 'his Lordship's sympathy'.

It is a great and holy gift,
 But (mournfully the bard confesses)
It will *not* give his son a lift,
 Or pay for Mrs. Timpkins' dresses.
One cannot *clothe* one's self you see
With e'en Viceregal sympathy.

Wife of my bosom, o'er the main
 You cannot go—Droop sweetly here!
What matter? Let us read again
 That cutting from the *Pioneer*.
Just think! We paupers—you and I—
Possess His Lordship's sympathy!

A MISSING WORD

Published in the *Pioneer*, 25 February 1886, as a letter to the editor which began: 'Sir,—A few days ago a correspondent in your columns wanted to know what happened to an "obnoxious mariner" in byegone days. He said the playful practice of dropping the O.M. on a desert island rhymed to something. So it does—a whole lot of things. Perhaps this may help . . . ' Signed 'The Musical Toon Tree'. Uncollected, but included in Scrapbook 3.

The bold buccaneer, who had scuttled too soon
(*Id est*,[1] ere obtaining the last, least doubloon)
Smack, brigantine, frigate, yacht, convoy or schooner was held by his crew an incompetent 'coon';
And, though he had brought them through gale and typhoon,
Had given them treasure—and maidens to 'spoon',
They were wont—like mad dogs at the full of the moon—
To turn on that Captain with cocked musquitoon;
To bind him and strip him to breeches and shoon;
Then, seeking some 'key' where the blue breakers croon
O'er the coral reef fringing the placid lagoon,
Where the 'pig' men call 'long'[2] is boiled, roasted or stewn
By the innocent native at morn and at noon;
Where life is affliction and death is a boon
(Such islands e'en now o'er the south seas are strewn)
They would drop there the Captain—a hapless *Maroon*.

L'ENVOI

Shah, Sultan, Prince, Kaiser, King, Negus, or Woon,[3]
You may search, if you like, from December to June,
Rack *Roget's Thesaurus* and read till you swoon,
But, unless you work in some allusion to 'dune',
I *don't* think you'll get a fresh rhyme to *Maroon*.

THE SEVEN NIGHTS OF CREATION

Published in the *Calcutta Review* for April 1886 (vol. lxxxii, no. clxiv, pp. 464-7), and in separate printing the same year. By permission of the BL. Signed

[1] *Id est*: that is.
[2] *long pig*: a human body.
[3] *Woon*: a Burmese title for governor.

'Rudyard Kipling'. Quoted in J. L. Kipling, *Beast and Man in India*, London, 1891, ch. xviii. Uncollected in this form, but the 'Fragment of a Projected Poem . . . to be called "The Seven Nights of Creation" ', which appeared in *Schoolboy Lyrics* in 1881, was collected in the Outward Bound, De Luxe, Sussex, and Burwash Edns. (See above, pp. 89-90.)

> Yusuf the potter told me this today,
> In the cool shadow of the Bhatti Gate,[1]
> When a red scorpion stung me and I railed,
> Breaking his mid-day slumber. Yusuf knows
> The tales of all men's tongues.
>
>   'Not His the fault
> Who fashioned all things fair and fit for man
> In those six days He laboured. That thy hand
> Fell on the worn, *reh*[2]-rotten brick which hid
> The evil thing, this much was God's design,
> The beast was fashioned otherwise.'
>   I wrapped
> Fresh melon-rind above my palm and laughed,
> Because I doubted Yusuf, being young
> And, so my brother *hulwaies*[3] tell me, proud.
> 'In the beginning there were seven days',
> Growled Yusuf from behind his lime-dyed beard,
> 'And seven nights. God laboured in the Light,
> Who is the Light of All Things. By His will,
> Who is the Power, Eblis[4] from the Pit
> Had power to labour in the night and make
> All things for our discomfort. God is great!
> Alone, afar, at noon-tide Eblis watched,
> Jealous of God, the All Sustainer's work—
> Saw the Great Darkness rent in twain and lit
> With Sun and Moon and Stars—beheld the Earth
> Heaved upward from beneath the Waters, green
> And trampled by the Cattle—watched the Sea
> Foam with the Children of the Waters—heard
> The voices of the Children of the Woods
> Across the branches. Saw and heard and feared,

---

[1] *the Bhatti Gate*: one of the thirteen gates of Lahore, on the south side of the city.
[2] *reh*: salt pollution in soil.
[3] *hulwaies*: confectioners.
[4] *Eblis*: the devil or chief of the apostate angels in Islamic mythology.

And strove thoughout those Seven Nights of Sin
To mar with evil toil God's handiwork.
O Hassan! Saving Allah there is none
More strong than Eblis. Foul marsh lights he made
To wander and perplex us—errant stars,
Wild devil-ridden meteors bringing plague—
Deserts of restless sand-drifts—icebound seas
Wherein is neither Life nor power to live—
Bound Devils to the snow-capped peaks (These vex
Earth with their struggles)—poured undying fire
Into the bosoms of the tortured hills,
And filled the belly of the Deep with life
Unnameable and awful at his will—
Sent forth his birds, the owl, the kite, the crow–
Grey wolves that haunt our village-gates at dusk
Made he his horses and his councillor
The hooded snake—in darkness wove the grass
That kills our cattle—made the flowers that suck
Man's life like dew drops—evil seeds and shrubs
That turn the sons of Adam into beasts
Whom Eblis snatches from the sword-wide Bridge.[5]
The thing that stung thee and its kind his hands
Fashioned in mockery and bitter hate—
Dread beasts by land and water all are his.
Each bears the baser likeness of God's work,
Distorted, as the shadow of thy face
In water troubled by the breeze.'
                                    But here
An Ape from off the *chuppar*[6] thatch that hangs
Above my stall, dropped swiftly down and stole
A double handful of sweet *balushai*,[7]
Then gibbered overhead among his kin.
I laughed (albeit half my stall was wrecked).
'Is *he* the work of Eblis?' Yusuf stretched
One lean forefinger to the painted shrine
Where Hanuman[8] the idol leaped and grinned
And all his living brethren frisked above:—

---

[5] *the sword-wide Bridge*: Al Sirat, the bridge no wider than the edge of a sword, over which those seeking to enter the Islamic heaven must pass.
    [6] *chuppar*: grass or straw thatch.
    [7] *balushai*: a kind of sweetmeat.   [8] *Hanuman*: Hindu god in monkey form.

'Eblis made Man—behold him—dung and filth
And refuse of the Pit. O Hassan! See
The men of Eblis worshipped by his sons!
Alone, afar, at noon-tide Eblis watched
The Seven Soils slow moulded into Man,
And feared the living clay God made his lord.
Then the last Night of Sin came down and cloaked
The young and tender world while Eblis wrought.
None knew the secrets of that Night but God.
'Tis writ the angels shuddered when they heard
Clamour and lamentation through the dark;
Cries of huge beasts whom Eblis slew to make
His Man more perfect; thunders from the Pit
And voices of the Devils and the Djinns
Rejoicing. It is written Eblis called
Three times to God to stay the flying Night.
Allah Al Bari[9] heard him (He is great!)
And held three times Her pinions till the cries
Ceased and the work was perfect.'
                                    Yusuf smiled,
Mocking the apes with pellets from his wheel:—
'Perfect. Then Eblis turned and saw his work
When the Great Darkness lifted. Thus he cried
Amid the laughter of the Sons of God:—
"Lo! what is this I make. Are these *his* limbs
Bent inward tottering 'neath the body's weight?
The body crutched by hairy spider arms,
Surmounted by a face as who should say
Mourning:—Why hast thou made me, wherefore breathed
Spirit in this vile body? Let me be.—
The strange black lips are working with a cry,
A cry and protest while the wrinkled palms
Are put forth helplessly and beat the dusk.
So did not my great foe when he was made.
I saw his eye quicken with sense of power,
I saw all wild things crouch beneath that eye;
God gave him great dominion over all,
And blessed him. Shall I bless my handiwork?
After thy kind be fruitful, lust and eat,
All things I give thee in the Earth and Air

---

9 *Al Bari*: the Creator (one of the ninety-nine names of God).

Only . . . depart and hide thee in the trees.
He rises from the ground to do my will
Dumb, limping, crippled. Can the being speak?
Stay, Thing, and thank me for thy quickening.
The great eyes roll—my meaning is not there
Reflected, as God's word was in the Man's.
I, Maker, bid thee speak in Adam's tongue,
Unto my glory and the scorn of God.

*   *   *   *   *

He plucks the grass-tufts aimlessly, and works
Palm within palm; then, for a moment's space
Breaks off rough bark and casts it on the ground!
Accursed, e'en as I am.
                                    Yet one curse
Shall sink him lower than the lowest. Stay!
Man! Inasmuch as thou art made my Man,
From all communion in the woodland tongue
With beast and bird for ever be debarred.
The Oxen bellow in a thousand keys,
There is one bellow to the ear of man:
The Lion from the rock-rift calls his mate,
And Adam hastening folds the fearless flocks,
Saying:—He roars for hunger. He is wroth—
So be it unto thee.
                                    Alas! the light
Is flaring forth to mock me. He, my Man,
Helpless, uprooting grass. While all the world
Is thick with life renewed that fills my ears
My last, my greatest work is mockery.
Depart O Ape! Depart and leave me foiled!' '

This tale told Yusuf by the Bhatti Gate,
Mocking the Apes with pellets from his wheel.
He bade me wrap the melon-rind anew,
And trust in God the Fashioner of Good,
Seeing the mighty works of Eblis brought
A half day's torment at the most—or stole
A double handful of sweet *balushai*.

PARTURIUNT MONTES

Published in the *CMG*, 26 April 1886, with heading: 'We learn from Simla that the members of the Financial Committee have already assembled, and are pulling themselves together for their struggle with the work which lies before them. Statistics of a most intricate and searching nature have been demanded. Of so elaborate a nature does the scrutiny promise to be, that a long time must perforce elapse before the necessary tabular statements and details can be prepared and placed in the hands of members; whilst the sifting of so enormous a mass of information will necessitate Herculean efforts on the part of the Committee.—*Pioneer*, April 20th.' Reprinted in the *Pioneer*, 29 April. No signature. Uncollected, but included in Scrapbook 3. A news item from Calcutta, dated 9 February, had announced the membership of the Indian Finance Commission (i.e. the Financial Committee now referred to by the *Pioneer*), with Mr C. A. Elliot, Chief Commissioner of Assam, as President. Its task was to review the whole pattern of expenditure by all Government departments, both imperial and provincial, throughout India. One of the members was the Honourable W. W. Hunter (see above p. 308). The title derives from Horace's *Ars Poetica*: 'Parturiunt montes, nascetur ridiculus mus' (The mountains are in labour; the birth will be a ridiculous mouse).

Scene: *The Simla Offices*. F——E C———E *discovered striking attitudes.*

CHORUS OF MEMBERS *rolling up shirt-sleeves:*

We are going to retrench! Yes! we're going to retrench,
    In a rigid, revolutionary style;
From the Judge upon his Bench, on his costly cushioned Bench,
    To the Babu and the Commissariat *Byle*![1]
(pp)   (Especially the Babu and the Byle)

(ff)   Let the fat Departments blench,
        We are yearning to retrench
           In a clip-and-cut, and skin-removing style!
        And when office doors are shut, we will get to business, but
        First we pull ourselves together and we smile.
                Ah! Yah!   (*They smile*)
        We must pull ourselves together and must smile.

Barcarole Extatique by PRESIDENT, *to official step-dance*:
      And *I* shall evolve a Report,
        Shall write you a splendid Report;

---

[1] *Byle*: bullock.

And 'neath my direction each para and section
    Shall sparkle with jewels of thought!
Ye Gods! it must be a Report
To set all the others at naught:
An elephant-folio, phototype-oleo,
    Guttenberg–Caxton[2] Report!

Recitative; HON'BLE W.W. *to music expressive of caution*:

The Hills are full of little birds.
What need of compromising words?
    We all know what we think—
Wherefore, I beg to move that we,
In sign of unanimity,
    Do wink a pregnant wink.

PRESIDENT

I second the motion with pleasure.

2ND MEMBER

But I an amendment propose.
Let each man advance, in slow measure,
    His thumb to the side of his nose.

Motion carried nem. con.[3] C————E *stand to order*, HON'BLE W.W.
    intones fortissimo through a paper trumpet:

Bring pens in sheaves and writing blocks in bales!
Pour out the ink-kegs into stable-pails!
Let blotting-pads in bushels strew the floor!
Produce your office-boxes by the score!
Pile on statistics till the tables creak,
(E—t and I can sift 'em in a week)
Each to his place! Draw out your cleanest pen,
Flourish it once, and—put it back again!
Drop down exhausted! Let the Public see
You're worth your salt! Now, taking time from me,

----

[2] *Guttenberg-Caxton*: Johann Gutenberg was the inventor of movable printing type;
William Caxton was the first English printer. The suggestion is that the Report will be of
a scale inconceivable in terms of former methods of production.
    [3] *nem. con.*: with no one dissenting.

Wipe with one trembling hand a toil-worn brow—
Then, all together, *make an awful row*!
Turn to the Plains! What ho there! Pipes and tabors!
Tell them about our Herculean labours.

FULL CHORUS OF C———E *to accompaniment of clinking despatch-
boxes:*

We have fled the toils of tennis; we are saving you your pennies;
On the mountain where our den is, we are slaving all the day:
And we think it only fitting, you should know that we are sitting,
While a sinful world is flitting off to dinner, dance and play.
Laughing men and maids invite us where Mahasu[4] woods delight us;
Notes for sylvan *fêtes* indite us, but we shun the gilded snare;
For we think upon our Duty, and are blind to Love and Beauty,
We despise the thought of *chuti*[5]—scoff at exercise and air.

Adagio, con molt exp:

We're a wonderful Committee; we deserve your praise and pity,
Ke-ind Christian fellow-citizens we hope you'll take the hint.
We are dying of exertion, and the lack of all diversion;
And should value the insertion of these sentiments in print.

CHORUS FROM THE PLAINS OF THE STEAMING THOUSANDS

There is a way of putting things
        Intrinsically great and grand,
That laughter and derision brings,
        And wakes irreverence in the land.
The office Anglo-Indian
Is *not* a sentimental man.

He knows, forgive the fact, your pay,
        Is some six times as much as his'n.
He works—at least eight hours a day,
        Perspiring in a sultry prison.
Whereas, whate'er your labours be,
Your summer heat is seventy-three;

[4] *Mahasu*: a resort 10 mls. from Simla.
[5] *chuti*: leave, dismissal.

And he demands it as his due,
> That you sit still and, if you can,
Produce, before the year is through,
> A sober practicable plan.
How does our dear Sam Gerridge[6] spout it?
'*We* works, but we don't 'owl about it.'

FAIR PLAY

Published in the *CMG*, 14 May 1886, with signature 'R.K.' and subtitle
'(Dulce est deSeepeere in loco)'—a pun on Seepee or Sipi and 'desipere' in
the Horatian tag 'It is sweet to play the fool upon occasion' (*Odes*, IV. xii). An
explanatory heading ran 'SIMLA, May 11.—The meeting of the Legislative
Council, to consider the Bankruptcy Bill, which was fixed for the 13th instant,
has been postponed till the 20th, on account of the Seepee Fair, which com-
mences on Thursday. *See yesterday's Telegram*.' Reprinted in the *Pioneer* and
Englishman, 17 May, and the *Pioneer Mail*, 19 May. Uncollected, but included
in Scrapbook 3. The fair held annually at Sipi, some six miles from Simla, was
one of the social events of the year. Europeans were welcomed by the local
Maharajah; the Viceregal Staff gave splendid lunch parties; and the 'Hill girls
assembled', it was said, 'from miles round to be bought as wives by the Hill
youth' (*CMG*, 16 May 1887).

The *jharan*[1]-coated subalterns
> Are mounted and away—
Shall we his Lordship's Councillors
> Be laggards more than they?
The Matrons of the Mountain haste,
> The jocund with the *jeldie*,[2]
Where Rockcliff spoons[3] Elysium,
> And Lowrie's Abergeldie.[4]

---

[6] *Sam Gerridge*: a character in T. W. Robertson's play *Caste* (first produced 1867).
See his speech in Act III, scene i: ' 'E's a pretty one for one of the workin' classes, 'e is!
'Asn't done a stroke o'work these twenty year. Now, I *am* one of the workin' classes, but I
don't 'owl about it. I work, I don't spout.'

[1] *jharan*: duster material with loud colourful checks, much affected for summer suits
and jackets, especially by military men.
[2] *jeldie*: lively.   [3] *spoons*: flirts with.
[4] *Rockcliff, Elysium, Lowrie's and Abergeldie*: hotels at Simla.

Ho! gallop up the Jakko[5] road!
    Hi! scuttle down the hill!
Let be your legislative load—
    The burden of the Bill!
Come ye who rule a people's fate,
    Old men with grizzled hair—
Pack up the hamper and the crate
    We ride to Seepee Fair.

There let us pass the foaming glass,
    In place of measures dry;
And form Select Committees on
    The *pâté* and the pie.
There let us bid the swings revolve,
    And frolic on the green,
As fits the trusted Ministers
    And Stewards of the Queen.

To horse, to horse, my aged ones!
    Staid senators and hoar—
For life is short, and laws are long—
    The steed is at the door.
And if men sneer, and if men scoff,
    'Tis little we shall care.
The Council of the Empire stands
    Postponed—for Seepee Fair.

A PARALLEL

Published in the *Englishman*, 20 May 1886. No signature. Uncollected, but
included in Scrapbook 3. (The text is missing from the Scrapbook, but the
space left has a heading '*Englishman*, May 20th; and this was the only poem to
appear in the *Englishman* on that date.)

A has a wife who loves him much
    And clings to him with fervour great;
But A's perversity is such
    He really seems to loathe his mate.
I, who am B, observe with pain
    A's brutal conduct and disdain.

[5] *Jakko*: mountain at Simla encircled by a road which made a favourite evening ride.

I, pining for a soul to love,
    Procure a small fox terrier, C;
When (who can tell the springs which move
    The canine mind?) she takes to me.
She shares my meal. Her nightly doze
    Is taken on my chest or toes.

So, for three long delightful days
    I thrill with selfish exultation;
I laud her most obtrusive ways,
    I drag her all about the station;
At office, dinner, walk, or ride,
    I like to have her at my side.

About my path, about my bed,
    Come sure and certain as the Fates,
The pattering feet, the wistful head,
    The liquid gaze that—irritates.
I fight against a growing chill;
    I strive to think I love her still.

My days grow void of all delight,
    She follows me to every place;
I cannot take my rest at night,
    She licks devotedly my face.
The tail that wags for none but me
    Becomes a meek monotony.

I make no other dog my care
    (I wish that I could tell her so),
Or wander off to places where
    A good fox terrier should not go.
I only want at times to be
    Alone with no one else but me.

I do not care for winning ways
    From six A.M. till ten at night;
I even shun her liquid gaze;
    I almost wish that she could bite.
I cannot thrash her off—I tried.
    It bound her closer to my side.

'Tis wrong to kill, 'tis vain to strike.
   I will not cast her off—as yet.
I have no reason for dislike.
   I *know* I ought to love my pet.
I know I am a heartless traitor
   Which makes me more than ever hate her.

DISTRESS IN THE HIMALAYAS

Published in the *CMG*, 21 May 1886, with signature 'R.K.' and heading 'A singular scarcity of men prevails this year at most of the Hill Stations of Upper India; owing to the number of men who have taken leave to England or Kashmir.—*Newsletter*.' Reprinted in the *Pioneer*, 24 May, and *Pioneer Mail*, 30 May. Uncollected, but included in Scrapbook 3.

> There's wailing on the Camel's Back;[1]
>   There's grief on Simla Mall;
> Blank horror thrills the Murree[2] Hills
>   And broods o'er Naini Tal.[2]
> The dances stop; the dinners drop;
>   The blatant bands are dumb:
> The maidens wait disconsolate
>   For men who never come.
>
> The 'rickshaws run—none run beside,
>   Uncavaliered they go;
> The only mails (Her Majesty's)
>   Accentuate their woe.
> Ah ha! they scorned our simple worth
>   In other, livelier years;
> Come, let us mock their misery,
>   And gloat upon their tears!
>
> Go, ask the bounding *barasingh*[3]
>   Where are your partners gone!
> Speak to the flying P and O,[4]
>   Or Thomas Cook and Son!

[1] *the Camel's Back*: road on a ridge to the north of the hill-station of Mussoorie.
[2] *Murree, Naini Tal*: two other hill-stations.
[3] *barasingh*: red deer of Kashmir.
[4] *P and O*: vessel of Peninsular and Oriental Steamship Company.

They hunt another quarry now,
  The men whose loss you grieve;
For half of them are in Kashmir
  And half at Home on leave.

For six short weeks each rover seeks
  A broader, bustling Mall—
A cool, electric-lighted Ind[5]
  Behind the Albert Hall.
What is the scent of deodars—
  The bray of G–ldst——n's[6] band—
To odours dear of London smoke,
  And tumult of the Strand?

They will return, I know them well,
  But *you* must eke till then
A semi-torpid season out
  With 'boys' and aged men.
The rawest thing in uniform,
  The rowdiest in check,
Shall save your dance from breaking down,
  Your picnic from a wreck.

Go up, bald-headed patriarchs!
  Time brings again your chance;
A dado of sweet wallflowers
  Is withering for a dance.
Fly, flaxen-headed innocence!
  Flirt while your Fate allows;
The Law is kind and does not bind
  A minor to his vows.

A LEVÉE IN THE PLAINS [LEVÉETY IN THE PLAINS]

Published in the *CMG*, 26 May 1886, with title 'Levéety in the Plains' (punning on 'levée' and 'levity' and contrasting with 'Distress in the Himalayas'—see preceding item). Unsigned. Collected in the Outward Bound, De Luxe,

---

[5] *A cool electric-lighted Ind*: a reference to the Colonial and Indian Exhibition held in South Kensington in 1886.
[6] *G–ldst——n*: Herr Felix von Goldstein (see above, p. 277).

Sussex, and Burwash Edns. In the *CMG* version the fifth stanza begins 'The whole Punjab there in sumshus garb were / Paradin',' The occasion described was the Queen's Birthday Levée held at Government House, Lahore, at 10.15 P.M. on 24 May 1886.

> Come here, ye lasses av swate Parnassis![1]
>   Kape cool me hid while me pen recalls
> That night av tormint whan all Lahore wint
>   To honour the Quane an' our great Sorr Charles.[2]
>
> There was music brayin' an' punkahs swayin',
>   An' men dishplayin' their uniform;
> An' the native ginthry they thronged the inthry;
>   An' oh, by Jabers! 'twas powerful warm!
>
> There was Colonels more there than I could score there,
>   In white an' khaki an' knots an' bows;
> An' the bowld Civilians they came in millions,
>   Meltin' away under toight dress-clo'es.
>
> There was gowld in plastrons[3] on epigastrons,[4]
>   An' stand-up collars that lay down flat;
> An' the Doctors splindid, wid swords attinded,
>   An' hearse-plumes wavin' above their hat.
>
> The whole Punjab there, in sum'shus garb there,
>   Paraded grandly the Aujence Hall;
> An' the *Shubadars*,[5] wid their midals and shtars,
>   Stud up to attintion forninst the wall.
>
> Thin spurs were scratchin' an' sword-belts catchin'
>   As they let the batch in at ten-fiftane,
> An' we stud perspirin' wid zeal ontirin'
>   To the greater glory av England's Quane.
>
> But oh! the dignity, the moild benignity,
>   Whin the Chief Coort Judges tuk the flure;
> A-standin' sinthry in the private inthry,
>   An' watchin' the rest av us march before.

---

[1] *Ye lasses* . . . : the Muses.

[2] *Sorr Charles*: Sir Charles Umpherston Aitchison, Lieut.-Gov. of the Punjab (see above, p. 288).

[3] *plastrons*: breast-coverings of facing cloth worn by Lancers.

[4] *epigastrons*: midriffs.   [5] *Shubadars*: i.e. subadars, native officers.

So some bowed nately, an' some too stately,
    An' some went noddin' aisy an' free;
An' some went trippin', an' some went skippin',
    But all went dhrippin' through the big Levee.

Thin down the stairway we ran for airway,
    An' tuk refreshments whan all was done;
Wid scabbards clinkin' an' men a-drinkin',
    An' the shtars a-winkin' to watch the fun.

OUR LADY OF REST

Published in the *CMG*, 15 June 1886, with signature 'R.K.' Collected in the
Outward Bound, De Luxe, Sussex, and Burwash Edns.

The wind in the pine sings Her praises,
    The snows of the North are Her seat,
The bluebells and little Hill-daisies
    Make gorgeous the ground at Her feet.
There is health in Her hand for the taking,
    There is peace on the calm of Her breast,
And we yearn to Her, sleeping and waking,
        Our Lady of Rest!

The Earth is hot iron beneath us,
    The Heavens are brazen above,
The winds of the Firmament seethe us
    With blasts from the Pit as they rove.
The cool and the shade have retreated,
    The levin-lit dust-clouds attest;
Our furnace is seven times heated,
        O Lady of Rest!

'I have built ye a marvellous palace,
    As chill and as green as the sea.
Come up—come away from the valleys;
    Inherit, my children, with me!'
Though the yoke of our servitude gall us,
    Laborious, burdened, unblest,
Dare we turn at Her voice, though She call us,
        Our Lady of Rest?

Not ours the silence and scorning,
    Not ours the fault of delay.
Clear twilight brings merciless morning,
    And night little rest after day.
For a handful of silver we sold us,
    White slaves from the Isles of the West,
And the chains of captivity hold us,
        Our Lady of Rest!

Be good to us out of Thy pity,
    For surely, in time, it shall be
That we fly from the sun-smitten city,
    That we win to the mountains and Thee;
And, at last, when the weary Plains leave us,
    When we climb the Himalayan crest,
From the smoke of our torments receive us,
        Our Lady of Rest!

STATIONARY

Published in the *CMG*, 21 June 1886. No signature. Uncollected, but included in Notebook 3.

Required, a hint for a summer's excursion;
    Will anyone proffer a word of advice,
Say where may a gentleman, bent on diversion,
    Be certain of pleasure at moderate price?

Dalhousie takes seventeen hours to go ter
    (How hard are good rhymes!) and is deluged with rain,
While the people who live on the top of Bakrota[1]
    Have a Mall of their own and are 'cuts'[2] with Potrain.[1]

And Murree's mere Pindi,[3] or something too near it,
    With babies and *Ayahs*[4] pervading the Mall—
A halting place solely for men who Kashmir it,
    With a season that isn't a season at all.

[1] *Bakrota, Potrain*: two of the peaks on which the hill-station of Dalhousie was built.
[2] *cuts*: i.e. not on speaking terms.
[3] *Pindi*: Rawalpindi.
[4] *Ayahs*: nursemaids, ladies' maids.

There's merry Mussoorie, *dégagée* and breezy—
    All tail and no head which is pleasant . . . perhaps;
Where life flows along in one big 'free and easy',
    And those who aren't 'Johnnies' and 'sportsmen' are 'chaps'.

There's Simla, a trifle less high than its prices,
    Where you *must* wear good clothes for six months of the year—
With a false reputation for long deceased vices—
    As dull as Dalhousie and ten times as dear.

Oh! what is the good of three-farthing frivolity,
    On the lee of a *Khud*[5] with the monkey and crow?
The wise man will seek metropolitan jollity,
    Will save up his leave for three seasons and go.

OF BIRTHDAYS

MS letter from John Lockwood Kipling on his birthday to Edith Plowden, dated Simla, 6 July 1886: 'Ruddy interrupts his scribbling to hand me with eyes alight, as they are when he has verse-spinning on hand,—a sonnet he has made.—Here it is.—[*gives text*] Pretty, isn't it?—wanting a little polish and finish perhaps, as first draughts of verses are apt to do. But I object to Ruddy across the table that it is scarcely perfect as a compliment.—Why shouldn't I have been once young like other people? . . . Today has been the boy's first day in Simla & he has been dashing about making calls. So there may be a touch of fatigue in his sonnet . . . '(KP 1/10).

    For us[1] Life's wheel runs backward. Other nests
        Are stripped of all their fledglings when our Fate
        Pitying may be, a childhood desolate,
    Brings home deferred,—unparted each one rests
        Beneath one roof.
                    But the year's fitful span
        Brings change & growth & half displeased you say
        Musing upon the babes of yesterday:
    'Behold, she is a woman; He a man.'

---

[5] *Khud*: deep valley, precipitous hillside.

[1] *us*: the Kipling family.

5. Kipling, *c.*1886. On the reverse of this portrait Kiplıng wrote ' "A kind of scrubbed boy—a lawyer's clerk." Merchant of Venice.'

Yet, spite of all, the childish wonder clings
    About our spirits when we hear him say—
    Our Father—'Children I was born to-day.'
And we return to nursery wonderings
    Back comes the childish question to the tongue
    Father a child!—Was Father ever young?

KING SOLOMON'S HORSES

Published in the *Calcutta Review* for July 1886 (vol. lxxxiii, no. clxv, pp. 204–5), with this heading: '*When the horses, standing on three feet and touching the ground with the edge of the fourth foot, swift in the course, were set in parade before him, King Solomon in the evening said:—"Verily, I have loved the love of earthly good above the remembrance of my Lord; and I have spent the time in viewing these horses till the sun is hidden by the veil of night. Bring the horses back unto me." And when they were brought back, he began to cut off their legs and their necks.—Al Korân.*' Signed 'Rudyard Kipling'. Uncollected. By permission of the BL.

The black Egyptian coursers of the sands,
Grey stallions from the North, the beasts I love,
Red-nostrilled, river-maned, I slew them all
As a child smites in anger. Oh! wise King!
And foolish past the folly of all fools.

Not anger wholly. Hiram[1] at the gate
Reined in his chariot crying:—'Let them go;'
And I, because I knew the minds of men,
Who cannot rule my own, bade strike afresh,
Assured the fame of such a sacrifice
Would spread to Tyre and the isles beyond.
My honour and not God's I sought herein—
My honour and men's wonder. Who but I
Dare slay a thousand horses of the best,
As Hiram slays his score of starveling goats
To Ashtaroth?[2]
               What sin was theirs who lie
Gaunt carcasses beneath the moonlight—speed,
Strength, and the glorious beauty of their kind?

---

[1] *Hiram*: King of Tyre, who provided cedars for the building of the Temple (1 Kgs: 5). [2] *Ashtaroth*: pagan goddess of fertility.

The thunder of the storm was in their feet;
The lightning of the storm was in their eyes;
The power of ten thousand men was theirs;
And one old man, chafed at his own neglect,
Has taken strength and beauty, speed and power.
Yea, they fought well. My reeking spearmen ran
Thrice from their furious onset, when we penned
The flying hundreds in the Palace Porch,
And I had slain the fairest steed of all—
The great grey stallion with the iron mane.
I chose him for my chariot ere the dusk
Fell and my wisdom left me. Mild was he;
Kingly as I have been. He bowed his neck
To the sharp point and stumbled at my feet,
Still kingly, pleading with great liquid eyes,
And died in silence.
                          Then I saw my sin
But dared not stay the slaughter. Hiram's eye
Alight with wonder at the gate forbade;
And some old lust of bloodshed spurred me on.
Wherefore I loosed my spearmen, till the Porch
Filled with the tumult of the flying steeds,
The screams of men and horses, kicks and blows;
The sharp, quick bubble of the stabbing-spears;
Fall of great hoofs that plashed in pools of blood
And the low gurgle of the dying. Last,
Out of the press, a red horse reared himself
Black with the sweat of horror, white with foam.
(Accursed be my knowledge of brute speech![3])
Crying:—'What sin is ours that we die
My brother?' Then I would have stayed the spears,
But that none heard me till the last was slain;
And I was left alone among the dead—
The raw, sick smell of blood upon the air—
And Hiram's voice across the silent court
Crying:—'All honour to King Solomon!'

All honour to the wisdom of the King!
Wrath and mad lust for honour—honour these!

---

[3] *my knowledge of brute speech*: later Jewish legend attributed to Solomon the power of understanding the speech of all birds and beasts.

Small profit unto God the sacrifice;
And to myself the gain of my own scorn.

All honour to the wisdom of the King!
The grey was beautiful above his kind,
And Hiram's fleet has sailed, nor brings again
Another steed as fair . . . Oh! most wise King!

CUPID'S DEPARTMENT

Published in the *Pioneer*, 20 July 1886, with signature 'R.K.' Reprinted in the
Pioneer Mail, 25 July. Uncollected.

Perched upon the Simla Ridge, as the clocks were warning ten,
Cupid watched the cavalcade of the office-going men;
Very wet his bow and quiver, dripping each ambrosial plume,
And a little touch of 'liver' filled his Godship's soul with gloom.

So he sneered to see them pass to the tin-topped roofs below—
'These', quoth he, 'are, one and all, my subordinates you know.
They may play at what they please—home and foreign policy—
C.S.I.'s[1] and C.I.E.'s[2]—but their work is under me.

Some have served me many years, faithful clerks and zealous they—
Some I pay in solid coin—some I owe a lifetime's pay;
On the honour of a god, it would make the saddest laugh,
Could he only read the roll of my Departmental Staff.

Silver-headed gentlemen, raw and reckless-riding youths,
Learn of me from four to ten, diverse valuable truths;
Each into my service pressed is, florid Youth and Dotage fading,
And the beauty of the jest is no one knows his rank or grading.

You may take it as a rule, for the comfort of your heart meant,
Kings are generally Pawns, Pawns are Kings in my Department;
All exceptions you must settle for yourself by Rule of Two—
If you chance to make an error, very much the worse for you.

[1] *C.S.I.'s*: Companionships of the Order of the Star of India.
[2] *C.I.E.'s*: Companionships of the Order of the Indian Empire.

All the office rules I keep out of my *employés'* sight,
They must puzzle out the Code for themselves by Nature's Light.
Yet, despite my rank injustice and the jobs I perpetrate,
My department is the largest and the leading one of State!'

Thus it was with mocking laughter when the clocks had stricken ten,
Cupid sent his blessing after all those office-going men:—
'Play at what you please my servants—home or foreign policy,
Ruling nations, building bridges—but your work is under me!'

A LOGICAL EXTENSION

Published in the *CMG*, 16 August 1886, with signature 'R.K.' and heading 'The horse, added Mr Thomas, was still fit for "purely processional purposes." *Vide* the *Pioneer*'s story of the Madras Scandals.' Uncollected, but included in Scrapbook 3. Through the summer of 1886 the *Pioneer* ran a series of articles on what it described as 'the Madras Scandals'. These centred on the charge that Mr H. E. Sullivan, the Senior Member of Council in Madras, had been guilty of serious malpractice, and that Mr Crole, the Collector of Madura, had been victimized because of his attempting to draw attention to the case. (For further details see notes to 'At the Bar', p. 338 below.) This poem deals with an unsavoury though minor episode, which was featured in the *Pioneer* for 7 August. Mr Crole had been suspended from his post, without pay; and Mr H. S. Thomas, a member of the Board of Revenue at Madras and an old friend of Mr Sullivan, had been appointed to enquire into Mr Crole's administration of the area. Mr Thomas had been at an earlier stage in his career the Collector at Tanipore, and as such Government Agent to the Ranees[1] there. Mr Crole had later held the same post, and at that time Mr Thomas had wanted to buy a horse from him, but was reluctant to pay the full price. He had offered an old horse of his own as part-payment; and when Mr Crole refused, he proposed that Crole should acquire the horse on behalf of the Ranees (i.e. at their expense), provide it with a home in their stables, and retain the purchase price as part-payment from him, Mr Thomas! Mr Crole had very properly refused. He had now been goaded into leaking the story, including the fact that Mr Thomas, while admitting that the horse had certain defects, had argued that it would none the less make a very handsome show-horse for processions.

> A horse? My charger's back is galled,
>   His knees are chipped, his hocks askew,

---

[1] *Ranees*: Hindu princesses.

I think he is the creature called
   By captious folk an 'utter screw',
And, spite of his declining years,
He jibs and shies and kicks and rears.

But if you helped him on behind,
   And propped him firmly underneath,
And led him (for the beast is blind)
   And patched his hide and filed his teeth,
I'm sure he'd be admired by all,
For purposes processional.

A wife? My daughter's form is rude,
   Her figure bad, her face the same,
Her chin retreats, her teeth protrude,
   Her eyes are green, her hair is flame.
But for processions—on my life—
You couldn't want a better wife.

A house? A hat? A dog? A gun?
   I've got the very things. I'll sell 'em,
They are all a trifle old, but none
   Would know it if you didn't tell 'em,
There—you can take them as they stand,
Processionally, off my hand.

The house fell in? The dog went mad?
   The rifle bust and you were blinded?
You seem to think your bargains bad,
   How singularly narrow-minded!
I should have mentioned my possessions
Are kept entirely for processions.

Why this appearance of disgust?
   This blow before? That kick behind?
I am a reprobate? I trust
   I am as godly as my kind.
Truth, Honour, Faith, I keep 'em all—
For purposes processional.

THE SONG OF THE DANCER

Published in the *CMG*, 7 September 1886, with heading: ' "With a form so wasted and worn, a spirit weary and faint, / A maiden danced in ragged robes and patches of powder and paint." "*G*" in *C. and M. Gazette—August 30th*.' No signature. Uncollected, but included in Scrapbook 3. Kipling's poem is a reply to G's 'Song of the Dance' which, modelled on Hood's 'Song of the Shirt', deplored the danger to health and spirits of perpetual waltzing.

What! Eternal condemnation for each innocent gyration,
　　Plus pneumonia and bronchitis and a ragged dress as well?
Keler-Bela, Strauss, Waldteufel,[1] with immortal souls you trifle,
　　For it seems your sweetest music opes the shortest cut to Hades.

This isn't said but hinted in the poem that you printed
　　On the thirtieth of August, and I've seen the thing before.
There's a certain form of tract (which is extremely inexact) which
　　Says in prose what 'G' has chanted of the perils of the Floor.

Does Dancing lead to Death then? Does one never stop for breath
　　then?
　　Do our wholesome English maidens deal in powder and in paint?
Do they fly where drinks are handy, to the 'simpkin'[2] and the brandy?
　　Are they all that 'G' has stated? I have met a few who ain't.

There are venerable dancers—senile, snowy-headed prancers,
　　Who are better in the whist-room—better still at home in bed.
But they frolic round the ball-room, taking up already small room,
　　Why should 'G' attack the youngsters? Why not preach to *these*
　　instead?

They were young long since, we know it. They are old, their faces
　　show it.
　　They have had their cakes and ginger; played the play and seen the
　　show,
And we feel '*bonjour lunettes*',[3] should entail '*adieu fillettes*',[4]
　　But it doesn't, and they linger all unwilling yet to go.

---

[1] *Keler–Bela. . . .*: three famous composers of waltzes—Kéler Béla (1820–82), Hungarian; Johann Strauss the Younger (1825–99), Austrian; and Émile Waldteufel (1837–1915), Alsatian.
[2] *simpkin*: champagne (with reference to G's lines 'With a form so wasted and worn, she scarce could stand on her legs, / A maiden waltzed in silken rags, supported only by "pegs" ').　　[3] *bonjour lunettes*: greetings, spectacles.
[4] *adieu fillettes*: goodbye, young girls.

'Ah! The insolence of Youth' they will make answer, but in sooth they
   Have a hundred consolations—money, girth and social standing.
We are paupers, slim, neglected—they are portly, rich, respected—
   Let us drive our aged rivals from the ball-room to the landing!

Now from evidence internal, the effusion in your journal
   Was the handwork of a lady (and exceeding well she sung)
Let her drop tractarian writing—join the great *jihad*[5] we're fighting—
   Swell the war-whoop of the Juniors—shout:—'The Ball-Room for
     the Young!'

FURTHER INFORMATION

Published in the *CMG*, 29 September 1886, with signature 'K' and heading
'("Lord Dufferin's Staff don't kiss." "Pioneer" *Sept. 23*)' Reprinted in the
Pioneer, 2 October, and *Pioneer Mail*, 6 October. Uncollected, but a copy
seems to have been printed specially for Lord Dufferin himself.[1] The *Pioneer*
of 23 September had carried an anecdote about Lady Dufferin's fancy dress
ball for children at Simla: 'A diminutive Miss approaches an equally diminutive
Master and enquires what he is. "I'm a Goverment House Aide-de-Camp",
answers the well-taught pigmy. "Oh den I must tiss you", rejoins the lady.
Autres temps, autres mœurs[2]—the little maid must have lived before her time.
Lord Dufferin's staff don't kiss.' Lord Dufferin's staff, headed by the Military
Secretary, the dashing Lord William Leslie de la Poer Beresford, VC, played a
central part in the social life of Simla; and when an amateur poet or poetess
wrote in the *CMG* of 6 October in defence of the asceticism attributed to them
in this poem, the paper noted that these 'very correct views . . . ought to
relieve the mind of those readers—if there were any such—who were harassed
by a suspicion of irony in "K's" effusion.'

      'And don't they really kiss you?' No!
      They'd blush if you asked them—ever so!
      At the slightest mention of social slips
      They turn clear pink to the finger-tips.
      Why, anything verging on innocent chaff
      Would shock the whole of Lord Dufferin's Staff;
        That Solemn and Serious Staff.

---

  [5] *jihad*: holy war against the infidel.

---

  [1] *Stewart and Yeats*, pp. 27–8, 451.
  [2] *Autres temps, autres mœurs*: other times, other manners.

'And pray, and what do the Gentlemen drink?'
From Whiskey they fly and from 'Simkin'[3] shrink;
But toast and water they merrily quaff,
For this is the way of Lord Dufferin's Staff;
  His rigidly temperate Staff.

'And don't they dance?' They think it wrong,
And wholly unfitting an *aid-de-cong*;
'Tis all you can do to raise a laugh,
Much less a waltz from Lord Dufferin's Staff,
  That Solemn and Serious Staff.

From six in the morning till ten at night,
The study of tongues is their sole delight;
And the Munshi[4] drones over *gain* and *kaf*[5]
To that ocean of learning, Lord Dufferin's Staff;
  His crushingly erudite Staff.

They seldom dine and they never sup.
They wear their jack-spurs wrong side up.
They always walk with their eyes on the ground,
They call P–l–ti's[6] the 'Devil's pound',
And frequently speak of Balls and dinners
  As traps for the Souls of benighted sinners.
'The lusts of the flesh are dross and draff',
  Say the whole of this verily Christian Staff,
   This painfully Virtuous Staff.

They are never seen on the Annandale course,[7]
They take no stocks in the legs of a horse.[8]
And the smoky din of a lottery night
Is rank perdition in their sight.
In fact, they are all too good by half
For this frivolous world are Lord Dufferin's Staff;
  This rigidly temperate, Solemn and Serious,
   prudish and passionless Staff.

---

[3] *Simkin*: champagne.   [4] *Munshi*: native teacher of languages.
[5] *gain and káf*: two letters representing Urdu phonemes difficult for Europeans to master.   [6] *P–l–ti's*: Peliti's, the famous café and confectioner's at Simla.
[7] *the Annandale course*: racecourse near Simla. Lord William was one of the best-known riders in India. (See below, p. 344.)   [8] *the legs of a horse*: cf. Ps. 147: 10.

ON A RECENT APPOINTMENT

Published in the *CMG*, 4 October 1886, with signature 'R.K.' and heading ' "The projectile having passed beyond the range of the earth's attraction, and the explosion of rockets at its base being insufficient to propel it further, must naturally revolve round the moon in interplanetary space, until the end of Time." *From the Earth to the Moon* (condensed).' Reprinted in the *Pioneer*, 6 October. Uncollected, but included in Scrapbook 3. The *CMG* for 29 September had reported that 'our Simla correspondent telegraphs that it is officially announced that Sir Charles Aitchison[1] will succeed Sir Steuart Bayley as Member of Council.' This appointment was an unexpected one: Sir Charles was already Lieutenant-Governor of the Punjab, a post to which a member of the Viceroy's Council might normally aspire *after* serving in that capacity. On 5 October the *CMG* had an article on 'The Simla Season', dated 30 September, which comments that 'The step by which a Lieutenant-Governor fades into the light of common day, and becomes a mere Member of Council, though it is not without precedent in the North-West Provinces, is new to us in the Punjab, and sets us speculating as to in how many years, if the playing back process be fairly carried out, we may expect to see Sir Charles jostling his juniors in the ranks of the Assistant Commissioner!'

<blockquote>

Oh! know ye not the rocket's flight—
    A whizz—an upward progress quick—
A spurt of fire 'gainst the night,
    And, after all, a burn-out stick
Falls, fields away, and sinks to rest,
Unnoticed, on earth's kindly breast.

Of old, our kings evanished so.
    They ruled and passed, and no one missed—
Dispersed to baser spheres and low
    'Mid groves of the Evangelist[2]
Or Kensington or Brompton—these
Received our Ex–authorities.

Nous avons changé tout cela[3]
    (Which means the old *régime* is changed)
No longer falls the full–poised star
    From that high orbit it has ranged.

</blockquote>

---

[1] *Sir Charles Aitchison*: see above, p. 288.
[2] *groves of the Evangelist*: St John's Wood.
[3] *Nous avons* . . . : we have changed all that.

But—*teste*[4] here His Honour's case—
Returns upon its godly race.

This year, he rules our province—next
    He will assist in framing laws—
Grow eloquent on code and text,
    And scuffle over point and clause.
By '92, unless I err,
He will be made Commissioner.

Divisions will his care confess
    For five full years. Thereafter he
In '97, more or less,
    Will find preferment as D.C.,[5]
When he will canter o'er the fields
And check the cess his district yields.

By nineteen twelve or twenty-four,
    When mind and body feel the brunt
Of ninety-seven years or more,
    He will become a junior 'stunt';[6]
And three-year men, with beardless faces,
Will help him through his maiden cases.

By nineteen-thirty—hopeful thought!
    With eighty years of work to show,
We shall behold His Honour brought
    To humble E.A.C.[7] you know.
And after that—if life remain—
His Honour will ascend again.

Why, Reader, dost thou hesitate
    To take my flawless theory?
Go, prove it on a school-room slate—
    Look up, oh Doubter, to the sky!
The comet's fiery passage run,
It spins for ever round the Sun.

[4] *teste*: witness.
[5] *D.C.*: Deputy Commissioner.
[6] *stunt*: Assistant [Commissioner]
[7] *E.A.C.*: Extra Assistant Commissioner (the humblest administrative grade).

AT THE BAR

Published in the *CMG*, 9 October 1886, with signature 'K.' and heading from the *Pioneer* of 25 September: 'Is it or is it not true that the hon'ble Mr H. E. Sullivan has violated the covenant of his order? His honour has been called in question. Yet he moves not.' Reprinted in the *Pioneer*, 11 October. Uncollected, but included in Scrapbook 3. The Madras scandals (see above, p. 331) and the *Pioneer*'s denunciation of them had now come to a head. After Mr Crole had been suspended from his duties without pay because (it was alleged) of insubordinate behaviour and intemperate language in his communications with the Government of Madras, his place as Collector of Madura was taken by a Mr Garstin. *He* had since been the victim of a dacoit attack, in which he had been robbed and beaten; and in the subsequent trial of suspects the suggestion arose that Crole had been in part responsible for instigating the attack. Crole's barrister, a Mr Norton, had denied this and suggested in turn that it was a report initiated by Mr Sullivan, the Senior Member of Council in Madras, as part of his vendetta against Crole. Sullivan brought a libel action, which was dismissed, not on the ground of truth or falsity in Norton's statement, but on the technical ground that that statement was privileged, having been made in a court of law. The trouble had begun with Crole's denunciations of what he saw as corruption among officials in Madras. Members of the Indian Civil Service had all signed a 'covenant' which defined their terms of service: to avoid the abuses of the previous century it forbade officials to own landed property in India or to engage in business transactions on their own behalf. Crole maintained that these terms had been violated, not least by Mr Sullivan who was said to have acquired a tea plantation known as Richings. Sullivan denied this, claiming that he had bought that property for his son and that he himself had no interest in it. When, however, the whole matter was referred to Lord Kimberley, the Secretary of State for India, he ruled that Sullivan did have a substantial interest in the estate, that Crole was right to raise the matter, that his intemperate language did merit punishment, but nothing as severe as that imposed, and that he should be reinstated forthwith in a comparable position, without any loss of pay or pension rights. There was a feeling that even now Sullivan was being protected by friends in high places: as Senior Member of Council he was the right-hand man of Sir Mountstuart Elphinstone Grant Duff, Lieutenant-Governor of Madras (well-known for his flamboyant—some thought boastful—speeches). In the event, however, the fear Kipling expresses—that Sullivan might act as Lieutenant-Governor for a time after Grant Duff's departure—proved unfounded. Lord Connemara arrived in due course to take over, and Sullivan left for England to explain himself as best he could to the Secretary of State. (Kipling was later to use some lines from this poem in his attack on Parnell in 'Cleared'—see *Barrack-Room Ballads*.)

Help for a Councillor distressed—a spotless spirit hurt!
Help for an honourable name sore trampled in the dirt!

From Mandalay to moist Bombay, oh listen to my song—
The *honourable* Sullivan has suffered 'grievous wrong'.

Four times his name was mentioned—oh, the burning black disgrace,
By that wicked Mr. Norton in the Garstin beating case.
Whereon he instituted suits and filed an affidavit;
And in favour of the barrister five learned judges gave it.

They gave it on a point of law—so let the question slide.
Another more important case is waiting to be tried—
Another and a larger Bench are asking, as their due,
Some simple explanations, Mr Sullivan, from you.

As the senior of a council incorruptible and just,
The honour of our Government was yours to hold in trust.
Men say the trust was broken—that the pledge was cast aside.
You have seen the charge in writing. Is that charge to be denied?

Now, hereafter, when Grant Duff shall quit a deeply thankful nation,
With a scrap-book full of speeches and a blasted reputation,
You will rule his thirty millions for a time—and understand,
Every moment of your rule, Sir, is an insult to the land.

You—a bye-word through the country from Peshawur to Ceylon,
You will govern Southern India when your worthy chief has gone—
You—the man of deft excuses—will your truthful pen deny
That Kimberley in black and white has given you the lie?

'But, in truth, he had an interest'—you'll remember what he wrote
On the Richings land-job business—'Tis a nasty thing to quote;
But you got the lie direct, Sir, in a curt official line.
And you took the insult meekly—bore the shame and made no sign.

There's a virtue in forbearance—but the time has come to show
You are much maligned and libelled, or to leave your post and go.
For the honour of your service, let us know you as you are;
'Is it guilty or not guilty?' Answer, prisoner at the Bar.

THE VINDICATION OF GRANT DUFF

Published in the *CMG*, 25 October 1886, with heading ' "So are they all, all
honourable men."—*See today's telegram*.' Unsigned and uncollected. The
Telegraphic Intelligence in the same issue (which would have been seen in
advance of publication only by the editorial staff, consisting of Kipling and E.
Kay Robinson) includes an item from Madras, on the review of his own
administration presented in a Minute, with some self-satisfaction, by Sir
Mountstuart Elphinstone Grant Duff at the conclusion of his term as Lieuten-
ant-Governor. It included comments on the Madras Scandals (see above,
pp. 331 and 338): 'As to the landholding of Madras civilians, he admits that,
until the time of his predecessor, the old rules had evidently slipped too much
out of sight. He proceeds:—"No doubt a vast amount of spiteful nonsense has
been talked and written about the sins in the matter of land of that very
honourable body of men, the Madras Civil Service, but I am sure all its mem-
bers will see that to transgress ever so little the rules about landholding is a sad
mistake, and one which enables its enemies to heap upon it all manner of false
accusations." '

> The man who digs himself a tomb
>   And hastes to drop forgotten in it,
> May justly, ere he meets his doom,
>   Address Creation in a Minute.
> It cannot harm a reputation
> Gone past all prospect of salvation.
>
> 'Oh! very honourable men'—
>   Thus writes the Ruler of Madras—
> 'Your "enemies" are happy, when
>   The bounds of right you overpass.
> And, since they are so spiteful—why,
> When you go wrong, the fact deny?
>
> All grossly patent forms of fraud
>   Are inexpedient, because
> They to our enemies afford
>   Excuse to prate of breach of laws.
> Don't blush, my friends! *I* also find
> How soon old rules slip out of mind.
>
> The Decalogue, for instance, is
>   A simple Code of Sections ten,

Yet we occasionally miss
   An odd commandment now and then.
Well—Laws are long and Life is short!
So, keep your trading out of Court.

Observe, I drop no word of blame,
   No syllable of censure mild;
Nor can men's "spiteful nonsense" shame
   My colleagues pure and undefiled.
But since the world is so abusive,
Don't make your land-jobs *too* obtrusive.

You see, a narrow-minded herd
   By spite and malice actuated,
Take views which are, we know, absurd
   Of lapses such as I have stated.
Wherefore, I do adjure you, then,
Keep straight *in public*, gentlemen.

Buy land in provinces afar—
   The sinful *Pioneer*[1] eschew;
Mistrust the wily *zemindar*[2]
   Who notes whate'er you say and do.
So shall each full of honours die
A pure and pensioned C.S.I.'[3]

Fit ending to a fit career—
   A dwindling reputation's close—
But, let us, while we scoff, revere
   The man who, even as he goes,
Paints in the shame with artist hand,
And flaunts the picture through the land.

---

[1] *The sinful Pioneer*: for the *Pioneer*'s campaign on the Madras scandals, see above, pp. 331 and 338.

[2] *the wily zemindar*: an allusion to the evidence against Sullivan presented by a *zemindar* (landlord) involved in the case.

[3] *C.S.I.*: Companion of the Order of the Star of India.

LUCIFER[1]

Published in the 2nd edn. of *Departmental Ditties* in the autumn of 1886, but not included in subsequent edns. of that volume. Holograph version in Pierpont Morgan Library. Collected in the Outward Bound, De Luxe, Sussex, and Burwash Edns. The MS and first published forms have ' "Side" ' for 'Pride' in l. 2 and 'mystic' for 'magic' in l. 5 of the first stanza. The 'black' epithet of the final stanza is 'short' in the MS and 'terse' in the 2nd edn.

Think not, O thou from College late deported,
        Pride goeth down
Among thy seniors—yea, though thou hast sported
        The B.A.'s gown,
And on thy Card the magic letters[2] stand
Which stamp thee of the Rulers of the Land.

St. Vincent Clare's Papa had lived before him,—
        Which always helps,—
So early in official life They bore him
        From fellow-whelps,
Destined to die or sicken in the slough
Of Lower India, to the Mountain's brow.

No fairyland is Capua[3]—still,'tis better
        Than other lands.
St. Vincent licked the stamp and signed the letter,
        And bound the bands
Of that foul, frail red tape which strangles ever
The honest energetic fool's endeavour.

So prospered greatly and forgat his father—
        Thereafter, big
With his own merits, grew to be a rather
        Conceited prig.
Facile the downward path,[4] O Clare! The Gods
Saw and prepared for him their briniest rods.

---

[1] *Lucifer*: cf. Isa. 14: 12: 'How art thou fallen from Heaven, O Lucifer, son of the morning!'   [2] *the magic letters*: ICS (Indian Civil Service).

[3] *Capua*: one of Anglo-India's nicknames for Simla. (In Roman times Capua was the chief city of Campania, famous for its wealth and luxury.)

[4] *Facile the downward path*: cf. Virgil, *Aeneid*, vi. 126: *facilis descensus Averno* (the descent to the nether world is easy).

'He is a c–d',[5] They murmured vexed and low;
        Yet said in love:
'No matter; give the boy another show;
        He may improve' . . .
'He is impossible.' The fiat went
Forth not so quickly as St. Clare's descent.

Cast out and doubly damned by that black epithet,
        He sought the Plains;
And now behind his door whoe'er so tappeth it,
        Another reigns:
While Vincent, as the punkah flickers o'er him,
Remembers—that his father lived before him.

ICHABOD

Published in the *CMG*, 9 November 1886, with signature 'Kingcraft' and sub-heading '(*See next column*)'. Uncollected. The title means 'The glory is departed'. Kingcraft, whose death was reported in October, had been for years the finest pony in India. ('Full of age and honour', wrote the *Indian Planter's Gazette and Sporting News*, 'the best horse of his day has been gathered to his fathers. . . . ') The 'next column' in the *CMG* carried an item headed 'A SPORTSMAN'S LAMENT'. It reported an advertisement for the Umballa Military and Hunt Meeting to be held on 16–18 December, with an assurance by the stewards, many of them officers in the Queen's Bays, that the steeple-chase course had been altered and made easier: 'The ditches are filled up, and all the rails removed. The fences are well sloped and bushed, and are well littered on the landing sides.' A correspondent, signing himself 'One of the Old School' deplores the degeneracy of the organizers: 'When we wept over the departure of the 9th Lancers, it was a great consolation to us, when a keen youth said "the Bays will fill their place." He was right, and in their zeal for filling things, they have filled in the ditches on the steeple course. . . . "The course has been altered and made easier." Shades of the 9th Lancers! When we shook our lances[1] and followed him who never returned when we crashed over boulders and nullahs[2] into ten thousand Afghans at Shahpur, it was *not* because we had been schooled over filled-in ditches. . . . ' And he invokes the support of well-known gentlemen-riders of North India in his protest. Kipling's authorship is attested by E. Kay Robinson, who tells us that the poem

---

[5] *c–d*: cad.

[1] *When we shook our lances* . . . : a reference to a charge by the 9th Lancers against overwhelming odds in the Chardeh Valley, near Sherpur or Shahpur and Kabul, in 1879, in the 2nd Afghan War. The commanding officer, Lieut.-Col. Cleland, was badly wounded in the attack.   [2] *nullahs*: dry watercourses.

achieved considerable notoriety: 'old steeple-chasers went humming it all over every station in upper India and swearing that it was the best thing ever written in English', while it was correspondingly resented by the Queen's Bays. ('Kipling in India', *McClure's Magazine*, vol. vii, no. 2, July 1896, pp. 105–6.)

Get a nervous lady's pony—get the oldest you can find—
Strap an ulster on the pommel—tie a bedding-roll behind;
To a Hanoverian Pelham[3] hitch a standing martingale[4]—
Then hang upon his jaws, my son, and listen to my tale.

Many ages since, my infant, we were green as Dehra[5] grass,
Though we lacked the shining silver we were millionaires in brass;[6]
And we gathered at Umballa when the 'seventies' were low,
And we rode like Helen Blazes in the days of long ago.

Those were times when life went swiftly both for rider and for horse—
When we sampled with our clavicles the texture of the course;
For the Stewards built the fences up to five-foot six or so,
And we 'pecked'[7] about those ramparts in the days of long ago.

Answer, man of many fractures,[8] William Beresford—Give ear.
'Bertie',[9] sweltering in Calcutta, Johnston, Humphreys, Percy Vere,
Did *you* fill these yawning ditches? Did *you* lay the railings low,
On the old Umballa race-course in the days of long ago?

Yea the ditches filled aforetime; but they filled with wrathful men!
Yea the railings were demolished by a bolter now and then!
More than once the 'well-bushed fences' sloped before the staggering
    blow
Of a puller, gazing skyward, in the days of long ago.

---

[3] *Hanoverian Pelham*: form of bit with curb and snaffle in one.

[4] *martingale*: a strap fastened at one end to the noseband, at the other to the girth, to prevent a horse from rearing or throwing back its head.

[5] *Dehra*: the capital of the Dehra Dun district, situated in a mountain valley 2,300 feet above sea-level: hence the greenness of the grass referred to.

[6] *brass*: effrontery (cf. 'brass neck').   [7] *pecked*: pitched forward.

[8] *man of many fractures*: Lord William Leslie de la Poer Beresford, VC, 9th Lancers, was Military Secretary to the Viceroy and a leading figure in sporting circles in India. An article in the *CMG*, 20 August 1888, in the series 'Our Gentlemen Riders', described him as an 'intrepid sportsman and daring rider who can boast a record of eight broken collar-bones, four concussions of the brain, and contusions innumerable'.

[9] *Bertie . . .* : Bertie Short, Frank Johnston, Percy Vere, and Humphreys were well-known members of the racing fraternity whose names frequently appear in 'Sporting Notes' from the *Indian Planter's Gazette and Sporting News*.

There was litter—lots of litter—spread about 'the landing side'
When a blown and basted leader checked his last half-hearted stride,
And the ruck came up behind him—and they made a holy show
On the old Umballa race-course in the days of long ago.

Many ages since, my infant, we were green as Dehra grass;
We were guileless as the morning—but we knew what riding was.
But a newer generation seem to make the pace more slow
Than we made it at Umballa in the days of long ago.

To an iron-bound ring-saddle nail a safety stirrup; then
Stitch a four-foot sofa-cushion just across your abdomen.
With a length of double stove-pipe guard your neck in case it breaks,
And—enter at Umballa, for the Military Stakes!

TWO LIMERICKS ON THE MADRAS SCANDALS

Almost certainly by Kipling are two limericks attributed to 'The Office Crow', published in the *CMG* on 20 November and 22 November 1886. Uncollected. For the matters alluded to, see above pp. 331 and 338. E. Kay Robinson recalls a tame crow which he and Kipling 'had picked up in a crippled condition in the road'. He became their 'Office Crow', and they considered opening a column in the paper for ' "Caws by the Office Crow", upon politics and things in general' ('Kipling in India', *McClure's Magazine*, vol. vii. no. 2, July 1896, p. 107).

(*a*) Our office crow, a most ill-mannered but perspicacious fowl, has, after a hearty meal on some back-numbers of the *Madras Mail*, delivered himself of the following. He calls it poetry:—

> There was an old man in a doolie[1]
> Who was pummelled by robbers unruly.
> When he said:—'On my soul
> 'Tis the work of one C—e!'
> The P——r jumped on him duly.

(*b*) That rude bird, the Office Crow, encouraged by our acceptance of his little contribution yesterday, continues to croak on matters of ancient history:—

---

[1] *doolie*: covered litter.

There once was a man of Madras
Who sold a 'Processional' ass.
    When they said:—'This is low!'
    He replied (says the Crow)
'These things are the rule in Madras!'

ALNASCHAR[1]

Published in the *CMG*, 23 November 1886, with signature 'R.K.' and heading from the previous day's paper reporting a *rise* in the value of the rupee: 'The rate of Exchange in Bombay on Saturday, November 20th was 1*s*. 6d., and the market was firm.' (Cf. pp. 298–9 above.) Uncollected, but included in Scrapbook 3.

So runs the telegram. Prepare
    The fatted calf—the firstling slay!
Wife of my Soul! Our meagre fare
    Shall be a Persian feast today.
The Widow's vintage[2] must be poured
This night above our humble board.

Bring forth the Bank-book—let us con
    The total of our savings small.
Draw draughts the London branch upon;
    Tomorrow we remit it all.
There is a tide—but no one knows
How soon it ebbs—how far it flows.

Methinks there is a suaver touch,
    A blander influence o'er the Earth;
The pauper East from Prome[3] to Cutch[4]
    Is radiant with returning mirth.
The very sky that hems us in,
Beams with a fine financial grin.

---

[1] *Alnaschar*: a beggar in the *Arabian Nights* who inherited a hundred pieces of silver, invested them in a basket of glassware, and then indulged in visions of the wealth he would acquire by cumulative trading. His final dream was of marrying the Vizier's daughter and then spurning her with his foot, at which point he kicked over his basket and broke all his wares.

[2] *The Widow's vintage*: Veuve Cliquot champagne (*veuve*: widow).

[3] *Prome*: city in lower Burma to the north of Rangoon.

[4] *Cutch*: area on the north-west coast of India.

The fervid Sun seems almost kind,
   My evening mutton almost tender;
Yea, at this moment, I could find
   Heart to believe my spouse is—slender.
Long vistas of enormous wealth
Confront me as I drink her health.

Now Thomas Timpkins—he my son,
   A lad of rare and curious parts—
Shall blossom as the seasons run
   Into a Bachelor of Arts.
Oxford in after years shall claim
A share of his illustrious name.

Amelia—Yes—a ladies' school
   At Brighton. Then, a year or twain
At Paris under Convent rule—
   Then to her parents' arms again.
And last—Oh joy for us and her!—
Wife of a full Commissioner.

And—let me see—my leave next year
   Is due. I really think we might—
Eh, Mrs Timpkins?—save a clear
   Three thou . . .
                The Cliquot's finished quite.
Alas! To think so poor am I—
A penny sets me leaping high!

A NIGHTMARE OF NAMES

Published in the *CMG*, 10 December 1886. Reprinted in the *Pioneer Mail*, 15 December. Unsigned and uncollected, but included in Scrapbook 3. The Burma War of 1885 had been quickly concluded, and the country was formally annexed on 1 January 1886. Vigorous resistance of a guerrilla kind was carried on, however, for several years, and the newspapers carried frequent reports of encounters between British troops and dacoits as the country was gradually pacified.

It was a wearied journalist who sought his little bed,
With twenty Burma telegrams all waiting to be read.
Then the Nightmare[1] and her nine-fold[2] rose up his dreams to haunt,
And from those Burma telegrams they wove this dismal chaunt:—

'Bethink thee, man of ink and shears,' so howled the fiendish crew,
'That each dacoit has one long name, and every hamlet two.
Moreover, all our outposts bear peculiar names and strange:
There are one hundred outposts and, once every month, they change.

If Poungdoungzoon and Pyalhatzee today contain the foe,
Be sure they pass tomorrow to Gwebin or Shway-my-o.
But Baung-maung-hman remember, is a trusted Thoongye Woon,
The deadly foe of Maung-dhang-hlat, Myoke of Moung-kze-hloon.

Poungthung and Waustung-chung are not at present overthrown,
For they are near the Poon beyond the Hlinedathalone;
While Nannay-kone in Ningyan is near Mecakaushay,
But Shway-zet-dau is on the Ma, and quite the other way.

Here are some simple titles which 'twere best to get in writing,
In view of further telegrams detailing further fighting:—
Malé, Myola, Toungbyoung, Talakso, Yebouk, Myo,
Nattick, Hpan-loot-kin, Madeah, Padeng, Narogan, Mo.

Pakhang, Samaitkyon, Banzé, Mine-tseil, Mine-the-Kulay,
Mantsankin, Toungbain, Bompan, Aeng, Naung, Banza, Kan-sau-
    mya.
Kteepauts, Salung, Enlay, Yindan, Nwa-Koo, Mahan-gyee-kin,
Kek-kai, Nat-lone, Salay, Toung-lone, Yihon, and lastly Tsin.'

It was a wearied journalist—he left his little bed,
And faced the Burma telegrams, all waiting to be read;
But ere he took his map-book up, he prayed a little prayer:—
'Oh *stop* them fighting Lord knows who, in jungles Deuce knows
    where!'

---

[1] *Nightmare*: in the archaic sense of a demon or incubus.
[2] *nine-fold*: attendant group of nine. Cf. *King Lear*, III. iv: 'He met the night-mare and her nine-fold.'

THE FAITHFUL SOUL

Published in the *CMG*, 13 December 1886, with headings: ' "The Hills Exodus is wrong in principle." *Calcutta Press.* / *"The Exodus question is to the Calcutta Press as a red rag to a bull." Press of Upper India.*' Unsigned and uncollected, but included in Scrapbook 3. The 'exodus' in question was the annual departure of the Government of India from Calcutta to Simla, at the start of the hot weather. The mercantile community, which remained in Calcutta throughout the year, saw no reason why the Government should not do the same: it deplored the additional costs incurred, and argued that in Simla the Government was out of touch with the country as a whole. The matter was hotly debated each year at public meetings and in the press, but Government practice did not change. (Cf. Kipling's poem 'A Tale of Two Cities', published in the *CMG* on 2 June 1887 as 'Love among the Ruins', and collected in the 3rd and subsequent editions of *Departmental Ditties.*)

In the nethermost silo of Sheol,[1] where Lawyers and Editors fry,
Was the soul of a turbulent pressman who had lately decided to die.
He had fought on the Exodus Question, and fought on the losing side,
So fired one white-hot leader—then fired a pistol and died.

In the nethermost silo of Sheol he settled himself at his ease,
For Sheol is Shiloh[2] to those who have laboured a public to please;
And the roar of the Great Blast-Furnace was sweet to his jaded brain,
For it seemed like the hum of the press-room he never need enter
        again.

But peace is forbidden in Sheol; and, after an œon or so,
The heart of the turbulent pressman was filled with an old-time
        woe—
With the fine, fierce ardour of conflict that harried his spirit on earth,
And he howled:—'I will settle the Question in the ultimate home of its
        birth.'

As a war-horse answers the bugle, or wild hawk stoops to its prey,
On the lines of the Exodus Question the Editor started the fray;
And proved to the joy of the Devils, in argument terse and clear,
The crime of remaining in Heaven for twelve months out of a year.

[1] *Sheol*: Hebrew name for hell.
[2] *Shiloh*: lit. place of rest.

He showed—while the spirits applauded—how most of their torments
    were bred,
Through 'want of touch' and 'the absence of a permanent, resident
    head'.
He dwelt on the value of Sheol—which some were disposed to deny—
And scoffed at 'the Capuan playground',[3] as he scoffed in the days
    gone by.

Though praising the present direction—since Satan deserved much
    thanks,
For his note on the Sub-Committee's report of the Kerosine
    Tanks—
His duty towards his fellows and conscience compelled him to state
The staff of subordinate Devils was slack and inadequate.

This rose from the crass indifference displayed by the Powers above,
In the state of the Lower Province, as he was prepared to prove.
By way of clinching the question, he quoted the ruling dry,
On a third reminder from Dives,[4] *re* roadways and water-supply.

Then, getting abreast of his business, an eloquent hour he spent
On showing that Sheol was made for the seat of the Government.
And, such is the force of statistics, the people of Sheol avowed,
Their own dry climate was better than rainbow and mist and cloud.

           *   *   *   *   *

Then the days of his torment ended. They called him up from
    beneath.
He rose with a sneer on his visage—a half-chewed pen in his teeth;
He trampled the amaranth blossoms, the breeze blew cheery and chill.
'What! Work in a perfect climate!' said he, 'I am d——d if I will.

I have lived on the dear old grievance, on Earth, and,—ahem—
    elsewhere,
At the public meetings down yonder, they vote me into the chair.
And, further, the principle's rotten. You ask me to sanction it—No!
As a practical permanent protest, I choose to remain below!'

---

[3] *Capuan playground*: cf. p. 342 above.
[4] *Dives*: the rich man in Luke 16 who called to Abraham from hell, asking him to send Lazarus to give him water to ease his torment, only to be told that between heaven and hell there was a great gulf fixed, so that the inhabitants of one could not pass to the other.

And the œons came and departed, and worlds that were young grew
     old,
And the Stars burnt out into ashes, and the Sun got dingy and cold.
In the nethermost silo of Sheol with pamphlet, oration, and pen
He threshed out the Exodus Question for ever and ever amen!

WITH A FAN TO THE MOTHER

Holograph version dated Xmas 1886 (KP 2/1).

> This is a fan for my mother
>   *No other*.
> Shall I then descant on its use
>   In manner diffuse.
> Maunder of passion and sighs
> And the light of your luminous eyes
> *I* am a novice these jobs on
> They are the stroke[1] of A Dobson.[2]
>
> No 'tis a chaperone's fan
>   Dreaded by Man—
> Signalling over the room
>   The signal of doom—
> When the hours of the night have grown small
>   At the end of a ball
> And Trixie the wilful demurs
> At the *hookum*[3] for carriage and furs—
> Wherefore your offspring would urge
> Use it dear mum for a scourge.

WITH A STUDY CHAIR TO THE PATER

Holograph version (KP 2/1). Undated, but it would seem to be a companion
piece to the preceding item. Xmas 1886?

---

[1] *stroke*: reading uncertain.

[2] *Dobson*: Henry Austin Dobson (1840–1921), a minor poet, author of verses 'On a
Fan that Belonged to the Marquise de Pompadour'.

[3] *hookum*: order.

'Tell mee where is Fancie bred
In ye Hearte or in ye Heade?'[1]
Surely neither heade nor Hearte
Fancie's Gifts to Men imparte:
Rather, saith ye thinkinge Minde,
Fancie cometh from behinde.
Beeswax in ye studie chair
Breedeth Fancies rich and rare
Inspiration never came
Save in fashion strange and tame—
Baito for ye laggard Thought
Or your Worke shall come to naught

Manie Yeeres have taught you this
What ye Use of Beeswax is,
(And if I your Thoughts should guide
Itt were neere to parricide)—
Wherefore I your Son Prepare,
Not ye Beeswax but ye Chair.

'YE PRINTER'S DEVIL, VERIE WYSE'

Holograph version, undated, without title, but with a drawing of a naked devil-
kin wearing spectacles. Signed 'Rudyard Kipling' (KP 2/1). The verses could
have been written for any of the Christmases when all four members of the
Kipling family were together in Lahore; but they could well be associated with
the two preceding items. Xmas 1886?

Ye Printer's Devil, verie wyse,
    And cladd but lightlie, as ye see,
(Sith those twinn glasses o'er his Eyes
    Make alle His winter Braverie)
Clomb from ye Pitt wherein Hee laye
To thinke alack! on Christmas Daye.

'And yt is verie harde to chuse',
    (Quoth Hee) 'what Things a Maiden loves
For There bin Farthingales and Shoos
    And fans & ruffs & muffs & gloves.

[1] *Tell-me* . . . : see *The Merchant of Venice*, III. ii.
[2] *Baito*: sit down.

I feare that these will not avail.'
(Whereatt Hee softlie bitte Hys Tayle)

'For Gloves must burste at Stitche and Seam
    And Fans will breake and Bootes decay
And Farthingales bee but a dream
    And mittens laste butt for a daye
When that my Sisters armes they grace'
(Whereat hee wepte a littel space)

'Behold itt is our fourfold Fate
    (Sith meals be needful now and then)
With fourfold force to transmutate
    Red golde from paper and from penn
What better gifte to give remains
Than these twinn masters of our braines?

Ye Penn whereby myselfe does live
    (Albeit in an humble sort)
Thyt Penn in boxes wil I give
    And paper lesst ye vagrom thought
Shall ere Shee fixe yt bee forgott—
Also a Blotter lest she blott.

And when ye Duste Storme bloweth Harde
    And inkie papers take 'em wings—
They by a Clippe shall be debarred
    From al unlicenced wanderings
These will I giv' quoth Hee—' 'Tis well'
And soughte again Hys inkie Hell

THE BALLAD OF AHMED SHAH

Holograph version, signed 'Rudyard Kipling', with holograph note 'written out
for "Bobby" Pringle.[1] Originally appeared in the I.P.G.[2] about 1886–7–8—
I've forgotten exact date.' (Library of Congress.) Lack of access to a complete
run of the *Indian Planter's Gazette and Sporting News* has made it impossible to

---

[1] *'Bobby' Pringle*: a sporting vet whom Kipling had known in Lahore.
[2] *I.P.G*: *Indian Planter's Gazette and Sporting News*.

locate the original published version. This copy was made years afterwards: the paper shows a watermark 1895 (*Catalogue of the Ballard Collection*, Philadelphia, 1935, p. 25).

> This is the ballad of Ahmed Shah
> Dealer in tats[3] in the Sudder Bazar,[4]
> By the gate that leads to the Gold Minār,[5]
> How he was done by a youth from Morar.[6]
>
> Ahmed Shah was a man of peace—
> His beard and his turban were thick with grease:
> His paunch was huge and his speech was slow
> And he swindled the subalterns high and low.
> Scores of subalterns came to try
> The tats that he sold—and remained to buy.
> Scores of subalterns later on
> Found that their flashiest mounts were 'gone'—
> Some in the front and some behind
> Some were roarers[7] and some went blind—
> Scores of subalterns over their 'weeds'
> Cursed old Ahmed and all his deeds.
> But Ahmed Shah in his gully sat still—
> And ever he fashioned a *Little Black Pill*!
>
> Yet a judgment was brewing for Ahmed Shah,
> Like a witch's cauldron, in far Morar
> And the youth that brewed it had eyes of blue
> And his cheek was beardless—and boundless too.
> Softly he mused o'er a trichi[8] thick:—
> 'By the Beard of the Prophet I've got the trick!'
> Then he rose from his chair with an artless grin
> And called the Battery Sergeant in:—
> 'Sergeant' he said 'Hast aught for me
> In the way of a "caster"[9] with lots of gee?'[10]
> The sergeant pondered and answered slow
> 'There's a red-roan gelding that's bound to go

---

[3] *tats*: country-bred ponies.   [4] *Sudder Bazar*: see above, pp. 181–3.
[5] *the Gold Minār*: the Sonari Masjid or Golden Mosque in Lahore.
[6] *Morar*: garrison town near Gwalior, some 200 mls. south of Delhi.
[7] *roarers*: horses suffering from disease which produces loud breathing due to narrowing of windpipe through inflammation.   [8] *trichi*: Trichinopoly cheroot.
[9] *caster*: horse considered no longer fit for service in the cavalry or artillery, and therefore sold by public auction.   [10] *gee*: horse; also with sense of 'go'.

At the next Committee. 'E aint no use
Excep' for kickin' recruits to the deuce,
'E's savaged two drivers last week an' now
'E's chained in the sick-lines.'
                              The subaltern's brow
Was puckered with thought for a moment. Then
The sergeant was richer by rupees ten.
'When the next Committee sits' quoth he
'O Sergeant buy up that brute for me.'

So the plot was laid and the long weeks passed
And the red-roan gelding was duly cast.
They led him in chains to the subaltern's stall
And gave him his gram[11] through a hole in the wall.
The subaltern mixed it. When morning came
The red-roan gelding was strangely tame.
He bit not nor kicked nor essayed to slay
And he and the sub went north that day
Till they came to the gully of Ahmed Shah
The man and the horse from far Morar.
The subaltern stated his funds were low
And he came—*mehrbáni*[12]—to 'sell *karo*'.[13]
Then Ahmed Shah with his eyes agog
Broke the Tenth Command in the decalogue
For the roan was a monster of size and thews
And stood over sixteen hand in his shoes.
'*Sahib kitna mangta?*'[14] With brow serene,
The subaltern softly answered '*Teen*'.[15]
He haggled an hour that dealer thrifty
Till the price was lowered to '*do sow fifty*'[16]
And the money was paid in greasy rupees
While the red-roan gelding drowsed at his ease.
The subaltern left him—and Ahmed smiled—
'By Allah, how mad is this pink-faced child
I will stuff that *ghorah*[17] with *atta*[18] and *goor*[19]
And sell him again to some English *soor*[20]
For a clear eight-fifty!' . . . and e'en as he spoke
The devil they'd drugged in the red-roan woke!

[11] *gram*: pulse crop used for feeding horses.   [12] *mehrbáni*: if you please.
[13] *karo*: do it quickly.
[14] *Sahib kitna mangta?*: How much does the sahib want?
[15] *Teen*: three (sc. 100 rupees).   [16] *do sow fifty*: two hundred and fifty.
[17] *ghorah*: horse.   [18] *atta*: flour.   [19] *goor*: molasses.   [20] *soor*: pig.

Then the head-ropes snapped and the heel-ropes drew
And the stallions squealed as the roan went through
And the saices[21] ran as men run for life
And the yard was troubled with equine strife
Till the berserk-rage of the beast was o'er
And he dropped to slumber at Ahmed's door!

Then a veil was lifted from Ahmed's eyes
As he raised the eyelids and punched the thighs
Felt the tense pulse slacken—the muscles still—
And fathomed the Trick of the Opium Pill!
His own old dodge that had brought him pelf
Had the subaltern turned against himself!

Did he swear? though his three best tats were lame
And half the city would hear of his shame.
Did he seek the law-courts? With down-cast eye
He hailed an ekka[22] that jingled by,
And drove to the Station where, filled with peace
The subaltern counted the greasy rupees.

What passed between them? I cannot say
The subaltern turns the question away
With an innocent laugh: but the men of Morar
Say he still gets ponies from Ahmed Shah.
Ponies to bet on—but not to buy—
Weeds to look at but devils to fly
And once in a while comes a tiny pill-box
Which the subaltern puts in his private till-box.
The Doctor abets him . . . Whenever I'm able
I plunge to my last clean shirt on their stable!

NEW YEAR RESOLUTIONS

Published in the *CMG*, 1 January 1887. Reprinted in the *Englishman*, 6 January. Unsigned and uncollected, but included in Scrapbook 3.

---

[21] *saices*: grooms.
[22] *ekka*: small one-horse carriage, much used by natives.

I am resolved—throughout the year
   To lay my vices on the shelf;
A godly, sober course to steer
   And love my neighbours as myself—
Excepting always two or three
Whom I detest as they hate me.

I am resolved—that whist is low—
   Especially with cards like mine—
It guts a healthy Bank-book—so
   These earthly pleasures I resign,
Except—and here I see no sin—
When asked by others to 'cut in'.

I am resolved—no more to dance
   With *ingenues*—so help me Venus!
It gives the Chaperone her chance
   For hinting Heaven knows what between us.
The Ballroom and the Altar stand
Too close in this suspicious land.
(*N.B.*) But will I (here ten names) abandon?
     No, while I have a leg to stand on!

I am resolved—to sell my horses.
   They cannot stay, they *will* not go;
They lead me into evil courses
   Wherefore I mean to part with—No!
Cut out that resolution—I'll
Try *Jilt* tomorrow on the mile.

I am resolved—to flirt no more,
   It leads to strife and tribulation;
Not that I used to flirt before,
   But as a bar against temptation.
Here I except (cut out the names)
x perfectly Platonic flames.

I am resolved—to drop my smokes,
   The Trichi[1] has an evil taste.

---

[1] *Trichi*: Trichinopoly cheroot, notoriously cheap and coarse.

I cannot buy the brands of Oakes;[2]
  But, lest I take a step in haste,
And so upset my health, I choose a
  'More perfect way' in pipes and Poosa.[3]

I am resolved—that vows like these,
  Though lightly made, are hard to keep;
Wherefore I'll take them by degrees,
  Lest my backslidings make me weep.
One vow a year will see me through;
And I'll begin with Number Two.

THE PLAINT OF THE JUNIOR CIVILIAN[1]

Published in the *CMG*, 7 January 1887, with heading ' "A handful of juniors just fresh out from home." *Vide Pioneer*'s definition of a "Junior Civilian".' No signature. Collected in the Outward Bound, De Luxe, Sussex, and Burwash Edns., with one stanza omitted (printed here in square brackets), and '*Indian Paper*' substituted for '*Pioneer*' in heading. The Public Services Commission, chaired by Sir Charles Aitchison (see above, pp. 288 and 336), was enquiring into the possible 'admission of natives of India to offices formerly reserved exclusively for members of the Covenanted Civil Service'. A report that the Junior (i.e. unpromoted) Civilians of the Punjab intended to ask the Commission to listen to the claims of the covenanted service itself provoked a tart comment from the *Pioneer* of 4 January: 'That a handful of juniors, fresh out from home, should be summoning Sir Charles Aitchison and his colleagues to Lahore to give evidence sounds queerly. . . .' On which the *CMG* commented on 6 January: 'The middle-aged men who, in these days, are called junior Punjab Civilians, are scarcely fresh from home. They wish they were: and wish still more they had never left home at all. And surely their grey hairs and long service, if not their official rank, entitle them to respect in the eyes of a Commission which has listened with interest to men whose standing is scarcely higher than a *chaprassie*'s.'[12] In the *CMG* version the last lines of stanzas 1 and 3 begin 'The *Pi* says I'm'; stanza 5 ends 'Writes / The *Pi*, I am "fresh out from Home" ', and line 7 of the last stanza begins 'The *Pi*' not 'The press'.

---

    [2] *Oakes*: Oakes Bros. and Co., tobacconists in London and Madras.
    [3] *Poosa*: tobacco from Pusa, an area in Behar where it was grown on an experimental basis.

---

   [1] *Civilian*: member of the Indian Civil Service.
   [2] *chaprassie*: office-messenger.

I have worked for ten seasons or more,
    In Settlement,[3] District, or Court;
I have served, with the rest of my corps,
    All over the Province, in short.
From Ismail accursed, to the Bar,
    From Jhang to Peshawur I roam,
And back from Kohat to Hissar;
        But—
    They tell me I'm 'fresh out from Home'!

I have loved, I have lost, twice or thrice;
    My weeds are 'long Dawsons with straw';[4]
I can sit fourteen–one[5] of shod Vice,
    And badger a pleader-at-law;
I can quote with precision the bulk
    Of Currie's delectable tome;[6]
I can coax a Hill Chief from a sulk,
        And—
    I find I am 'fresh out from Home'.

I can flirt with the girls at the well
    In dialect rude and uncouth;
I can force a fat *Khattri*[7] to tell,
    By accident, half of the truth.
I can chew like a Rajah my *pân*,[8]
    I can slang with a *Naqqal* or *Dôm*,[9]
I can say, 'Térá músha Pathan!'[10]
        Yet—
    They tell me I'm 'fresh out from Home'.

That Home I have quitted an age.
    (Ten Junes in the District seem long),

---

[3] *Settlement*: review of tax assessments for Land Revenue over a specified area.

[4] *long Dawsons with straw*: Dawsons were a brand of cheroot, and the cheaper varieties often had straw mouthpieces.

[5] *fourteen–one*: a horse fourteen hands, one inch, in height.

[6] *Currie's delectable tome*: Fendall Currie was the author of a number of commentaries on Indian law. His *Indian Code of Criminal Procedure* and *Indian Law Examination Manual* went through several editions.

[7] *Khattri*: 'one of the trading class' (Sussex Edn.).

[8] *pân*: 'nut rolled in betel leaf' (Sussex Edn.).

[9] *Naqqal or Dôm*: 'low castes' (Sussex Edn.).

[10] *Térá músha Pathan*: How are you, Pathan? (colloq.)

For I sailed when 'Our Boys'[11] was the rage,
   And 'Tommy, make room'[12] was the song;
There's a patch on the top of my pate
   That needs not the care of the comb,
And thirteen-eleven's my weight;
       Though—
   They tell me I'm 'fresh out from Home'.

I have worn my first saddle and second
   Clean down to the wood of the tree;
And D.C.'s[13] a dozen I've reckoned
   Have managed my transfers and me;
I am learned in roadways and cess,
   In *rabi*[14], rice-huskers, and loam—
Over thirty, but nevertheless,
       Write
   The papers, I'm 'fresh out from Home'.

[I have grievances many and sound,
   That blossom and bloom with the years;
And imminent dangers surround
   Myself and my 'juvenile' peers
Who remember when Davies[15] was lord,
   When Egerton[16] passed o'er the foam,
Ere Aitchison[17] came—the abhorred;
       Still—
   We learn we are 'fresh out from Home'.]

Oh, babes of the Punjab Commission,[18]
   Oh, sucklings of ' '73',[19]
Consider our humble position,
   Remember what juniors we be!

---

[11] *'Our Boys'*: a comedy by H. J. Byron, produced at the Vaudeville Theatre in 1875.

[12] *'Tommy, make room'*: 'Tommy make room for your uncle', sung by W. B. Fair, was one of the music-hall hits of the 1880s.   [13] *D.C.'s*: Deputy Commissioners.

[14] *rabi*: crops sown after the rains and reaped in the following spring.

[15] *Davies*: Sir Robert Henry Davies, Lieut.-Gov. of the Punjab 1871–7.

[16] *Egerton*: Sir Robert Eyles Egerton, Lieut.-Gov. of the Punjab 1878–82.

[17] *Aitchison*: see above, pp. 288 and 336.

[18] *the Punjab Commission*: body of civil, military and judicial officers responsible for the administration of the Punjab.   [19] *'73*: the year of their appointment.

Oh, lads without standing or credit,
Nous[20], influence, *ukal*,[21] *aplomb*,
The press, in its wisdom, hath said it:
We
Are all of us 'fresh out from Home'.

PERSONAL RESPONSIBILITIES

Published in the *CMG*, 31 January 1887, with heading ' "Those mechanical means by which alone the Government coffers can be replenished." *See Viceroy's speech to Dufferin Fund, on 26th instant.*' Unsigned and uncollected, but included in Scrapbook 3. The *CMG* for 29 January gave the full text of Lord Dufferin's speech in Calcutta at the second Annual General Meeting of the Countess of Dufferin's Fund (on which, see below p. 363). In the course of it he spoke as follows: 'No one knows better than myself the difficulty of obtaining money in India . . . but let me tell the Lady President[1] of the fund, that it will probably prove a far more graceful, as well as more successful method to throw herself on the generosity of the Indian people, than, as I have been obliged to do, to resort to those mechanical means by which alone the Government coffers can be replenished.' This was received with 'Laughter and loud cheers'.

Nay, not 'mechanical' my Lord—
    A personal and private glow
Pervades us when our humble hoard
    Is 'cut' by twenty dibs[2] or so.
Least of your subjects, store immense I
Set monthly by Your Excellency.

For when I pay my little dues,
    I wonder where the money goes;
And read the papers for the news,
    Or write to ventilate my woes.
Because I sink my money in
The firm of 'Queen and Dufferin'.

[20] *Nous*: intelligence.
[21] *ukal*: intelligence, spirit. Cf. letter begun 28 November 1885 to Margaret Burne-Jones. 'Ukhál is difficult to translate exactly—it means all that goes to make up a Man'. (KP 11/6.)

---

[1] *the Lady President*: Lady Dufferin.
[2] *dibs*: money (slang); here presumably pieces of money.

Oft in some ultra loyal mood
　　I tender newly coined rupees;
In case His Excellency should
　　Befoul his gloves with dirt and grease.
By arts like these, I strive to win
The friendship of Lord Dufferin.

But, when the red *chaprassi*[3] brings—
　　Magnificent in marge and line
A letter, hinting awful things,
　　From some respected friend of mine,
Because my tax is overdue,
Then much, my Lord, I mourn for you.

My friend is kindest of the kind,
　　I meet him oft—I know him well—
It ne'er would cross *his* courteous mind
　　To threaten me with dungeon cell.
Who drove him, therefore, into sin?
He answers sadly:—'Dufferin'.

And when some 'unearned increment'
　　Is added to my modest stipend—
Like Achan[4] in the fateful tent
　　So I—a neatly-worded lie penned—
Secrete my gold untaxed, and smile
With glee ungodly at my guile.

Now, I was nurtured in a creed
　　That hates a lie and scorns a theft;
Who makes me traitor to my breed,
　　Of truth and honour both bereft?
Who vulcanized my moral skin?—
My business partner—Dufferin.

---

　　[3]　*red chaprassi*: official Government messenger.
　　[4]　*Achan*: see Josh. 7: 21 in which Achan confesses his sin: 'When I saw among the spoils a goodly Babylonish garment and two hundred shekels of silver, and a wedge of gold of fifty shekels weight, then I coveted them and took them; and behold, they are hid in the earth in the midst of my tent, and the silver under it.' He was thereupon stoned to death.

And when I pay that tax no more,
　　And pass beyond the fires they kindle,
St Peter at the half-shut door
　　Will tax me with my latest swindle.
But I shall answer:—'Let me in!
Refer the debt to Dufferin.'

And thus the Silver Chain hooks on
　　Our destinies diverse in tether;
And Frederick Temple Hamilton,[5]
　　And You and I, and they together,
Are linked in ties, occult, unreckoned,
Of last year's Act,[6] surnamed the Second.

FOR THE WOMEN

Published in the *CMG*, 18 February 1887, with heading, 'Ave Imperatrix,
Moriturae Te Salutant!' (Hail, Empress; those women about to die salute
thee)—a modification of the traditional formula of greeting to Caesar by gladi-
ators entering the arena. Unsigned. Reprinted in the *Pioneer*, 22 February.
Stanzas 5 and 6 were used as a heading for Chapter 10 of *The Naulahka* (1892)
and published in a collection of Rhymed Chapter Headings from the book in
the same year. The poem itself was collected in the Outward Bound, De Luxe,
Sussex, and Burwash Edns. with one stanza omitted (printed here in square
brackets). In 1885 Lady Dufferin had launched an appeal fund, with which her
own name was associated, for supplying female medical advice and instruction
to the women of India. They suffered both from medical ignorance and from
the difficulty of providing access for male doctors, because of the seclusion
imposed on them by rules of purdah. This poem appeared on the same page of
the *CMG* as a report of the laying of the foundation-stone of Lady Aitchison's
Hospital for Women in Lahore, under the general auspices of Lady Dufferin's
Fund.

We knit a riven land to strength by cannon, code,[1] and sword;
We drove the road for all men's feet, we bridged the raving ford;
We cleared the waste of force and wrong, we bade the land be still;
And whereso'er that will was good, we wrought the people's will.

---

[5] *Frederick Temple Hamilton*: i.e. Frederick Temple Hamilton Hamilton-Temple
Blackwood, Earl of Dufferin.
[6] *last year's Act*: the Income Tax Bill, which was technically Act No. 2 of 1886 (East
India Parliamentary Papers).

---

[1] *code*: i.e. legal code.

The Wisdom of the West is theirs—our schools are free to all.
The strength of all the West is theirs, to prop them lest they fall;
And men may say what things they please, and none dare stay their
      tongue.
But who has spoken out for these—the women and the young?

Who know but you, O men we taught, and men who teach us now,
Co-heirs of our eight hundred years, and . . . Servants of the Cow[2]—
Who know but you the life you cloak, secure from alien stare?
Are all our gifts for men alone, or may your women share?

Small wish have they for learning's light or Wisdom of the West;
Small wish have you that they should learn, or we should break their
      rest.
But—pitiless as when He spoke, untempered, quick to slay—
The curse God laid on Eve is theirs for heritage to-day.

You know the 'Hundred Danger Time' when, gay with paint and
      flowers,
Your household Gods are bribed to help the bitter, helpless hours;
You know the worn and rotten mat whereon the mother lies;
You know the *sootak*[3] room unclean, the cell wherein she dies—

Dies, with the babble in her ear of midwife's muttered charm,
Dies, 'spite young Life that strains to stay, the suckling in her arm,
Dies in the three-times-heated air, scorched by the Birth-fire's
      breath,
Foredoomed, you say, lest anguish lack, to haunt her home in death.[4]

These things you know, and more than these—grim secrets of the
      Dead,
Foul horrors done in ignorance, by Time on Folly bred.
The women have no voice to speak, but none can check your pen—
Turn for a moment from your strife and plead their cause, O men!

[Help now—for your own sakes give help. Look! since the world
      began
Was never people walked apart—the woman from the man,
And you are rich in all our lore, you make our thoughts your own—
But, by the mothers of your race, you cannot rise alone.]

    [2] *Servants of the Cow*: a jibe at the reverence paid by Hindus to the cow as a sacred animal.
    [3] *sootak*: birth, and the impurity or defilement associated with it by Hindus.
    [4] *to haunt her home*: i.e. as a *churel*—the ghost of a woman who has died in childbirth.

Help here—and not for us the boon and not to us the gain;
Make room to save the babe from death, the mother from her pain.
Is it so great a thing we ask? Is there no road to find
When women of our people seek to help your womenkind?

No word to sap their faith, no talk of Christ or creed need be,
But woman's help in woman's need and woman's ministry.
Such healing as the West can give, that healing may they win.
Draw back the *purdah*[5] for their sakes, and pass our women in!

BY HONOURS

Published in the *CMG*, 22 February 1887, with signature 'R.K.' and heading
' "The meteoric shower of honours which has descended upon the just and
unjust this year, not only makes it almost impossible for us to know 'Who's
Who in '87' but has driven some weaker minds to the verge of insanity."—
Extract from a Calcutta letter.' Uncollected, but included in Scrapbook 3. A
Jubilee Honours list had been published in Calcutta on 16 February, and was
featured in the *CMG* for 18 February. Honours awarded included those of the
Order of the Star of India (Knights Grand Commanders, Knights Com-
manders, Companions), the Order of the Indian Empire (Knights Com-
manders, Companions) and the Order of St Michael and St. George. Indian
awards included titles of Hereditary Rajah, Sadh Nawab Bahadur, Rajah
Bahadur, Nawab, Rajah, Rani, Khan Bahadur, Rai Bahadur, Rao Bahadur,
Khan Sahib, etc. A new title had also been created, by which recognition was
given to. eminent distinction in learning among Hindus and Muslims. 'For
Hindus the title is Mahamahopadhyava and for Mahommedans Shams-ul-
Ulama.'

I dare not take my walks abroad, my friends I dare not see
Where once I used to speak to them, and they would speak to me.
My friends are ochre, black, and white, I count them by the score;
But till I learn last week's *Gazette* I may not meet them more.

How runs the Doctor's newest name, Mahai—? Mahout—? Moham—?
Mohunt—? Mahomedpudmini, Illuminated Sham?
Dewan-i-Khas or Sri[1] Diwan is Smith unless I err.
No! Smith's Mir Munshi got the Sri, and Smith himself's the Sir.

---

[5] *purdah*: literally, a curtain screening women from sight of strangers; more generally,
the Indian system of secluding women.

---

[1] *Sri*: honorific title.

So Mrs Smith is Lady S. and Jones's wife likewise;
Or was it Jones who finished up the batch of C.S.I.'s?[2]
Or was he made a 'Rajah Rao'? Alas! my addled brain
Has mixed him with a Borah Shroff.[3] Bring out the list again!

Smith, B.C.S.,[4] K.C.S.I.,[5] Jones, C.I.E.,[6] C.E.[7]
Brown, Robinson, collectively, K.C.G.M.C.B.[8]
That's better! Gul Mahommed 'Rao'; Asraf Mahommed 'Rai';
And 'Raja' Babu Chatterjee . . . or was *he* C.S.I.?

Once more, though madness hover near, that awful list I scan!
Asraf Mohammed seems to be a 'Rai Bahadured Khan',
And Chatterjee's a 'Shish Mahal', 'tis plain as printers' ink;
And Pundit Prem Nath Guru Dutt is 'Brevet Thakur Spink'.[9]

I wonder why, in wriggling fire is limned the Honours roll,
(Sirdar Khansamah!)[10] and my thoughts slip, eel-like, from control.
Rai, Rao, Dewan, Nawab, C.B., K.C.I.E., Mahout-
Bahadur flash across my brain—a gorgeous golden rout.

What ha! What ho! Why stare ye so, oh Lords and Ladies gay?
What means the whisper in the air:—'His mind has given way!'
I am not mad—Rai, Rubee, Rais, Sub Titular Nawab!
Why cramp my limbs with clanking chain; my frame in maniac's garb?

I am not mad. Psst! Shwye ya Min! Daulat-Inglishia[11] D——!
Who said, Sir Knights, I am not mad? Bring on your Dukes[12]—I am!

---

[2] *C.S.I.'s*: Companions of the Order of the Star of India.
[3] *Borah Shroff*: Big Money-lender.
[4] *B.C.S.*: Bengal Civil Service.
[5] *K.C.S.I.*: Knight Commander of the Order of the Star of India.
[6] *C.I.E.*: Companion of the Order of the Indian Empire.
[7] *C.E.*: Civil Engineer.
[8] *K.C.G.M.C.B.*: a conflation of K.C.M.G. (Knight Commander of the Order of St Michael and St George) and C.B. (Companion of the Order of the Bath).
[9] *Thakur Spink*: a pun on 'Thakur', meaning Rajput noble, and Thacker, Spink and Co., Kipling's Calcutta publishers?
[10] *Sirdar Khansamah*: Chief Butler.
[11] *Daulat-Inglishia*: British sway.
[12] *Dukes*: perhaps a pun on 'dukes' as a slang word for 'fists' but I suspect a usage meaning 'handcuffs'.

THE LOVE THAT DIED

Published in the *Englishman*, 2 March 1887, with signature 'G.L.' and heading ' "Call it what you please," said the Major. "One half of it's idleness and the other half is liver." "*The Confessions of Lieutenant Dawking*".' Uncollected, but included in Scrapbook 3.

Look! It was no fault of mine. Read a story plainly writ
Caroline was Caroline: I was—very badly hit.
Caroline alone possessed all the heart within my breast.

So I mused upon her face—ventured into verse of course.
Lay my racket in its place—at his picket stood my horse.
And my shot-gun in its baize[1] slumbered two-and-twenty days.

Yearnings dark and inchoate troubled next my lonely life—
Visions of a future state tempered by a charming wife
Drove me to a Bank Book, which proved me anything but rich.

Tennyson I read with zeal; Browning's 'Men and Women' eke—
Scoffed at those who could not feel passion such as paled my cheek.
Thought of Caroline, and so felt exceeding hipped[2] and low.

Down my dexter shoulder ran torment it were vain to hide—
Anguish past the lot of man crumpled up my dexter side.
Sleeping after tiffin lit Tophet[3] in my tummy's pit.

Awful visions came by night; heavy drowsiness by day—
Little specks of coloured light seemed before my eyes to play.
To my door a Doctor drove. 'See,' quoth I, 'a prey to Love.'

He was burly, brutal, plain; (I am slender, love-sick, young)
He to my disgust and pain punched my ribs and saw my tongue.
'Write above my tomb', I sighed, ' "Twas for Caroline I died." '

Foul prescriptions men made up for a pill as blue as I,
Something in a coffee-cup racked my soul with agony,
But the shoulder I confess seemed to pain a little less.

[1] *baize*: baize-lined gun-case.
[2] *hipped*: depressed.
[3] *Tophet*: a place of perpetual fire; hence hell.

Then the beefy man and coarse smackt me on my fragile back,
Bade them saddle up my horse, never *quite* a lady's hack
(Weeks of idleness and gram[4] had not made him more a lamb.)

Heavens! How he scattered dust! Heavens! How I puffed and blew!
There are times when lovers must be in thought to love untrue.
All my heart and soul I own centered on that brute alone.

Knees were flayed and frame was sore, but the shoulder and the side
Ceased from twingeing any more, and my body's torment died;
With it, horrible to say, fled my spirit's gloom away.

Gone the tender thoughts and rare! Gone the yearnings vague and
    sweet!
Blown to bits by outer air; trampled 'neath a horse's feet.
Yea! the loathsome brew I quaffed seemed a very Lethe's[5] draught.

Was it liver? Was it love? In another, better land
I may yet the skein unrove; but, at present, as we stand,
Caroline is Caroline. I am Me and Me is Mine.

DIANA OF EPHESUS[1]

Published in the *Englishman*, 18 March 1887, with signature 'G.L.' Collected
in 3rd edn. of *Departmental Ditties*, 1888, but not included in subsequent edi-
tions of that volume. The poem remained uncollected thereafter until it
appeared in the Sussex and Burwash Edns., although a short extract figured as
the heading to 'Venus Annodomini'[2] in *Plain Tales from the Hills*. It may be that
'Diana' was too recognizable as a figure on the Simla social scene.

Ephesus stands—you may find it still—
On the lee of a verdurous, pine-clad hill,
And once in a twelve-month, the folk below
Flock to the pines and the upland snow—
Flee from the sunshine, the glare, and the dust,
For the good of their souls—as is right and just.

[4] *gram*: a pulse crop used for feeding horses.
[5] *Lethe*: river of forgetfulness in underworld in classical mythology.

[1] *Diana of Ephesus*: There was a famous temple of Diana at Ephesus in Asia Minor,
with a statue of the goddess which was said to have fallen from Olympus. Cf. Acts 19:
23–35.
[2] *Venus Annodomini*: a pun on Venus Anadyomene (rising from the sea) and *Anno
Domini* (in the year of our Lord) used as slang for old age.

She fell from Heaven—as all aver,
From the lap of Olympian Jupiter;
And so descended to govern us
Men of the City of Ephesus.

She ground us under Her dainty heel,
She bound us slaves to Her chariot-wheel,
She levied taxes and toll and cess
For Her sumptuous shrine and Her golden dress;
And we paid them merrily—ever thus
Is the use of the People of Ephesus.

And the years went on, as the years must do,
But our great Diana was always new—
Fresh and blooming, and young and fair,
With azure eyes and with aureate hair;
While all the people who came and went
Offered Her praise to Her heart's content.
So we said in our pride[3], as the years rolled by;—
'Our Great Diana can never die!'

But once—ah me!—when Her shrine was lit
And we danced to the Goddess who governed it,
When the music thundered[4] and, far and wide,
Our lamps made day on the mountain-side,
When the incense thickened, the trumpets brayed,
Came the terrible vengeance of Time delayed!
The clear voice faltered—the lithe form stooped—
The white hands wavered—the bright head drooped—
The trumpets quavered,[5] the lights burned blue,
And the Goddess died—as Goddesses do.
And all we could see in the twilight dim
Was a visage meagre and pointed and grim—
A hard, lined brow, and a mouth grown old,
And a ripple of bad, discoloured gold
From the folds of the chiton;[6] and so we cried:—
'What shall we do now Diana hath died?'
Wherefore we mourned till the morrow—thus
True to its idols is Ephesus.

---

[3] *pride*: 'hearts' (*Englishman*)'   [4] *thundered*: 'maddened' (*Englishman*).
[5] *quavered,*: 'ceased as' (*Englishman*).   [6] *chiton*: dress.

Then we dragged Her out of the City's bound,
And cast Her into the Stranger's Ground.
We cleansed the shrine from the offerings stale,
We gilt the pillars and altar-rail,
We lit fresh fires and called on Jove
For another Diana to praise and love;
And e'en as our call[7] went up on high,
Another Diana dropped out of the sky,
Stepping at once to the old one's place
With the light of the Godship about her face.
And we gave Her power to govern us
Men of the City of Ephesus.

The City is old as the pines above,
Old as the mountains, as old as Love;
And I am as old as a man may be
Ere he pass from the pines to the Unknown Sea,
And I serve, as I served in the years gone by,
The Great Diana who fell from the sky.
The yoke of Her priesthood is heavy to bear
Though the Great Diana be always fair.
But, after a season,[8] and none know when,
Our Goddess must die in the sight of men.
We must bear Her forth to the grave that waits
In the ground Unclean, by[9] the Temple gates,
While Her name is forgot and Her face likewise,
For another Diana drops out of the skies,
And we make obeisance and hail Her thus:—
'Queen of the City of Ephesus'.

And howso clearly I know the end
Of the love we give and the money we spend;
And howso clearly Diana foresees
That terrible day when the trumpets cease;
And howso clearly the grave be made,
Where the bones of our old-time Queens are laid;
And howso clearly the City knows
Whither the path to Her Temple goes,

---

[7] call: 'prayer' (*Englishman*).
[8] after a season . . . : 'after a while—in a year or ten' (*Englishman*).
[9] by: 'past' (*Englishman*).

These things are certain—I still obey
The great Diana who rules today,
The City with me, and She in state
Looks out o'er the path to the Temple gate,
And takes our homage and hears us cry:—
'Our Great Diana can never die!'
For this is our custom.
                                    Endeth thus
The tale of Diana of Ephesus.

A BUDGET ESTIMATE

Published in the *CMG*, 31 March 1887, with signature 'R.K.' Reprinted in the
Englishman, 5 April. Uncollected, but included in Scrapbook 3. The *CMG* for
28 March reported the issue of the annual Budget Statement in the form of a
Minute in the *Gazette* by the Financial Member of Council, Sir Auckland Col-
vin, and offered this summary: 'Expenditure has exceeded, or is expected to
exceed, the income in 1885–86 by £2,801,726; 1886–87 by £1,048,900;
1887–88 by £1,231,300. These are the bare results shown by the figures, and
they are certainly not promising; but then comes in the beauty of Indian
finance in general, and of the Famine Insurance Fund in particular. By a piece
of very simple manipulation, described as "the transfer to loan of charges
otherwise debitable to revenue under the head of Famine Insurance" the
account is balanced, and even a small surplus displayed.' The full and compli-
cated Financial Statement was printed in the *CMG* on 30 March.

Don't knight him yet! He read it through
    From end to end and back again—
He was the only person who
    Could stand beneath the fearful strain;
And this, so far as he discerns,
Is what the Indian Public learns:—

THE SURPLUS

'Cheer up my fellow-countrymen!'
Writes C–lv–n of the Silver Pen,
'If Two and Two were always Four
We might a Deficit deplore;
But since, with some success, I strive
To write them down, at least, for Five,
I may assert with modest pride
We have a Surplus on our side.

ITS MANUFACTURE

Still, *entre nous*,[1] I quite admit
The suit financial does not fit.
But if I shear the pants away
And use them for the waistcoat, say;
Or, Decency forbidding, deck
With coat-tail ends your tattered neck,
Or stitch across your manly breast
Some trifling fragments from the vest;
Or deftly take the seat to trim
Your wideawake's[2] much-fingered brim
(I trust I make my meaning clear)
That suit will serve another year,
Nay further—as my Statement shows—
Leave wherewithal to wipe your nose.

THE EXPLANATION

A certain widely-spread desire
To, reverently of course, inquire
Into that wild and whirling dance
Which vulgar herds have dubbed 'Finance',
Is not unnatural, and I
Will meet your curiosity.
Intelligence like yours will seize
At once such patent facts as these:—
The Estimated Surplus lies
Co-ordinate with my Revise.
The Budget Estimate, you see,
Makes up the working Trinity.
Whereas—the simplest mind may judge it—
Deductions from the Previous Budget
Bring, *ipso facto*,[3] in their train
The Surplus Estimates again.
But next year's Surplus keeps in view
The Deficit of '82
Which, when transferred to Loan Account,
Links on the *last* Revised amount

---

[1] *entre nous*: between ourselves.
[2] *wideawake*: soft felt hat with wide brim.
[3] *ipso facto*: by that very fact.

For Sterling Loans which, *per se*,[4] range
In inverse ratio to Exchange,
And, *ex necessitate*,[5] call
For next year's Budget Scheme. That's all.

THE CONCLUSION

N.B.—I merely pause to mention
I haven't got the chee—intention
To raise your Income-Tax, *as yet*.
The fish may wait for next year's net.
Meantime, accept five hundred quid
On paper. Pay as you are bid.
Don't mind the scrappy, patchy dressing—
It looks all right in front. My blessing
And this advice;—abstain from solvin'
The ways and works of
                            Yours,

                            A. C–LV–N.'

IN THE CASE OF RUKHMIBHAIO

Holograph draft in Scrapbook 1. A fair copy, uncompleted, appears on p. 305 of the Scrapbook; and I have supplemented this with lines (printed here in square brackets) from rough drafts on pp. 310–11. (Among the other fragments in his draft are phrases like 'But you cannot fathom a contempt more deep than speech is', 'Sari-swaddled cattle', and 'wedded in her infantage, under code inhuman'.) Undated: April 1887? The case is one on which Kipling commented several times, always with indignation. Rukhmabai—the spelling of her name is variously rendered—was an educated Hindu who had been married in her childhood, but had never lived with her husband Dadaji. He had now sued for restitution, or rather institution, of marital rights, which she resisted on the grounds that he had not means to support her, that he was suffering from disease, and that he was immoral in his way of life. A verdict was given in her favour in September 1885, the judge indicating that 'it would be a barbarous, a cruel and revolting thing to do, to compel a young lady, under these circumstances, to go to a man whom she dislikes.' The case went to appeal, however, and in the *CMG* for 9 April 1886 Kipling writes with anger of the higher court's ruling that according to Hindu law Rukhmabai was bound to

---

[4] *per se*: by themselves.
[5] *ex necessitate*: by necessity.

join her husband now, regardless of the circumstances: 'The whole case fur-
nishes a convincing instance of the utter rottenness of the law; and is a suf-
ficient answer for those who clamour that the East and the West shall be
treated on an equal footing. A society that tolerates such a law . . . is a society
that places itself, by the cowardly cruelty of that law, below all civilisations.'
(KP 28/3, p. 16.) Rukhmabai still refused to join her husband, and in the
CMG for 11 March 1887 Kipling writes with indignation of her being sen-
tenced to six months' imprisonment for contempt of court, and of the lack of
any protest from the native press (KP 28/3, p. 89). On 16 April he denounced
the attitude of the *Indian Mirror* which he accused of accepting the humiliating
status quo for Hindu women while urging political reforms to give more power
to Indian men (KP 28/3, p. 102).

> Gentlemen reformers with an English Education—
>   Lights of Aryavarta[1] take our heartiest applause,
> For the spectacle you offer of an 'educated' nation
>   Working out its freedom under 'educated' laws.

> Laudable your sentiments, eloquent your diction,
>   For your flowing periods, all our language racked is.
> May a brutal Briton ask:—'Wherefore then the friction
>   'Twixt the golden Principle and the grubby Practice.'

> Gentlemen reformers, you have heard the story
>   Weighed the woman's evidence—marked the man's reply.
> Here's a chance for honour, notoriety and glory!
>   Graduates of culture will you let that chance go by?

> [You can lecture government, draught a resolution—
>   Sign a huge memorial[2]—that Calcutta saw.
> Never such an opening for touching elocution—
>   As the text of Rukhimbai, jailed by Hindu law]

> What? No word of protest? Not a sign of pity?
>   Not a hand to help the girl, but, in black and white
> Writes the leading oracle[3] of the leading city:—
>   'We the Indian nation, *we* hold it served her right

---

[1] *Aryavarta*: the area inhabited by the Aryans; i.e. North India.
[2] *a huge memorial*: cf. p. 263 above.
[3] *the leading oracle*: the *Indian Mirror*, published in Calcutta.

Wherefore, gracious government, let her do her sentence:
  Learn the majesty of Law, teach our erring wives—
By a six months' sojourn in a common prison pent—hence
  She and they are cattle at our service all their lives.'

Gentlemen reformers, you can understand the loathing
  That would fill your bosoms did a *mehter*[4] claim to share
On the strength of velvet skull-cap and a suit of [snowy clothing
  Your name and rank and prospects and a seat beside your chair]

[Very hard it is to keep in bounds of decent moderation—
  And grief to smother epithets unseemly out of place
When excellent reformers chose to call themselves a nation
  And clamour for equality beside the higher race.

It is then the brutal Briton feels an impulse, wild, unruly—
  That tingles in the toe nails of a non-official boot—
Lumps in one mean heap of cruelty the graduate and cooly—
  And the old race-instinct answers to the clamour:—Hut you brute.

Which is barbarous and savage but the graduate of culture
  May console himself with thinking of the proverb wise and old
'Though you paint him as a peacock, still the vulture is a vulture'—
  And the dôm[5] is still an outcast though you plate his back with
    gold.]

IN THE MATTER OF A PROLOGUE

Published in the *CMG*, 9 June 1887, with heading ' "The best actors in the
world either for tragedy, comedy, history, pastoral, pastoral-comical, histori-
cal-pastoral, tragical-historical, tragical-comical-historical pastoral, scene
individual, or poem unlimited." Vide *Hamlet, and* next column.' Unsigned and
uncollected, but included in Scrapbook 3. An adjacent column contained the
verse prologue which, as reported in the same issue, had been spoken at the
opening of the new Gaiety Theatre at Simla the previous week with the com-
edy *Time Will Tell*. 'Before the rising of the curtain, a prologue in which refer-
ence was gracefully made to the past history of the Simla Stage, was delivered
by Mrs Deane, one of our favourite actresses. The prologue, written by Major
Deane, was very well received, and enthusiastically applauded.'

---

[4] *mehter*: sweeper.
[5] *dôm*: member of a very low caste who performed such duties as carrying dead
bodies, removing carrion, etc. (Glossary to 6th edn. of *Departmental Ditties*, London,
1891.)

For past performances, methinks 't were fit
To let the patient Public give the *chit*;[1]
Albeit, scarce their memory can score
Your triumphs since the season 'seventy-four'
When Lytton[2] ruled the roast, and—so 'tis sung—
The Empire[3] and the Amateurs[4] were young.
You, then as now, were Irvings, Barretts, Keans,[5]
For you the local Stansfield[6] painted scenes.
The lenient eyes of Marquises and Earls
Watched, then as now, your not too girlish girls,
And deftly praised, with diplomatic guile,
The high-strung pathos that provoked a smile.
Survivors of a score of Simla years—
Hot for fresh praise and panting for fresh cheers—
Why tell us this? Full oft have we confessed
Your renderings are better than the best.
But Smith today is gone, and gone is Jones—
He of the nut-brown curls and dulcet tones.
'Macready'[7] Boffkins left in 'seventy-eight',
And Burbles is a Minister of State.
Yea, these are gone, and Time, the grim destroyer,
Already blurs their photoes in your *foyer*,
Though Boffkins' sneer throughout the Hills was known,
And Burbles' *Faust* was mentioned in Ceylon*.

> *   'Whose fame beyond their own abode,
>   Extends—for miles along the Haarlem Road.'[8]

---

[1]   *chit*: letter of recommendation.

[2]   *Lytton*: Lord Lytton, Viceroy 1876–80. He had been an enthusiastic patron of the old Gaiety, where Kipling himself had acted in more recent years.

[3]   *The Empire*: the Royal Titles Act of 1876 had proclaimed Queen Victoria Queen-Empress of India, so that the formal title of Indian Empire could be said to date from then.   [4]   *the Amateurs*: Simla Amateur Dramatic Club.

[5]   *Irvings, Barretts, Keans*: great actors of the London stage–Henry Irving (1838–1905); Wilson Barrett (1846–1904); Edmund Kean (1789–1833).

[6]   *Stansfield*: Clarkson Stanfield, a famous scene-painter of the early and mid-19th-cent. theatre in London.

[7]   *'Macready'*: William Charles Macready (1793–1873), another famous actor of the London stage.

[8]   *Whose fame*: See Oliver Wendell Holmes's attack in *Astraea: The Balance of Illusions* (1850) on upstart New York critics and the local authors they discover and acclaim: 'Titanic pigmies, shining lights obscure . . . / Whose wide renown beyond their own abode / Extends for miles along the Harlaem Road.' (*Complete Poetical Works*, London, 1895, p. 336.) Apart from the spelling of 'Harlem', Kipling quotes the couplet in the form in which it is cited in Bayard Taylor's *The Echo Club and other Literary Diversions* (Boston, 1876). This collection of parodies had been a favourite book of his.

Sweet must it be to you, remembering these,
To gild afresh half-faded memories,
Belaud the past and, in the praise you paste,
Praise most yourselves—the Perfect and the Chaste!
Why 'chaste' amusement?[9] Do our morals fail
Amid the deodars[10] of Annandale?[11]
Into what vicious vortex do they plunge
Who dine on Jakko[12] or in Boileaugunge?[13]
Of course it's 'chaste'! Despite the artless paint,
And P–mm's[14] best wig, who dares to say it ain't?
Great Grundy! Does a sober matron sink
To infamy though rouge and Indian Ink?
Avaunt the thought! As tribute to your taste,
WE CERTIFY THE SIMLA STAGE IS CHASTE.
Mellowed by Age, and cooled by tempering Time,
We find it venerable and sublime.

But newer generations take their seats
Unversed in Boffkins' or in Burbles' feats;
And these, perhaps, exacting babes, may say:—
'The audience, not the actors, judge the play'
Nor think that lady-critic over bold,
Who said not 'Time will tell' but 'Time hath told.'

QUANTITIES OF 'EM

Published in the *CMG*, 15 June 1887, with signature 'R.K.R.' and headings
' "Her name was Thălĭa and not Thālia." *v.* Philothespian's letter yesterday. /
"*Exegi false quantitatum aere audacius*" / "I have played off a false quantity
bolder than brass" Horace (Simla Edition) / *v.l.*[1] "I have only exaggerated a

---

[9] *Why 'chaste' amusement*: the prologue had contained the line 'The Stage here offers
an amusement chaste'.
[10] *deodars*: Himalayan cedars.
[11] *Annandale*: wooded glen near Simla.
[12] *Jakko*: mountain at Simla.
[13] *Boileaugunge*: western area of Simla.
[14] *P–mm*: Pymm, Williams and Co., Hairdressers and Perfumers, Calcutta and
Simla.

---

[1] *v.l.*: *varia lectio* (variant reading).

false quantity audacious and airy." Horace (Lahore Edition).' (Cf. Horace, *Odes*, III. xxx.) Uncollected, but included in Scrapbook 3. The *CMG* on 14 June had carried a letter by 'Philothespian' headed 'The Latin of Olympus':[2] 'Sir, on behalf of the poor Muse of Comedy whose name has been taken in vain by the author of the Prologue on the occasion of the first performance in the Simla New Gaiety Theatre, it should be pointed out that her name was Thaleīa and not Thālia as in the line "the pliant mien of Thālia's face". If the actors of Olympus don't know the name of their own patrons—what can do?' The nine Muses, daughters of Mnemosyne, most of whose names are mispronounced in his poem, were Terpsichore (dancing), Melpomene (tragedy), Thalia (comedy), Erato (the lyre), Euterpe (flute-playing), Calliope (epic poetry), Polyhymnia (sacred song), Urania (astronomy), and Clio (history).

> Oh! Do you know the Muses nine
> The daughters of Jove and Mnemosyne?
> And have you heard how they play the deuce
> With 'longs' and 'shorts' at Olympūs?
> They waltz around on the boarded floor
> To pay their homage to Terpsichore;
> They act a tragedy—this I ween
> *Not* under the guidance of Melpomene;
> While Comedy—H'm—if it prove a failure
> Is—pardon the rhyme—disowned by Thalia;
> The love that never was taught by Plato
> They learn to express from the fair Erato
> While writers of *vers de société* chirp
> At the foot of the footstool of Miss Euterpe,
> Though singers and actors can hardly hope
> For a line on the tablets of Calliope,
> And barely two of the crowd aspire
> To follow the calm-eyed Polyhymnia,
> Or turn to the Heavens and bother their crania
> With profitless watching the stars, like Urānia.
>
> Which things—that the last may be hurried more quickly o-
> ver—move the wrath of the scornful and sick Clio,
> Who wails, through our pen, from Parnassian glades:—
> 'This is classical knowledge in Simla, Oh Hades!'

[2] *Olympus*: the abode of the gods in classical mythology: Anglo-Indian nickname for Simla.

TAKING A HINT

Published in the *CMG*, 18 July 1887, with subtitle 'And its Fatal Conse-
quences' and heading '(*Vide Recent Judgment of C——— H— C—)*'. Unsigned
and uncollected, but included in Scrapbook 3. The *CMG* for 15 July had criti-
cized a decision of the Calcutta High Court in what was called the Meherpur
Fishery Case. A young Assistant Magistrate had tried sixty-eight people for
fishing in a private lake, after they had been warned by the police that fishing
was prohibited. He had sentenced all between the ages of 16 and 45 to be
flogged and the others to undergo two months' imprisonment. The High
Court overturned his decision, held that no crime had been committed since
the fish were wild fish in a natural lake, and severely rebuked the young Magis-
trate for the punishment he had imposed. The language used by the Chief Jus-
tice was humiliating, and the *CMG* took the view that such a public rebuke was
calculated to bring the administration of the country into contempt. It illus-
trated this by an article on the case in the Calcutta Press which implied 'that
those who may deem themselves aggrieved by punishment inflicted in the
name of the law might well revenge themselves with their own hands upon its
individual ministers'.

'Come let us slate the Magistrate,
    The District Judge no less—
"Young persons"[1] they, from whose mad sway
    The ryots[2] ask redress.
Yea, let us print the scornful hint
    About the D.S.P.;[3]
And straightly curse that most perverse
    And juvenile D.C.'[4]

They cursed them free, judicially
    In judgment and report.
They took the District Judges' list
    To make a Bench's sport.
They bullied then these luckless men
    In divers ways and harsh;
And, while they wrote, with grateful throat,
    The people cried:—'*Shabash!*'[5]

---

[1] *"Young persons"*: the Chief Justice in his comments on the Assistant Magistrate's
action used the phrase 'a young person in his position'.
[2] *ryots* (or *raiyats*): peasants, tenant farmers.
[3] *D.S.P.*: District Superintendent of Police.
[4] *D.C.*: Deputy Commissioner.   [5] *Shabash!*: Bravo! Well done.

And argued thus ('t is obvious
    They took too hasty views;
For Oriental discontent
    Runs fast in Europe shoes):—
''Tis plain indeed, from what we read,
    Whatever we may do
To *Sahibs* like these, is sure to please
    One Judge and, may be, two.'

The Magistrate, respected late,
    Was chased by wild Vakils.[6]
The Zemindar[7] would oft *shikar*[8]
    The 'Stunt'[9] among the *bhils*.[10]
When they had slain a Judge or twain,
    They looked for honour, but
That budding hope a slip-knot rope
    Incontinently cut.

A PROLOGUE

Spoken by Kipling's sister Trix at a theatrical performance at Snowdon, the
Commander-in-Chief's[1] residence at Simla, on 25 July 1887. Printed on a
programme card for the occasion (KP 28/3); published in the *Pioneer*, 1
August 1887, with two couplets omitted (printed here in square brackets);
reprinted in the *Pioneer Mail*, 7 August. Unsigned and uncollected, but
included in Scrapbook 3. The performance took place in a new ballroom
specially designed to serve as a theatre, and was attended by a large audience
including the Viceroy and Lady Dufferin. It was in aid of Lady Roberts's fund
for providing summer homes in the Hills for nursing sisters who were to be
brought out from Britain, in a scheme she had initiated, to provide skilled
nursing in European military hospitals in India in an attempt to reduce the
high mortality rate among British troops.

So please you, Gentlefolk, a drama slight
Awaits your verdict on our opening night.
But, ere the call-bell rings, we pray you take
In all good part the humble plea we make

---

[6] *Vakils*: pleaders, attorneys.   [7] *Zemindar*: landlord.   [8] *shikar*: hunt.
[9] *Stunt*: Assistant (Collector).   [10] *bhils*: marshes or ponds.

[1] *the Commander-in-Chief*: Sir Frederick Roberts (see above, p. 282).

For mercy at the hands of those who know
Exactly how a comedy should go.
And they are many, and their cold grey eyes
Note every weakness from the curtain's rise.
They scoff at halting bye-play and rejoice
To hear the agonizing Prompter's voice;
Mark where the hare's foot trenches on the crow's
And damn an actor for too red a nose;
Then, where the 'rickshaws block Peliti's[2] door,
Remark: 'We never saw such stuff before!'
To these stern critics we appeal for ruth,
By virtue, not of excellence, but youth.
For we are young—behold, the paint still new
Shows that but yesterday our playhouse grew.
Forgive us then, if side-slips slide uncertain,
Or all too hasty falls the half-trained curtain,
Or from your eyes by unrehearsed mishap,
Our leading ladies vanish down a trap.
Such little accidents, it stands to reason,
Might mar the first performance of the season.

Thus, having met all possible detractors,
We will *not* ask you to excuse our actors.
Some you know well; their art in bye-gone years
Has moved the Gaiety to mirth and tears,
Brought as the 'act-drop' closed upon the scene,
To English lips, the Moslem cry of *Din*![3]
We borrowed them—we glory in the crime—
And hope to *play*giarise a second time.
The others who portray poor Lucia's[4] griefs,
Are all, in their respective lines,—*the Chiefs*![5]
The *Army List* eluciadates this fact.
And now to tell you how we came to act.
Who said—'To please yourselves'?—No! I deny it.
Who ever acts for pleasure? Just you try it!

---

[2] *Peliti's*: famous café and confectioner's in Simla.

[3] *Din*: 'the faith'—cry of excited Muslims—punning here on the names of Major and Mrs Deane, veterans of the Simla theatre. (Cf. p. 375 above.)

[4] *Lucia*: the performance included an operatic burlesque, *Lucia di Lammermoor*.

[5] *the Chiefs*: i.e. army men, under command of Sir Frederick Roberts, the Commander-in-Chief.

Men say, who simmer in the Plains below,
That Simla people frivol. Be it so.
Let us admit that, as the Plains assert,
The Maidens of the Mountain sometimes . . . flirt,
While Matrons dance, and others, wilder still
Give picnics at the back of Summer Hill.
And bold, bad sportsmen on a lottery-night
Sit up till morning dims the candle-light.
But *we* are good. *We* scorn the flighty crew.
We frivol with a serious end in view:
And here forgive me if my trifling rhyme
Take graver accents for a little time.

You know, who know the Army, first of those
Strong lines that wall the Empire from her foes
Stands—'to attention' ready for the sign—
One Thomas Atkins, Private of the Line.
His business is—well, never mind the rest;
You men who lead him know his business best!
But, 'ere that work begins, 'neath Indian skies
Too oft alas! our faithful warder dies.
[The hot Sun wars above him and beneath
The steaming Earth reclaims the Dragon's Teeth],[6]
The chill of night, the fever of the town,
The sickness of the noon-day strikes him down.
Nor him alone. The leaders and the led
Swell that great army of the untimely dead
Who knew no battle save one hopeless fight
With Death, beneath the punkah in the night.
Is this an idle story in your ears?
Look back! How reads the record of past years?
Think for a moment, while your memory traces
The long procession of the dead lost faces.
See! Year on year the dreary record runs—
Strong men and boys—friends, lovers, husbands, sons,
Cut down upon the threshold of Life's Gate
Who might have lived, but that help came too late.

---

[6] *the Dragon's Teeth*: the armed men (who in classical legend sprang from the earth when it had been sown with the teeth of a dragon which guarded the well of Ares, the god of war).

Help came too late. The care sad comrades gave
Was rough as ready, and unskilled to save.
And O! it asks the tenderest care to stay
The spirit poised between the Night and Day.
That care, if woman's skill and woman's toil
May from the Slayer wrench the destined spoil—
[By night-long watches in the dim-lit ward
Arrest the downward stroke of Azrael's[7] sword—]
That care is theirs by right who freely give
Their lives to guard the land wherein we live.
Let be the Dead gone down beyond recall;
Turn to the Living. Help them lest they fall!
Fight Death with money—money that can buy
The soft, cool, soothing touch, the sleepless eye,
The woman's art that coaxes and commands
The fevered mouth and weak and trembling hands.
Buy these—for all the healing lore men know
Fails, lacking these, to bind the soul below.
Help us herein, who strive in some small measure
To weave a purpose in the threads of Pleasure—
To meet both Simla's and the Soldier's needs
And make light Mirth the handmaid of Kind Deeds.

But here some justly wearied man may say:—
'We didn't want a sermon. Where's your play?'
So I, who trespass on your patience, cease.
Ohé! Behind there! *Psst!* Ring on the piece!

CONCERNING A JAWÁB[1]

Published in the *CMG*, 6 August 1887, with signature 'E.Y.', and heading
' "There was no other man in the case at all. She said she had simply changed
her mind—had done so for a long while, but didn't like to tell me for fear of
hurting my feelings. So I gave back the letters and it's all over." *Extract from a
Private Letter.*' Uncollected, but included in Scrapbook 3. 'After' is a revised
version of 'The Attainment' or 'Escaped!', written in May 1882 (see above,
p. 148.)

---

[7] *Azrael*: the angel of Death in Islamic legend.

[1] *Jawáb*: reply; more specifically, a refusal to a proposal of marriage.

BEFORE

By all the mighty Oaths that Love can frame,
    And all the Penalties by Love imposed,
I swore to Him that Love should be the same
    Till Time's weak wings and Time's worn Eyelids closed.
These things, in scorn of Time, I swore to prove,
    But Time, in scorn of Me, my Love hath killed,
    And, for this Treason, leaves my Heart unfilled,
Lest Treason find a Comfort in new Love.

Alas! Long Usage schools the fettered Speech
To that sweet Creed, outlived an Age ago,
Since Time hath checked his Flight to edge my Doom.
Dull Cowardice sets Freedom out of Reach.
While Pity wails:—'For Love's Sake be it so.'
And Passion's Corpse-Light flickers o'er Love's Tomb.

AFTER

Peace, by Time's Mercy, in the Heart of Me,
    The Peace that springs of very Weariness;
As One Wave-rescued looks upon the Sea
    So look I on the Day of my Distress.—
A Power defied that stretches forth weak Hands
    To hold Me who am passed from out Its Reach—
    An angry Wave that thunders on the Beach,
But takes no Trophy of the scornful Sands.

Yea, Peace hath come again and I am free,
And all the Old is dead and cannot rise,
And all the New awaits Me, pure, untrod.
As One Wave-rescued turneth from the Sea
Landward to rest Him, so turn I my Eyes
From past Things to the Future, thanking God.

THE WITCHING OF TEDDY O'NEAL

Published in the *CMG*, 14 September 1887, with signature 'R.K.' Uncollected.

Teddy O'Neal went up the Hill:
        Heart of my heart was Teddy O'Neal,
For the light of the Good Folk was over his path,
And the music called him from dune and rath,[1]
And I could not stay him, delay him, nor pray him
        To fly from the witch-wives, my Teddy O'Neal.

Teddy O'Neal went up the Hill:
        Best of the Best was Teddy O'Neal,
Drawn by the cords that the Good Folk make,
With a heart on flame for the music's sake;
But I knew there was danger for Teddy, a stranger,
        In the Court of Finvarra,[2] my Teddy O'Neal.

Teddy O'Neal went up the Hill:
        Fair as the morning was Teddy O'Neal,
He danced with the witch-wives, one, two, three,
He tasted their wine and he turned from me
From me while I pleaded, he speeded nor heeded;
        Of the wine of Finvarra drank Teddy O'Neal.

Teddy O'Neal sank down on the Hill.
        The Black Rath swallowed my Teddy O'Neal,
And I prayed to the Saints as I stood without
And heard through the hill side the rattle and shout
Of the feast that they gave him, and I could not save him;
        For a witch-wife was charming my Teddy O'Neal.

Teddy O'Neal came down the Hill,—
        Not my brother, my Teddy O'Neal,
The kiss of the witch-wife was red on his mouth;
He turned from my table in hunger and drouth,
For the Good Folk had crowned him, and bound him and wound him
        In the Spell of Finvarra, my Teddy O'Neal.

Teddy O'Neal is back in the Plains—
        The flesh of the body of Teddy O'Neal;
But his lips are closed and his voice is still,
And I know that his heart is straining up Hill
To the witch-wife he strayed with and stayed with and paid with
        The price of his soul, my poor Teddy O'Neal.

[1] *rath*: enclosure made by strong earth wall, to serve as fort and residence for a chief.
[2] *Finvarra*: Fionnbharr, king of the fairies in Irish folklore.

ITU AND HIS GOD

Published in the *CMG*, 10 October 1887, with signature 'K'. Uncollected, but included in Scrapbook 4. One of Kipling's contributions to the *CMG* on 6 May 1887 read as follows: 'There has been a "revival" on a large scale in far off Kafiristan[1] by reason of the displeasure of the great god Kysh, who last month loosed a great stone from a glacier on a congregation of the Oash Gool and killed thirty of them as they were praying to him. Then, says our devout correspondent, came Oatta, Bishop of the God of Kysh, and a very holy saint from the Himalayas, and told the men of Oash Gool that Kysh was angry with them, and unless offerings were made, they would be accounted followers of Aram and Yaboosh, which being translated means Satan. . . . ' (For an interest in primitive religion comparable with that registered in this poem, see 'The Sacrifice of Er-Heb' in *Barrack-Room Ballads*.)

> Itu, who led the Oash Gul to war,
> Carved a great image from the mountain-pine,
> Strung beads upon its neck and smeared its cheeks
> With blood of slaughtered beasts, and called it God,
> And set it in a cavern of the Hills,
> Alone, and save for him who knew the path
> Between the glacier and the sliding shale,
> Remote, unseen and unapproachable.
>
> Between the Council and the Day of Fight,
> Between the Choosing and the Sacrifice,
> Between the full-thought Plan and that he did,
> Itu made pilgrimage across the snows
> That guard the glacier and the sliding shale,
> And called upon his God with mighty cries,
> And looked into the white-shell eyes for sign.
> And slew the beasts, and made the altar smoke,
> Alone and in the cavern of the Hills.
>
> And, as the night-wind sang about the rocks,
> Or as the hill-stream thundered in the cleft,
> Or as the river groaned beneath the snows,
> So Itu read the answer of his God,
> And warred against the foe or held his hand.

[1] *Kafiristan*: an area of eastern Afghanistan including part of the Hindu Kush mountain range.

But once the mountain where the Cavern is
Was troubled as a man is vext in sleep,
And stirred a little, blindly, heaved a flank,
Then fell afresh to slumber. When the day
Broke desolate across the desolate snows,
And the affrighted eagle sought her nest,
An hour quitted, lost beneath the drift,
The great, unwinking-eyed, pine-carven God
Lay in the valley, riven, splintered, marred
And soiled with muddy water from the streams,—
A log across the torrent.
                                Itu came,
With him a score of ewes for sacrifice,
And heads of enemies in wicker arks,
Wherefrom the blood dripped softly on the snow,
And incense stolen from the Devil-Shrine,
Which is beyond the hills of Ao-Safai.—
But lo! his God was fallen from the cave,
A log across the torrents of the hills.

Then Itu called him by his Name of Praise,
His name of Pleading, and the Third Great Name
The Name of Power; but the water lapped
About his ears, and rippled on his back,
And frothed among his feet, and he lay still,
Esteeming more the mud and broken trees
Than twenty ewes or bleeding human heads,
Or Itu, leaning from the crag above,
And whispering to him, in the Third Great Name.

So Itu flung the wicker arks away,
And freed the ewes to die among the snows,
And, stepping from the boulder to the pine
Disthroned, and from the tree-trunk to the mire,
Smote once, and twice and thrice, the white-shell eyes
And cut the neck and set the head adrift
And hewed the body, weeping while he smote
Because his God was fallen from the cave.

Then he returned to lead the Oash Gul
Out of the Temple to the war, but first
Struck Kysh and Yabosh, very terrible,

Red-eyed, smoke-blackened, by the altar steps
Before the priests could stay him. Hom he struck
Between the eyes, and loosed the Silver Crown
Which is the diadem of Hom the Wise;
Nor stopped before the murky shrine of Thar
Who rules the births of men. So he was bound
By all the priests of Kysh and Hom and Thar,
And set upon a boulder in the snows
And pierced with arrows till, that night, he died,
Blaspheming his own God with white-shell eyes,
Yabosh and Kysh and Hom and Thar the Maid,
And all the priest-hood of the Oash Gul,
Because his handiwork was carven pine.

And, later, the snow-leopard took his bones,
And spread them where the wild horse herds in spring,
And gave his skull to please her cubs awhile;
And men forebore to speak on Itu's name
Who cursed the great Gods of the Oash Gul,
Because he made a God without the priests,
That was no God, but fell as pine-trees fall,
Between the glacier and the sliding shale.

THE NIGHT OF POWER

Holograph draft, uncompleted, on diary page for 1 January[1] 1888, with marginal sketches of a hookah, a kukri,[2] a railway engine, two profiles, and an Indian scene with a low building and a tree (Library of Congress). The fragment is of interest firstly because it gives so clear a view of Kipling in the process of composition—his cancellations are shown here in square brackets, with double square brackets for cancelled variants within cancelled lines; and secondly, because it anticipates the themes of the story 'How Fear Came' in *The Second Jungle Book* (1895). That story, first published in 1894, tells how Tha made the tiger master of the jungle, then deposed him for killing a fellow animal, and replaced him first by the ape, and then by Man who was Fear to the inhabitants of the jungle. But the tiger, to compensate for his lost supremacy, was allowed one night of power each year when Man feared him and was his victim.

---

[1] *1 January*: the fact that the poem appears on this diary page does not necessarily mean it was written on that date. 'The Song of the Women', which was published in the *Pioneer* on 17 Apr. 1888, is drafted in the Diary pages for 8, 9, and 10 Jan.; but this does suggest 1888 as the year of composition.   [2] *kukri*: Gurkha knife.

In the beginning when the earth was new
[God] Thár[3] made the Tyger monarch till he slew
[An angel] Thar's uncle wandering in human shape
[Across] Among the wood-ways. Then was crowned the Ape
Who walked unseemly till he made the name
Of King of Beasts a [mocking] scoffing and a shame.
[Then] ⎰Thereafter⎱ through the ⎰listening woods ⎱ the mandate ran
       ⎱So,   ⎰   ⎱trembling earth ⎰
Henceforth [of all things made] obey ye for your ruler man"
And with the word fell fear as [fire flies] fires pass   and Thâm
In [later] latter summer through the [plu] [sere] dry plumed grass   Thár
Great fear there was of this poor naked thing
Couched in the caves who knew not he was King
[But trembled at the ⟦beasts who⟧ thunder ⟦in the⟧ of the cries]
[Only the Tyger mindful of his fall
Was void of fear and]
Only the Tyger mindful of his fall
Fled to the wilds and had no fear at all,
[But underneath the stars ⟦in piteous wise⟧ up to the skies
⟦Wailed for his sovereignty⟧ Moaned for his sovereignty in piteous
     wise]
But nightly [moaning] roaring 'neath the new made sky,
Cried out [alone] to Thar for his lost sovereignty
And Thár who is as faithful as the rains,
[And] Who draws[4] the swarming blackbuck on the plains,
Who sends the wind that makes the devils flee,
And [sleeps] bids the <   >[5] [flower] bloom abundantly
And <   >[6] [gave] teaches man to [take] mat the grass and make,
[Such shelter] Strong shelters that the wild-pig cannot break
[And lights the sun to call the]
[Who was before the oldest and shall ⟦be⟧ live
After the youngest ⟦climb⟧ ⟦di⟧ pass:]

Caetera desunt.[7] Try again some other night

       Thar heard the [cry] plaint

---

    [3] *Thár*: cf. 'Itu and his God', lines 65–71 (p. 388 above). Cf. also the god 'Tha, the
First of the Elephants' in 'How Fear Came'.
    [4] *draws*: reading uncertain.   [5] : illegible.   [6] : illegible.
    [7] : *Caetera desunt*: the rest is missing.

THE MAN AND THE SHADOW

Published in the *Week's News*, 4 February 1888. Unsigned. Collected in the Outward Bound, De Luxe, Sussex and Burwash Edns. with one stanza omitted (printed here in square brackets). In the *Week's News* version the last line of the tenth stanza reads 'Doing *budli*[1] for his betters'; line 4 of the eleventh stanza has 'dire' for 'open'; and line 6 of the last stanza reads 'I should think his end alas!'

If it were mine to choose
A single gift from Fate,
I would not ask for Rank or Fame,
I would not seek a knighted name—
Give me, for office use,
One good subordinate.

Up the steep Official Stair
    With rapidity amazing
    Clomb, his seniors bedazing,
    Into Heights of Glory blazing,
With the Stars that mortals wear
    On their dress-coat breasts at Levées,
    Hastings Clive Macaulay[2] Bevys.

And they stood below and cursed—
    All the Juniors of his calling—
    With a fluency appalling,
    Betting on his chance of falling;
Prayed to see the bubble burst
    Of the reputation first-class
    Of this Idler of the worst class.

In his office, scorned of all,
    Saddle-hued, grotesque of feature,
    Worked a weird, bi-racial creature,
    Far too humble-souled to meet your

---

[1] *Doing budli*: acting as substitute or locum tenens.
[2] *Hastings Clive Macaulay*: names of great significance in the history of British India: Warren Hastings (1732–1818), the first Governor-General; Robert Clive (1725–74), who established British supremacy in Bengal by his victory at Plassey in 1757; Thomas Babington Macaulay (1800–59), member of Supreme Council 1834–8, who was largely responsible for the imposition of English patterns of education on India.

Eye—Concepcion Gabral;
   Santu Ribiera Paul
   Luz Concepcion Gabral.

[What he did I cannot say.
     Did he give or take instruction,
     Break the eggs[3] for Bevys' suction,
     Work that highly paid deduction
Which—while sparing Bevys' pay—
     Cut in graduated stages
     Everybody's else's wages?]

This I know, and this is all:
     For his labours unremitting
     Came a recompense befitting
     Bevys, *plus* a well-paid flitting
Into Burmahorbengal;
     But Concepcion, the able,
     Stirred not from the office-table.

This I know, and this is all:
     There were hints unfit for hinting,
     There was speech unfit for printing,
     There were protests without stinting,
Heard in Burmahorbengal—
     Crudely, nudely, rudely, rawly,
     Saying, 'Take back this Macaulay'.

In the brutal, bitter wit
     Much affected east of Suez,
     Where the Englishman so few is,
     And a man must work or rue his
Incapacity and quit,
     Fell innumerable bastings
     Upon Clive Macaulay Hastings.

With the Hand of Common Sense
     On the Waistband of Despair, they
     Raised that ruler high in air, they
     Stripped him miserably bare, they

---

[3] *Break the eggs*: cf. the saying 'Teach your grandmother to suck eggs'.

On the soft flesh of Pretence
    In the face of India, smacked him,
    Then, as shop-boys say, they 'sacked' him.

You may find him still to-day
    'Twixt Peshawur[4] and Colaba,[5]
    Derelict without a harbour,
    A civilian Micawber[6]
(Spare the rhyme who read the lay!)
    In 'officiating' fetters,
    Doing duty for his betters.

And—oh, irony supreme!
    All the Gods who rule the Nation
    Have withheld the explanation
    Of his open degradation
From the man they justly deem
    An administrative novice
    Trusting blindly to his office.

This I know, and this is all
    (*He* is ignorant as ever)
    And if Fate decrees he never
    Meet again the humble, clever,
Quick-to-grasp-ideas Gabral,
    Sure am I his end, alas!
    Will be madness or—Madras.[7]

STRUCK ILE

Published in the *Pioneer*, 4 February 1888, with signature 'R.K.' and headings:
' "Two years ago Sir A. Colvin,[1] in introducing the Income Tax Bill, des-
cribed that year as the last of the fat kine.[2] He said that the lean kine were
come in."—*Vide Mr Westland's Financial Statement, Jan. 30th.*' / ' "Peace,

---

[4] *Peshawur*: city on the North-West Frontier.

[5] *Colaba*: promontory and area of city of Bombay.

[6] *Micawber*: see *David Copperfield* for Mr Micawber's perpetual hope that something would turn up.

[7] *Madras*: 'the benighted Presidency' in the eyes of North India men.

[1] *Sir A. Colvin*: Sir Auckland Colvin, formerly the Financial Member of Council, but now Lieut.-Gov. of the North-West Provinces with his headquarters in Allahabad.

[2] *fat kine*: see Gen. 41.

peace, such a small lamp illumes on this highway, / So dimly, so few steps in front of our feet." *The Song of the Bower*.'[3] Reprinted in the *CMG*, 7 February, and *Pioneer Mail*, 8 February. Uncollected, but included in Scrapbook 4. James Westland, Comptroller and Auditor General and Head Commissioner of Paper Currency, was serving as a Member of Council at this time. The *Pioneer* for 28 January 1888 reported his speech on the financial situation, and the full text was printed in the issue for 30 January. Westland proposed a tax on all imported petroleum, in addition to a 25% increase in the Salt Tax.

W– stl–nd, the bank-note man,
    Holding the Treasury keys,
Promised 'to pay the bearer'
    Eighty crores[4] of rupees,
And C–lv–n was caught up to Allahabad-Valhallahabad of L.G.'s.

W–stl–nd, the bank-note man,
    Proved in a lucid way
Nobody ought to be wrath if
    Government couldn't pay;
And C–lv–n leaned from the bar of Heaven and cheered him on to the
        fray.

W–stl–nd, the bank-note man,
    Served up the usual hash,
Added a grain of salt, and
    Drew pro-notes for the cash;
Devastating the P——r with seven columns[5] of trash.

A scrape from the golah's[6] mouth—
    A tea cupful of the brine—
A crutch and a stay and we pull through the day,
    And blunder along the line,
While Krishna[7] W–stl–nd tootles his flute to C–lv–n's starveling kine.

W–stl–nd, the bank-note man,
    Trusting to Time and Chance,
Tinkered the leak with a kerosine-can
    In the name of paraffinance;
And C–lv–n lighted a hurricane lamp to shine on the dreary dance.

---

³ *The Song of the Bower*: by Dante Gabriel Rossetti.

⁴ *crores*: tens of millions.

⁵ *seven columns*: the text of Westland's speech and an account of the debate in Council ran to seven and three-quarter columns in the *Pioneer* for 30 January.

⁶ *golah*: storehouse for salt or grain.

⁷ *Krishna*: Hindu deity, one of the incarnations of Vishnu the Preserver, often represented as playing a flute.

Knaust[8] *where we lack the nous*[9]—
   Thora mutti-ki-tel[10]—
A pinch and a shift and away we drift
   With a dying wind in the sail;
But what shall we do when the cruize is run and the last, least catspaws fail?

Here is a study in oils—
   Naught in the world could be fairer—
W–stl–nd making his Bearer pay,
   Instead of 'paying the bearer',
And an Empire starting a *bunnia*'s[11] shop, as the *pice*[12] grow rarer and
   rarer.

A BALLADE OF BAD ENTERTAINMENT
[A BALLADE OF DAK-BUNGALOWS][1]

Published in the *Week's News*, 11 February 1888, under title 'A Ballade of
Dak-Bungalows.' Unsigned. Holograph version with drawing of fowl, signed
'R.K.' and dated February 1889 (Houghton Library, Harvard University).
Collected with minor revisions in the Outward Bound, De Luxe, Sussex, and
Burwash Edns.

      A wanderer from East to West,
         From Mandalay to Matheran,[2]
      By itch of loaferdom possest,
         I scour the plains of Hindustan.
      Dismissed the fragrant *gariwān*,[3]
         I clamour at each hostelry:
      'What, ho! within there, *be imân!*'[4]
         '*Khodawund, siruf murghi hai!*'[5]

---

[8] *Knaust*: a reference to the Lamp Warehouse of Theodore Knaust in Bombay.
[9] *nous*: intelligence.   [10] *Thora mutti-ki-tel*: a little kerosine.
[11] *bunnia*: corn merchant, shopkeeper.
[12] *pice*: copper coins of very small value.

---

[1] *Dak-Bungalows*: accommodation provided by the Government for officials travelling
on business; available to other travellers on payment of a fee. *Dak*: stage of journey.
[2] *Matheran*: a hill-station some 50 mls. from Bombay.
[3] *gariwān*: driver (collected edns.).
[4] *be imân*: man without faith (collected edns.).
[5] *Khodawund, siruf murghi hai*: Heaven-born, there is only fowl (collected edns.).

The days repeat the sorry jest—
    The dusty drive, the dreary barn.
'All things await the Sahib's behest,
    Borne through his slave Mohammed Jan.'
And after? Hear the wild *tūfān*
    Among the cockerels as they fly!
What comes of that false feigned *élan*?
    '*Khodawund, siruf murghi hai!*'

Though in ten thousand fashions messed
    They bear the *Janwar ki nishan*,[7]
The bold black legs, the bony crest,
    The flesh more tough than sailors' yarn.
Oh, land of *uttr*[8] and of *pân*,[9]
    For this poor corpse thy children cry,
Loud as the mullah shouts *azán*,[10]
    '*Khodawund, siruf murghi hai!*'

L'ENVOI

Prince! (Here the wearied bard will rest
    From long 'a' rhymes.) If Famine fan
The flames of Fury in your breast,
    And grievously you smite your man,
For his one answer, this I can
    Add to your comfort: An he die,
You shall be told by all his clan:
    '*Khodawund, siruf murghia hai!*'[11]

INSCRIPTION IN COPY OF *PLAIN TALES FROM THE HILLS* PRESENTED TO MRS HILL

Mrs Edmonia Hill describes in her article 'The Young Kipling', *Atlantic Monthly*, vol. clvii (1936), pp. 406–15, how she and her husband became

---

[6] *tūfān*: uproar (collected edns.).
[7] *Janwar ki nishan*: mark of the beast (collected edns.).
[8] *uttr*: attar, perfume (Sussex and Burwash Edns.).
[9] *pân*: nut wrapped in betel leaf, for chewing.
[10] *azán*: the call to prayer (collected edns.).
[11] *Khodawund, siruf murghia hai*: Heaven-born, he is only dead (collected edns.).

friendly with Kipling after he moved from Lahore to Allahabad, and how, on 2
March 1888, he presented her with a copy of *Plain Tales from the Hills* with this
inscription (ibid., p. 407).

> Between the gum pot and the shears,[1]
>   The weapons of my grimy trade,[2]
> In divers moods and various years
>   These forty foolish yarns were made.
>
> And some were writ to fill a page
>   And some—but these are not so many—
> To soothe a finely moral rage
>   And all to turn an honest penny.
>
> And some I gathered from my friends
>   And some I looted from my foes,
> And some—All's fish that Heaven sends—
>   Are histories of private woes.
>
> And some are Truth, and some are Lie,
>   And some exactly half and half,
> I've heard some made a woman cry—
>   I *know* some made a woman laugh.
>
> I do not view them with delight
>   And, since I know that you may read 'em,
> I'd like to thoroughly rewrite,
>   Remould, rebuild, retouch, reword 'em.
>
> Would they were worthier. That's too late—
>   Cracked pictures stand no further stippling.
> Forgive the faults.
>
>   *March* '88
>   To Mrs Hill
>   From Rudyard Kipling

---

[1] *the gum pot and the shears*: scissors and paste (cf. p. 255 above).
[2] *my grimy trade*: journalism.

6. Kipling in his later years in India. 1887–8? (Cf. frontispiece.)

THE VANISHING FIGURE

Published in the *Week's News*, 10 March 1888. Unsigned and uncollected, but included in Scrapbook 4.

Helen Montfaucon, née Snape,
　　Moved me to passionate love—
Hers was a figure of exquisite shape,
　　Hers was the voice and the eye of a dove.

Wholly untinted her face,
　　Wholly ungilded her hair—
She held pearl-powder and rouge a disgrace
　　She it was told me so. Hence my despair!

No, neither powder of rice,
　　Rouge nor bronzed locks were her line,—
Hers was a figure of rarest device
　　Perfect in contour—Milosian,[1] divine.

What was it happened? Who knows?
　　I can but faintly suggest—
Maybe in waltzing I held her too close
　　Close to the violets pinned on my breast.

There was a pin 'neath the flowers,
　　Something went off with a gasp—
Sighed like a sibillant gas-jet. Great Powers!
　　Helen Montfaucon grew lean in my clasp.

Shrivelled, shrank, dwindled, went small,
　　Said that the room was too hot—
Fled from the cloak-room, and fled from the ball.
　　I saw her going. Her figure was not!

There are advertisements. Yes.
　　Can they mean anything? No.
Say, was it possible . . . Helen's ball dress
　　Hid ought less solid than Helen below?

---

[1] *Milosian*: from the Venus de Milo.

VERSE HEADING TO 'THE "KINGDOM" OF BOMBAY'

Published in the *Pioneer*, 10 April 1888. Reprinted in the *Pioneer Mail*, 11 April; *CMG*, 12 April; and *Week's News*, 14 April. Unsigned and uncollected, but the sequel, 'Bombaystes Furioso', is included in Scrapbook 4. The first heading reads 'All classes and creeds are alike interested in a policy (the transfer of Sind[1] to the Punjab) which strikes a mortal blow at the future growth and prosperity of the Kingdom of Bombay.—*Times of India*,[2] April 5th.' The story derides the overweening pretensions of Bombay as revealed in this description of the Presidency as a Kingdom; and the second heading reads:

Who are they that bluff and blow among the mud-banks of their
    harbour?
Making mock of Upper India where the High Gods live alway?
Grey rats of Prince's Dock[3]—more dull than oysters of Colaba[4]—
Apes of Apollo Bunder[5]—yea, *bacilli* of Back Bay![6]
                  Swinburne[7] (adapted)

VERSE HEADING TO 'BOMBAYSTES FURIOSO'

Published in the *Pioneer*, 16 April 1888. Reprinted in the *Pioneer Mail*, 18 April, and *Week's News*, 21 April. Unsigned and uncollected, but included in Scrapbook 4. A follow-up to 'The "Kingdom" of Bombay', provoked by an injudicious response by the *Times of India*.

Oh! what will Your Majesty please to wear—
    Shoddy or fustian or piebald gown?
Will Your Majesty look at *our* bill of fare?
    Will Your Majesty wait till we take you down?

            Bombastes Furioso[1] (adapted)

[1] *Sind*: the territory of Sind was at this time under the jurisdiction of the Bombay Government.   [2] *Times of India*: published in Bombay.

[3] *Prince's Dock*: one of the main docks in the harbour area at Bombay.

[4] *Colaba*: a promontory and area of the city at Bombay.

[5] *Apollo Bunder*: famous landing place at Bombay harbour.

[6] *Back Bay*: large bay between the Malabar and Colaba promontories at Bombay.

[7] *Swinburne*: see the opening of stanza 2 of his poem 'The Commonweal': 'What are these that howl and hiss across the strait of westward water?'

[1] *Bombastes Furioso*: burlesque by William Barnes Rhodes, published in 1810. The name 'Bombastes' derives from 'bombast', and 'Furioso' (as in *Orlando Furioso*) means 'raging' or 'in madness'.

LIBERAVI ANIMAM MEAM[1]

Published in the *Week's News*, 21 April 1888, with heading ' "The Bishop of Bombay is displeased with Society because it encourages the sinful game of 'Tommy Dodd' at Charity Bazaars."—*Pioneer*, April 14th.' Unsigned and uncollected, but included in Scrapbook 4. The Bishop had written to the press protesting against the use of this game at a Fancy Fair held by Lady Reay, the wife of the Lieutenant-Governor of Bombay, in aid of the Cama Hospital for woman and children. The *Pioneer* went on to comment: 'For the benefit of the uninitiated, it may be explained that "Tommy Dodd" is a compromise between roulette and the race game: four small leaden horses struck on the four points of a weather-vane, a barrel-head divided into compartments for the staking of rupees, and . . . an energetic lady to control the bank, are all that is requisite to play it.'

My name is Tommy Dodd,
(Tommy Dodd)
And I scorn the Bishop's rod
(Tommy Dodd),
You may find me spinning free
At each Charity Squeejee—
'Stakes confined to one rupee.'
(Tommy Dodd) *Bis*[2]

And the Bishop he may write,
He may write:
Yea, in lawn-sleeved black and white
Urge the fight,
And in language erudite
Lash the gambling appetite
Of Society polite.
(Tommy Dodd).

But ere Bishops wielded crook,
(Tommy Dodd),
Ere they cursed by Bell and Book
(Tommy Dodd),
I—or some one like me—taught
Man the hope of gain for naught;
But they called *my* worship 'Sport'.
(Tommy Dodd).

[1] *Liberavi* . . . : I have freed my spirit (Saint Bernard).
[2] *Bis*: twice.

Since your little race began
          (Tommy Dodd),
I have swayed the soul of man;
          (Tommy Dodd),
Crozier, rochet, mitre, pall,
I am stronger than them all,
And shall flourish when they fall
          (Tommy Dodd).

Dam the Indus[3] in its bed
          (Tommy Dodd),
Blanket Kinchinjunga's[4] head
          (Tommy Dodd),
Skid a glacier, cork a crater,
Make the Morning Sun rise later,
And—I'll own that you're the greater
          (Tommy Dodd).

Spokeshave ever failing human,
          (Tommy Dodd),
Turn the heart of man from woman,
          (Tommy Dodd),
Cleanse the Earth of evil in it,
Pinion Passion's wings with sinnit,[5]
And—I'll abdicate this minute
          (Tommy Dodd).

While the breath of man endures
          (Tommy Dodd),
There's an older Law than yours:
          (Tommy Dodd),
He will quit your highest altars
For the Chance that clicks and falters
Where the croupier reads the psalters
          (Tommy Dodd).

[3] *Indus*: one of the great rivers of North India.
[4] *Kinchinjunga*: one of the great peaks of the Himalayas.
[5] *sinnit*: braided cord.

Here's my answer to your cry
(Tommy Dodd),
'See the little horses fly!
(Tommy Dodd),
Open bank and we'll begin,
Let the whirring needle spin,
Try your luck—*you're sure to win!*'
(Tommy Dodd).

NEW SONGS AND OLD (extract)

Published in the *Pioneer*, 30 April 1888, with signature 'Eliphaz the Tema-nite',[1] in reply to a protest 'Songs Old and New' by 'L.L.' in the *Pioneer* for 26 April. Reprinted in the *Pioneer Mail*, 2 May, *CMG*, 3 May, and *Week's News*, 5 May. Uncollected, but included in Scrapbook 4. (Cf. 'Music for the Middle-Aged', pp. 220–2 above.)

You would fain see a return to the 'golden days of song' when it was fashionable to sing of 'Annie Laurie'. So far as my poor memory serves me, that young lady's face was 'the fairest That ever sun shone on'. I put it to you, as a husband, as a father, as a bachelor—conceive the positive inhumanity, in this weather, of suggesting the possibility of sunshine upon any face that you took an interest in. The brow 'like the snowdrift', the 'neck like the swan' and the devotion that depends on these, where would they be after ten minutes exposure? Burnt up, Sir, burnt up—freckled, tanned, blistered, destroyed. No, if we must sing 'Annie Laurie' in the land of our exile, we will sing it thus:

The *cus-cus tattie's*[2] soothin',
With water sluicin' through,
'Twas there that Annie Laurie
Ga'ed me—a waltz or two.

Annie Laurie never gives anything else these days . . . How shall we sing the old songs in a strange land . . . ? . . . Once more what would you? Abolish the new and restore to their throne the songs of the past? 'Nature brings not back the mastodon, nor we those days.'[3] The ancient

---

[1] *Eliphaz the Temanite*: one of Job's comforters. See Job 2: 11.
[2] *cus-cus tattie*: door or window screen made of dry grass roots. (See above, p. 218.)
[3] *Nature brings not back* . . . : see Tennyson, 'The Epic', ll. 36–7.

ditties would fall flat in youngling ears. Something indeed might
be done, if we restored them so to speak; wrote them up to date,
injecting into their pulseless veins the mordant arsenic of local colour.
'Our grandmothers,' you write, 'sang of the "Miller's Lovely
Daughter".' Let us take 'Allen Water' and see how the last verse would
go under the above conditions:—

> By the swirling Sutlej[4] water
>   When my three months' leave was o'er,
> There I sought the Colonel's daughter
>   But she smiled no more.
> For the Autumn fever caught her,
>   And the funeral left at three—
> By the muddy Sutlej water,
>   None so dead as she.

Something like that, eh? You have one of the oldest tragedies in the
world, new dressed. *Placetne Domini?*[5] . . . Let us try over another of
your favourites—'Auld Robin Gray'. 'Indefiniteness' was the vice you
complained of was it not? Does *this* suit you?

> An' I had been at Simla a week an' something more,
>   When I saw that bad boy Jamie come a ridin' to my door—
> I saw that bad boy Jamie—I could na' think it he.
>   Says he:—'I've hooked a fortnight here to get a glimpse of thee.'
> I gasped:—'How *dare* you do it?' We had heaps of things to say.
>   He took a lot of kisses and he stayed through half the day,
> But how could I be angry, for it's not my fault, you see,
>   If Auld Robin Gray would insist on weddin' me.

Get some lady friend to sing this, as an encore verse, and note how the
hopeless passionate wail of the last line suits the words. . . . You would
force upon a thin-blooded generation, the blatant boisterousness of
'Drink to each lass'. We sing it otherwise:—

> Let the ice crash! Here's to each mash![6]
> Sip to your tarts[7] in a *nimbu esquash*[8] . . .

[The distraught multitude of toilers] are . . . likely to take the inspiring
chorus with which you so effectively close your sermon, and sing it in
this manner:—

---

⁴ *Sutlej*: one of the great rivers of the Punjab.
⁵ *Placetne domini?*: does it please you, masters?   ⁶ *mash*: conquest (slang).
⁷ *tarts*: young women (slang), without the modern sense of prostitutes.
⁸ *nimbu esquash*: lime squash.

Should mere acquaintance be forgot and never brought to mind?
We'll give a dinner to the lot—they're done with when they've dined!
So ask the crew to dine my wife—yes, get the brutes to dine,
And . . . don't *kallie* the *degchies*[9] for the sake of Auld Lang Syne.

TO THE ADDRESS OF W.W.H.

Published in the *Pioneer*, 1 June 1888, with signature 'R.K.' Reprinted in the
Pioneer Mail, 3 June. Uncollected, but included in Scrapbook 4. William Wilson Hunter (see above, pp. 308 and 315) has retired at the age of forty-seven
after a distinguished career in India. He was known to be the author of a series
of articles now appearing in *The Times*, which roused Kipling's ire because of
their sympathetic treatment of the Indian National Congress. 'Hunter my own
W.W. has risen in the West and wishes to be taken *au grand serieux*,'[1] he wrote
to Mrs Hill on 27 May. 'Tisn't good for Hunter to be so taken and I am preparing a little *bandillero* [*sc. banderilla?*[2]] for him which will appear in the *Pi* and
will hurt him a few. . . . I like, I admire Hunter immensely but . . . not as a
statesman.' (KP 16/2.) Hunter replied in a letter of July 1888, on his attempt
to place a poem of Kipling's in a London magazine as requested by his mother:
'I have also received your little pasquinade in the *Pioneer* sent to my address. It
is, I think, to be regretted that you devote to clever trifles of this sort talents
which are capable of much better things. They practically fix your standard at
that of the gymkhana and the mess-room, and give point to the Philistines'
sneer, "See how these literary men love one another!" As regards myself, I
know what my work in life is, and I turn neither to the left nor right for praise
or blame. . . . ' (F. H. Skrine, *The Life of Sir William Wilson Hunter*, London,
1901, pp. 374–5.) In spite of this clash, Hunter wrote a favourable review of
the third edition of *Departmental Ditties* in the *Academy* for 1 September 1888.
(See *Kipling: The Critical Heritage*, ed. Roger Lancelyn Green, London, 1971,
pp. 38–41.) There is a marked proof of the poem in the Library of Congress.

'Oh, Hunter, and Oh blower of the horn,[3]
　　Harper . . . and thou hast been a rover too.'

---

[9] *kallie the degchies*: 'tin' the pots and pans (with a thin layer to avoid taste from the brass).

[1] *au grand sérieux*: very seriously indeed.
[2] *banderilla*: barbed dart used in bullfighting.
[3] *Oh, Hunter . . .* : Isolt's greeting to Sir Tristram in Tennyson's 'The Last Tournament', ll. 540–1; with the capital 'H' emphasizing the pun on Hunter's name.

Out of Sir Tristram of old days is born
    Sir Bors[4] in big burgeois;[5] but we, we knew
You in the past and, therefore, laughter-torn,
    Admire the patent stereoscopic view
Of Krishna[6] tooting dirges; but, you bet,
We catch the wink above the flageolet.

Our 'pard-like spirit',[7] beautifully bland—
    Proteus[8] most passionate of Peterhoff[9]—
Our dear delightful humbug—so you stand,
    Kutcha[10] Cassandra-wise five oceans off,
And preach your latest gospel to the land!
    Are you in earnest? Pardon if we scoff.
We took your measure by the foot-rule grim!—
'Who hath no faith, men have no faith in him.'

We know that—bless you—but they do not know
    Who take you for a sort of Simla Sphinx
Across the water. Shall we tell them so?
    That would be cruel. Gracious! When one thinks
Of all the somersaults you used to throw
    To set the land agiggling, printers' inks
Pale on the roller.—'Viceroy's sympathy'—
'More English than the English.'[11] Doctor, fie!

How dare you bluff the British public thus?
    You know as well as we the inner meaning
Of all this demos-demonstration stuff—
    The Oriental's sudden liberal leaning
To ballot-blatherumskite picked up from us—
    You know exactly what the veils are screening.
You know which side your roti-oti's[12] buttered—
Let's seek the reason of the words you've uttered.

---

[4] Sir Bors: another knight of the Round Table, who had visions of the Grail and other portents; probably cited here as a type of visionary.

[5] burgeois: sc. bourgeois, a size of printer's type.

[6] Krishna: Hindu deity, one of the incarnations of Vishnu the Preserver, often represented as playing a flute.   [7] pard-like spirit: from Shelley's Adonais, l. 280.

[8] Proteus: tender of the flocks of Poseidon, god of the sea, with knowledge of all things but also with the ability to assume different shapes to elude his questioners.

[9] Peterhoff: the viceregal residence at Simla, prior to the building of the Viceregal Lodge on Observatory Hill.   [10] Kutcha: temporary, unreliable.

[11] Viceroy's sympathy . . . : fragments of earlier pronouncements of Hunter's. Cf. p. 308 above.   [12] roti-oti: bread and so on.

You saw that London town was very large—
    That men might splash therein and make no sound,
That lighted matches on the Thames's marge
    Were by the sullen tide untimely drowned,
And all the splendours of your star-bossed targe
    Drew small attention from the folks around.
Through Fleet-Street fog, methinks, your sun loomed pale—
What price the crooning pines of Ann–nd–le?[13]

You mused upon the radiant Kulu[14] snows
    That rim with cream the Heaven's turquoise bowl,
You mused upon the window-tapping rose,
    Fresh born that morning for your button-hole,
And the long downward sweep all Simla knows,
    Where the red Arab[15] tittupped to his goal,
And you, delighting twenty willing ears,
Did stately prance to Council with your peers.

Fresh fame you sought. But of all roads to Fame
    Why choose the worst—the Press? You knew the trade
Too well, too well, when in old days you came
    To wield a lambent and most courteous blade.
(It smashed my cutlass once).[16] And did the game
    Repay the lamp-oil? Answer, now 'tis played—
Hunter, by *shouk*[17] and *kam*[18], by cult and ism,
I charge thee, flee the Sink of Journalism!

Observe! One rabid dog—one King with cancer[19]—
    Three islands hoisted Heavenward in red flame—
Two blown-on frauds—one burnt-up ballet-dancer
    (With illustrations) Mrs Some One's shame—
Ten only roads to peace—the last Bonanza—
    Gladstone and Naldire's tablets[20]—all the same:
Pepsine from porkers—Nervine brewed by Bunter;
And there's your daily Rag. . . . Now *why* add Hunter?

[13] *Ann—nd—le*: Annandale, a wooded glen and racecourse near Simla.
[14] *Kulu*: area to north of Simla.
[15] *the red Arab*: Sir Frederick Roberts's favourite mount. (Cf. *Something of Myself*, p. 57.)   [16] *It smashed my cutlass once*: reference unidentified.
[17] *shouk*: favourite pursuit, bent.   [18] *kam*: work.
[19] *one King with cancer*: the Emperor Frederick III of Germany, who died a fortnight later, and whose illness was the subject of almost daily bulletins.
[20] *Naldire's tablets*: a patent medicine for worms and fleas.

You're far too good! Ask L—g,[21] ask Arn–ld,[22] ask
    The S——le and the S——ge[23] where men call
Who nightly gibber 'neath the penny mask,
    And scribble crudities on Time's blank wall,
How golden is the guerdon of their task.
    Hark! From the weltering Strand the news-boys bawl:—
'Murder in Paddin'ton! Revoltin' Story!!
'Untin' in Injia!' Hunter is *this* glory?

You wrote as Statesman? There are scores of fools
    To pole the yawing *buggalow*[24] of State
And, summing up the average of their rules,
    They don't do *too* much harm, for God is great;
And, somehow something always skids and cools
    A crazy *ticca*.[25] Let the Empire wait,
'Twill never take you *au grand sérieux*. Think!
Your record? Insincerity and ink.

You skirmished on the outskirts of the show—
    You beat the big side-drum (it was your own)
For twenty years. Aha! you know we know.
    Climb down before that gorgeous gaff is blown.
But to no meaner level—ten times no!
    You have the Talents in the napkin stown—
The Three Great Gifts, beyond all gifts of earth,
To move men's hearts to sorrow or to mirth.

The Eye that sees, the Golden Pen, the Touch
    Keen as the whip-thong on a leader's ear,
Light as a woman's granted kiss—so much
    And twice so much is yours. But, Doctor dear,
There's not a single Stunt[26] twixt Prome[27] and Cutch[28]
    Would take your word for aught save Gazetteer;[29]

---

[21] *L—g*: Andrew Lang (1844–1912), journalist and man of letters.
[22] *Arn–ld*: Sir Edwin Arnold (1832–1904), educationalist, journalist, and author of poems on Indian topics.
[23] *The S——le and the S——ge*: the Savile and Savage Clubs, frequented by literary men.   [24] *buggalow*: boat.
[25] *ticca (gharry)*: hired carriage.   [26] *Stunt*: Assistant.
[27] *Prome*: city in Lower Burma to north of Rangoon.
[28] *Cutch*: area on north-west coast of India.
[29] *Gazetteer*: Hunter had compiled the *Imperial Gazetteer*, a statistical survey of the Indian Empire.

And *that* not wholly. Yet you have the power
To make us all your bond-slaves in an hour.

Shifty and sunshine-loving child of Ayr-
    Iavata,[30] you have japed your little jest.
Hands that could paint us Sinai's trumpet-blare,
    Lips that would sneer at Sinai's quivering crest,
Come out o' that! Your work lies other where,
    And leads to Power the brightest and the best.
Rule—what *is* Rule? Let statesmen pose and grovel,
Doctor doctissimme,[31] bring out your novel![32]

O BAAL,[1] HEAR US!

Published in the *Pioneer*, 19 July 1888, with signature 'R.K.', subtitle 'A Metri-
cal Forecast', and heading ' "An attempt should be made to prepare a moral
text-book based upon the fundamental principles of natural religion, such as
may be taught in all Government and non-Government colleges"—*Vide* Reso-
lution in this week's *G——tte of I——a*.' Reprinted in the *Pioneer Mail*, 22 July,
and *CMG*, 23 July. A passage from the Chorus of the Indian Pantheon was
used as a heading to Chapter xix in *The Naulahka* (1892), published in a collec-
tion of *Rhymed Chapter Headings for Naulahka* in the same year, collected in
Songs from Books (1912), and included in the successive 'Inclusive Editions' of
his verse. The poem itself was collected in the Outward Bound, De Luxe,
Sussex, and Burwash Edns., with the heading attributed to 'Resolution of the
Indian Government' and with some passages excised (printed here in square
brackets). There had been a good deal of press comment in the course of the
year on the report of an Education Commission, which had commented *inter
alia* on problems of discipline in Indian schools and colleges, and on the fact
that education there concentrated on the acquisition of knowledge to the neg-
lect of moral training. Its proposals included the suggestion that a textbook of
ethics of a non-sectarian nature should be prepared for use in schools. 'And
who', asked the *CMG* on 15 June 1888, 'is to write or compile all these guides
for morals? The founders of Christianity, and Mahomedanism, and Buddhism,

---

[30] *Ayr-Iavata*: a pun on 'Ayr'—since Hunter had connections with the south-west of
Scotland, his grandfather having been an Ayrshire schoolmaster—and 'Aryavarta', the
territory inhabited by Aryans—i.e. North India.

[31] *Doctor doctissime*: most learned doctor. The *Pioneer* and *Pioneer Mail* printed the
nominative form 'Doctissimus' instead of the vocative—much to Kipling's chagrin when
he realized the mistake. He corrects it in the Scrapbook version.

[32] *your novel*: Hunter did publish a work of fiction, *The Old Missionary* (1890), with
considerable success.

---

[1] *Baal*: the god of the Phoenicians and other Semitic peoples of the Middle East;
hence a false god to the Hebrews.

and Hinduism, have all in their own grand ways set their hands to "moral text-books", yet none of these will quite meet the general view in this land. . . . ' A Resolution of the Indian Government published in the *Gazette of India* for 14 July provoked Kipling to the comment, in a letter to Mrs Hill, 'Ah me! Here comes a thundering Govt resolution about education. I must wire an abstract to the Pioneer and write a skit on it afterwards . . . ' (KP 16/3.) His abstract, a full-length article on 'The Educational Policy of the Indian Government' appeared on 17 July, and included this item: 'On the subject of moral edu-cation it is remarked:—"Attention has again been called to the proposal by the Education Commission that an attempt should be made to prepare a moral text-book, based upon the fundamental principles of natural religion, such as may be taught in all Government and non-Government colleges. The Govern-ment of India and the Secretary of State entertained doubts as to the wisdom of this recommendation at the time . . . but circumstances have since occurred[2] which have suggested to both authorities the desirability of making the attempt." '

Scene: A Palace in Cloudland.[3] MORAL TEXT-BOOK COMMITTEE *discovered at a round table, singing.*

> Moralists we,
> From over the sea,
> From the land where philosophers plenty be—
> From the land that produced no Kants with a K,
> But many Cants with a C.
> Where the Hodmadod[4] crawls in its shell confined,
> The Symbol exalted of Fetterless Mind,
> And Arithmetic sits on her throne of pride
> As Theology personified.
> We have fished in the Lake,
> And the Worm wouldn't bite.
> Our preachers have covered
> The Pit from our sight.
> By the wisdom of Comte[5]
> We have learned to devise
> Our own little roofs, and
> Dispense with the skies.

---

[2] *circumstances have since occurred*: these had included a much-publicised riot at the Madras Christian College, during which Brahmin students had assaulted and insulted their Professors. This trouble broke out on 30 April 1888.

[3] *Cloudland*: Cf. Nephelococcygia or Cloud-Cuckoo-Land in Aristophanes' *The Birds*; with some reference also to *The Clouds*, in which he satirized new fashions in philosophy.   [4] *Hodmadod*: snail in shell.

[5] *Comte*: Auguste Comte (1798–1857), French philosopher who rejected metaphysics and revealed religion in favour of a religion of humanity.

The Gods and the Godlings
On dust-laden shelves
Repose for a sign.
We are all Gods ourselves!

(*Confidentialissimo*)
And so we come here
With gum-pot and shear—
Devoid of convictions, but blessed with long faces,
From every land's vext Book
To clip out a text-book
Which gives us 'religion on natural bases'.

PRESIDENT (*solo, tremolo*)

In Afric's sunny clime the slave
   Assuages both catarrh and grief
By blowing of his nose upon
   The Moral Pocket-handkerchief.

His fetich grins beneath the tree—
   A skull, three rags, an ostrich-feather;
He turns aside to us who give
   Good texts and textile goods together.

Ber-etheren, ere ye stain the pen,
   Think of that joyous Afrikander;
What saith the Chief of Married Men?[6]—
   'Sauce for the goose will suit the gander.'

(*Flourish of silver trumpets*)

In the name of the Great God Fudge,
   I charge ye take good heed
To weigh and sift and sniff and judge
   The merits of every creed,
That no man may your wage begrudge,
   That your fame may be great indeed.
Who have gotten a God at the Government's nod
   In the land where the deities breed!

---

[6] *the Chief of Married Men*: Solomon, who had seven hundred wives and three hundred concubines (1 Kgs. 11: 3).

The COMMITTEE *fall to their labours. The* INDIAN PANTHEON *rises behind them in red fire.*

CHORUS OF THE INDIAN PANTHEON

We be the Gods of the East,
   Older than all—
Rulers of Greatest and Least,
Rulers of Mourning and Feast,
Rulers of Man and of Beast.
   How shall we fall
Whose feet are made firm on men's necks—whose hands hold
    their heart-strings in thrall?

SEMICHORUS

Over the strife of the schools
   Low the day burns;
Back as the kine to the pools
   Each one returns
To the life that he knows, where the altar-flame glows, and the
    tulsi[7] is trimmed in the urns.

CHORUS

Will they gape for the husks that ye proffer,
   Or move to your song?
And we—have *we* nothing to offer
   Who held them so long
In the cloud of the incense, the clash of the cymbal, the blare
    of the conch and the gong?

PRESIDENT (*jubilantissimo*)

We'll get the text-book ready as quickly as we can
For the Ary—for the Ary— for the Ary-an![8]

SECRETARY

I'll go and hunt the Vedas[9] while you play with the Ko-ran[10]
For the Ary— for the Ary— for the Ary-an!

---

[7] *tulsi*: basil plant considered sacred by Hindus.
[8] *Aryan*: see above, p. 287.
[9] *Vedas*: sacred writings of the Hindus.
[10] *Koran*: the holy book of Islam.

DUET AND DANCE

Oh, isn't it nice to root out Vice, and usher Virtue in!
And isn't it sad a cultured lad should stumble into sin!
We'd like to have him moral; but, oh, where shall we begin
With the Ary— with the Ary—with the Ary-an?

CHORUS OF COMMITTEE

Help the Ary— help the Ary— help the Ary-an!
Three-and-thirty million Gods don't improve a man!
Wait till we have forced our potted morals in a can
Down the Ary— down the Ary— down the Ary-an!

PRESIDENT (*patter-song with piccolo accompaniment*)

Take a little Rabelais—just a garlic hint;
Out of Locke and Bacon steal something fit to print.
Grind 'em down with Butler,[11] add morsels of Voltaire;
Don't forget the 'Precious Fools'[12] sketched by Molière!

Robert Elsmere,[13] Mallock,[14] Hume,[15] Gibbon (on his knees).
Knock the Ten Commandments out if they fail to please;
Substitute the Penal Code—sections underlined.
There you have a perfect book to form the infant mind!

(Encore verses may be introduced here according to the taste of the singer or the educational policy of the Government of India.)

[AERIAL CHORUS OF INVISIBLES (*Stringed instruments only*)

(Con spirit)

The kine went forth to the clover
In the flush of the morning-tide,
But long ere the day was over
They suffered from pains inside—

---

[11] *Butler*: Joseph Butler (1692–1752), Bishop of Bristol and then of Durham, moral philosopher and theologian.

[12] *Precious Fools*: *Les Précieuses ridicules*, a comedy satirizing contemporary follies.

[13] *Robert Elsmere*: a novel by Mrs Humphrey Ward, published in 1888, which emphasized the social mission of Christianity while rejecting its miraculous elements.

[14] *Mallock*: William H. Mallock (1849–1923), a novelist of ideas, author of *The New Republic, or Culture, Faith and Philosophy in an English Country House* (1877) and *The New Paul and Virginia, or Positivism on an Island* (1878).

[15] *Hume*: i.e. David Hume, the philosopher.

(Retard)

They laid them down in the clover—
    They swelled and they bust and they died.

Now was it the fault of the clover
    That tenders its bloom to the bees?
And how did the kine come over
    From the scant, dry grass of the leas,
To eat and to burst in the clover
    That never had injured the bees?

(Con molt. exp.)

They had opened the gates to the clover,
    They said it would fatten the kine;
But never a man could discover
    It was wrong for cattle to dine
On the windy and wine-red clover,
    Too fair—too free—and too fine. *(bis)*[16]]

The COMMITTEE *conclude their labours, and produce Moral Text-Book
wrapped in a white handkerchief.*

CHORUS

Now whoso sneers
At our paste and shears
May go, if he can, to the Deuce!
We have built for the Pagan
A first-class Dagon[17]
For strictly official use.

[(*They dance round the M.T.B. with appropriate gestures.*)]

CHORUS OF ADMIRING ARYAVARTA[18] (*organ, plagal cadence*[19])

When Dagon was builded of old
    By the Demons who wrought in a day,

[16] *bis*: twice.
[17] *Dagon*: a god of the Philistines, according to the Old Testament; represented as half-man, half-fish. The newspaper versions have reading 'First-Grade'.
[18] *Aryavarta*: the land inhabited by the Aryans—i.e. North India—but used here as a collective noun for the race.
[19] *plagal cadence*: progressing from the subdominant to the tonic chord, as in the singing of 'Amen'.

His forehead was brazen, his belly[20] was gold,
   And his throne was the red river-clay—
   [And the tempest dissolved it away—]
But our masters are wiser than they.

(*Trumpets*)

For when Dagon was builded anew,
   By the breath of their order they made him;
   By the froth of their ink-pots they stayed him,
   In cut-paper frills they arrayed him,
The subtle, the supple, the new,
   Who is greater than scourges or rods—
     An olla podrida[21]
     Of Faiths and Fifth[22]-Reader,
   The Friend of all Possible Gods!

[COMMITTEE (*scattering text-books abroad*)

It's bound in cloth and it's one rupee,
   And a very good thing you'll find it.
It may almost pass for—what you please,
   If nobody gets behind it.

(*Grand general walk-round of* COMMITTEE. *Bundles of M.T.B. under their arms; hats over one eye.*)

We don't know anything about it at all,
   But here's the book you see;
So we'll supply the school and cry:
   'Are you there Mor-al-i-tee?'

(*Kick-dance in order of Seniority*)

(*f*)   We don't care anything about it at all,
   For devil a faith have we;
But we'll all look sly and gaily cry:
   'Are you there Mor-al-i-tee?'

BOUQUETS, BLUE-FIRE, GENERAL REFORMATION AND CURTAIN.]

---

[20] *belly*: 'body' in newspaper versions.
[21] *olla podrida*: Spanish dish of meat, beans, sausages, etc.; hence a miscellany or mixture.
[22] *Fifth*: 'first' in newspaper versions.

VIRGINIBUS PUERISQUE¹

Published in the *Pioneer*, 13 August 1888, with signature 'R.K.', subtitle 'A Second-Rate Farce', heading 'Dedicated with all possible respect and admiration to the D–cc–n M——g C——y C–mm—tee', and subheading from Browning's 'The Statue and the Bust': 'And the sin I impute to each frustrate ghost / Is the unlit lamp and the ungirt loin, / Though the issue in sight was a Vice, I say / You of the Virtue, we issue join / How goes it? *De te fabula.*'² Reprinted in the *Pioneer Mail*, 19 August. Uncollected, but included in Scrapbook 4. On 16 April 1888 the *Pioneer* reported that the Nizam or Prince of Hyderabad, the greatest and wealthiest of the Native States (i.e. states which did not come under direct British rule), had dismissed his Home Secretary and Minister of Public Works, Abdul Huq, 'pending an explanation by him of his connection with the Hyderabad Mining Company, whereby the Government, parting for 99 years with their mineral interests gratis, purchase 12,500 shares for £150,000, and the company pays the concessionaires £850,000 for the concession, out of their capital of £1,000,000 sterling. . . . ' From this point on the scandal was a matter of frequent comment in the Indian and British press, and a Select Committee was established by the House of Commons to enquire into the affairs of the Hyderabad (Deccan) Mining Company. It became clear from the public hearings that the concessionaires, Mr Watson and a Mr Stewart (now deceased) had conspired with Abdul Huq to defraud both the Hyderabad Government and British shareholders. The shares sold to the Nizam himself, for example, were part of a large block given to Abdul Huq as a gift in reward for his services; but the Nizam was given to understand that they were bought on the open market, and their sale was effected through a number of stockbrokers to give the impression of brisk trading. The allocation of £850,000 worth of shares to the concessionaires was clearly outrageous, and there were other irregularities in the conduct of the company's affairs. The British Agent at Hyderabad, the Indian Government, and the Secretary of State for India had all been involved at one stage or another in the negotiations for the concession, and there was widespread criticism of their failure to exercise more effective control. As the time approached for the Committee to report, there were persistent rumours that the Government was anxious to suppress any adverse comments on senior British officials. The *Pioneer* printed a full summary of the Report on 11 August 1888, but described it as 'about as disappointing a thing as could well be imagined', since it confined itself to obvious facts such as the concessionaires having pocketed vast sums the Nizam's Government never intended them to have, and obvious conclusions such as the need for Residents in Native States to look more carefully to the interests of those they were supposed to protect and advise: it did nothing to

---

¹ *Virginibus Puerisque [canto]*: [I sing] to maidens and boys (Horace, *Odes*, III. i. 4). The implication is that the subject-matter is free from offence.

² *De te fabula [narratur]*: the story [is told] about yourself (Horace, *Satires*, I. i. 69–70).

clear away the suspicions of carelessness and incompetence on the part of senior officials, or to confirm such suspicions and deliver a rebuke.

Scene: Exterior of the I—a Office on a remarkably shady day. Enter CHOR-US OF INDIGNANT SPECULATORS, *too angry to be particular about their rhymes, singing:*

> Who shall restore us the leaves
> That the Huqster hath eaten,
> Or who shall arraign us the thieves
> To be properly beaten?

> Where is the grim guillotine—
> The sawdust and platter—
> For W–ts–n? Too long hath he been
> A joy to his hatter!

> We are sold and we feel it acutely,
> A scorn and a hissing.
> The Heathen hath had us astutely—
> Our eye-teeth are missing!

> Let no man survive to record
> The way we were snaffled!
> Let the paid share[3] be turned to a sword—
> Its drop to a scaffold.

ECHO OF A VOICE FROM H–D–R–B–D; *con brio*:

> 'Tis oh for a day of the days that are dead
> And a dead and a done with land,
> For a tusker trained[4] and a *budmash*[5] brained
> At the wave of a Monarch's hand!

> Yea, a *hathi musth*,[6] and a spirt of dust,
> A trumpet shrill and loud—
> A kick and a thud and a gout of blood,
> And the deep drawn breath of the crowd.

---

[3] *the paid share*: as opposed to those unpaid for by Abdul Huq and the concessionaires.

[4] *a tusker trained*: a traditional punishment in princely states in an earlier era was for the malefactor to be trampled to death by an elephant.

[5] *budmash*: evil-doer.   [6] *hathi musth*: frenzied elephant.

'Twere ended then in the sight of men,
    The lie and the loss and the theft:
They might pluck the wrong or the right from the long
    Keen tusks sent in to the heft.

SEMI-CHORUS OF VENERABLES FROM NOWHERE IN
PARTICULAR:

Gently does the trick, my lad, gently does the trick,
To the moral hide, my lad, suit the moral stick;
    Bulls in China-shops are bad,
    Gently does the trick, my lad,
    Yes, we own, it's awful sad,
        But
        Gently does the trick!

Easy on the trawl, my lad—easy on the trawl!
You may smash expensive nets with too great a haul.
    What's the use of damning eyes?
    Drop the personalities,
    Will you kindly summarize
        And
    Easy on the trawl!

CHORUS OF C–MM—TEE *in conclave assembled*:

Tenderly, ah! tenderly, oh!
    Water the lightning and muffle the thunder!
pp)   Somebody whisper to Henry:[7] 'Lie low.'
    Somebody bund up Apollo—the Bunder.[8]
Tenderly, ah! tenderly, oh!
Over the pimples triumphant we go!

INDIGNANT SPECULATORS *to staccato accomp. of kicks on door panels, and with British pronunciation*:

    'More light,' quoth dying Goethe,
        And We demand the same;
    For why should You be shirty
        If They are not to blame?

---

[7] *Henry*: Sir Henry James (1828–1911), lawyer and statesman, chairman of the Select Committee.

[8] *Apollo—the Bunder*: a bund was a dam or embankment; the Apollo Bunder was a famous landing-place at Bombay; but the reference here is obscure.

C–MM—TEE *from behind closed doors, to hymn tune*:

> More light is sometimes trying,
> And You have clean forgot
> That Goethe lay a-dying
> While We are on the spot!

C–MM—TEE *emerge in guise of nigger minstrels, their faces extensively blackened, supported by a précis-writer on £70 a year, and the Consciousness of Rectitude. Topical song by* PRESIDENT, *tambo*[9] *and steps*:

> When you sit by chance on a hornet's nest,
> And they're all there—very much there.
> To leave 'em alone is by far the best,
> For they're all there—very much there!
> The friends and the relatives come to see,
> And Sheol[10] wakes in the old oak tree,
> And Deuce knows what the end may be
> There—very much there!

CHORUS

> We're all there—very much there!
> O koorong[11] with the whole affair,
> It's dicky[12] in front and it's dicky behind.
> But we'll get inside and pull down the blind,
> And the rude little boys will please not to stare
> When we're all there—very much there!

Solo, banjo and bones,[13] S–R R–CH—D T–MPLE,[14] *to very careful walk-round of* C–MM—TEE:

> Right foot! lef' foot! Hop light Loo,
> Here am a fuss—dere am a muss! What am a nig to do?
> Down de middle an' back again—
> *Keep de sugar out o' de rain,*
> Mind de aigs upon de floor an'—hop light, Loo!

---

[9] *tambo*: tambourine.
[10] *Sheol*: Hebrew word for hell.
[11] *O koorong*: *au courant*: thoroughly conversant.
[12] *dicky*: tricky, risky, 'dicey' (slang).
[13] *bones*: thin strips of ivory or bone, a pair of which was held between the fingers of each hand and clattered together.
[14] *S–r R–ch—d T–mple*: Sir Richard Temple (1826–1902), Conservative MP, former Anglo-Indian administrator, member of the Select Committee.

(CHORUS *and complete break-down*)

Hop light, Loo! Here's a how-de-do!
Razors am a flyin' in de air!
   Sot de cream behind de do'
   Or de storm'll turn it sho',
   Trim de lamp a little low,
   Massa likes to hab it so—
Listen to de thunder in de mawnin'!

Solo, H——Y L——CH–RE[15] in pink shirt.

Down in Demerara when we roll de sugar keg,
Every darkey hoppin' on a gummilastic leg,
Massa Trufle James an' me, Massa Monkey Dick,
Keep de bar'l a rollin to de Lee-vee!

CHORUS

Keep de bar'l a rollin' slow,
Tech him lightly wif your toe,
'R else you're sure to bust de show—
Nurse de bar'l a rollin' to de Lee-vee!

CHORUS OF VENERABLES, *more insistently:*

Bring not grey hairs with sorrow down to Woking—
   Stir not, touch not, ask not, see not. Be wise
Ye know not what or whom ye are invoking.
   Shut down the trap and . . . simply summarize!

The C–MM——TEE *summarize with the help of précis-writer:*

   We find it so—exactly thus
      According as you was,
   Henceforward this peculiar biz
      Is obviously because:
   The subject and the predicate
      Are generally plain,
   But major premisses are facts
      Not easy to retain.
   Observe the rule that seems to hint
      But really does not mean,

---

[15] *H——y L——ch–re*: Henry du Pré Labouchere (1832–1912), journalist, radical politician, member of the Select Committee; founder of the weekly journal *Truth* which exposed many fraudulent enterprises.

Avoid all fuss, be warned by us,
  And—keep your fingers clean!

(The voices die into silence. W–TS–N, A—L H–Q *and the Others study the Report with tears of envy)*

W–T S–N, *solo in character*:

Claude Duval[16] rode over the heath,
  Over the heath when the moon was low,
He emptied a shoehorn o' Nantes[17] beneath
  The gibbet that creaks when the night-winds blow.
'You in the chains there, ready to fall,
Give me your blessing!' quoth Claude Duval.

Claude Duval rode over the heath,
  Over the heath to the Liverpool Mail,
Guard in the bucket armed to the teeth
  Pointed the blunderbuss—turning pale.
'Dog eat dog were a terrible sin—
What would they say at the *Black Bull* Inn?'

Dick the driver must bully and brag,
  Bully and brag for the sake of the coach,
Claude Duval has taken the swag—
  Cool as a lawyer and sound as a roach.
Deftly he opens the mail-bags all:
'Look to your priming', says Claude Duval.

Claude Duval has galloped away,
  Galloped away in the night of the years;
But Claude Duval of the present day
  He is the gentleman everyone fears:
Justice is silent and *Truth* sings small
Under the pistol of Claude Duval.

[16] *Claude Duval*: famous highwayman of the late 17th cent.
[17] *shoehorn o' Nantes*: appetizer of French brandy.

Voice of PRESIDENT OF C–MM—TEE *from the flies*[18]—*Cadenza*
Expostulatzione:

I live on Table Mountain[19] and my name is Truthful James,
   I am not versed in rigging shares or any sinful games;
I hope you'll take our penny-farthing version of the 'shine'
   That broke up that society upon the Deccan Mine.

*(The Stage darkens gradually to Gounod's 'Funeral March of a
Marionette'.)*

CURTAIN

A JOB LOT

Published in the *Pioneer*, 1 September 1888, with signature 'R.K.', subtitle
'(NOT to be sung at Snowdon[1] Theatre)', and headings: ' "The present Com-
mander-in-Chief in India is a fine soldier, who has earned the national grati-
tude by his public services, and endeared himself to the Army by his untiring
devotion to its interests. But among the penalties of Sir Frederick Roberts'
exalted position is the control of a vast patronage, and this it is impossible to
deny is not always so disposed as to disarm unfriendly criticism, and to secure
for his bestowals that unfailing respect which is so desirable."—*Vide "Pioneer"*
yesterday.' / 'She was bland, passionate and deeply religious, painted in water-
colours, was first cousin to Lady Jones, and of such is the Kingdom of Hea-
ven.' Reprinted in the *Pioneer Mail*, 2 September, and *CMG*, 4 September.
Uncollected, but included in Scrapbook 4. Years afterwards Kipling recalled
the episode: 'The *Pioneer* editorially, but cautiously as a terrier drawing up to a
porcupine, had hinted that some of Lord Roberts' military appointments at
that time verged on nepotism. It was a regretful and well-balanced allocution.
My rhymed comment (and why my Chief passed it I know not!) said just the
same thing, but not quite so augustly. . . . I don't think Lord Roberts was
pleased with it, but I know he was not half so annoyed as my chief proprietor!'
(*Something of Myself*, pp. 73–4.) The immediate issue was the choice of
Lieutenant-Colonel Neville Chamberlain as a military representative on a
mission being sent to Afghanistan on the invitation of the Amir, when more

---

[18] *flies*: gallery running along sides of stage above the wings space.
[19] *I live on Table Mountain*: see Bret Harte's poem 'The Society upon the Stanislaus',
with the opening lines 'I reside at Table Mountain, and my name is Truthful James; / I
am not up to small deceit, or any sinful games; / And I'll tell in simple language what I
know about the row / That broke up our society upon the Stanislow.'

[1] *Snowdon*: the Commander-in-Chief's residence at Simla. Cf. p. 380 above.

distinguished officers were said to be available. Chamberlain, who had served on Roberts's Staff in the Second Afghan War, and had then acted as his ADC, was the nephew of his friend and former chief, Field Marshal Sir Neville Chamberlain.

> They really were most merciful,
>   They praised his winning ways,
> His little feet that merrily
>   Trip on from baize to bays;
> They glorified the new canteen,[2]
>   They called him 'Tommy's Pride',
> But O they said his patronage
>   Was sometimes misapplied!

> They passaged all about the fact—
>   Right shoulder out and in—
> They did their very best to save
>   H–s Ex—ll—cy's skin:
> They sandwiched smack and blandishment,
>   Like best Italian ice;
> But still they drew attention to
>   That too notorious vice.

> They hemmed and hawed, they sidled off,
>   They sidled up again:
> One hand upon the laurelled head,
>   The other on the cane;
> And while he heard with sweet content
>   The praise that was his due,
> On legs that never fled the fray
>   *Whish*, fell the big bamboo!

> And through the sighing deodars[3]
>   A little whisper stole;—
> 'Why, for the quadrilateral man,
>   Select the roundest hole;

---

[2] *the new canteen*: in an attempt to encourage temperance in the Army Roberts had urged the creation of Regimental Institutes with a range of facilities in place of the old 'wet canteens' where soldiers went simply to get drunk.

[3] *deodars*: Himalayan cedars.

And wherefore thrust the polygon
    Into the crescent's curve,
Since other folk have other eyes,
    And other eyes observe?

Perpend, retreat, refrain, reform,
    Oh man of Kandahar,[4]
For even pocket-Wellingtons[5]
    May carry things too far.
We cannot judge the influence,
    The fact alone we see,
And if the *P——r* is wrath,
    Oh Lord what *must* you be!'

CHORUS

We've heard it before, but we'll drink once more,
    While the Army sniffs and sobs
For Bobs[6] its pride, who has lately died,
    And is now succeeded by Jobs.[7]

HANS BREITMANN[1] AS AN ADMINISTRATOR

Published in the *Pioneer*, 15 September 1888, with signature 'R.K.' and sub-heading 'With all apologies to C. G. Leland'. Reprinted in the *CMG*, 18 September, and *Pioneer Mail*, 19 September. Uncollected, but included in Scrapbook 4. On 10 May 1888 a native paper, the vernacular weekly *Rajyab-hakta*, had accused a British official in the Bombay administration of taking bribes, alleging that 'we have personally seen a bag of Rs [rupees] 20,000 placed in the railway carriage of the Political Agent, Kathiawar, by a Raja.' The

[4] *man of Kandahar*: one of Roberts's most famous achievements was his forced march from Kabul to Kandahar and his defeat of the Afghans there in 1880.

[5] *pocket-Wellingtons*: an allusion to Roberts's diminutive stature.

[6] *Bobs*: Roberts's nickname.

[7] *Jobs*: appointments of unsuitable or unqualified persons for reasons of private interest or profit.

[1] *Hans Breitmann*: the hero of *The Breitmann Ballads* by C. G. Leland (1824–1903), which appeared from 1857 onwards. Written in broken English with an admixture of German, they record the experiences and reflections of a hard-drinking, hard-fighting immigrant to the United States. Kipling enjoyed them to excess.

Bombay Government had written to the native paper asking for details. In reply the editor named the former Political Agent for Kathiawar, Colonel L. C. Barton, but indicated that the only witnesses had been two men whose names he had now forgotten. When pressed further the editor gave impertinent or evasive replies, and denied on 15 August that any charges of bribery had in fact been made. The Bombay Government then issued a Resolution dated 7 September, setting out the documents in the case with its conclusion: 'The Government having instituted an enquiry into the specific allegations . . . find it impossible to take action upon charges so vague and stale, the truth of which is on the face of them so improbable. The editor's letter, dated the 15th ultimo, virtually amounts to a recantation of his specific accusation, and no further action need, therefore, be taken in regard to it.' (*Bombay Gazette*, 8 September 1888.) The Bombay Government was sensitive on such matters since one of its senior officials, Mr Arthur Crawford, was currently under investigation on charges of corruption; but the *Pioneer* was sharply critical of it for engaging in such a correspondence on the character of one of its officers, and still more for publishing a Resolution on the matter. When it became clear that there was no case to answer, the Government should, said the *Pioneer*, have brought a libel action or else dropped the matter completely: 'We cannot imagine anything more feeble or more mischievous than the line that has been taken . . . ' (*Pioneer*, 11 September 1888).

> Hans Breitmann vent to India—
>   Dere vasn't no demonsdration—
> He bummed along in a B and O
>   To look at de Aryan nation;
> But Himmel's[2] face had a shiny smile
>   As if it knowed de thing,
> Und liddle shtars coom out und vinked
>   At Breitmann on de ving.

> Hans Breitmann went to India—
>   Drey drop him at Bombay—
> He hoonted aroun' for de Gofernor,
>   On top of a buggy-shay.
> '*Darwaza bund*',[3] de porter said—
>   Der Breitmann speak him fair:—
> 'Dere vasn't any sooch a man,
>   Und if dere vas—I'm dere!

---

[2] *Himmel*: the heavens.
[3] *Darwaza bund*: not at home.

I seek a shenuine Deutscher,[4]
    Dey say he runs dis show,
Und arguin' on a door-mat
    Is dwice so mean ash slow—
Derefore!' He shvore ein *juron*[5]
    De liddlest dot he knew—
De porter faint mit horror und
    De Breitmann pass through.

He found de crate Herr Gofernor
    In bens and ink geshpilt
Wrop up in adminisdration—
    Likevise in a plazin' kilt.
'Die Färb'[6] sind mir nicht unbekannt—
    But I guess de green haf ran
Into die red und vhite und plue',
    Remark de Breitmann.

Dey sat him down on a sofa,
    Dey gafe him a long cigar,
Vhile de Gofernor dell of troubles
    Mit bapers in Kathiawar—[7]
Und vhen he haf grasp de inwardness
    Und lighted another schmoke,
Mit his feet on de top of de dable
    'Tvas so de Breitmann shboke:—

'Now bist du Scotch or Deutscher
    Or bist du both—in shpots,
It's bedder to vork on a brinciple
    Vhich I'll pring down to dots:
For de more dot brinciple's acted on
    Und trifen home to de heft,
De less vill you be hong up to dry,
    Und de less vill you get left.

---

[4] *a . . . Deutscher*: a German. Lord Reay, the Lieut.-Gov. of Bombay from 1885 to 1890, was the son of Eneas, Baron Mackay, and Maria, daughter of Baron Fagel, privy councillor of the Netherlands. He lived in Holland till the age of 36, becoming a British citizen in 1877 after his succession to his father's title.

[5] *ein juron*: an oath.   [6] *Die Färb* . . . : the colours are not unknown to me.

[7] *Kathiawar*: native state in north-west of the Bombay Presidency.

Dere's a certain sort of cussin'
    Dot bolidicks mostly breeds—
Slanganderin' men by nations
    And drowin' mud on deir creeds;
But dot's legitimate pizness
    For, since de world pegan,
Lager, de girls and de *gali**[8]
    Ish more dan meat to a man.

He'll shvear at de Pope und Kaiser
    He'll shvear at his frau, by shings!
Und ven his frau shvears back at him,
    He'll shvear at afery dings!
Und 'lowin' for human nadure
    De notion's safe und sound,
So long as de man mit grievance
    Joost sloshes his shvearin' around.

But vhen subjectif cussin'
    Tevelops a tefinite line
Und begomes objectif libel,
    Fidelicit:—"Schmitt is a schwein!"
De Schmitt dot is called a schwein-pick,
    Howefer his bolidicks lean,
Vill call on de Herr Redakteur[11]
    Und say:—"Vot Hell you mean?"

Nun! Oonder your vay of pizness—
    I put de matter in prief—
A snigglin', snoopin' schwein-blatt[12]
    Have called your servant a thief;
Und when you asked for de proofments
    Und found dot dere vasn't none,
Insdeat of bustin' de druckerei[13]
    You leaf dat schwein-blatt alone.'

* I gannot dell how Hans haf himself bewrapped roun' de intrigasity of de Oriental philologische *bât*,[9] pecause he vas most dimes at de Yacht Cloob, samplin brandy-smash from de metaphysical stand-point. Boot he is a bequisitif rooster, and I guess he picked it oop from de grisettes—same as in Paris pefore de War.

FRITZ SCHWACKENHAMMER[10]

[8] *gali*: abusive language.
[9] *bât*: word, language.
[10] *Fritz Schwackenhammer*: a friend of Breitmann's who figures as a commentator on several of the Ballads in Leland's volume.   [11] *Redakteur*: editor.
[12] *schwein-blatt*: swine of a news-sheet.   [13] *druckerei*: printing office.

De Gofernor look at de ceilin'—
    De Gofernor look on de floor,
He never vas so behondelt
    By voman or man pefore.
'Now dere was a custom in Kansas'[14]—
    Hans schmile a derrible schmile—
'For sublimatin' de kultur
    Und puttin' a gloss on de style.

Ve passed a simple rulin'
    To raise de tone of de blace,
Und nailed a gratis copy
    To every forme und case:—
"De man dot publishes ardicles
    Peyont his politishescope
De Viligance Committee
    Sub-edits . . . mit a rope!"

Und dot vas in "bleedin' Kansas",[15]
    Vhere men are ge-built in de raw—
Und foorst dey empty deir bistol
    Und den enquire de Law;
But no one was called a horse-thief
    Mitout a mountain of proof,
For de only case of libel
    Ve hanged from his office roof.

Gut! Toornin' again to your trouble,
    Vhich you have so mooch bemessed,
De man dot vas tarred in de paper
    Haf folded his vings in de West;[16]
Und, since dot paper haf shwallowed
    Its statement hump and paw,
Onless you vass heeled und ready,
    Vhy Devil und all did you draw?

[14] *Kansas*: the *CMG* for 16 Aug. had carried a news item about a lynching in Kansas.

[15] *"bleedin' Kansas"*: a propaganda phrase widely current before the American Civil War, to describe the predicament of Kansas as a battleground between slavery and anti-slavery interests; but here used to indicate the prevalence of simple gun-law.

[16] *Haf folded his vings in de West*: Col. Sir Lionel Chase Barton went on the Supernumerary Unemployed List on 3 Jan. 1886: in effect, this meant that he retired.

Potzblitz!¹⁷ and dou art a Deutscher!
Herr Gott!¹⁸ and a Baron too!
Mit a lien on de Sherman nation
  Vhich makes it *Reayson-de-blu*¹⁹
Dot you shouldn't be so spread-eagled
  Und hung by der heels to bleed,
But I guess I haf taught you somedings.'

*   *   *   *   *

Here endet de Breitmannleid.²⁰

THE SUPPLICATION OF KERR CROSS, MISSIONARY

Published in the *Pioneer*, 29 September 1888, with signature 'R.K.' and head-
ing '(Let us get a good sized gun and fight in earnest . . . The Portuguese will
no doubt refuse to allow [it]¹ to enter the country, but we must try. Let us wire
home and ask the Government to help us thus far, for, if necessary, we must
try and smuggle a gun in. What right have the Portuguese to act hand in hand
with the Arabs to close up this truly fine country and enslave its tribes? Mr
Moir goes . . . to wire home for a cannon and a Mr Ran goes to Natal to buy a
second. May God prosper them in their endeavours!—*Vide extract from "Daily
News", next column*.)' Reprinted in the *Pioneer Mail*, 3 October. Uncollected,
but included in Scrapbook 4. The *Daily News* item consisted of a letter from
the Revd Dr Kerr Cross of the Free Church Mission, dated from Livingstonia,
Lake Nyassa, East Central Africa, Karonga, on 2 July 1886. It described an
episode in the war against Arab slavers: Dr Cross had acted as surgeon in a
night march and dawn attack made by a small force from the African Lakes
Company on an Arab village. They had had to retire with numerous casualties,
the fortifications proving much stronger than expected, and in the passage
quoted Cross is not making a personal statement but summarizing the views
expressed in the council of war that followed—though it is clear that he
endorses them. (For an account of the episode see Margery Perham, *Lugard:
The Years of Adventure*, London, 1956, pp. 115–25.)

---

¹⁷ *Potzblitz*: damnation! (or some comparable oath.)
¹⁸ *Herr Gott!*: Lord God!
¹⁹ *Reayson-de-blu*: *raison de plus*: all the more reason (with a pun on 'Reay').
²⁰ *Breitmannleid*: the song of Breitmann.

---

¹ [*it*]: 'us' in heading, but 'it' is the reading in the actual extract from the *Daily News*.

TUNE—'Christchurch' (Ouseley)[2]

Father of Mercy, who hast made
    The sun by day, the moon by night,
To show the course of British Trade
    And cheer the Gospel-teaching white,
Tho' we attack with fire and sword,
The heathen press us hard, O Lord!

We smote at dawn, in stealthy wise,
    The walls were high—they would not flee:
Thou knowest when a sparrow dies—
    Thou knowest that I climbed a tree,[3]
And there in Thy dear name I prayed
To speed the bullet and the blade.

But where wast Thou? Our broken fray
    Recoiled in blood and flame and smoke—
Perchance Thine eyes were turned away
    On other, unregenerate folk,
While steadfastly we did Thy work—
Are *we* less worth than Jew or Turk?

Comfort Thy Church in her distress
    Where, lacking Grace and grape,[4] she faints—
Karonga in the Wilderness
    Is wet with life-blood of Thy saints.
The heathen rage against us, but
Let not our prayerful throats be cut!

The spirit that by Thee was given
    How can we quickest take away?
Thou knowest, Lord, that we have driven
    The hissing lead through bleeding clay;
But slight the wounds of small-arm fire,
They will not die as we desire.

---

[2] *Ouseley*: Sir Frederick Arthur Gore Ouseley (1825–89), English church musician, scholar, and composer of sacred music.

[3] *I climbed a tree*: Cross established his First Aid Post some distance from the fortification, and while waiting for the wounded, he writes, 'I climbed a tree on my right and had a view of the whole.'   [4] *grape*: grape-shot.

A minister of Christ, I kneel
   Before Thy altar to beseech
One seven-pounder—rifled—steel—
   Ten-grooved[5] and loading at the breech:
Thereto, for Thou dost all things well,
Much ammunition—shot and shell.

Hot with our rage, the shot shall bring
   Thy mercy to the shrieking camp,
The shells shall Thy salvation sing,
   (Vouchsafe the fuses be not damp!)
And, since they need repeated slaughters,
Send case,[6] dear Lord, for closer quarters.

Moreover all that land is fair,
   And certain slaves in bondage lie,
And we would pitch our pastures there
   And smite the owners hip and thigh,
For they from out Thy Fold have gone
To serve the Whore of Babylon.[7]

How canst Thou care for such as these—
   Just God who lovest us so well—
The Arab and the Portuguese,
   The Heretic and Infidel?
We will possess their land. Do Thou
To each new gun spare sights allow.

Creator of the countless suns,
   We spread the message of the Cross,
Grant that we smuggle safe those guns
   And horribly avenge our loss!
So shall we teach, by death and dearth,
Goodwill to men and peace on earth.

---

[5] *Ten-grooved*: altered to 'Three-grooved' in margin of Scrapbook 4.

[6] *case*: case-shot.

[7] *the Whore of Babylon*: the Roman Catholic Church, according to extreme Protestant interpretations of Rev. 17–19. There were serious conflicts between the adherents of Protestant and Catholic missions in the early history of Uganda.

THE WAY AV UT

Published in the *Pioneer*, 8 October 1888, with signature 'R.K.' and headings
' "The Black Mountain Expedition[1] is apparently to be a teetotal affair.—Vide
Civil and Military, October 5th." / "A charge of Ghazis[2] was met by the Royal
Irish[3] who accounted for the whole of them . . . " / "The Royal Irish then car-
ried the position."—*Pioneer*, today.' Reprinted in the *Pioneer Mail* and *CMG*,
10 October, and *Week's News*, 13 October. Uncollected, but included in
Scrapbook 4. The last three lines of stanza 4 were later incorporated, with
slight modifications, in 'Belts' in *Barrack-Room Ballads*.

I met wid ould Mulvaney[4] an' he tuk me by the hand,
Sez he:—'Fwhat *kubber*[5] from the front, an' will the Paythans[6] stand?'
'O Terence, dear, in all Clonmel such things were never seen,
They've sint a Rigimint to war widout a Fiel' Canteen!

'Tis not a Highland Rigimint, for they wud niver care—
Their corp'rils carry hymn-books an' they opin fire wid prayer—
'Tis not an English Rigimint that burns a Blue Light[7] flame—
'Tis the Eighteenth Royal Irish, man, as thirrsty as they're game!'

An' Terence bit upon his poipe an' shpat behin' the door.
''Tis Bobbs',[8] sez he, 'that knows the thrick av makin' bloody war.
Ye say they go widout their dhrink?' 'An' that's the trut' ' sez I.
'Thin Hiven help the muddy Kheyl[9] they call an Akazai![10]

I lay wid thim in Dublin wanst, an' we was Oirish tu,
We passed the time av day an' thin the belts wint *whirraru*:
I misremember fwhat occurred but, followin' the shtorm,
A *Freeman's Journal Supplemint* was all *my* uniform.

[1] *The Black Mountain Expedition*: a punitive campaign carried out in Oct. and Nov.
1888 in an area of the North-West Frontier where two British officers and some Gurkha
soldiers had been murdered by tribesmen.
[2] *Ghazis*: fanatical Muslim warriors.
[3] *the Royal Irish*: the 18th Foot, the Royal Irish Regiment.
[4] *Mulvaney*: one of the 'Soldiers Three' who figure in many of Kipling's Army stories
of this period.   [5] *kubber*: news.
[6] *Paythans*: Pathans, tribesmen of North-West Frontier.
[7] *Blue Light*: member of temperance society known as the Good Templars.
[8] *Bobbs*: sc. Bobs: Sir Frederick Roberts, the Commander-in-Chief.
[9] *Kheyl*: clan or tribe, used here for a member of same.
[10] *Akazai*: the Akazais were one of the tribes involved.

They're rocks upon parade, but O in barricks they are hard—
They're ragin' tearin' devils whin there's ructions on the kyard;
An' onless they've changed their bullswools[11] for baby's socks, I think
They'd rake all Hell for grandeur—an' I *know* they wud for dhrink!

An' Bobbs has sint thim out to war widout a dhrop or dhrain—
'Tis he will put the *jildy*[12] in this dissolute campaign:
They'd fight for frolic half the year, but now their liquor's cut
The wurrd'll go:—"Don't waste your time! The bay'nit an' the butt!"

Six hundher' stiffin'[13] throats in front—tu hundher' lef' behind
To suck the pickins av the cask whiniver they've a mind!—
I wud *not* be the Paythan man forninst the *sungar*[14] wall,
Whin those six hundher' gentlemin projuce the long bradawl!

They'll all be dhry—tremenjus dhry—an' not a dhram to toss—
Divils of Ballydavel, holy saints av Holy Cross;
An' holy cross they all will be from Carrick to Clogheen,
Thrapeesin' afther naygur-*log*[15] widout a Fiel' Canteen.

Will they be long among the hills? My troth they will not so—
They're crammin' down their fightin' now to have ut done an' go;
For Bobbs the Timp'rance Shtrategist has whipped thim on the
        nail[16]—
'Tis cruel on the Oirish but—ut's Murther on the Kheyl!'

TO SAVE TROUBLE

Published in the *Pioneer*, 18 October 1888, with subheading 'Respectfully
Dedicated to the Native Press, with Apologies to "The Curse of Doneraile" '.[1]
Reprinted in the *Pioneer Mail*, 24 October. Unsigned and uncollected, but

---

[11] *bullswools*: leather boots (Army slang).
[12] *jildy*: liveliness, speed.　　[13] *stiffin'*: cursing.
[14] *sungar*: stone breastwork.　　[15] *naygur-log*: nigger people.
[16] *whipped thim on the nail*: probably a variant of the Army slang phrase 'to whip on a
peg', meaning to put on a charge, with an implied pun here on 'charge'. There may also
be a reference to the Scots colloquial phrase 'off the nail' meaning 'tipsy'.

---

[1] *The Curse of Doneraile*: a 19th cent. Irish poem, which survives in several versions.
The bard Cormac O'Kelly had his watch stolen when he was visiting Doneraile in
County Cork, whereupon he wrote a poem cursing every aspect of the town and its inha-
bitants: 'May fire and brimstone never fail / To fall in showers on Doneraile; / May all
the leading fiends assail / The thieving town of Doneraile; / . . . May every pestilential
gale / Blast that curst spot called Doneraile', etc., etc.

included in Scrapbook 4. On 9 October the *Indian Mirror* (see above, p. 257) had published a denunciation of Lord Dufferin, claiming that he had 'failed in every respect as a Viceroy'. On 13 October the *Pioneer* commented that, all things considered, this condemnation was 'a singularly complete performance and deserve[d] all credit. His Excellency is cursed from the sole of his foot to the crown of his head, in his domestic, his foreign and his financial policy: for all that he has said and not said, for every measure that has been passed during his rule, and for every pie of income tax collected during the same period. He is damned for the Finance Committee,[2] doubly damned for the Public Service Commission,[3] and trebly damned for giving his assent to the Calcutta Municipal Act.[4] Most of all is he devoted to infamy for subtly setting Hindu against Mahomedans . . . Curiously enough he has not been condemned for the floods in Lower Bengal . . . ' Kipling leaps to his defence by offering, ironically, a curse on the Viceroy so compendious as to render supererogatory any further attacks by the Native Press.

> True patriots, let us now begin
>   To curse our ruler Dufferin.
> The British rifle guards our skin,
>   But prey for all is Dufferin.
> *Iswasti*,[5] on enlightened prin-
>   ciples demolish Dufferin.
> The Tree of Power we strove to shin,
>   Who thrust us from it?—Dufferin.
> Who sowed dissension 'twixt the Hin-
>   du Muslim peoples?—Dufferin.
> Who killed our kine,[6] who taxed our tin,[7]
>   Who butchered Burma?[8]—Dufferin.
> With fawning speech and eye-glassed grin
>   Who swindled Asia?—Dufferin.
> Who sinned the Last, the Nameless Sin,
>   Nor heard *our* clamour?—Dufferin.

[2] *the Finance Committee*: because it had authorized the introduction of Income Tax.

[3] *the Public Service Commission*: because it had disappointed hopes that the Indian Civil Service would be thrown open to Indians.

[4] *the Calcutta Municipal Act*: because it had involved wealthy inhabitants of Calcutta in paying municipal as well as national taxes. 'Just conceive', wrote the *Indian Mirror*, 'that, under the benign administration of Lord Dufferin . . . the people have to pay house-rate twice over, one to the Municipality and another to the Income Tax Office.'

[5] *Iswasti*: for that reason, therefore.

[6] *Who killed our kine*: a controversy over 'Cow-Killing' by Muslims and Europeans was raised by Hindus who saw the animal as sacred.

[7] *who taxed our tin*: a reference to the introduction of Income Tax, 'tin' being slang for 'cash'.

[8] *Who butchered Burma?*: a reference to the Burma War of 1885, the annexation of the country in January 1886, and the subsequent years of struggle against dacoits.

Who failed *our* high regard to win?—
    The 'mediocre' Dufferin.
Collinga[9] turned him outside in,
    And Bow Bazar[9] scorned Dufferin.
Today, the nations, piebald, brin-
    dled, rise to spit at Dufferin.
Thrice thirty million crore[10] Divin-
    ities assist them, Dufferin!
From fat Ganesh[11] to Kali[12] thin
    The High Gods yelp at Dufferin.
The curse of Hume[13] and Budrudin
    Tyabji[14] wither Dufferin.
From Boileaugunge[15] to high 'Knockdhrin'[16]
    May houses fall on Dufferin;
May Oriental and Penin-
    sular ships sink with Dufferin;
And every blotch on Naaman's[17] skin
    Defile the flesh of Dufferin.
His wife[18] that helped our women kin
    Whelm in the Doom of Dufferin.
She wrought our cloked *zenanas*[19] in,
    Then damned be Lady Dufferin!
Oh blast 'em all, hoof, hide and fin,
    The progeny of Dufferin!
Six Sixty-six[20]—the Man of Sin[21]
    Das[22]—*wuh*[23]—the It—the Dufferin!
By sap and mine, by pit and gin,
    Befoul the fame of Dufferin,

---

[9] *Collinga, Bow Bazar*: areas of Calcutta.   [10] *crore*: ten million.

[11] *Ganesh*: in Hindu mythology a fat-bodied, elephant-headed god, son of Siva the Destroyer and Reproducer who is one of the manifestations of Brahm, the supreme being.   [12] *Kali*: a terrible goddess in Hindu mythology, wife of Siva.

[13] *Hume*: Allan Octavian Hume (1829–1912), a retired Indian Civil Servant and a champion of the Indian National Congress, of which he was one of the founders.

[14] *Budrudin Tyabji*: a Muslim activist from Bombay, and an important member of the Congress.   [15] *Boileaugunge*: the western area of Simla.

[16] *Knockdhrin*: well-known residence on Simla Mall.

[17] *Naaman*: on Naaman's leprosy, see 2 Kgs. 5.

[18] *His wife*: on Lady's Dufferin's efforts on behalf of the women of India, see above pp. 361 and 363.   [19] *zenanas*: women's quarters.

[20] *Six Sixty-six*: see Rev. 13: 18: 'Let him that hath understanding count the number of the beast: for it is the number of a man; and his number is Six hundred three score and six.'   [21] *the Man of Sin*: the Antichrist (2 Thess. 2: 3).

[22] *Das*: that (German).   [23] *wuh*: that one (Hindustani).

Let 'Albions'[24] clack and 'Harrilds'[24] spin
   Pye—dis—and *dele*[25] Dufferin!
Till English voters hear the din
   And love us loathing Dufferin:
Till all the earth from Hull to Minn-
   eapolis damns Dufferin;
For flying pen and wagging chin
   Shall surely ruin Dufferin.
Thus, lowly walking, may we win
   To freedom—free of Dufferin.
We love the Queen, but not a pin
   Our loyal breed loves Dufferin!
He would not worship Us—to flin-
   ders smash, and bury Dufferin!
And write above that reeking bin:
   'Here lies our shame and Dufferin!'

'IMPERIOUS WOOL-BOOTED SAGE'

Holograph version, untitled and unsigned (Library of Congress). Edmonia Hill, in her article 'The Young Kipling' in the *Atlantic Monthly*, vol. clvii (1936) quotes (p. 411) from a letter she wrote in 1888: 'I never saw anyone more devoted to children [than Kipling], and alas there are so few in this station; all old enough have been sent to England, but Dr and Mrs J. Murray Irwin have a darling little girl[1] who is my godchild. When she comes to the house there is nothing R. will not do to amuse her . . . On her birthday he wrote to accompany my small gift a gay little verse beginning 'Imperious wool-booted sage, / Tho' your years as men reckon are three, / You are wiser than ten times your age / And your faithfullest servants are we." '

Imperious wool-booted sage
   Tho' your years as men reckon are Three
You are wiser than ten times your age,
   And your faithfullest servants are we.

---

[24] *Albions, Harrilds*: printing machines. The Albion Iron Press, hand-operated, was placed on the market in 1822 but remained in use for certain purposes throughout the 19th cent. Harrild and Sons were major manufacturers of printing machines in Britain.

[25] *Pye, dis, dele*: printing house terms, *Pye*: mess up or break up (e.g. a forme of type); *dis*: distribute the component parts (e.g. individual pieces of type): *dele*: delete.

[1] *a darling little girl*: the Irwins' daughter Edna Florine was baptized in Allahabad in Dec. 1885. Her birthday is thought to have been in Oct.

Oh fluffy Philosopher small
   You can't read our rhymes it is true,
For dinner and play is your All
   And Creation is—you!

You cry for the moon and—you get it,
   You laugh and our spirits have mirth,
And the least of your orders we set it
   O'er everything else upon earth.

We know we are older—we may be
   More wise than yourself O my sweet
But today you are Queen of us Baby
   And we come with our gifts to your feet.

A SONG OF ADDRESSES

Published in the *Pioneer*, 15 December 1888, with subheading '(Dedicated, without permission, to the C–lc–tta M–n–c–p–l–ty)'. Reprinted in the *Pioneer Mail*, 19 December. Unsigned and uncollected, but included in Scrapbook 4. Lord Lansdowne, the new Viceroy, arrived in Calcutta on 8 December 1888. The *Pioneer* for that day printed what was claimed to be the draft of an Address to be presented to him by the Calcutta Municipality, pleading for 'a moderate and timely concession' in the sphere of government, for the 'unofficialising of the administration' in enlightened centres like Calcutta, and for the 'granting of a larger voice to the unofficial community'. On 13 December the *Pioneer* printed the final text of the Address, which was delivered that day. Respectful in tone and less political in emphasis than the draft had been, it none the less alluded to 'the reasonable aspirations of the non-official community both European and native', and hoped for the passing of such measures as would 'harmoniously broaden the foundations on which rests the undoubted loyalty of the people of India to the Throne of our most Gracious and beloved Queen-Empress'.

We represent the Ward of Bow Bazar![1]
   We're the dolphins of the Hugli[2] on the roll!
We're the crests of Kinchinjunga,[3] we're the sons of Holy Gunga,[4]
   And we come to guide Your Lordship's infant soul!

[1] *Bow Bazar*: area of Calcutta.
[2] *Hugli*: western channel of River Ganges, linking Calcutta to the Bay of Bengal.
[3] *Kinchinjunga*: one of the highest peaks of the Himalayas.
[4] *Holy Gunga*: the River Ganges, sacred to Hindus, which reaches the sea at Calcutta.

(CHORUS) They're the pinks[5] of Ooltadunga,[6] they're the pearls of
                Holy Gunga,
            And they'll edify His Lordship's simple soul!

You will please to take your orders, Sir, from us,
    You will kindly let us warn you of your slips,
As the stewards tried and trusty of the sewage-sodden *busti*[7]
    You will reverence the wisdom of our lips.
(CHORUS) He will learn to govern nations through their lucid
                lucubrations,
            Who will jump upon his stomach if he trips.

We're your festive fellow-subjects. *Hari ji*![8]
    We're a fid[9] of every 'longshore breed and *clique*—
From the quite-played-out Caucasian to the Jew and the Eurasian
    And the Chinaman, Armenian and Greek.
(CHORUS) He will gaze upon the faces of his fellow-subject races,
            And will bow before their fine unblushing cheek.

We're the rocket-politicans of Bengal,
    We're the patent gas and atmospheric ram!
We're the Product nickel-plated of a postulate misstated,
    And an Aspinal[10]-enamel-painted sham!
(CHORUS) Yes, a paralytic camel done with Aspinal enamel
            And a dangerous and homicidal sham.

But we'll teach you how to govern as you ought
    From Peshawur[11] to the Coromandel[12] main.
We will all instruct Your Lordship in the duties of your wardship,
    And will regulate the measures of your reign.
(CHORUS) They will first expound his duty from Peshawur unto
                Ooty[13]
            And then, perhaps, will flush a city drain.

---

[5] *pinks*: 'swells' (slang).   [6] *Ooltadunga*: area of Calcutta.
   [7] *busti*: one of the 'separate groups of huts in the humbler native quarters of Calcutta,
the sanitary state of which has often been held up to reprobation' (*Hobson-Jobson*).
   [8] *Hari-ji*!: Lord God! (lit. Lord Krishna).   [9] *fid*: plug or lump.
   [10] *Aspinal*: the inventor of an oxidized enamel paint; hence a type of enamelling.
   [11] *Peshawur*: city on North-West Frontier.
   [12] *Coromandel*: south-east coast of India.
   [13] *Ooty*: Ootacamund, a hill-station in South India.

(GENERAL CHORUS)

When they've pointed out the path he ought to tread,
  And declared their views on Franchise and Reform,
They may rinse a reeking *kintal*,[14] they may even dare to hint all
  Their roads are not unflooded after storm.
They may mulct in more than lucre *gowlis*[15] thrice convict of *phuka*,[16]
  And may segregate their lepers in a *gaum*,[17]
But at present they're explaining the Entire Art of Reigning
  To the trumpet and the cymbal and the shawm.

(ENCORE VERSE)

When the Eatanswill[18] of Asia knows its place
  And the value of each copper Pott and Slurk,[19]
It may drop unbalanced bluster for the *jaroo*[20] and the duster—
  It may even—settle down to do its work!

THE LAW OF LIBEL

Published in the *Pioneer*, 22 December 1888, with heading ' "Perhaps the
belief was true but not the rumour. Possibly belief and rumour were
unfounded. But is it so great a sin in a public journal to lend voice to the
people, &c? Where the absolute verity is nearly impossible of attainment by the
instituted tribunals, how much more so by the poor journalist! He can only go
upon the rumour and the proof of rumour ought to absolve him in court."
Comment of a Native paper on a recent libel-suit'. Reprinted in the *Pioneer Mail*,
26 December. Unsigned and uncollected, but included in Scrapbook 4. (I
have incorporated autograph corrections to the Scrapbook version.) A modi-
fied form of stanza 1 was used as a chapter-heading for Chapter vi of *The Nau-
lahka* (1892), and included in a volume of *Rhymed Chapter Headings for
Naulahka* the same year. Kipling's contempt for the way the Native Press
abused its freedom under British rule was reinforced by his observation of how
such things were ordered in the Native States. 'Note this fact . . . ', he writes
in *Letters of Marque*, no. xix, published in the *Pioneer*, 28 February 1888: 'With
the exception of such journals as, occupying a central position in British terri-
tory, levy blackmail from the neighbouring States, there are no independent

---

[14] *kintal*: cesspool or sewage ditch ? I have not succeeded in finding a translation of
this term.   [15] *gowlis*: ? *galis*: lanes, alleys.
   [16] *phuka*: ? *phok*: rubbish, vegetable waste, especially from sugar-cane.
   [17] *gaum*: village settlement.
   [18] *Eatanswill*: see the account of the Eatanswill by-election in *Pickwick Papers*.
   [19] *Pott and Slurk*: the editors of the two rival political newspapers in Eatanswill.
   [20] *jaroo*: broom.

papers in Rajputana. A King may start a weekly, to encourage a taste for Sanscrit and high Hindi, or a Prince may create a Court Chronicle; but that is all. A "free press" is not allowed, and this the native journalist knows. With good management he can, keeping under the shadow of our flag, raise two hundred rupees from a big man here, and five hundred from a rich man there, but he does not establish himself across the Border. To one who has reason to hold a stubborn disbelief in even the elementary morality of the native press, this bashfulness and lack of enterprise is amusing. . . . A year spent among native States ought to send a man back to the Decencies and the Law Courts and the Rights of the Subject with a supreme contempt for those who rave about the oppressions of our brutal bureaucracy.' (*From Sea to Sea*, London, 1900, vol. i, pp. 195–6.)

To the State of Kot-Kumharsen where the wild dacoits abound,
    And the Barons live in castles on the hills,
Where the tiger and the cactus in alternate streaks are found,
    And the Raja cannot meet his monthly bills,
    Where the Agent[1] Sahib Bahadur[2] shoots the black-buck for his
        larder
        From the tonga[3] which he uses as *machân*,[4]
Babu Bunkum Bandar Bose took his Harrilds and his Hoes,[5]
    And proprieted the *Bewaquf Tufan*.[6]

'Twas a paper for the masses who were nearly all Hindu,
    With a taint of touchy Thakur[7] fighting blood;
'Twas a journal dealing largely with affairs that were not true,
    And disseminating ill-considered mud.
    'Twas a *pukka*[8] People's issue, 'twas a four-page pica[9] tissue
        Of turtle-headed infants' ghouls and *djinns*,
    And aspersions sepia brown on the *mullah*[10] of the town,
        And a record of the Agent's grosser sins.

[1] *Agent*: British representative in Native State.
[2] *Bahadur*: term of respect.
[3] *tonga*: light two-wheeled vehicle, drawn by two ponies.
[4] *machân*: platform to shoot from.
[5] *Harrilds and Hoes*: printing machines. For Harrild and Sons, see p 435 above. Robert Hoe and his son Richard were significant figures in the development of the printing industry in the USA, especially in the design of machines for newspaper production.
[6] *Bewaquf Tufan*: lit. ignorant storm.
[7] *Thakur*: Rajput noble.
[8] *pukka*: genuine.
[9] *pica*: a size of printer's type giving six lines to the inch.
[10] *mullah*: Muslim religious teacher.

It was read by all the Nation for a range of eighty miles,
    It was studied in the only Middle School,
It exposed with crushing irony the Viceroy's many wiles
    And it always praised the King's 'enlightened rule'.
    For the silky-soft Diwan[11] bought that *Bewaquf Tufan*
      At a price beyond its market-value far,
    And the Raja privy purse would the proper funds disburse
      When the Babu brought his *nuzzer*[12] to durbar.

So it cursed *per* M.A. Standard once a week, with monthly pauses
    For Dewali,[13] Christmas Day and Durga Pujah,[13]
And it published paper State reform in annotated clauses,
    And it yearly found its State subvention huger;
    And the public puzzle-headed read its pica double-leaded,
      And talked of *Kali Yugas*[14] and *nukshan*,[15]
    For it printed all the rumours of administrative tumours
      And corruption did the *Bewaquf Tufan*.

Yea, it cursed the shining Agent as it cursed the British Raj,
    And it pounded every Viceroy into jelly,
And it swore the Public Works had slain a porker[16] in the Taj,[17]
    And shut the Jumma Masjid[18] up at Delhi;
    And the yarns of want and war that it learned in the *bazar*
      Were duly reproduced with running notes,
    But since the mild Diwan held the *Bewaquf Tufan*
      It was death against the Barons owning votes.

But a noble sense of duty brought about the final smash,
    When a heavy falling-off among the readers
Led the silky sweet Diwan to haggle hotly o'er the cash,
    And suggest increased *empressement*[19] in the leaders,
    For unlucky Bander Bose with a dripping pen arose
      And stated (which was truth or very near)

---

[11] *Diwan*: chief minister of Native State.   [12] *nuzzer*: ceremonial gifts.
[13] *Dewali and Durga Pujah*: major Hindu religious festivals.
[14] *Kali Yuga*: an era of darkness and degeneration, in which virtue deteriorates and mankind becomes depraved.   [15] *nukshan*: offence, injury.
[16] *had slain a porker*: thus polluting a holy building, the pig being an unclean animal in the eyes of Muslims.   [17] *the Taj*: the Taj Mahal in Agra.
[18] *the Jumma Masjid*: the great mosque at Delhi.
[19] *empressement*: eagerness, urgency.

Neither Pharphar nor Abana[20] filled the Raja Sahib's *Zenana*,[21]
    But he kidnapped wives within the British sphere.

'Twas the gossip of the City, it demanded cess unstinted,
    'Twas a duty half the Court had tried to fill,
It was truer than the rumour of the previous week that hinted
    At a Native-State-annexatory bill;
    But that flossy-mild Diwan dropped the *Bewaquf Tufan*,
      As we drop the pail of thrice-defiling tar,
    And, since British law obtains but in British ruled domains,
      Said the Raja of the journal briefly, '*Mar!*'[22]

Woe is me for Habeas Corpus or a trial by jury—
    Or the lesser risk of Judge and one appeal!
There was laughter 'mong the Barons—in the Raja's heart was fury—
    In the Palace yard the clink of spur and steel;
    And the Harrild and the Hoe heard the howl of 'Birchee do!'[23]
      As the lean Mahratta lances raised the thatch;
    And I grieve to say that same broke in twenty points of flame
      Through the medium of a common sulphur match.

So they fused, with execrations, quite a hundred pounds of plant,
    And they hunted for the Staff without avail,
For the Journal to the Border made a record-cutting slant
    Till his women (under torture) showed his trail.
    Then that Raja's Bodyguard rode relentlessly and hard,
      And they caught him, half a mile from British ground,
    And the gentle *thanda pench*[24] with a double-action *kench*[25]
      Made him swoon and juice of chillies brought him round.

---

[20] *Pharphar nor Abana*: i.e. his own territories. See 2 Kgs. 5: 12, where Naaman, captain of the host of the King of Syria, asks 'Are not Abana and Pharphar, rivers of Damascus, better than all the waters of Israel?'

[21] *zenana*: women's quarters.

[22] *Mar*: beat or kill; in this context 'clobber it'.

[23] *Birchee do*: give it the spear.

[24] *thanda pench*: lit. 'cool twist'. Some form of torture, probably involving a stick tightening a tourniquet round the head. Cf. 'At Howli Thana': 'I saw the mark of a string on the temples of Iman Baksh. Does the Presence know the torture of the Cold Draw?' (*Soldiers Three and Other Stories*, Uniform Edn., p. 263)

[25] *kench*: pull.

Then the Barons from their castles and the Raja from his throne
    Descended to elucidate the point
As to subtler forms of libel and the less obtrusive bone
    That a knee and rope and *charpoy*[26] may disjoint.
        'Curse not the King in bed for a bird shall tell', they said,
            'And specially avoid the use of print.'
        And that unreported trial was succeeded by a phial
            Of mustard oil, a *Kobiraj*[27] and lint.

Now the Harrild and the Hoe are lying still at Kot-Kumharsen,
    The ashes of the office thatch among,
And since the lyric stage no more can count on David Carson,[28]
    I have ventured to compose this little song.
        How the law of libel runs under British flags and guns,
            Is a blot that every litho[29] slang-sheet knows:
        How that self-same law obtains in a petty King's domains
            Must be patent now to Bunkum Bander Bose.

TO THESE PEOPLE

Holograph verses addressed to Professor and Mrs Hill who had befriended
Kipling at Allahabad and invited him to share their house there. Signed
'Rudyard Kipling' and dated 25 December 1888 (Library of Congress). Hill
('Alex') was Professor of Science at the Muir Central College in the University
of Allahabad. Edmonia ('Ted') Hill suffered a severe illness in late 1888 and
early 1889, and the couple decided to return on leave to her family home in
Beaver, Pennsylvania, when she was well enough to travel. They planned to
sail to San Francisco via Burma, Singapore, Hong Kong, and Japan, and they
would subsequently return to India via England. In the event Kipling accom-
panied them on their voyage to San Francisco on his own return to England,
but that arrangement had not been envisaged when he wrote this poem.

        'Peace upon Earth to people of good will'
            So runs the song of eighteen hundred years
        Caught by the drowsy shepherds on the hill
            From Regents of the Spheres.

[26] *charpoy*: bedstead.   [27] *Kobiraj*: physician.
[28] *David Carson*: a music-hall entertainer who seems to have specialized in Indian
impersonations; author of song 'The Bengalee Baboo'.
[29] *litho*: produced by lithography, i.e. by a method of printing from stone or metal
plates which have been made ink-receptive.

Now we have lost the Babe among the straw
   That men, too wise, thresh out of Death and Birth;
But year by year the old sweet changeless Law
   Rings downward to the Earth.

Wherefore so long as mortal life endures,
   To that Beyond we doubt and dream of still,
Peace upon earth and all goodwill be yours
   O household of goodwill!

And none the less because so near to Youth
   The hand that fails your merits in confessing
And none the less because so far from truth
   The heart that shapes the blessing.

Against the petty round of wearing strife
   You gave me refuge very dear and new—
The tender courtesies of daily life
   Unwavering, sweet and true.

Forgoing much you opened wide your doors
   And made me welcome past all worth or right—
An inky gamin doing inky chores
   And doing 'em at night!

You heard the egotistic tongue that jumped
   From babbling joy to beer-begotten gloom,
Nor shuddered when cheroot in hand I stumped
   Your dainty drawing room.

Do I write jestingly? Believe me no—
   Between the lines a deeper meaning lies
And heartier thanks than best Blue Black can show
   Or pen anatomize

Help, Comfort, Sympathy and Kindness lie
   Beyond all scribbling though I set apart
A thirty page edition of the *Pi*[1]
   And filled it—from my heart

[1] *the Pi*: the *Pioneer*.

I thank you for I hold you very dear—
    Science and Housewifry who made me guest,
And more than guest, for half a happy year—
    And veil my thanks in jest

Behold! The stranger in your gates calls down
    A mighty Blessing—yea, a note of credit
Available at every sea and town
    As you and yours shall tread it

All good encompass you from East to West
    Till utmost East becomes the West extreme,
What time you take your giant pleasure-quest
    To lands whereof I dream.

For you shall China's wave take softer mood,
    And Yeddo[2] yield her choicest 'broideries,
And Halcyons hastening from their haunts shall brood
    O'er North Pacific seas.

Most rare medicaments on every breeze
    Shall steal beneath the awnings for your sake
Till tortured temples find unbroken ease,
    And burning brows forget the way to ache.

Rangoon shall strew her rubies at your feet,
    New skies shall show uncharted constellations,
And gentle earthquakes in Japan shall meet
    Your rage for observations.

No plate of all the gross shall frill or blur,[3]
    Your trunks shall 'scape unclean *douane-darogahs*,[4]
Though gems and *netschies*,[5] curios and fur
    Shall cram your Saratogas.[6]

---

[2] *Yeddo*: former name of Tokyo.
[3] *No plate . . .* : Hill was an enthusiastic amateur photographer. Cf. pp. 450–2 below.
[4] *douane-darogahs*: chiefs of Customs stations.
[5] *netschies*: ? netsuke (Japanese carved toggles of wood or ivory).
[6] *Saratogas*: large travelling trunks.

So shall you fare, while happy omens bless,
    By land and sea, thrice proof against all harms,
Till . . .
        Alex finds himself an F.R.S.[7]
And Ted her Father's arms.

NEW LAMPS FOR OLD

Published in the *Pioneer*, 1 January 1889. Reprinted in the *Pioneer Mail*, 2 January. Unsigned. Collected in the Outward Bound, De Luxe, Sussex, and Burwash Edns. Some lines are adapted in 'The Conundrum of the Work-shops', published in the *Scots Observer*, 13 September 1890, and collected in *Barrack-Room Ballads*.

When the flush of the new-born sun fell first on Eden's green and
    gold,
A Lying Spirit sat under the Tree and sang, 'New Lamps for Old!'
And Adam waked from his mighty sleep, and Eve was at his side,
And the twain had faith in the song that they heard, and knew not the
    Spirit lied.

They plucked a lamp from the Eden-tree (the ancient legend saith),
And lighted themselves the Path of Toil that runs to the Gate of
    Death;
They left the lamp for the joy of their sons, and that was a glorious
    gain,
When the Spirit cried, 'New Lamps for Old!' in the ear of the branded
    Cain.

So he gat fresh hope, and builded a town, and watched his breed
    increase,
Till Tubal[1] lighted the Lamp of War from the flickering Lamp of
    Peace;
And ever they fought with fire and sword and travailed in hate and
    fear,
As the Spirit sang, 'New Lamps for Old!' at the change of the
    changing year.

---

[7] *F.R.S.*: Fellow[ship] of the Royal Society.

[1] *Tubal*: see Gen. 4: 22.

They sought new lamps in the Morning-red, they sought new lamps in
    the West,
Till the waters covered the pitiful land and the heart of the world had
    rest—
Had rest with the Rain of the Forty Days, but the Ark rode safe above,
And the Spirit cried, 'New Lamps for Old!' when Noah loosened the
    Dove.

And some say now that the Eden-tree had never a root on earth;
And some say now from an eyeless eft our Father Adam had birth;
And some say now there was never an Ark and never a God to save;
And some say now that Man is a God, and some say Man is a slave;

And some build altars East and West, and some build North and
    South;
And some bow down to the Work of the Hand and some to the Word
    of the Mouth.
But wheresoever a heart may beat or a hand reach forth to hold,
The Spirit comes with the coming year, and cries, 'New Lamps for
    Old!'

And the sons of Adam leave their toil who are cursed with the Curse
    of Hope,
And hang the profitless past in a noose of the thundering belfry's rope,
And tear the branch from the laurel-bush with feastings manifold,
When the cry goes up to the scornful stars, 'New Lamps! New Lamps
    for Old!'

Though all the lamps that ever were lit have winked at the world for
    years,
The sons of Adam crowd the streets with laughter and sighs and tears;
For they hold that new, strange lamps shall shine to guide their feet
    aright,
And they turn their eyes to the scornful stars and stretch their arms to
    the night.

And the Spirit gives them the Lamp of War that burns at the cannon-
    lip,
As it blazed on the point of Tubal's blade and the prow of the battle-
    ship;

And the Lamp of Love that was Eve's to snatch from Lilith[2] under the
   Tree;
And the Lamp of Fame that is old as Strife and dim as Memory;

And the Lamp of Faith that was won from Job, and of Shame that was
   wrung from Cain;
And the Lamp of Youth that was Adam's once, and the cold blue
   Lamp of Pain;
And last is the terrible Lamp of Hope that every man must bear,
Lest he find his peace ere the day of his death by the light of the Lamp
   Despair.

We know that the Eden Lamp is lost,—if ever were Eden made,—
And the ink of the Schools in the Lamp of Faith has sunk a world in
   the shade;
But ever we look for a light that is new, and ever the Spirit cries,
'New Lamps for Old!' and we take the lamps, and—behold, the Spirit
   lies!

THE QUESTION OF GIVENS

Published in the *Pioneer*, 18 January 1889, with subheading '(*Vide* Accounts of
the Mississippi Disaster)' and half-stanza from 'Jim Bludso':[1] 'And sure's
you're born they all got off / Before the smoke-stacks fell, / And Bludso's
ghost went up alone / In the smoke of the Prairie Belle'. Reprinted in the *Pio-
neer Mail*, 23 January. Unsigned and uncollected, but included in Scrapbook 4.
The *Englishman* (14 January), the *Pioneer* (16 January), and the *CMG* (15 and
17 January) all carried items on the loss of the steamer *John Hanna*, which was
destroyed by fire on the Mississippi at Plaquemines, Louisiana, on 24
December 1888. The fire was discovered about midnight; the cargo of cotton
burned 'with fearful rapidity'; and 'within three minutes of its discovery the
vessel was one sheet of flame from stem to stern'. The pilot ran the boat ashore
so that some crewmen and passengers made their escape, but others stuck in
the mud and were roasted to death by the conflagration, while others again met
their death on board. The pilot jumped into the water and swam to safety,
whereupon the steamer drifted downstream with more loss of life. Among
those who perished was another pilot, Bob Smith, who had saved many lives in

---

[2] *Lilith*: Adam's first wife, according to Rabbinical tradition. D. G. Rossetti describes
her revenge on Adam and Eve in his poem 'Eden Bower', published in 1870.

[1] '*Jim Bludso*': 'Jim Bludso of the Prairie Belle' from *Pike County Ballads and Other
Poems* by Colonel John Hay (1838–1905).

a previous disaster by sticking to his post on a burning steamer. His behaviour then, and that of Bludso who had '[held] her nozzle agin' the bank / Till the last soul got ashore', seem to have provided Kipling with his models for 'Givens'.

> Sir, with the scalpel[2] and delicate knives
>   Hacking a hole in the guinea-pig's brain,
> Versed in the Why of our poor little lives,
>   Study the papers and kindly explain.
> Something seems wrong in the scheme that you drew—
> Please reconstruct your Creation anew.

> Yes, I am sure that the Lord is a fiction,
>   Yes, I am sure from a germ-blob of earth,
> Slowly we clomb into dress-clothes and diction,
>   Sat on a chair and told lies of our birth:
> I'm one Ascidian[3] and you are another—
> What about Givens, my erudite brother?

> What about Givens? Hell Fire's exploded—
>   He did his best in a close imitation—
> Held a lit steamer with cotton-bales loaded
>   Hard on the bank, for the people's salvation—
> Burned like an onion and broke as he died
> Nature's first law which is:—'Keep a whole hide.'

> What was the motive that led him to danger?
>   Why did he stick to the wheel like a fool?
> Why did he trouble to rescue the stranger
>   When he might jump in the stream and be cool?
> Death could be found in a prettier way,
> Why did he plump for an Auto da Fé?[4]

---

[2] *Sir, with the scalpel*: the poem is an attack on the view propounded by Charles Darwin in *The Descent of Man* (1871) that 'man is descended from some less highly organised form' of life and that there is no basis for the belief 'that man is the work of a separate act of creation'. Darwin refers (2nd edn., 1874, p. 603) to Dr Brown-Séquard's demonstration that 'if certain animals are operated on in a particular manner, their offspring are affected'; and these animals are identified as guinea-pigs in the index (ibid., p. 647).

[3] *Ascidian*: minute marine invertebrate animal, seen as link in chain of evolution. Cf. Darwin, op. cit., p. 609: 'In the dim obscurity of the past we can see that the early progenitor of all the Vertebrata must have been an aquatic animal . . . more like the larvae of the existing marine Ascidians than any other known form.'

[4] *Auto da Fé*: lit. act of the faith; execution of sentence of the Inquisition, usually by burning.

What was the instinct—acquired or inherited?
   Dim recollection of Sunday-School teaching?
Desperate rush to the Fate that he merited?
   Practical finish of Methody preaching?
He was a deck-hand—it wasn't his pidgin[5]
Rashly to riot in flames or religion.

Though you shall read in a work of devotion
   Something that says there is no love exceeding
Death for a friend's sake, *that* wasn't his notion:
   He held the wheel while the rest fled unheeding.
Deck-hands and passengers love in their station—
What shall we think of this Type-Aberration?

Mark him, defunct now, a *lusus naturae*,[6]
   Say he was mad or suggest he was drunk.
Write on his tombstone:—'He tasted Death's fury
   Long ere he died, too uncultured to funk.'
Add there:—'*Resurgat*[7]—as wheat haulm or tree.'
So much for Givens—but what about Me?

Hand back that God that you diddled me out of—
   Hand back the prayer-book you said was a sham—
Give me some Power I haven't a doubt of—
   Something almighty to bless and to damn!
Deuce take your atoms and test-tubes that smell—
Givens won Heaven by walking through Hell!

If he comes out in the Dark on the far side—
   Finds there is neither Gold Doorway nor Throne—
He will steer straight for some unannexed starside,
   Start, on his merits, a Heaven of his own.
Sidney[8] will help him, while you on the earth
Write to the *Times* of a new planet's birth.

---

[5] *pidgin*: business.
[6] *lusus naturae*: freak of nature.   [7] *Resurgat*: let him rise again.
[8] *Sidney*: Sir Philip Sidney. The reference is to the famous story of how Sidney, dying of wounds, passed a cup of water to another wounded man with the words 'Thy necessity is greater than mine'.

So! You can prove me an anthropoid whats-its-name,
  Post-proto-blasto-Caesarian It—
Work your philosophy, gentlemen—rot's its name—
  Try it on Givens and Givens won't fit.
All that you know of the Earth, Sky or Sea
Doesn't account for that fellow—or Me!

'I THANK YOU MRS COLVIN'

Holograph verses by Kipling, sent as Mrs Hill's thanks for a present of fruit
during her illness (Library of Congress). Mrs Colvin was the wife of W. M.
Colvin, a leading advocate of the High Court in Allahabad. Undated: January
1889?

I thank you Mrs Colvin
for the fruits in juice disolvin'
& I ate the grapes and oranges with will
& I'd like another basket
Any time I choose to ask it,
& I'm always yours sin [cerely Mrs Hill.]

A BALLADE OF PHOTOGRAPHS

Holograph version, signed 'Rudyard Kipling', in an album of photographs by
Professor Hill. A note by Mrs Hill in 1921 reads: 'In the late summer of
1888 . . . Mrs Hill was interested in a Bazaar which was to be given at Allaha-
bad in February 1889, for the benefit of Trinity Church. As the Hills were
great photographers, Mrs Hill decided to present two books (to be raffled) of
her own work. Mr Hill had made many beautiful negatives of Indian scenes—
Mrs Hill . . . printed and mounted the photographs and called upon young
Kipling who was always ready to help—to write some verses.' The Hills kept
one of the volumes for themselves, with Kipling's first version of this poem.
The other, with the final version, was duly raffled, and Kipling wrote to Mrs
Hill in February 1889 that 'Colonel Dodd tells me that a Colonel Lang (loca-
lity unknown) won the album of photographs. I hope he may be worthy of the
trouble taken over it. Don't you.' (KP 16/4.) Both albums are now in the
Library of Congress, with Mrs Hill's note quoted above (cf. KP 27/6).

Behold, O Fortune-favoured one
To whom this dainty book may fall,
Pachmarri, Muttra, Brindabun
Shall rise before you at your call—
Benares' ghât, the Agra hall,
And verdant slopes of Ranikhet,
Are yours to gaze upon in all
The pomp of full-plate cabinet.[1]

Mussoorie woods and boulders dun,
Dead homes of Kings, and streams that crawl
League-broad beneath a burning sun,
And green, bamboo-embattled wall—
A silver tarn, a floating yawl,
Squat shrine and Muslim minaret,
Are yours, at price exceeding small
In pomp of full-plate cabinet

And have you ne'er let Fancy run
Athwart the East we hold in thrall;
And have you ne'er with rod or gun
Left dusty Lines or dreary Mall?
Then turn the page where torrents brawl
And Nature's sumptuous throne is set
'Twixt giant rock and leafage tall
In pomp of full-plate cabinet.

L'ENVOI

Prince or Princess, now you have won
This book with gorgeous views beset,
Procure a camera and run
Yourself to full-plate cabinet.

VERSES ON THE CHARLEVILLE HOTEL, MUSSOORIE

The album retained by the Hills (see above, p. 450), contained holograph verses by Kipling inscribed under two photographs of the Charleville Hotel, Mussoorie, where he had visited the Hills in June 1888. The first, under a

---

[1] *cabinet*: a particular size of photograph, about seven inches by five.

photograph of the office, reads 'And there were men with a thousand wants / And women with babes galore— / But the dear little angels in Heaven know / That Wutzler[1] *never* swore'. The second is inscribed under a photo with the caption 'Quarters at the Charleville. April–July 88.' (Library of Congress.)

> A burning sun in cloudless skies
>   And April dies,
> A dusty mall—three sunsets splendid—
>   And May is ended,
> Grey mud beneath—grey cloud o'erhead
>   And June is dead.
> A little bill in late July
>   And then we fly.

THE IRISH CONSPIRACY

Published in the *Pioneer*, 18 February 1889, with heading 'The Maharajah Dhulip Singh[1] has issued a manifesto addressed to the Princes and people of India. In it he declares that there are supporters in Europe and America who are ready to form an army for the overthrow of British rule in India; but a fund of four million pounds is necessary for the purchase of munitions in order to carry out that object. Besides the Punjabis, the Irish soldiers serving in British regiments in India would assist in the movement.—*Vide Reuter's telegram in "Pioneer" of 15th instant.*' Reprinted in the *Pioneer Mail*, 20 February. Unsigned and uncollected, but clearly by the same hand as 'The Way uv It'. (Mulvaney[2] was in any case Kipling's property, and the *Pioneer* would not have allowed anyone else to appropriate him.) A later holograph copy, signed 'Rudyard Kipling', is in the Strange Africana Library, Johannesburg.

> I went to ould Mulvaney wid the Friday's *Pioneer*,
> I grup him by the shoulther-strap—sez I to him:—'Look here,
> There's rumours av conspiracy an' fire an' rape an' ruin,
> Expaytiate upon ut, man—fwhat *are* the Oirish doin'?'

---

[1] *Wutzler*: H. Wutzler, manager of the hotel.

[1] *Dhulip Singh*: born 1837, son of Maharajah Ranjit Singh, the last independent ruler of the Punjab. The Sikh Wars were fought during his minority; the Punjab was annexed by Britain; and he lived for most of his life in England with great ostentation. After an official enquiry into his debts in 1880 he turned against Britain, but was prevented from revisiting India in 1886 when he issued an inflammatory proclamation to the Sikhs; he flirted with Russia as a potential ally, and died in Paris in 1893.

[2] *Mulvaney*: see above, p. 431.

7. Sketch of Kipling by his father, February 1889 (KP 2/1). Kipling wrote to Mrs Hill on 23 February that 'the Pater shot me as I was writing; and the result was a lovely pen and ink, and a blue stump sketch—just head and pipe; the former frowning & the latter fuming. It's a great deal more characteristic than any photo.' (KP 16/4.)

You break your Colonels' hearts out here, you turn your Captains
    grey,
You're breakin' heads in Doblin for O'Brien[3] and Tay Pay,[4]
You're only safe in action or Kilmainham[5] or the Clink,[6]
But fwhat's this latest devilment av Mister Julup Sink?'

Mulvaney tuk the paper, an' he hild ut to his eyes,
An' read about battalions all languishin' to rise,
He shuk the black dudeen[7] out on the armpit av his fist,
'The naygur-man is right', sez he. 'By God, we wud assist!

If only Mister Julup, wid his di'monds in his hat,
Wud pass the time av day forninst the "rebils" at Cherat,[8]
There's rookies from Blackwaterton, an' toughs from Cullyhanna,
Wud trate His Royal Highnuss in a most amazin' manner.

An av there come an accident by reason av their fun,
An' av his head and joolry was both pulled off in one,
The bhoys wud steal a baggage-thrain, an' bribe a gyard to take
The corpse on to Jullundur for the Connaughts[9] there to wake.

But av they didn't waste him, an' the Connaughts let him be,
The Leinsters[10] at Calcutta are conshumin' for a shpree,
They'd wet him in the Hugli an' they'd dhry him in the Strand.
For they'd run him wid their terriers through his patrimonial land.

But fwhat's the good av *bukhin*'?[11] Av he wants to see us rise
Let him write to Bobbs[12] Bahadur[13] for a fortnight's field-supplies,
An' ship a handy army av tin thousand to Bombay—
Thin call the Oirish rigiments—there's six av us[14]—his way.

---

   [3] *O'Brien*: William O'Brien (1852–1928), an Irish politician, one of the leaders of the Home Rule movement.
   [4] *Tay Pay*: T. P. O'Connor (1848–1929), another leading Irish nationalist, politician and journalist.   [5] *Kilmainham*: Irish gaol.
   [6] *the Clink*: prison (slang); but more especially cells for soldiers undergoing punishment. Cf. 'Cells' in *Barrack-Room Ballads*: 'I'm here in the Clink for a thundering drink and blacking the Corporal's eye'.   [7] *dudeen*: clay pipe with short stem.
   [8] *Cherat*: military station near Peshawur on the North-West Frontier, where the Royal Irish Fusiliers were stationed.   [9] *Connaughts*: the Connaught Rangers.
   [10] *Leinsters*: the Prince of Wales's Leinster Regiment.
   [11] *bukhin'*: talking.   [12] *Bobbs*: Sir Frederick Roberts, the Commander-in-Chief.
   [13] *Bahadur*: honorific title.
   [14] *six av us*: the Irish infantry regiments then serving in India were the Royal Irish Regiment (cf. p. 431 above), the Connaught Rangers, the Leinster Regiment, the Royal Irish Fusiliers, the Royal Dublin Fusiliers, and the Royal Munster Fusiliers.

Wud we come? Ay, Jumpin' Moses, we wud so an' niver fear ut—
The Doblins an' the Munsters, an' the Kickin' Harse[15] from
      Meerut—
The Aigle[16] an' the Elephint,[17] the Harrp[18] an' Maple leaves[19]
Wud start a Noah's Arrk among his Continintal thieves.

We'd work the job wid illigance, an' sentimint an' taste,
For the di'monds on his hat-band an' the im'ralds round his waist.
I've seen his father's porthrait—av the son is dhressed to suit,
Begad, he's simply dhrippin' wid onmitigated loot!

Rise! Faith, we'd rise to Hiven an' we'd smash the guard-gate in
For the half av fwhat he carries on his Russia-leather skin!
Four million pounds in sov'reigns—it wud strike a woman dumb—
Betune six Oirish Regiments! Pershuade the man to come!'

                    *   *   *   *   *

Mulvaney dhropped the paper an' he dhropped the laughin' too,
An' black as rain on Malin Head[20] the features av him grew;
The bugles in the barrick-square were blowin' for parade,
He slipt into his 'coutrements an', swearin' cold, he said:

'I take no thought for Julup, I cud mash him in my fist,
But I'd like to catch the renegade who said that we'd assist;
Av I met the two tomorrow, I wud put the naygur by,
But I'd rip the livin' hide off from the swine that tould that lie!'

[15] *Kickin' Harse*: probably a reference to the 8th (King's Royal Irish) Hussars, then stationed at Meerut.

[16] *Aigle*: the Royal Irish Fusiliers wore the emblem of an eagle on their buttons and waist-plates, to commemorate their capture of the Eagle of the 8th French Light Infantry at Barossa in the Peninsular War.

[17] *Elephint*: the Connaught Rangers wore an elephant on their collar-badges, as did the Royal Dublin Fusiliers who combined it with a tiger.

[18] *Harrp*: three of these regiments, the Royal Irish Regiment, the Royal Dublin Fusiliers, and the Connaught Rangers had a harp as part of their insignia.

[19] *Maple leaves*: the Leinster Regiment wore two maple leaves as part of their insignia (its 1st Battalion having originally been the Royal Canadian Regiment).

[20] *Malin Head*: promontory on north coast of Donegal.

INSCRIPTION IN COPY OF *IN BLACK AND WHITE* PRESENTED TO MRS HILL

The *Kipling Journal*, no. 189 (March 1974), reported the sale of the collection of the late David Gage Joyce in Chicago on 23–4 September 1973: 'The most interesting item was a copy of *In Black and White* . . . with the following verses on the title-page in Kipling's hand.' (p. 2.) They were signed 'the Author'.

> To Mrs 'Ill at Belvidere[1]
> I 'umbly dedicate this 'ere,
> An' if she do not like the same
> It is the Author wot's to blame.
> But if she thinks 'em rather fine
> The credit's hern an' none o' mine
> Because it was her Smile wot made
> Me take a pleasure in my trade.

INSCRIPTION IN COPY OF *WEE WILLIE WINKIE* PRESENTED TO MRS HILL

Holograph inscription in copy of *'Wee Willie Winkie' and Other Child Stories* presented to Mrs Hill in March 1889. Published in her article 'The Young Kipling', *Atlantic Monthly*, vol. clvii (April 1936), p. 414. Facsimile of first fifteen lines of original in American Art Association Catalogue, 22–4 April 1924 (Dalhousie University Library). A draft in Cornell University Library has some preliminary lines on her request for an inscription: 'As idle as a bard may be / I drift across a lazy sea / And wrap each India sundered sense / In triple web of Indolence / And roll a sleep be-sodden eye / Between the ocean and the sky / But you demand a verse to end / The last of six small books[1] I penned / A servant of the *Pioneer* / A month ago at Belvidere.[2] / What shall I write? They lie who say / I set my foot in India . . . / Behold the sixth small book of mine / That ends the silly series / But ask me not for rhymèd line / I only drink and sleep and dine'. There are other cancelled scraps as well.

---

[1] *Belvidere*: the Hills' house at Allahabad.

[1] *six small books*: the six volumes of Kipling's stories published in the Indian Railway Library series in 1888–9—*Soldiers Three*, *The Story of the Gadsbys*, *In Black and White*, *Under the Deodars*, *The Phantom Rickshaw*, and *Wee Willie Winkie*.

[2] *Belvidere*: see note to previous poem.

I cannot write, I cannot think
I only eat and sleep and drink.—
They say I was an author once
I know I am a happy dunce
Who snores along the deck and waits
To catch the rattle of the plates,
Who drowns ambition in a sea
Of Lager or of Tivoli[3]
I cannot write, I cannot sing—
I long to hear the meal-bell ring—
I cannot sing—I cannot write
I am a Walking Appetite.

But you insist and I obey.
Here Goes!
        In steamer *Madura*[4]
Now rolling through a tepid sea
March 10th
        To Mrs Hill
            From me
A journalist unkempt and inky
With all regards,
            Wee Willie Winkie.

VERSE FRAGMENTS AND LIMERICKS

The first three of these holograph drafts seem to have been written on *The City of Peking*, on which Kipling and the Hills sailed from Yokohama to San Francisco in May 1889. The second three also seem to date from early 1889, but I cannot date them more precisely (Library of Congress).

(*a*)   She wandered round the blessed world:
      She watched the sunset she:
   O'er hills, incarnadine, impearled
      Agate and lazuli:
   Strange climes she saw and stranger folk
      And fish of alien seas.

---

[3] *Tivoli*: a brand of beer.
[4] *Madura*: the ship on which Kipling and the Hills sailed from Calcutta on 9 Mar.

(*b*) I played with a lady at Euchre
And did all I knew for to roochre
     But spite of my play
     At the end of the day
She won and I promptly forsoochre.

(*c*) I know a young lady from Beavor
And not for the world would I grieve her
     But it runs in my head
     That she scares[1] herself dead
For no one's allowed to relieve her

(*d*) There was a small boy who was proud
And smoked where he wasn't allowed
     Till a java cigar
     Lit the bestest so*far*
And he quit—in a Pillar of Cloud.

(*e*) What shall we do with a king who is dead
     He governed us well while life was in him:
Lay him in state on his royal bed,
     In the paper shrouds the poets spin him:
        Turn to the prince who is crowned today:
        And shout for

(*f*) And will you give me love for love
     And troth for troth said he?
Ay, Love for love and troth for troth
     And heart for heart quoth she.

And will you give me life for life
     And soul for soul quoth he:
Ay, soul for soul, with seas between,
     Till end of love quoth she.

THE OWL

In letter from Kipling to Mrs Hill, postmarked 12 June 1889, from San Francisco where he had parted from the Hills after their voyage together: 'In the meantime please look over a copy of the verses I sent to the Bohemian Club [of

---

[1] *scares*: reading uncertain.

San Francisco] when they made me an honorary member. The totem of the
club, wh. you will find throughout its rooms is an owl.' (*Bohemian Club Library
Notes*, no. 9, June 1961, pp. 2–4; with facsimile of letter and poem.)

Men said, but here I know they lied,
    The owl was of a sullen clan
Whose voice upon the lone hillside
    Forboded ill to mouse and man—
A terror noiseless in the flight,
A hooknosed hoodlum of the night.

But I have found another breed,
    An owl of fine artistic feelings,
A connoisseur of wine & weed
    Who flutters under frescoed ceilings
Nor scorns to bid the passing guest
Abide a season in his nest.

I saw him on the staircase sit
    And blandly wink at jibe & joke,
An arbiter twixt wit & wit,
    A god enshrined in baccy smoke
While round his pedestal there beat
The clamour of his servants' feet.

Some toiled in journalistic fetters
    And some in stocks—and stand up collars—
Some worked his will in Art & letters
    And some their own with things called dollars.
Whate'er they ran or wrote or drew
The owl was monarch of the crew.

With humour bright as Frisco air
    In speech as dry as Frisco sand,
He blithely bade me welcome there
    And stretched a claw to take my hand
Whereat I found acceptance free
Among his jovial company.

A wanderer from East to West
  A vagrant under many skies,
How shall a roving rhymester best
  Requite O owl thy courtesies?
Accept in lieu of laboured stippling
A simple 'Thank you'
                                signed R. Kipling.

VERSES ON FRUIT PLATES

Having crossed the United States on his own, Kipling rejoined the Hills in
Beaver, Pennsylvania. Mrs Hill recorded in her diary for August 1889 how she
had been painting a series of dessert plates with a design of wild flowers to take
back to India: 'One day Mr Kipling . . . demanded china and paint. We won-
dered what project was being evolved in that fertile brain and now we know,
for he has put upon six fruit plates some clever verses, about ten lines each,
which he painted directly on the china without any notes. His subjects are
Plums, Peach, Berries, Watermelon, Apples, Grapes.' ('The Young Kipling',
Atlantic Monthly, vol. clvii (April 1936), p. 415.) The originals are in the
Library of Congress. Thirty years afterwards Kipling could not recall painting
them, but Mrs Hill and her sister Caroline gave firm testimony to his author-
ship (KP 23/11).

PLUMS

Children of ye Garden We
Simple and of low Degree.
Such as chuse Us ere our Time
Suffer Paines unmeet for Rhyme
Such as eat Us overmuch
Suffer like ye other Such.
Purblind Race of toiling men
Lap Us round with Pye-Crust—then
Served with Sugar and with Cream
Ye shall find Us what we Seem.

THE PEACH

Ye Garden's royal Pride am I.
A Queen of Beauty manifold,
Y-clad in Crimson dasht with Golde

And crowned by every Summer Skie.
Take ye my Largesse merrilie
Nor dread this Giving shall grow small.
Ye Trellis on ye Sun-warmed Wall
Hath hundreds not less Faire than I.

BERRIES

We be gamins of the Wood
Who claim the Bramble's brotherhood,
A feeble folk in russet dressed
Of all Earth's children littlest.
The brown Bear knows us where we hide
By river-bank or mountain-side—
The settler's baby, brown as he,
Espies where our battalions be
And shameless peddles at the mart
Red jewels warm from Nature's heart.

THE WATERMELON

I sprawl in the sunshine & grow
                    (Ho! Ho!)
I am seen of the small boy afar
                    (Ha! Ha!)
At night he appropriates me
                    (Hee! Hee!)
He eats—and is sure he will die
                    (Hi! Hi!)
And the Earth with its sorrow and sin
                Continues to spin.

APPLES

By Cause of Us was Eden lost
        (Ye ancient Legend saith)
And Adam by ye Heavenly Post
        Was driven forth to Death

Thys is our Sin (or Hers that pluckt)
        Yet doe our Orchards make

Almost an Eden reconstruct
    And guiltlesse of ye Snake.

For underneath ye laden Boughe
    That fretts ye Summer Skie
In more than Eden Idlenesse
    Ye Citie Folk may lie.

And catche (in murmur of ye Bees)
    An Echoe of ye Town,
And marke from out ye Sleepie Trees
    Fat Apples tumbling downe.

GRAPES

Wee have sett, sith Time began
Madnesse in ye Minde of Mann,
Soe that Hee shoulde sinke—alas!—
Lower than ye Kine att Grasse.—
Yet for all oure past Misdeede
Wee be of a noble Breede—
Emerald and Purple dyed,
Rome's delight and Gallia's Pride
    An ye doubte our High Pretence
    Eate of Us in Innocence

CAROLINE TAYLOR

Typescript of poem written by Kipling in the late summer of 1889, during his
stay with Mrs Hill's family at Beaver (Cornell University Library). Caroline
Taylor, one of 'Ted's' sisters with whom Kipling fancied himself in love, had
attempted to rake up the fallen leaves which lay deep on the walks round the
college of which Dr Taylor was president. She over-tired herself, and Kipling
improvised this poem—a parody of Whittier—while conversing with her father
that afternoon. (MS note to this effect by Mrs Hill: KP 16/4.)

Caroline Taylor for Conscience sake
Went to the tool-house and hooked a rake,

Hooked a rake as the sun went down
Over the chimneys of Beavertown.

Up the pathway in whispering sheaves
The wind was blowing the autumn leaves.

Caroline Taylor in sore distress
Said, 'Good land, what an elegant mess',

Stalwart John, with a wink in his eye
Fled to Rochester speedily—

Said to himself as he skimmed the pike—
'Now Miss Carrie kin do as she like.'

Caroline Taylor for conscience sake
Went to work with that terrible rake.

Brushed the litter from path and bed
Till hands were aching and face was red.

Over the chimneys of Beavertown
Softly sarcastic the Sun looked down.

Caroline Taylor with holy wrath
Went for the leaves on the garden path.

Gathered them up in neat little mounds
Over the face of her father's grounds.

John, the hand, and Billy the horse
Had gone on a picnic together of course.

Caroline Taylor as daylight passed
Murmured 'The garden is fixed at last'.

Caroline Taylor for weariness sake
Lay till the midnight wide awake—

Raked from midnight till half past six
Phantom gardens she never could fix.

Rose in the morning heavy eyed,
Looked at the garden paths and cried.

For the wind had blown in the night and spoiled
All the neatness for which she toiled.

Under the apple trees russet and brown
Swiftly and softly the leaves came down.

Over the trim kept paths they whirled
As though there had never been rake in the world.

Caroline Taylor with patient mien
Said 'I must rake that garden clean'.

Raked that day from ten to four,
Raked the next day an hour or more.

Raked the next day—but woe is me
Wrote on the fourth for a famed M.D.!

While over the chimneys of Beaver Town
Sweetly remorseless the leaves came down.

                  *   *   *   *   *

Caroline Taylor's work is o'er
And the rake is back of the tool-house door.

She dabbles in medicines, white and black
And lies on her couch with a pain in her back.

The Moral of which is *never try*
To be more tidy than Earth and Sky.

A BALLADE OF INDIAN TEA

Typescript copy of poem sent from New York to Julia Taylor, Mrs Hill's other sister, just before Kipling sailed for England on 25 September 1889 in *The City of Berlin*, together with 'Ted', Caroline, and their cousin Edgar (Library of Congress). Professor Hill had gone on to England ahead of them. On 16 September Kipling had written to Mrs Hill from Boston, telling her to 'rest easy in regard to that tea': 'If all New York holds a single pound of Kangra Valley[1] that will I get for you to cheer you on your weary way across the Atlantic' (KP 16/4); and on 17 September he reported that he had 'scoured Boston—and secured some Assam tea' (ibid.).

> I wander East, I wander West,
>   I wander where the ferries be—
> I wander, like a man possest
>   From Zero to Infinity—
>   From Harlem to the moaning Sea
> I tramp the city o'er and o'er—
>   In hopeless search of Indian tea,
>   Kulu, Assam, or Palampore.
>
> Joy turns to sorrow in my breast,
>   I lunch at noon with Misery,
> Because of woe, untold, unguessed,
>   That parts me from Humanity.
> What share have I in revelry,
> Who clamour at each grocer's door—
> 'For Pity's sake, some Indian tea
> Kulu, Assam, or Palampore!'
>
> They said that 'mild Oo Long'[2] was best
>   Or Congou[2] grown in far Tamsui[3]—
> They tempted me with many a chest
> Packed by the gentle Japanee.
> Yet one (his name was Cassidy
>   His venerable head was hoar)
> Cried:—'Sir *I've* got some Indian tea,
> Kulu, Assam, or Palampore!'

L'ENVOI

> Princess, enjoy with girlhood's zest
> When strikes the hour of half past three,
> The fragrant cup that with your guest
>   You sip in Pennsylvaniee.

---

[1] *Kangra Valley*: a tea-producing area in the north-east of the Punjab, near Dalhousie.
[2] *Oo Long, Congou*: varieties of black tea from China.
[3] *Tamsui*: a treaty-port in Formosa (Taiwan).

This day to other lands I flee,
Yet, ere the steamer takes me o'er
Remember, by that Indian tea,
Myself, as well as Palampore.

IN THE CITY OF BERLIN

Holograph poem written on a dinner menu card of the SS *City of Berlin* during
the voyage from New York to Liverpool. The card is dated 26 September 1889
(Library of Congress).

There were passengers thirty and three
And they sailed along o' we
On the North Atlantic Sea
 In the *City of Berlin*.

And they none of 'em laughed or spoke—
(They were far too queasy to smoke)
And they couldn't stomach a joke
 In the *City of Berlin*.

When from New York we flew
They eat[1] through the whole me*new*
And later retired from view
 On the *City of Berlin*

The Stewardess smiled a smile
Of pity mingled with guile
And dealt them their basins awhile
 On the *City of Berlin*

And they cursed in various tones
The lockers of Davy Jones
And the air was full of their groans
 On the *City of Berlin*

They commended their souls to the Lord
As the wind of the ocean roared
And we took the spray on board
 Of the *City of Berlin*

[1] *eat*: *sic*; sc. ate.

But we (who are Never Ill)
We watched 'em load & unfill
And laughed—we are laughing still—
    On the *City of Berlin*

There were passengers thirty and three
A grisly crowd to see
And they sailed along o' we
    On the *City of Berlin*

'THERE ONCE WERE FOUR PEOPLE AT EUCHRE'

Holograph version dated 30 September [1889], with note '9:35. Had a good hand at Euchre' (Library of Congress). Written on the *City of Berlin*.

There once were four people at Euchre
Who played for mere Love—not for Lucre—
    But the row that they made
    O'er each diamond & spade
Was suggestive of warfare not Euchre.

VERSES FROM A LETTER TO ANDREW LANG

Soon after his arival in London early in October 1889, Kipling met Andrew Lang (1844–1912), the influential man of letters—poet, reviewer, classical scholar, folklore expert, and collector of fairy-tales—who introduced him to other literary men at the Savile Club. Lang and H. Rider Haggard (1856–1925), who was also a member, were then co-operating on *The World's Desire*, a romance about Odysseus; and in these verses, dated 26 October, Kipling prefigures a report in the American press by Bret Harte's 'Truthful James' (see above, p. 421) on a possible joint lecture-tour by Lang and Haggard in America to promote this work. (*Rudyard Kipling to Rider Haggard*, ed. Morton Cohen, London, 1965, pp. 26–7.)

I reside at Table Mountain and my name is Truthful James
I am not versed in lecturin' or other sinful games.
You will please refrain from shooting while my simple lyre I twang
To the tale of Mister Haggard and his partner Mister Lang.

They were high toned litterateurs and two most unhappy men
For they started to enlighten our enlightened citizen;
And thanks to the reporter who the interviewing fixed
Mister Lang with Mister Haggard got inextricably mixed.

Now our sunward-gazing nation gets its information slick
From the daily mornin' journal—an' it reads darnation quick
So if that information be inaccurately wild
Some eighty million citizens are apt to be beguiled.

In the ears of Mister Haggard whom they hailed as Mister Lang
The societies of Boston ethnologically sang
And they spoke of creature-legends, and of totem, myth and sign
And the stricter law of Metre—Mister Haggard answered '*Nein*'.

Then emboldened by his silence which was painful and extreme
They discoursed of gnome and kelpie and the imp that steals the
        cream
And of pornographic poems (which the same he never knew)
And they bade him chaunt a rondel—Mister Haggard then withdrew.

His subsequent adventures form no part of this concern—
It is to the other person Mister Rangard Hang we turn;
Our sunward-gazing nation fell upon him in a mass
Demanding little stories of his friend Umsloppogas[1].

The Prohibition Party made him lecture on the fate
Of the female Cleopatra[2] who imbibed her poison straight
While the Theosophic centres[3] were revolving round his knees
And suggesting further volumes on some forty further 'Shes'.[4]

But the straw that broke that camel was Chicago's mild request
For a Zulu dance[5] in character—appropriately dressed
And vain is approbation when the path to glory leads
Through a wilderness of war-whoops and a wardrobeful of beads.

[1] *Umsloppogas*: Umslopogaas was an African warrior who figured heroically in Haggard's *Allan Quatermain* (1887).
[2] *Cleopatra*: the heroine of Haggard's *Cleopatra* (1889) committed suicide by drinking poison from a golden goblet.
[3] *Theosophic centres*: the Theosophical Society, founded in New York in 1875, sought to investigate Eastern religions and spiritualism.
[4] *Shes*: the heroine of Haggard's *She* (1886) enjoyed supernatural powers, and, having bathed in a magical fire of life, had lived for over two thousand years.
[5] *Zulu dance*: Zulus, whom Haggard had known in South Africa, figure in *King Solomon's Mines* (1885) and other of his romances.

In the 'Iroquois'[6] at Buffalo that partnership broke up
To the melancholy music of a six-shot boudoir Krupp[7]
And the waiters on the staircase counted pistol shot and oath
While the partners argued hotly if the States could hold 'em both.

They collaborate in Yarrup[8] where men know them who from which
And by latest information they are striking of it rich
But when evening lamps are lighted and the evening paper rustles
Still they pick forgotten bullets from each other's gluteal muscles.

VERSE LETTER TO SIDNEY LOW (extract)

Sidney Low (1857–1932), the editor of the *St. James's Gazette*, had expressed
willingness to publish sketches or short stories by Kipling, but he also sug-
gested that he might sign a contract for regular work; and Andrew Lang seems
to have suggested a similar arrangement with the *Daily News* or *Pall Mall
Gazette*. Kipling, however, was afraid of frittering himself away on piece-work,
and he dreaded putting his head back in the old noose of journalism; where-
fore, he told Caroline Taylor, he had 'refused in a brief poem of five stanzas
the St. James's Gazette offer of a permanent engagement' (copy of undated
fragment of letter in KP 16/5, which Professor Pinney attributes to November
1889). The following stanza is preserved in a letter from Low in the Library of
Congress, in which he says it comes from 'an unpublished poem of 40 lines'
written on this occasion.

> There is gold in the News they call Daily,
>   There is pence in the sheets of Pall Mall,
> But I whistle in front of them gaily
>   And softly consign them to—well,
> If *you*, Sir, had suffered my anguish
>   Alone, 'neath a tropical sun,
> You'd let every newspaper languish,
>   Ere making a contract with one.

---

[6] *'Iroquois'*: the Iroquois Hotel had recently opened in Buffalo, NY, which Kipling
had visited in the course of his American tour.

[7] *Krupp*: product of the German armaments firm of that name.

[8] *Yarrup*: Europe.

IN PARTIBUS[1]

Composed 11 November 1889. Published in the *CMG*, 23 December 1889, with signature 'Rudyard Kipling'. Reprinted in the *Pioneer*, 25 December, and *Week's News*, 28 December, both with heading 'Mr Rudyard Kipling, who was understood not to be always satisfied with life in India, is apparently at times dissatisfied with England. The following amusing doggerel . . . will find many sympathetic readers.' Collected in *Abaft the Funnel* (1909), and the Sussex and Burwash Edns. In spite of the exhilaration of success and sudden recognition, and in spite of the fact that Rider Haggard was to prove a lifelong friend, Kipling was inclined to take a jaundiced view of some of the literary circles in which he now moved, and he was also suffering from loneliness and depression with the Hills' (and Caroline's) departure for India on 25 October. It was in this mood that he wrote this 'doleful ditty' on 11 November, an 'evil— evil day' when he woke to find 'the gloom of the Pit upon the land, a yellow fog through which the engines at Charing Cross whistled agonizedly to each other'. 'It was called *In Partibus* and was the wail of a fog-bound exile howling for Sunlight' (letter to Mrs Hill, KP 16/5).

> *The 'buses run to Battersea,*
> *The 'buses run to Bow,*
> *The 'buses run to Westbourne Grove,*
> *And Notting Hill also;*
> *But I am sick of London Town,*
> *From Shepherd's Bush to Bow.*

> I see the smut upon my cuff,
> And feel him on my nose;
> I cannot leave my window wide
> When gentle Zephyr blows,
> Because he brings disgusting things,
> And drops 'em on my 'clo'es'.

> The sky, a greasy soup-tureen,
> Shuts down atop my brow.
> Yes, I have sighed for London Town
> And I have got it now:
> And half of it is fog and filth,
> And half is fog and row.

---

[1] *In partibus* [sc. *infidelium*]: in countries [of the infidels].

And when I take my nightly prowl,
    'Tis passing good to meet
The pious Briton lugging home
    His wife and daughter sweet,
Through four packed miles of seething vice,
    Thrust out upon the street.

Earth holds no horror like to this
    In any land displayed,
From Suez unto Sandy Hook,[2]
    From Calais to Port Said;
And 'twas to hide their heathendom
    The beastly fog was made.

I cannot tell when dawn is near,
    Or when the day is done,
Because I always see the gas
    And never see the sun,
And now, methinks, I do not care
    A cuss for either one.

But stay, there was an orange, or
    An aged egg its yolk;
It might have been a Pears' balloon[3]
    Or Barnum's[4] latest joke:
I took it for the sun and wept
    To watch it through the smoke.

It's Oh to see the morn ablaze
    Above the mango-tope,[5]
When homeward through the dewy cane
    The little jackals lope,
And half Bengal heaves into view,
    New-washed—with sunlight soap.

[2] *Sandy Hook*: promontory marking the entrance to New York harbour.

[3] *a Pears' balloon*: presumably one of the many advertising devices used on behalf of Pears' Soap.

[4] *Barnum*: Phineas T. Barnum (1810–91), famous American showman. The Barnum and Bailey Circus visited London in 1889.

[5] *tope*: grove.

It's Oh for one deep whisky-peg
    When Christmas winds are blowing,
When all the men you ever knew,
    And all you've ceased from knowing,
Are 'entered for the Tournament,
    And everything that's going'.

But I consort with long-haired things
    In velvet collar-rolls,
Who talk about the Aims of Art,
    And 'theories' and 'goals',
And moo and coo with womenfolk
    About their blessed souls.

But that they call 'psychology'
    Is lack of liver-pill,
And all that blights their tender souls
    Is eating till they're ill,
And their chief way of winning goals
    Consists of sitting still.

Its Oh to meet an Army man,
    Set up, and trimmed and taut,
Who does not spout hashed libraries
    Or think the next man's thought,
And walks as though he owned himself,
    And hogs his bristles short.

Hear now a voice across the seas
    To kin beyond my ken,
If ye have ever filled an hour
    With stories from my pen,
For pity's sake send some one here
    To bring me news of men!

The 'buses run to Islington,
    To Highgate and Soho,
To Hammersmith and Kew therewith,
    And Camberwell also,
But I can only murmur 'Bus!'[6]
    From Shepherd's Bush to Bow.

---

[6] *Bus*: enough (Sussex Edn.).

MY GREAT AND ONLY[1] (extract)

Kipling's account of his discovery of the London music-halls, and of his composing a song to be performed at one of them, was published in the *CMG* on 11 and 13 January 1890, but it had been written the previous November. Collected in *Abaft the Funnel* (1909) and in the Sussex and Burwash Edns. (Kipling having marked galley proofs for the Sussex in 1930). On 15 November 1889 he recorded in a diary-letter to Mrs Hill that he had 'dined at the Italian restaurant and after dinner concluded to go to Gatti's Music Hall.[2] This opened a new world to me and filled me with fresh thoughts—surely the people of London require a poet of the Music Halls' (KP 16/5). On 16 November he 'woke early & lay in bed till the bath was hot ruminating over Music Halls. Then . . . wrote for the C&MG a thing called "A Legend of Great Honour"—an exposition of Music Halls' (ibid.) . This was to be published as 'My Great and Only', in which Kipling defends the music-hall song as a popular art form conveying 'basic and basaltic truths' about human nature, and gives a fictional account of his own experiment with the genre—foreshadowing the Barrack-Room Ballads on which he was to embark early in 1890:

I glanced at the gallery—the Red-coats were there. The fiddle-bows creaked, and, with a jingle of brazen spurs, a forage-cap over his left eye, my Great and Only began to 'chuck it off his chest.' Thus:—

> 'At the back of Knightsbridge Barricks,
>   When the fog was gatherin' dim,
> The Life Guard talked to the Under-cook,
>   An' the girl she talked to 'im.'

'*Twiddle-iddle-iddle-lum-tum-tum,*' said the violins. '*Ling-aling-aling-a-ling-ting-ling,*' said the spurs of the Great and Only, and through the roar in my ears I fancied I could catch a responsive hoof-beat in the gallery. The next four lines held the house to attention. Then came the chorus and the borrowed refrain. It took—it went home with a crisp click. My Great and Only saw his chance. Superbly waving his hand to embrace the entire audience, he invited them to join him in:—

---

[1] *My Great and Only*: from the hyperbolic formulae used by Masters of Ceremonies in introducing music-hall performers.

[2] *Gatti's Music Hall*: opposite Kipling's rooms in Villiers Street. See *Something of Myself*, p. 81, for the origin of *Barrack-Room Ballads* in 'the smoke, the roar, and the good-fellowship of relaxed humanity at Gatti's.'

'You may make a mistake when you're mashing a tart,[3]
But you'll learn to be wise when you're older,
And don't try for things that are out o' your reach,
And that's what the Girl told the Soldier,
Soldier! Soldier!
An' that's what the Girl told the Soldier.'

I thought the gallery would never let go of the long-drawn howl on 'Soldier.' They clung to it as ringers to the kicking bell-rope. Then I envied no one—not even Shakespeare. I had my house hooked—gaffed under gills, netted, speared, shot behind the shoulder—anything you please! With each verse the chorus grew louder, and when my Great and Only had bellowed his way to the fall of the Life Guard and the happy lot of the Under-cook, the gallery rocked again, the reserved stalls shouted, and the pewters twinkled like the legs of demented ballet-girls. The conductor waved the now frenzied orchestra to softer Lydian strains.[4] My Great and Only warbled, *piano*:—

'At the back o' the Knightsbridge Barricks,
When the fog's a-gatherin' dim,
The Life Guard waits for the Under-cook,
But she don't wait for 'im.'

'*Ta-ra-rara-ra-ra-rah*!' rang a horn clear and fresh as a sword-cut. 'Twas the apotheosis of virtue.

'She's married a man in the poultry line
That lives at 'Ighgate 'Ill.
An' the Life Guard walks with the 'ousemaid now,
An' (*awful pause*) she can't foot the bill!'[5]

Who shall tell the springs that move masses? I had builded better than I knew. Followed yells, shrieks and wildest applause. Then, as a wave gathers to the curl-over, singer and sung-to filled their chests and hove the chorus, through the quivering roof—horns and basses drowned and lost in the flood—to the beach-like boom of beating feet:—

---

[3] *mashing a tart*: flirting with a girl. Cf. p. 403 above.

[4] *softer Lydian strains*: the Lydian mode of Greek music, associated with Lydia in Asia Minor, was characterized by soft pathos. Cf. Milton's 'L'Allegro': 'And ever against eating Cares, / Lap me in soft *Lydian* Aires.'

[5] *she can't foot the bill*: a reference to the practice by which young women in service would pay soldiers to walk out with them in the full splendour of their uniforms.

'Oh, think o' my song when you're gowin' it strong,
  And your boots are too little to 'old yer,
And don't try for things that are out of your reach,
  And that's what the Girl told the Soldier,
      Soldier! Soldier!

Ow! (Hi! Yi! Wha-hup! Phew! Whit! Pwhit! Bang! Whang Crr-rash! There was ample time for variations as the horns uplifted themselves and ere the voices came down in a foam of sound.) *That's what the Girl told the Soldier!*[6]

Providence has sent me many joys, and I have helped myself to others, but that night, as I looked across the sea of tossing billycocks and rocking bonnets—my work—as I heard them give tongue, not once, but four times—their eyes sparkling, their mouths twisted with the taste of pleasure—I felt that I had secured Perfect Felicity. . . . The chorus bubbled up again and again throughout the evening, and a Red-coat in the gallery insisted on singing solos about 'a swine in the poultry line' whereas I had written 'man', and the pewters began to fly, and afterwards the dark street was vocal with various versions of what the girl had really told the soldier, and I went to bed murmuring: 'I have found my Destiny.'

[6] *That's what the Girl told the Soldier*: for a further stanza see Ortheris's song in 'Love-o'-Women', *Many Inventions*, 1893:

    'Oh, do not despise the advice of the wise,
      Learn wisdom from those that are older,
    And don't try for things that are out of your reach—
      An' that's what the Girl told the Soldier!
        Soldier! Soldier!
    Oh, that's what the Girl told the Soldier!'

APPENDIX A

'The Carolina' and 'The Legend of The Cedar Swamp'

These two very early poems by Kipling survive as literary curiosities. (See p. 4 above.)

(*a*)   THE CAROLINA

Holograph version in Kipling Collection, Dalhousie University Library, signed 'J. R. Kipling',[1] with note by its former owner 'Written when Rudyard Kipling was nine years of age. . . . ' The paper on which it is written, however, bears the watermark 1876 (Stewart and Yeats, p. 4), and Kipling's tenth birthday was on 30 December 1875, so that he must have been at least ten when he wrote it.

> Aūrŏrā[2] rose in a cloudless sky
> And looked on all so beamingly
> Portsmouth's dark walls stood out so bright
> Amid the flood of beaming light
> A vessel from the harbour came
> The Carolina was her name
> With Stun'sails set and royals too
> Over the billows she lightly flew
> Three hundred souls bouds[3] for London town
> Each one doomed Alas! to drown
> For o'er the deck Death's dark shape hung
> Loud and weird were the songs he sung
> The sun had set there came clouds and rain
> The ship was never seen again
> She had sunk on a rock and then gone down
> With 300 souls bound for London town
> She had sunk like lead with no canvas rent
> And never a spar or catline bent

---

[1] *J. R. Kipling*: his full name was Joseph Rudyard Kipling.
[2] *Aūrŏrā* thus in the MS, marking two false quantities out of three! Clearly he had not been introduced to Latin at this stage.
[3] *bouds*: *sic*; sc. bound.

The waves sighed mid the masts of the wreck
And fishes darted athwart the deck
Down, down, she lies full 50 fathom down
Does the Carolina bound for London town

(*b*)   THE LEGEND OF THE CEDAR SWAMP

Holograph version, signed 'J. R. Kipling' in the Bancroft Library, University of
California at Berkeley, with note in an unidentified hand 'by Rudyard Kipling
/ written beside me at my brother's / & given me when / he was 9 years / of
age.' This item bears many resemblances to the MS of 'The Carolina': 1876?

Darkness lay thick where e'er we trod
Alone with Nature and with God
Deep bogs were many round our way
And here t'was half night and half day
The Toucan's chatter was all we heard
No other sound through the forest stirred
We stumbled on o'er tree trunks dank
And up to our knees in the ooze we sank
Now and anon in the green slime rose
Then sunk again the caïman's nose

The night came on it darker grew ⎫
O'er rotten logs ourselves we threw ⎭
On our wretched couch we silent lay ⎫
And patiently waited till break of day ⎭
The caïman routed among the slime ⎫
Oh t'was an aweful, sickening time ⎭
The vapours rose mid the tree trunks dim ⎫
And fever crept o'er every limb ⎭
The cedar swamp was dark and drear ⎫
Nought to see still less to hear ⎭
Day came I rose and looked around ⎫
Four corpses lay stretched out on the ground ⎭
I staggered on-ward where I knew not ⎫
T'was but to leave the cursed spot ⎭
Onwards still onwards I bent my flight ⎫
Walking Walking by day & night ⎭

Four toucans ever fly with me
Away, away, away I flee
T'is vain they fly where'er I go
What have I done that they follow me so,

A voice in the forest thundered
Vile wretch it is thy doom
Far better were it for thee
That thou wert in thy Tomb

Four corpses lie unburied
And they can never rest
Until by priestly hands
The mouldering skulls are prest

The deed was done the bones up rose
The blood within my body froze
A fiery cross shone in the sky
And ended all the mystery
The[1] trapper boy rowed to the skeleton's shore
Time passed—he was never heard of more

[1] *The*: reading uncertain.

APPENDIX B

Contents of Notebooks and Early Editions

Notebook 1

'The Story of Paul Vaugel' ['Paul Vaugel'] (conclusion only); 'Les Amours Faciles'; 'How it seemed to Us'; 'A Dedication' ['The Dedication of this Book which is written to a Woman']; 'Change'; 'A dominant Power'; 'A profession of Faith'; 'Sir Galahad'; 'A Creed' ['In the Beginning']; 'The Quest'; 'Commonplaces'; 'Greeting'; 'The trouble of Curtiss who lodged in the Basement'; 'Our Lady of Many Dreams (Old Style)'; 'Our Lady of Many Dreams (New Style)'; 'The letter written Up in the Attic'; 'After long years' ['A Locked Way']; 'Two lives'; 'After the promise'; 'A promise'; 'I Believe'; 'Discovery'; 'Mon Accident!'; 'His Consolation' ('So be it—you gave me my release'); 'After the Fever'; 'His Consolation' ['Their Consolation'] ('Alas! Alas! it is a tale so old'); 'The Tryst in Summer' ['A Tryst']; 'Escaped!' ['The Attainment'; 'Concerning a Jawáb: After']; 'Song for two Voices' ['Song (For Music)'] ('Follow and faint not'); 'Θάλασσα, Θάλασσα' ['Land-Bound']; 'Parting' ['In the Hall']; 'Patience' ['Prescience'; 'The Widower']; 'The Reaping'; 'A Craven'; 'Understanding'; 'A Reminiscence' ['To You']; 'A Voyage'; 'Woking Necropolis' ['Severance']; 'What the Young Man's Heart said to Him'; 'Satiety'; 'Confession'; 'Lo! I am crowned'; 'El Dorado'; 'The Sign of the Withered Violet' ['The Sign of the Flower']; 'A Morning Ride'; 'Les Amours de Voyage'; 'Out of Sight'; 'As far as the East is set from the West'; 'The Pious Sub's Creed'; 'The Sudder Bazar'; 'With a Locket'; 'A Murder in the Compound'; ' "What makes my heart to throb & glow?" (North India version)' ['From the Hills']; 'Divided Allegiance'; ' "Way Down the Ravi River" '; 'A Valentine' ['A Song of St. Valentine'; 'Au Revoir']; 'There's tumult in the Khyber' ['On Fort Duty'] (incomplete).

Notebook 2

'Given from the Cuckoo's Nest'; 'Paul Vaugel' ['The Story of Paul Vaugel']; 'Change'; 'Bring me a message of hope, O Sea' ['A Question'; 'By the Sea']; 'How it seemed to us'; 'A dominant power'; 'How the day broke'; 'Les Amours faciles'; 'The Page's Song'; 'Failure'; 'Ave Imperatrix' (printed text); 'The Trouble of Curtiss who lodged in the Basement'; 'After the Promise'; 'Run down to the sea, O river' ['Land-Bound'; 'Θάλασσα! Θάλασσα!']; 'Song (For Music)' ['Song for Two Voices'] ('Follow and faint not'); 'In the Hall'

['Parting']; 'Prescience' ['Patience'; 'The Widower']; 'Escaped' ['The Attainment'; 'Concerning a Jawáb: After']; 'Discovery'; 'A profession of Faith'; 'Two Lives'; 'A Locked Way' ['After long years']; 'A Promise'; 'Greeting'; 'Where the Shoe pinches'; 'A Creed' ['In the Beginning']; 'Their Consolation' ['His Consolation'] ('Alas, alas! it is a tale so old'); 'A Tryst' ['The Tryst in Summer'].

Notebook 3

First Series: 'The Dedication of this Book which is written to a Woman' ['A Dedication']; 'How the Goddess Awakened'; 'Sir Galahad'; 'Failure'; 'Waytinge' ('Doubte not that Pleasure cometh in the Ende'); 'Pro Tem.'; 'After the Promise'; 'Greeting'; 'Cavé'; 'How the Day Broke'; 'Reckoning'; 'Two Lives'; 'Change'; 'An Auto da fé'; 'A Question' ['By the Sea']; 'Our Lady of Many Dreams'; 'The Ballad of the King's Daughter'; 'The Page's Song'; 'A promise'; 'A locked way' ['After long years']; 'Les Amours Faciles'; 'The Trouble of Curtiss who lodged in the Basement'; 'The Message' ['The Page's Message']; 'How it seemed to Us'; 'Venus Meretrix' ['For a Picture']; 'I Believe'; 'A Dominant Power'; 'Two Players'; 'The Wooing of the Sword'; 'Where the Shoe Pinches'; 'Mon Accident!'; 'Haste' ['The Flight']; 'Discovery'; 'A profession of Faith'; 'His Consolation' ['Their Consolation'] ('Alas! Alas! it is a tale so old'); 'Four Sonnets': 'In the Beginning' ['A Creed'], 'A Tryst' ['The Tryst in Summer'], 'The Quest', 'The Attainment' ['Escaped!'; 'Concerning a Jawáb: After']; 'An Ending'.

Second series: 'Prescience' ['Patience'; 'The Widower']; 'The Reaping'; 'A Craven'; 'Θάλασσα, Θάλασσα' ['Land-Bound']; 'A voyage'; 'Severance' ['Woking Necropolis']; 'Satiety'; 'Parting' ['In the Hall']; 'The Story of Paul Vaugel' [Paul Vaugel] (incomplete); 'The Sign of the Flower' ['The Sign of the Withered Violet']; 'Rejection'; 'The Reading of the Will' ['Reading the Will']; 'El Dorado'; 'Crossing the Rubicon'.

'To You' ['A Reminiscence'].

Sundry Phansies

'Dedication' ['A Dedication'; 'The Dedication of this Book which is written to a Woman']; 'How the Goddess Awakened'; 'A Ballad of the King's Daughter'; 'Reckoning'; 'Cave!'; 'Quaeritur' ('Is Life to be measured by grains'); 'Missed!'; 'Crossing the Rubicon'; 'The Reading of the Will' ['Reading the Will']; 'An Auto-da-fé'; 'Waytinge' ('Doubte not that Pleasure cometh in the End'); 'Solus cum Sola'; 'Chivalry (?)'; 'Les Amours Faciles'; 'The Flight' ['Haste']; 'Conspiracy'; 'Two Players'; 'Failure'; 'By the Sea' ['A Question']; 'The Page's Song'; 'The Page's Message' ['The Message']; 'How the Day Broke'; 'Pro Tem.'; 'Song (for two voices)' ('I bound his soul'); 'The Story of Paul Vaugel' ['Paul Vaugel']; 'How it Seemed to Us'; 'For a Picture' ['Venus

Meretrix']; 'A Visitation' ['The Second Wooing']; 'Change'; 'Brighton Beach';
'Resolve'; 'L'Envoi' (Rhymes, or of grief or of sorrow').

USCC (1881–9)

'A Legend of Devonshire', 'Disappointment', and 'The Excursion' (30 June
1881); 'De Profundis: A Ballade of Bitternesse' and 'The Pillow-fight' (23 July
1881); 'Index Malorum' and 'A Mistake' (1 November 1881); 'Waytinge'
('Waytinge! wearilie waytinge') and 'Told in the Dormitory' (5 December
1881); 'Told in the Dormitory' (cont.), 'Romance and Reality', 'The Knight
Errant', and 'Ave Imperatrix' (20 March 1882); 'Told in the Dormitory' (cont.)
and 'The Worst of It' ['The Jam-Pot'] (3 June 1882); 'Donec Gratus Eram'
(24 July 1882); 'Follicular Tonsilitis' ['The Song of the Sufferer'] (11
December 1882); 'The Song of the Exiles' (15 October 1883); 'On Fort Duty'
(28 March 1884); 'The Ride of the Schools' ['The Boar of the Year'] (30
October 1884); 'The Battle of Assye' (2 July 1886); 'A Ballad of Burial' and 'In
Spring Time', both from *Departmental Ditties* (29 October 1888); 'Inscribed in
a Presentation Copy to the Common Room of "Echoes" ' (27 March 1889).

Schoolboy Lyrics (1881)

'Lo! as a little child'; 'The Dusky Crew'; 'The Night Before'; 'Two Sides of
the Medal'; 'This Side the Styx'; 'Reading the Will' ['The Reading of the
Will']; 'An Echo'; 'Caret'; 'Roses'; 'The Lesson'; 'The Song of the Sufferer'
['Follicular Tonsilitis']; 'The Front Door'; 'Fragment of a Projected Poem',
'Conventionality'; 'Envy, Hatred and Malice'; 'A Legend of Devonshire';
'Illusion, Disillusion, Allusion'; 'Overheard'; 'From the Wings'; 'Credat
Judaeus'; 'Solus cum Sola'; 'Missed'; 'Requiescat in Pace'.

Echoes (1884)

' "A new song, sirrah?" '; 'A Vision of India'; 'The City of the Heart'; 'The
Raiyat at Home' ['The Indian Farmer at Home']; 'The Flight of the Bucket';
'Laocoön'; 'Nursery Rhymes for Little Anglo-Indians'; 'Tobacco' ['Unpub-
lished Sonnet by Keats: To a Pipe']; 'Appropriate Verses on an Elegant Land-
scape'; 'His Consolation' ('So be it, you give me my release'); 'The Cursing of
Stephen'; 'Jane Smith'; 'Nursery Idyls'; 'Sonnet (*On being rejected of One's
Horse*)'; 'Kopra Brahm'; 'The Sudder Bazar'; 'Commonplaces'; 'Quaeritur'
('Dawn that disheartens the desolate dunes'); 'London Town'; 'Himalayan';
'Our Lady of Many Dreams'; 'A Murder in the Compound'; ' "Way Down the
Ravee River" '; 'Amour de Voyage'; 'Failure'; 'How the Day Broke'; 'A
Locked Way' ['After Long Years']; 'Land-Bound' ['Θάλασσα, Θάλασσα'];
'The Ballad of the King's Daughter'; 'How the Goddess Awakened'; 'The
Maid of the Meerschaum'; 'Estunt the Griff'; 'Cavaliere Servente'.

Items known to be by Trix are 'Children of Nature'; 'The Bearing of the Vine'; 'Hope Deferred'; 'Egoism'; 'On Sorrow'; 'To You, Love'; 'On True Friendship'. On 'Jane Smith', see above, pp. 29–30.

Quartette (1885)

'Divided Allegiance'; 'At the Distance'; 'A Tragedy of Teeth'; 'The Second Wooing' ['A Visitation']; 'From the Hills' [' "What makes my heart to throb & glow?" (North India version)'].

APPENDIX C

Dates of Poems of the Period 1879–89 included in the Definitive Edition of Kipling's Verse

The following table gives the dates of first publication, and dates of composition where these are known, of poems of this period which are included in the Definitive Edition.

1882

20 Mar. 'Ave Imperatrix', *USCC*, no. 8.

15 June 'The Widower' ['Patience', 'Prescience'], Notebook 1; *CMG*, 8 August 1887.

1884

16 Dec. 'The Moon of Other Days', *Pioneer*.

20 Dec. 'Some Unpublished Maxims of Hafiz', *Pioneer*.

1885

27 Jan. 'To the Unknown Goddess', *Pioneer*.

20 Mar. 'In Springtime' ['In the Spring Time'], *Pioneer*.

8 July 'My Rival', *Pioneer*.

13 July 'Possibilities', *Pioneer*.

19 Aug. 'Divided Destinies' ['The Divided Destinies'], *Pioneer*.

22 Aug. 'The Mare's Nest' ['The Legend of the Lilly'], *Pioneer*.

8 Oct. 'The Undertaker's Horse', *CMG*.

1886

30 Jan. 'The Rupaiyat of Omar Kal'vin', *CMG*.

9 Feb. 'Army Headquarters', *CMG*.

16 Feb. 'Study of an Elevation, in Indian Ink', *CMG*.

23 Feb. 'A Legend of the Foreign Office' ['A Legend of the F.O.'], *CMG*.

3 Mar. 'The Story of Uriah', *CMG*.

9 Mar. 'Public Waste', *CMG*.

16 Mar. 'The Post that Fitted', *CMG*.

23 Mar. 'The Man Who Could Write', *CMG*.

30 Mar. 'Pink Dominoes', *CMG*.

6 Apr. 'A Code of Morals', *CMG*.

13 Apr. 'The Last Department', *CMG*.

16 Apr. 'The Plea of the Simla Dancers', *CMG*.

30 Apr. 'The Legend of Evil' ii (' 'Twas when the rain fell steady'), letter of 30 Apr. 1886 to E. K. Robinson (KP 17/25); as chapter-heading in John Lockwood Kipling, *Beast and Man in India*, 1891.

'With Scindia to Delhi', letter of 30 Apr. to E. K. Robinson (v. above); *Barrack-Room Ballads*, 1892.

16 June 'Pagett, M. P.', *Pioneer*.

June 'A General Summary', *Departmental Ditties*, 1st edn.

'The Lovers' Litany', *Departmental Ditties*, 1st edn.

'Arithmetic on the Frontier', (couplet quoted *CMG*, 9 July 1885) *Departmental Ditties*, 1st edn.

'Giffen's Debt', *Departmental Ditties*, 1st edn.

July 'The Explanation' ['The Legend of Love'], *Calcutta Review*, vol. lxxxiii.

15 Sept. 'Two Months: September' ['In September'], *CMG*.

11 Oct. 'Delilah', *CMG*.

10 Nov. 'The Fall of Jock Gillespie', *CMG*.

Oct./
Nov. 'A Ballad of Burial', *Departmental Ditties*, 2nd edn.

'A Ballade of Jakko Hill', *Departmental Ditties*, 2nd edn.

'The Overland Mail', *Departmental Ditties*, 2nd edn.

'L'Envoi' ('The smoke upon your Altar dies'), *Departmental Ditties*, 2nd edn.

24 Dec. 'Christmas in India' ['Latter Day Carols: The Dyseptic in India'], *Pioneer*.

1887

21 Apr. ' "As the Bell Clinks" ', *CMG*.

4 May 'What the People Said' ['A Jubilee Ode (Punjabi Peasant's Point of View)'], *CMG*.

9 May 'Municipal' ['The D.C.'s Story'], *CMG*.

2 June 'A Tale of Two Cities' ['Love among the Ruins'], *CMG*.

7 June 'La Nuit Blanche' ['Natural Phenomena'], *CMG*.

13 Aug. 'Blue Roses' ['Misunderstood'], *CMG*.

15 Aug. 'An Old Song' ['The Frame and the Picture'], *CMG*.

1888

2 Jan. 'What Happened', *Pioneer*.

7 Jan. 'The Grave of the Hundred Head', *Week's News*.

21 Jan. 'The Lament of the Border Cattle Thief' ['The Border Cattle Thief'], *Week's News*.

Jan. Chapter Headings, *Plain Tales from the Hills* (including 'By the Hoof of the Wild Goat', which Kipling later printed as a separate poem, and two headings which he later enlarged to form separate poems— 'Hadramauti' and 'Tarrant Moss').

'The Love Song of Har Dyal' in 'Beyond the Pale', *Plain Tales from the Hills*.

3 Mar. 'The Ballad of Fisher's Boarding House', *Week's News*. (Completion

1888

recorded in diary entry of 22 Feb.: see *Catalogue of the Works of Rudyard Kipling Exhibited at the Grolier Club*, New York, 1930, item 575, p. 181 and Plate XXIX.)

17 Apr. 'The Song of the Women', *Pioneer*.

Apr. 'Two Months: June' ['Two Months: In June'], *Departmental Ditties*, 3rd edn.

1 Sept. 'The Ballad of Boh Da Thone', *Week's News*.
(Referred to in letter of 27 May 1888, KP 16/2.)

26 Oct. 'The Masque of Plenty', *Pioneer*.

21 Nov. 'The Betrothed' ['The Meditation of William Kirkland'], *Pioneer*.

Nov. 'A Dedication' ['L'Envoi'] ('And they were stronger hands than mine'), *Soldiers Three*.
Refrain of 'Troopin' ' as heading to 'The Big Drunk Draf' ', *Soldiers Three*.

Nov./
Dec. 'The Winners' ['L'Envoi'] ('What is the moral? Who rides may read'), *The Story of the Gadsbys*.

7 Dec. 'One Viceroy Resigns' ['One Word More'], *Pioneer*.

1889

Nov. 'The Ballad of the King's Mercy', *Macmillan's Magazine*.

Dec. 'The Ballad of East and West', *Macmillan's Magazine*.
(Finishing composition 8–9 Nov., KP 16/5.)

APPENDIX D

Additional Poem: 'The year wears by at last'

On 4 June 1903 a Mrs E. M. Morton, née Davey, wrote to Kipling asking him whether he would, as a favour, initial a poem which she enclosed and which, she wrote, 'has been among my treasures for more years than I care to think— You will remember it and all the circumstances under which it was written. I never thought of parting with it but circumstances alter cases'; and she explained the financial problems that made her think of selling it (KP 23/13). Kipling refused her request, but a typed copy of this poem has been preserved with the correspondence. Mrs Morton has been tentatively identified by Professor Pinney as a former governess in the Tavenor Perry household at the time Kipling frequented it. Date uncertain: 1881–82? (This poem came to my attention too late for it to be included in its proper sequence following 'Rejection' on p. 113 above.)

> The year wears by at last—
>   The long days go
> And pain is over past
>   And past is woe.
> Oh friend, ill cannot last for aye!
>   Oh friend, the darkest night must fade away
>   Into dawn's glow.
>
>
> Old hopes are hard to kill,
>   Old passions burn
> Old strivings stir us still
>   *Old loves return.*
> Oh friend, ill cannot last thro' life!
>   Oh friend there is an ending to all strife
>   Whereto all yearn!
>
>
> Peace for the aching brain,
>   Rest for strained eyes,
> When Love returns again
>   And past joys rise.
> When tired hearts are joined, true souls close knit
>   And Love is King, who changeth not a whit
>   When evil flies.

Oh friend the time is near
   The dark is white
To sunrise—while the drear
   Cold blank of night,
Kindles with dawn—have patience yet a space.
   Ere God brings thy love to thee face to face
      And all is right.

INDEX OF TITLES

[Entries in square brackets represent alternative titles.]

INDEX OF FIRST LINES